T. J. B. Spencer was born in 1915 and educated at the Lower School of John Lyon, Harrow. He graduated at the University of London and served from 1941 to 1946 in the Army in North Africa. After holding appointments at King's and University colleges, London, he became Professor of English at the Queen's University of Belfast (1955–8). He was then appointed Professor of English Language and Literature at the University of Birmingham, and, in addition, Director of the Shakespeare Institute in 1961.

Professor Spencer's other books include *Fair Greece, Sad Relic* (a study of English philhellenism from Shakespeare to Byron, reprinted in 1986 by Denise Harvey & Co. in Athens), *The Tyranny of Shakespeare, Byron and the Greek Tradition, From Gibbon to Darwin, Shakespeare: The Roman Plays*, and other contributions to scholarship and criticism. He was general editor of the *Modern Language Review*, the quarterly journal of the Modern Humanities Research Association. For Penguin he edited *Shakespeare: A Celebration 1564–1964*, and was general editor of the New Penguin Shakespeare and the Penguin Shakespeare Library; for these series he edited *Romeo and Juliet, Hamlet* and *Elizabethan Love Stories*.

Professor Spencer died in 1978.

# SHAKESPEARE'S
# PLUTARCH

★

THE LIVES OF JULIUS CAESAR,
BRUTUS, MARCUS ANTONIUS,
AND CORIOLANUS
IN THE TRANSLATION OF
SIR THOMAS NORTH

★

EDITED, WITH AN INTRODUCTION,
GLOSSARY, AND
PARALLEL PASSAGES FROM
SHAKESPEARE'S PLAYS,
BY T. J. B. SPENCER

PENGUIN BOOKS

PENGUIN BOOKS

Published by the Penguin Group
Penguin Books Ltd, 27 Wrights Lane, London W8 5TZ, England
Penguin Books USA Inc., 375 Hudson Street, New York, New York 10014, USA
Penguin Books Australia Ltd, Ringwood, Victoria, Australia
Penguin Books Canada Ltd, 2801 John Street, Markham, Ontario, Canada L3R 1B4
Penguin Books (NZ) Ltd, 182–190 Wairau Road, Auckland 10, New Zealand

Penguin Books Ltd, Registered Offices: Harmondsworth, Middlesex, England

First published in Peregrine Books 1964
Reprinted in Penguin Books 1968
3 5 7 9 10 8 6 4 2

Copyright © T. J. B. Spencer, 1964

Printed in England by Clays Ltd, St Ives plc
Set in Monotype Bembo

Except in the United States of America, this book is sold subject
to the condition that it shall not, by way of trade or otherwise, be lent,
re-sold, hired out, or otherwise circulated without the publisher's
prior consent in any form of binding or cover other than that in
which it is published and without a similar condition including this
condition being imposed on the subsequent purchaser

# CONTENTS

# INTRODUCTION

## Plutarch the Biographer

PLUTARCH's collection of *Parallel Lives of the Greeks and Romans* is one of the great books of the world. He provided a vision of Greece and Rome which held the imagination of Europe for centuries. He saw history in terms of human character; and interpreted Antiquity to the modern world as a state of existence in which outstanding men moulded events by their personal decisions and by the inevitable tendencies of their characters. It is probable that from the sixteenth century onwards his writings have done more than those of any other ancient author to make familiar the great men and great happenings of Antiquity and to provide the material for other imaginative works about Greece and Rome.

The *Parallel Lives* of Plutarch consist of twenty-three pairs, each pair being followed by a 'comparison'. Not all these 'comparisons', however, are extant. There are a few extra *Lives*, without a companion, and probably about a dozen more were written by Plutarch but have been lost. He compiled the work from a great number of sources and must have had access to a large library of Greek and Roman literature and history. Occasionally he mentions his authorities for his statements. Many of the books from which he obtained information have not survived; so we cannot judge his reliability except on general grounds.

His intention and method in the *Parallel Lives* he explains at the beginning of his *Life of Alexander* (which Shakespeare may well have read, because the 'parallel' to Alexander is, of course, Julius Caesar). Readers must remember, he says,

*that my intent is not to write histories, but only lives. For the noblest deeds do not always show men's virtues and vices; but oftentimes a light occasion, a word, or some sport, makes men's natural dispositions and manners appear more plain than the famous battles won wherein are slain ten thousand men, or the great armies, or cities won by siege or assault.*

As a historian of Greece, Plutarch was brilliant. But as a historian of Rome, he had several limitations. He was himself a Greek, a philosopher and rhetorician, one who had little direct experience of the Roman world and its language and literature. He passed most of his life in provincial Greece, in the time of the Roman Empire, a life of quiet self-cultivation under the *Pax Romana*. He drew his ideals from the Hellenic past, not from the Roman world, past or present. There is very little evidence in his *Parallel Lives* that he really admired the Romans. In each pair the Greek worthy is generally more attractively drawn than the Roman. The character of Alcibiades, for example, is certainly represented with more sympathy and understanding than that of Coriolanus.

But in spite of his antipathies, the events in Roman history which led to the rise of Julius Caesar, the republican reaction attempted by Cassius and Brutus, and the struggle for supremacy between Marcus Antonius and Octavius Caesar – these were not remote from Plutarch. He was a contemporary of the Emperor Nero (who was born in A.D. 37 and ruled from 54 to 68), as he says at the conclusion of his *Life of Antonius* (p. 295); but his great-grandfather Nicarchus had told him what the people of his native place, Chaeronea, suffered at the time of the battle of Actium 31 B.C. (p. 262); and his grandfather Lampryas provided him with stories of Antonius's extravagances in Alexandria with Cleopatra (p. 204).

# North the Translator

Plutarch was a voluminous writer, and all his works, philosophical as well as biographical, were greatly admired in Europe in the sixteenth century. The *Lives* were early translated from Greek into Latin, at that time the language of every educated person. In 1559 they were translated into French by Jacques Amyot (1513–93), whose work is commonly regarded as one of the masterpieces of sixteenth-century French prose (see Sainte-Beuve, *Causeries du Lundi*, 20 August 1851). This was the version which Thomas North used in order to produce his English *Plutarch* of 1579, when Shakespeare was in his mid-teens.

On the title-page of his book North candidly stated the source of his translation:

*The Lives of the noble Grecians and Romans, compared together by that grave learned Philosopher and Historiographer, Plutarch of Chaeronea: Translated out of Greek into French by* JAMES AMYOT, *Abbot of Bellozane, Bishop of Auxerre, one of the King's privy counsel, and great Amner of France, and out of French into English, by* THOMAS NORTH.

The *Plutarch* was the last of the three major works of translation undertaken by North. He had already published *The Dial of Princes* (1557), a fictional version of the memoirs of the Emperor Marcus Aurelius (the now famous *Meditations* were not yet in print), and *The Moral Philosophy of Doni* (1570), a collection of fables of oriental origin. He had become, therefore, an experienced translator when he turned to Plutarch's *Lives*. He was then about thirty years older than Shakespeare. He seems to have been a good modern linguist, for his various translations were made from the Spanish, Italian, or French – though we have no means of knowing his competence in the classical languages. He had travelled abroad; he became a Justice of the Peace for the County of Cambridgeshire; and by 1591 he had achieved sufficient prosperity and reputation to be knighted by Queen Elizabeth (to whom he affectionately dedicated the third edition of the *Lives* in 1603).

As a translator North's workmanship was vigorous rather than skilful. He often follows his French version word for word without paying much attention to the English idiom. Sometimes he does not understand what he is translating, or does not think what he is doing. Sometimes he merely mistranslates. He had nothing like the scholarship, the care, and the thoroughness of his master Amyot.

But when all his limitations have been exposed, North remains an astonishingly successful translator, able to interest the reader by

the directness of his language and the rough strength of his narrative.
He has a taste for vivid graphic language, even where his French text
uses plain or commonplace terms. 'The Empire of Rome was in
garboil and uproar', he writes (p. 105), where Amyot had mildly said:
'*L'empire de Rome fut troublé.*' 'But this holdeth no water' (p. 109)
is his version of '*mais ils ne disent pas la vérité*'. 'My fists may walk
once again about thine ears' (p. 110) represents '*je te rompe la tête à coups
de poing*'. He gave his translation a vivid contemporary tone for his
Elizabethan readers by his straightforward identification of things of
antiquity with rough-and-ready equivalents in sixteenth-century
life. He boldly uses the technical nautical terms (*brigantine, carect,
pinnace, hoise sail, clap on sail, loof, yarage*) and the names for military
dress (*cassock, murrion, sallet*), not strictly appropriate, but acceptable.
Sometimes North could not find contemporary equivalents and fell
back upon an old-fashioned military vocabulary (*coat-armour, lists,
target*). Occasionally the absence of equivalent English words led
him into some awkward paraphrases: *fencers at the sharp, sword players
to fight at the sharp, fencers at unrebated swords* are his efforts to get
over the lack of the word *gladiators*. The appointment of Julius Caesar
as *chief bishop of Rome* is surprising and perhaps misleading until we
remember that North is translating Amyot's *souverain pontife*, that
is, the Latin *Pontifex Maximus*. In general North's translation gains
considerably by his unaffected and unpretentious use of contemporary
terms and the familiar idiom.

One further peculiarity of North as a translator deserves to be
mentioned. Plutarch, who was thoroughly familiar with the literature
of his country, occasionally quotes from the Greek poets, especially
from Homer – allusively, sometimes almost proverbially. North's
translations of these quotations seem to be his own. He seems to
have thought it appropriate to give them in a mock-archaic style, a
kind of bogus Chaucerian language (see, for example, pp. 133, 146).
In some cases the effect is ludicrous; and when it was imitated by
Shakespeare in *Julius Caesar*, it was received with Brutus's comment:

*Ha, ha! how vilely doth this cynic rhyme!* (p. 147)

# Shakespeare and North's Plutarch

For anyone who was venturing upon extended dramatic treatment of an episode of Roman history, Plutarch, it must be acknowledged, was incomparable. Suetonius, the only possible rival as a biographer, dealt with a narrow range of characters – the first twelve Caesars, from Julius to Domitian – and although his narrative is vivid and anecdotal he is altogether lacking in the geniality and penetration of Plutarch.

But Shakespeare seems to have taken a long time before coming to read Plutarch. *A Midsummer Night's Dream* contains an episode in the story of Theseus, whom Shakespeare calls Duke of Athens. Oberon accuses Titania of misconducting herself with Theseus.

> *Didst thou not lead him through the glimmering night*
> *From Perigenia, whom he ravished?*
> *And make him with fair Aegles break his faith,*
> *With Ariadne and Antiopa?*                    (II, I, 77)

For this information Shakespeare seems to have looked at the *Life of Theseus*:

*For some say, that Ariadne hung herself for sorrow, when she saw that Theseus had cast her off . . . and they think that Theseus left her because he was in love with another, as by these verses should appear:*

> *Aegles the nymph was lov'd of Theseus,*
> *That was the daughter of Panopeus.*

But Shakespeare did not have to go very far; for Theseus is the first *Life* in the book, and these names come in the early pages.

It seems likely that Shakespeare began to read, or re-read, Plutarch about the time he was writing *Henry V*. Perhaps he was not greatly impressed by the accuracy of the 'parallels' between each Greek and Roman worthy. He must, surely, have been thinking of their inadequacies when he made Fluellen establish his immortal comparison between Alexander of Macedon and Harry of Monmouth (IV, 7, 25–51).

> I warrant you sall find, in the comparisons between Macedon and Monmouth, that the situations, look you, is both alike. There is a river in Macedon; and there is also moreover a river at Monmouth: it is called Wye at Monmouth; but it is out of my prains what is the name of the other river; but 'tis all one, 'tis alike as my fingers is to my fingers, and there is salmons in both. If you mark Alexander's life well, Harry of Monmouth's life is come after it indifferent well: for there is figures in all things.

And, as a specimen of a Plutarchan parallel, Fluellen offers:

> Alexander, God knows, and you know, in his rages, and his furies, and his wraths, and his cholers, and his moods, and his displeasures, and his indignations, and also being a little intoxicates in his prains, did, in his ales and his angers, look you, kill his best friend Cleitus.

Gower: Our king is not like him in that: he never killed any of his friends.

Fluellen: It is not well done, mark you now, to take the tales out of my mouth, ere it is made and finished. I speak but in the figures and comparisons of it: as Alexander killed his friend Cleitus, being in his ales and his cups; so also Harry Monmouth, being in his right wits and his good judgments, turned away the fat knight with his great-belly doublet.

But although Shakespeare may have seen the weakness of Plutarch's scheme of putting a life of a Greek alongside a life of a Roman, a careful study of the plays in relation to Plutarch's narrative shows how much Shakespeare respected Plutarch's powers of characterization by significant detail. Yet when we consider the impact of Plutarch upon Shakespeare, we need to remember that the world's literature was then much more limited than it is now. For one thing, there were no great novelists; and in an age when there were no great novels Plutarch could pass as skilful in the description and delineation of character. Plutarch compared very favourably, certainly, with what Shakespeare could find in John Lyly's *Euphues* or Sir Philip Sidney's *Arcadia*. We may assume, from the evidence of his close following of Plutarch, that Shakespeare had a high estimate of his literary and historical merit. In this respect Shakespeare was in the company of Rabelais, Montaigne, Saint-Evremond, Montesquieu, and Rousseau.

Shakespeare was also appreciative of North's language and he adapted many of his best passages to his own dramatic purposes. He made no effort to go beyond North for many important speeches in the plays, and it is natural for us to regard these borrowings from North as a compliment to his literary merits. Certainly he paid to no other of his books the same respect as he did to North. He followed North, moreover, even more closely in the later plays (*Antony and Cleopatra* and *Coriolanus*) than he did in *Julius Caesar*. The description of Cleopatra's first meeting with Antony on the river Cydnus (p. 201), the death of Cleopatra (p. 291), the speech of Coriolanus to Aufidius (p. 337), are examples of Shakespeare's careful adaptation of North's words to the exigencies of blank verse and the actors' art of speaking. His dependence upon North occurs, then, not in the days of literary apprenticeship but at the peak of his intellectual and artistic powers. But the odd thing is that it was not only North's best passages that he adapted; he also versified passages of only average merit, as if it were an economy of effort to do so. Shakespeare certainly felt at liberty to invent wholesale, whenever the material in North was inadequate. Two striking examples in *Julius Caesar* are the speeches of Brutus and Mark Antony in the Forum. Here North's Plutarch provides nothing of Shakespeare's language; and indeed the sources of Antony's speech have been sought elsewhere – in the history by Appian, which had been translated in Shakespeare's time as *An Ancient History and Exquisite Chronicle of the Roman Wars, both Civil and Foreign* (1578). It is probable that Shakespeare looked at other books of Roman history besides Plutarch. But none of them can have given him the literary excitement of North. It is worth remembering, too, that in Shakespeare's time the *Lives* were confined to large and cumbrous folios. There were no convenient selections comparable to the present volume; neither did there exist any handy edition of the complete work, such as the six manageable Tudor Translations (1895) or the ten pocket volumes of the Temple Classics (1898) – or the others mentioned in the Bibliography on

p. 20. Shakespeare, when he read Plutarch, had to have a very heavy folio in his hands. One reads 1010 folio pages in the 1579 edition before coming to the death of Cleopatra (but Shakespeare doubtless knew what to look for in Plutarch, as we do). The reading of North was rather a serious thing for a busy man of the theatre, probably his most serious experience of the bookish kind.

Julius Caesar had been the subject of many tragedies before Shakespeare, about 1599, turned from his series of English historical plays (the three parts of *Henry VI*, *Richard III*, *Richard II*, *King John*, the two parts of *Henry IV*, and *Henry V*) to explore Roman history. It can be presumed that he went to Plutarch knowing that Julius Caesar was a suitable character for a tragedy. His many references to Caesar in plays written before *Julius Caesar* show that Shakespeare viewed him with admiration and awe, even though it was also possible to mock Roman arrogance. Falstaff compares himself to 'the hook-nosed fellow of Rome' who said 'I came, saw and overcame'; and for Rosalind the love of Celia and Oliver was as sudden as 'Caesar's thrasonical brag' (see pp. 71–2).

For the composition of this play Shakespeare carefully read the lives of *Caesar*, *Brutus*, and *Marcus Antonius*. For the most part he followed the *Brutus*, though Acts I and II and the first scene of Act III also derive from the *Caesar*. The passages from Shakespeare and the cross-references at the foot of the page in this edition will enable the reader to follow Shakespeare's progress through his Plutarch. His reliance on the *Brutus* rather than the *Caesar* may be due to the fact that Plutarch is not at his best with Julius Caesar, a character whom he did not understand and did not like. Plutarch saw the inevitability of monarchical rule in Rome as he plainly said (pp. 77, 165). But he looked back with nostalgic admiration to the past of his own country and its brilliant small city-states; and he respected the republican virtues of Rome. Caesar was the cause of the downfall of the Republic, and Plutarch does not refrain from expressing his disapproval. It seems that Shakespeare did not get all he needed from the *Caesar*, and worked more closely and more sympathetically with the *Brutus*.

On the other hand there is a physical vividness about the *Life of Marcus Antonius* which shows Plutarch at his best and which seems to have been stimulating to Shakespeare. We, too, respond to Plutarch's description of Antony's personal appearance (p. 177) and manner of speech (p. 175). We, too, can accept inconsistency in the moral values by which we are to judge Antony and his love. Plutarch praises Antony for generosity and endurance, and then blames him for cruelty and extortion. He does not conceal a certain enthusiasm for Cleopatra, a Greek who got the better of a Roman; but yet he reprobates Antony for falling under her influence: 'The extremest mischief of all other (to wit, the love of Cleopatra) lighted on him, who did waken and stir up many vices yet hidden in him' (p. 199). Yet it was from Plutarch that Shakespeare learned to allow Cleopatra, at a moment of great dramatic tension, to fill our imagination with the vision of Roman grandeur, dignity, and resolution.

> *And then, what's brave, what's noble,*
> *Let's do it after the high Roman fashion,*
> *And make death proud to take us.*
>
> (IV, 15, 86)

In *Antony and Cleopatra*, Shakespeare's most remarkable extension of the materials he found in the *Life of Marcus Antonius* was in the development of the character of Enobarbus (who, as Aenobarbus, is only mentioned very briefly in Plutarch, pp. 228, 294). Enobarbus's function in the play is obvious: he is a commentator, the voice of common sense, a link between the audience and the main characters. But he is far more than a chorus. His desertion and death are deeply moving, and his final scene (IV, 9) throws light on the character of Antony and preserves our sympathy at a time when we may begin to feel exasperation with his weakness. The loyalty of Enobarbus does not merely give an opportunity for a display of Antony's typical generosity but also elevates the dignity of his character when the play needs it. Enobarbus has been, in the eyes of the audience, a plain dealer and blunt soldier who sees through Cleopatra's amorous manoeuvres just as he sees through the Triumvirs' political manoeuvres. We have therefore a special confidence in his two great moving scenes: the description of Cleopatra on Cydnus (II, 2) and his death from a broken heart (IV, 9). He understands the weaknesses of Antony – one 'whom ne'er the word of "No" woman heard speak'; and he gives his opinion of his general with soldier-like candour:

*He will to his Egyptian dish again.*

Thus although Aenobarbus is an insignificant person in Plutarch, a careful reading of the *Life of Marcus Antonius* shows that Shakespeare had absorbed a great deal of the miscellaneous information he found about Antony into building up the character and dramatic function of Enobarbus.

*Coriolanus* is an entirely different kind of story from *Julius Caesar* and *Antony and Cleopatra*, and in this, the most austere of his tragedies, Shakespeare treated his source very carefully. His deviations from Plutarch are all in the direction of theatrical effectiveness. In the great scene of supplication outside the walls of Rome, he added the parts of Virgilia and the young Marcus; and he was thus able to make the appeal to be directed towards Coriolanus's natural instincts as a husband and a father, and not only as a son. In small details, too, Shakespeare increases the dramatic life of some of the episodes he takes very closely from Plutarch. Coriolanus asks for the release of a Volscian prisoner who had been his host; but Shakespeare adds the detail that, in spite of his good intentions, he has forgotten his name (p. 312). One can see the theatrical tact here. It is slightly deflating. Coriolanus is generous; but ineffectually so. And just as he created Enobarbus in *Antony and Cleopatra* for the purpose (at least partly) of giving a standard of equanimity, shrewdness, normal affection, and common sense, so he developed the character of Menenius from a mere hint in Plutarch: 'The Senate ... did send unto them certain of the pleasantest old men and the most acceptable to the people among them. Of those Menenius Agrippa was he who was sent for chief man of the message from the Senate' (p. 303).

Apart from the three Roman plays the most important part of Shakespeare's work drawn from Plutarch is *Timon of Athens*, probably written about the same time as *Coriolanus*. The story of Timon occurs as a digression in the *Life of Marcus Antonius* (pp. 263–6), and the almost exact repetition of Timon's epitaph (p. 266) shows that Shakespeare had his copy of North's *Plutarch* open beside him as he wrote; though in the case of this play there are probably sources other than Plutarch to be taken into account.

# This Edition

The four *Lives* in this volume were the main sources of *Julius Caesar*, *Antony and Cleopatra*, and *Coriolanus*, and contributed something to *Timon of Athens*. For reasons of space it has regrettably not been possible to include the Parallels between Dion and Brutus, Demetrius Poliorcetes and Marcus Antonius, and Alcibiades and Coriolanus, though these may well have interested Shakespeare. The Parallel of Alexander the Great and Julius Caesar is not extant. There are other *Lives* that Shakespeare may well have read or looked at – *Theseus*, *Alcibiades*, *Pompeius*, *Cato* (the Younger), and *Cicero*. But there is no convincing evidence of this. The 1603 edition of North's *Plutarch* contains a *Life of Octavius Caesar*, which Shakespeare might have consulted to supplement the *Life of Marcus Antonius* when he was writing *Antony and Cleopatra*; it is a dull thing, however, and not by Plutarch.

North's translations of the four *Lives* are here printed in a way that is intended to make the narrative as readable and unencumbered as possible. Anyone who has acquired a taste for the quality of North's writing from this book can turn to one of the reprints, fuller and more archaically presented, listed on p. 20.

The text follows the folio edition of 1595. Where the printer of 1595, in setting up his type from a copy of the 1579 edition, seems accidentally to have dropped a word or made a trivial substitution, the apparently correct reading of 1579 has been restored. The text of 1595 has been collated with those of 1579 and 1603. In the four *Lives* now reprinted the differences between the three editions are of little significance, though there are one or two genuine corrections in 1603 (see pp. 25, 33). It is not known which of these three editions

Shakespeare read. His *Julius Caesar* was written before the 1603 edition appeared.

In the sixteenth century printers used a variety of spellings for the same word. In most instances, however, the spelling nowadays customary in any word was also one of those used for it in the sixteenth century. It does not much impair the text, therefore, to normalize the inconsistent spelling of the original by printing it according to the consistent modern system. There are a few obsolete forms and words; the meanings of most of these are obvious from the contexts, but a brief Glossary is provided on p. 363. More troublesome than obsolete words are familiar words which have changed their meaning, such as *careful* (full of anxiety), *commodity* (profit), *conceit* (opinion), *convinced* (found guilty), *incontinently* (immediately), *misery* (miserliness), *nice* (scrupulous), *policy* (trickery), *table* (picture), *tuition* (protection), and so on. A number of such words are included in the Glossary.

Punctuation offers more difficulty than spelling. North's syntax and sentence patterns are not those of modern prose. It is impossible therefore merely to 'modernize' the punctuation; and a reader unaccustomed to sixteenth-century books would find much of the original punctuation a hindrance. The editor hopes that the punctuation here used will help the reader to take the meaning of North's sentences, sometimes rather involved, with as little stumbling as possible. Paragraphing and the setting out of the speeches and letters have also been introduced in order to facilitate reading.

Names of persons and places have generally been retained in the forms used by North and his printer. They have not been amended in accordance with correct classical usage, except where the sixteenth-century forms have been thought to be misleading. Most editors of Shakespeare have 'corrected' his classical proper names (for example, in *Julius Caesar*, IV, 3, Varro and Claudius, instead of Varrus and Claudio). North's forms have, however, been rendered consistent.

North's errors and mistranslations have not been corrected or noted; but one or two corrections of what are probably printer's errors have been admitted: 'reason' for 'treason' (p. 348), 'Fulvia, Antonius' wife' for 'Fulvia, and Antonius' wife' (p. 194).

North (or perhaps his printer) provided a kind of running summary of the text, printed in the margins of the book. Thus, the first few pages of the *Life of Julius Caesar* have the following summary as side notes: 'Caesar joined with Cinna and Marius', 'Caesar took sea and went unto Nicomedes, king of Bithynia', 'Caesar taken by pirates', 'Junius, praetor of Asia', 'Caesar's eloquence', 'Caesar loved hospitality', and so on. The side notes are of interest because Shakespeare's eye may have been caught by them as he turned over the pages of the folio. They do not, however, often add anything to the text and they have had to be omitted from this edition (except in a few instances where they are included as a parenthesis or as a footnote).

The passages from Shakespeare's plays given at the foot of the page are those in which his language or his treatment of an episode follows North. A few passages are given when it is of interest that he has deliberately departed from North. The text of the Globe Shakespeare has generally been followed, except in a few instances where that text is now thought to be wrong in departing from the originals. But in the quotations here given, the stage-directions follow those printed in the folio edition of Shakespeare's plays in 1623. In the texts of Shakespeare now current these original stage-directions have in some cases been amplified or amended by editors with the help of North's *Plutarch*. To insert these additions here would, of course, obscure the reader's sense of the relation between Shakespeare and North.

# BIBLIOGRAPHY

NORTH's translation of Plutarch's *Lives* was first published in 1579 and reprinted in 1595, 1603 (with additional lives), 1612, 1631, 1657, and 1676. The complete work has been reprinted in several forms in modern times: 6 vols., 1895, edited with an introduction by George Wyndham (Tudor Translations); 10 vols., 1898, edited by W. H. D. Rouse (Temple Classics); 8 vols., 1928 (Shakespeare Head Press, Oxford); 5 vols., 1929 (Nonesuch Press). *Selected Lives from the Lives of the Noble Grecians and Romans*, 2 vols., 1963, edited by Paul Turner (Centaur Press), includes sixteen of them and nine are included in *Plutarch: The Rise and Fall of Athens*, translated by Ian Scott-Kilvert (Penguin Books).

The principal editions of selections of the *Lives* illustrating Shakespeare are: *Shakespeare's Plutarch*, edited by W. W. Skeat (1895); *Four Lives from North's Plutarch*, edited by R. H. Carr (1906); *Shakespeare's Plutarch*, edited by C. F. Tucker Brooke (2 vols., 1909); *Narrative and Dramatic Sources of Shakespeare*, edited by Geoffrey Bullough, Vols. V and VI, *Classical Plays* (1964–6). These all contain material valuable for the study of Shakespeare's use of Plutarch. Other helpful books are: R. C. Trench, *Plutarch. His Life, his Parallel Lives, and his Morals* (1874); M. W. MacCallum, *Shakespeare's Roman Plays and their Background* (1910; new edition 1967); J. A. K. Thomson, *Shakespeare and the Classics* (1952); *Shakespeare Survey*, Vol. X (1957), edited by Allardyce Nicoll. For a general study of North and his contemporaries as translators, see F. O. Matthiessen, *Translation. An Elizabethan Art* (1931).

I am grateful to my colleagues at the Shakespeare Institute, Miss Roberta Buchanan, Mr P. J. Frankis, and Dr Stanley Wells, for much help in the preparation of this edition.

T. J. B. SPENCER

*The Shakespeare Institute*
*University of Birmingham*

# THE LIFE OF JULIUS CAESAR

At what time Sylla was made lord of all, he would have had Caesar put away his wife Cornelia, the daughter of Cinna Dictator. But when he saw he could neither with any promise nor threat bring him to it, he took her jointure away from him. The cause of Caesar's ill will unto Sylla was by means of marriage. For Marius the elder married his father's own sister, by whom he had Marius the younger; whereby Caesar and he were cousin-germans. Sylla being troubled in weighty matters, putting to death so many of his enemies, when he came to be conqueror, he made no reckoning of Caesar.

But he was not contented to be hidden in safety, but came and made suit unto the people for the priesthoodship that was void, when he had scant any hair on his face. Howbeit he was repulsed by Sylla's means, that secretly was against him; who when he was determined to have killed him, some of his friends told him that it was to no purpose to put so young a boy as he to death. But Sylla told them again that they did not consider that there were many Marians in that young boy.

Caesar, understanding that, stale out of Rome, and hid himself a long time in the country of the Sabines, wandering still from place to place. But one day, being carried from house to house, he fell into the hands of Sylla's soldiers, who searched all those places and took them whom they found hidden. Caesar bribed the captain, whose name was Cornelius, with two talents which he gave him. After he had escaped them thus, he went unto the sea side and took ship, and sailed into Bithynia to go unto King Nicomedes.

When he had been with him a while, he took sea again, and was taken by pirates about the isle of Pharmacusa. For those pirates kept all upon that sea coast, with a great fleet of ships and boats. They asking him at the first twenty talents for his ransom, Caesar laughed them to scorn, as though they knew not what a man they had taken, and of himself promised them fifty talents. Then he sent his men up and down to get him this money, so that he was left in manner alone among these thieves of the Cilicians – which are the cruellest butchers in the world – with one of his friends and two of his slaves only. And yet he made so little reckoning of them that, when he was desirous to sleep, he sent unto them to command them to make no noise. Thus was he eight-and-thirty days among them, not kept as prisoner, but rather waited upon by them as a prince. All this time he would boldly exercise himself in any sport or pastime they would go to. And other while also he would write verses and make orations, and call them together to say them before them; and if any of them seemed as though they had not understood him or passed not for them, he called them blockheads and brute beasts, and laughing threatened them that he would hang them up. But they were as merry with the matter as could be, and took all in good part, thinking that this his bold speech came through the simplicity of his youth. So when his ransom was come from the city of Miletum, they being paid their money, and he again set at liberty, he then presently armed and manned out certain ships out of the haven of Miletum, to follow those thieves, whom he found yet riding at anchor in the same island. So he took the most of them and had the spoil of their goods; but, for their bodies, he brought them into the city of Pergamum; and there committed them to prison, whilst he himself went to speak with Junius, who had the government of Asia, as unto whom the execution of these pirates did belong, for that he was Praetor of that country. But this Praetor, having a great fancy to be fingering of the money, because there was good store of it, answered that he would consider of these prisoners at better leisure. Caesar, leaving Junius there, returned again unto Pergamum, and there hung up all these thieves openly upon a cross, as he had oftentimes promised them in the isle he would do, when they thought he did but jest.

Afterwards, when Sylla's power began to decay, Caesar's friends wrote unto him, to pray him to come home again. But he sailed first unto Rhodes, to study there a time under Apollonius the son of

Molon, whose scholar also Cicero was, for he was a very honest man and an excellent good rhetorician. It is reported that Caesar had an excellent natural gift to speak well before the people; and, besides that rare gift, he was excellently well studied, so that doubtless he was counted the second man for eloquence in his time, and gave place to the first because he would be the first and chiefest man of war and authority, being not yet come to the degree of perfection to speak well, which his nature could have performed in him, because he was given rather to follow wars and to manage great matters; which in the end brought him to be lord of all Rome. And therefore, in a book he wrote against that which Cicero made in the praise of Cato, he prayeth the readers not to compare the style of a soldier with the eloquence of an excellent orator, that had followed it the most part of his life.

When he was returned again unto Rome, he accused Dolabella for his ill behaviour in the government of his province; and he had divers cities of Greece that gave in evidence against him. Notwithstanding, Dolabella at the length was dismissed. Caesar, to requite the good will of the Grecians, which they had showed him in his accusation of Dolabella, took their cause in hand when they did accuse Publius Antonius before Marcus Lucullus, Praetor of Macedon; and followed it so hard against him in their behalf that Antonius was driven to appeal before the Tribunes at Rome, alleging to colour his appeal withal, that he could have no justice in Greece against the Grecians.

Now Caesar immediately won many men's good wills at Rome through his eloquence in pleading of their causes; and the people loved him marvellously also, because of the courteous manner he had to speak to every man and to use them gently, being more ceremonious therein than was looked for in one of his years. Furthermore, he ever kept a good board, and fared well at his table, and was very liberal besides; the which indeed did advance him forward, and brought him in estimation with the people. His enemies judging that this favour of the common people would soon quail when he could no longer hold out that charge and expense, suffered him to run on, till by little and little he was grown to be of great strength and power. But in fine, when they had thus given him the bridle to grow to this greatness and that they could not then pull him back, though indeed in sight it would turn one day to the destruction of the whole state and commonwealth of Rome, too late they found that there is not so little a beginning of any thing, but continuance of time will soon make it strong, when through contempt there is no impediment to hinder the greatness. Thereupon Cicero, like a wise shipmaster that feareth the calmness of the sea, was the first man that, mistrusting his manner of dealing in the commonwealth, found out his craft and malice, which he cunningly cloaked under the habit of outward courtesy and familiarity.

'And yet,' said he, 'when I consider how finely he combeth his fair bush of hair, and how smooth it lieth, and that I see him scratch his head with one finger only, my mind gives me then that such a kind of man should not have so wicked a thought in his head as to overthrow the state of the commonwealth.'

But this was long time after that.

The first show and proof of the love and good will which the people did bear unto Caesar was when he sued to be Tribune of the soldiers (to wit, colonel of a thousand footmen), standing against Caius Pompilius, at what time he was preferred and chosen before him. But the second and more manifest proof than the first was at the death of his aunt Julia, the wife of Marius the elder. For, being her nephew, he made a solemn oration in the market-place in commendation of her, and at her burial did boldly venture to show forth the images of Marius; the which was the first time that they were seen after Sylla's victory, because that Marius and all his confederates had been proclaimed traitors and enemies to the commonwealth. For when there were some that cried out upon Caesar for doing of it, the people on the other side kept a stir and rejoiced at it, clapping of their hands, and thanked him for that he had brought as it were out of hell the remembrance of Marius' honour again into Rome, which had so long time been obscured and buried. And where it had been an ancient custom of long time that the Romans used to make funeral orations in praise of old ladies and matrons when they died, but not of young women, Caesar was the first that praised his own wife with funeral oration when she was dead; the which also did increase the people's good wills the more, seeing him of so kind and gentle nature.

After the burial of his wife he was made Treasurer under Antistius Vetus Praetor, whom he honoured ever after; so that when himself came to be Praetor, he made his son to be chosen Treasurer. Afterwards, when he was come out of that office, he married his third wife Pompeia, having a daughter by his first wife Cornelia which was married unto Pompey the Great.

Now for that he was very liberal in expenses, buying, as some thought, but a vain and short glory of the favour of the people – where indeed he bought good cheap the greatest things that could be – some say that, before he bare any office in the commonwealth, he was grown in debt to the sum of thirteen hundred talents. Furthermore, because he was made overseer of the work for the highway going unto Appius,* he disbursed a great sum of his own money towards the charges of the same. And on the other side, when he was made Aedilis, for that he did show the people the pastime of three hundred and twenty couple of sword players and did besides exceed all other in sumptuousness in the sports and common feasts which he made to delight them withal, and did as it were drown all the stately shows of others in the like that had gone before him, he so pleased the people and won their love therewith that they devised daily to give him new offices for to requite him.

At that time there were two factions in Rome, to wit, the faction of Sylla, which was very strong and of great power, and the other of Marius, which then was under foot and durst not show itself. But Caesar, because he would renew it again, even at that time when, he being Aedilis, all the feasts and common sports were in their greatest ruff, he secretly caused images of Marius to be made and of victories that carried triumphs; and those he set up one night within the Capitol. The next morning, when every man saw the glistering of these golden images excellently well wrought, showing by the inscriptions that they were the victories which Marius had won upon the Cimbres, everyone marvelled much at the boldness of him

* Corrected in the 1603 edition to 'the highway called Appius' way'. [Ed.]

that durst set them up there, knowing well enough who it was. Hereupon it ran straight through all the city; and every man came thither to see them. Then some cried out upon Caesar, and said it was a tyranny which he meant to set up, by renewing of such honours as before had been trodden under foot and forgotten by common decree and open proclamation; and that it was no more but a bait to gauge the people's good wills, which he had set out in the stately shows of his common plays, to see if he had brought them to his lure, that they would abide such parts to be played and a new alteration of things to be made. They of Marius' faction on the other side, encouraging one another, showed themselves straight a great number gathered together, and made the mount of the Capitol ring again with their cries and clapping of hands; insomuch as the tears ran down many of their cheeks for very joy when they saw the images of Marius; and they extolled Caesar to the skies, judging him the worthiest man of all the kindred of Marius. The Senate being assembled thereupon, Catulus Luctatius, one of the greatest authority at that time in Rome, rose and vehemently inveighed against Caesar, and spake that then which ever since hath been noted much: that Caesar did not now covertly go to work, but by plain force sought to alter the state of the commonwealth. Nevertheless Caesar at that time answered him so that the Senate was satisfied. Thereupon they that had him in estimation did grow in better hope than before, and persuaded him that hardily he should give place to no man, and that through the good will of the people he should be better than all they and come to be the chiefest man of the city.

At that time the chief Bishop Metellus died; and two of the notablest men of the city, and of greatest authority, Isauricus and Catulus, contended for his room. Caesar, notwithstanding their contention, would give neither of them both place, but presented himself to the people and made suit for it as they did. The suit being equal betwixt either of them, Catulus, because he was a man of greater calling and dignity than the other, doubting the uncertainty of the election, sent unto Caesar a good sum of money to make him leave off his suit. But Caesar sent him word again that he would lend a greater sum than that, to maintain the suit against him.

When the day of the election came, his mother bringing him to the door of his house, Caesar, weeping, kissed her and said:

'Mother, this day thou shalt see thy son chief Bishop of Rome, or banished from Rome.'

In fine, when the voices of the people were gathered together and the strife well debated, Caesar won the victory and made the Senate and noblemen all afraid of him, for that they thought that thenceforth he would make the people do what he thought good.

Then Catulus and Piso fell flatly out with Cicero, and condemned him for that he did not bewray Caesar when he knew that he was of conspiracy with Catiline and had opportunity to have done it. For when Catiline was bent and determined, not only to overthrow the state of the commonwealth, but utterly to destroy the Empire of Rome, he scaped out of the hands of justice for lack of sufficient proof, before his full treason and determination was known. Notwithstanding, he left Lentulus and Cethegus in the city, companions of his conspiracy; unto whom whether Caesar did give any secret help or comfort, it is not well known. Yet this is manifest, that when they were convinced in open Senate, Cicero, being at that time Consul, asking every man's opinion in the Senate what punishment they should have, and every one of them till it came to Caesar, gave sentence they should die, Caesar then rising up to speak made an oration, penned and premeditated before; and said that it was neither lawful, nor yet their custom did bear it, to put men of such nobility to death – but in an extremity – without lawful indictment and condemnation; and therefore that, if they were put in prison in some city of Italy, where Cicero thought best, until that Catiline were overthrown, the Senate then might at their pleasure quietly take such order therein as might best appear unto their wisdoms. This opinion was thought more gentle, and withal was uttered with such a passing good grace and eloquence, that not only they which were to speak after him did approve it, but such also as had spoken to the contrary before revoked their opinion and stuck to his, until it came to Cato and Catulus to speak. They both did sharply inveigh against him, but Cato chiefly; who in his oration made Caesar suspected to be of the conspiracy and stoutly spake against him, insomuch that the offenders were put into the hands of the officers to be put to death.

Caesar coming out of the Senate, a company of young men, which guarded Cicero for the safety of his person, did set upon him with their swords drawn. But some say that Curio covered Caesar with his gown and took him out of their hands. And Cicero self, when the young men looked upon him, beckoned with his head that they should not kill him, either fearing the fury of the people, or else that he thought it too shameful and wicked a part. But, if that were true, I marvel why Cicero did not put it into his book he wrote *Of his Consulship*. But certainly they blamed him afterwards, for that he took not the opportunity offered him against Caesar, only for over-much fear of the people, that loved him very dearly. For shortly after, when Caesar went into the Senate, to clear himself of certain presumptions and false accusations objected against him, and being bitterly taunted among them, the Senate keeping him longer than they were wont, the people came about the Council house and called out aloud for him, bidding them let him out. Cato then, fearing the insurrection of the poor needy persons, which were they that put all their hope in Caesar and did also move the people to stir, did persuade the Senate to make a frank distribution of corn unto them for a month. This distribution did put the commonwealth to a new charge of five hundred and fifty myriads. This counsel quenched a present great fear, and did in happy time scatter and disperse abroad the best part of Caesar's force and power, at such time as he was made Praetor and that for respect of his office he was most to be feared.

Yet all the time he was officer he never sought any alteration in the commonwealth; but contrarily he himself had a great misfortune fell in his own house; which was this.

There was a young nobleman of the order of the Patricians called Publius Clodius, who lacked neither wealth nor eloquence, but otherwise as insolent and impudent a person as any was else in Rome. He became in love with Pompeia, Caesar's wife, who misliked not withal; notwithstanding she was so straitly looked to, and that Aurelia, Caesar's mother, an honest gentlewoman, had such an eye of her that these two lovers could not meet as they would, without great peril and difficulty.

The Romans do use to honour a goddess which they call the Good Goddess, as the Grecians have her whom they call *Gynaeceia* (to wit, 'the goddess of women'). Her the Phrygians do claim to be peculiar unto them, saying that she is King Midas' mother. Howbeit the Romans hold opinion that it is a nymph of wood married unto god Faunus. The Grecians, they say also that she was one of the mothers of the god Bacchus, whom they dare not name. And for proof hereof, on her feast day the women make certain tabernacles of vine twigs and leaves of vine branches; and also they make, as the tale goeth, a holy dragon for this goddess, and do set it by her. Besides, it is not lawful for any man to be present at their sacrifices, no not within the house itself where they are made. Furthermore, they say that the women in these sacrifices do many things amongst themselves, much like unto the ceremonies of Orpheus. Now when the time of this feast came, the husband, whether he were Praetor or Consul, and all his men and the boys in the house do come out of it, and leave it wholly to his wife, to order the house at her pleasure; and there the sacrifices and ceremonies are done the most part of the night; and they do besides pass the night away in songs and music.

Pompeia, Caesar's wife, being that year to celebrate this feast, Clodius, who had yet no hair on his face and thereby thought he should not be bewrayed, disguised himself in a singing wench's apparel, because his face was very like unto a young wench. He finding the gates open, being secretly brought in by her chamber maid that was made privy unto it, she left him and ran to Pompeia her mistress to tell her that he was come. The chamber maid tarried long before she came again, insomuch as, Clodius being weary waiting for her where she left him, he took his pleasure and went from one place to another in the house, which had very large rooms in it, still shunning the light, and was by chance met withal by one of Aurelia's maids, who, taking him for a woman, prayed her to play. Clodius refusing to play, the maid pulled him forward and asked him what he was. Clodius then answered her that he tarried for Abra, one of Pompeia's women. So Aurelia's maid, knowing him by his voice, ran straight where the lights and ladies were, and cried out that there was a man disguised in woman's apparel. The women therewith

29

were so amazed that Aurelia caused them presently to leave off the ceremonies of the sacrifice and to hide their secret things; and having seen the gates fast locked, went immediately up and down the house with torch light to seek out this man; who at the last was found out in the chamber of Pompeia's maid, with whom he hid himself. Thus Clodius being found out, and known of the women, they thrust him out of the doors by the shoulders.

The same night the women told their husbands of this chance as soon as they came home. The next morning there ran a great rumour through the city how Clodius had attempted a great villainy and that he deserved not only to be punished of them whom he had slandered but also of the commonwealth and the gods. There was one of the Tribunes of the People that did indict him, and accuse him of high treason to the gods. Furthermore, there were also of the chiefest of the nobility and Senate that came to depose against him, and burdened him with many horrible and detestable facts, and specially with incest committed with his own sister, which was married unto Lucullus. Notwithstanding, the people stoutly defended Clodius against their accusations; and this did help him much against the judges, which were amazed and afraid to stir the people. This notwithstanding, Caesar presently put his wife away; and thereupon, being brought by Clodius' accuser to be a witness against him, he answered, he knew nothing of that they objected against Clodius. This answer being clean contrary to their expectation that heard it, the accuser asked Caesar why, then, he had put away his wife.

'Because I will not,' said he, 'that my wife be so much as suspected.' And some say that Caesar spake truly as he thought. But others think that he did it to please the common people, who were very desirous to save Clodius. So Clodius was discharged of this accusation, because the most part of the judges gave a confused judgment, for the fear they stood one way of the danger of the common people if they condemned him, and for the ill opinion of the other side of the nobility if they did quit him.

The government of the province of Spain being fallen unto Caesar for that he was Praetor, his creditors came and cried out upon him, and were importunate of him to be paid. Caesar, being unable to satisfy them, was compelled to go unto Crassus, who was the richest man of all Rome and that stood in need of Caesar's boldness and courage to withstand Pompey's greatness in the commonwealth. Crassus became his surety unto his greediest creditors for the sum of eight hundred and thirty talents. Whereupon they suffered Caesar to depart to the government of his province.

In his journey it is reported that, passing over the mountains of the Alps, they came through a little poor village that had not many households and yet poor cottages. There, his friends that did accompany him asked him merrily if there were any contending for offices in that town, and whether there were any strife there amongst the noblemen for honour. Caesar speaking in good earnest, answered: 'I cannot tell that,' said he, 'but for my part, I had rather be the chiefest man here than the second person in Rome.'

Another time also when he was in Spain, reading the history of Alexander's acts, when he had read it he was sorrowful a good while after, and then burst out in weeping. His friends seeing that, marvelled what should be the cause of his sorrow. He answered them: 'Do ye not think,' said he, 'that I have good cause to be heavy, when King Alexander, being no older than myself is now, had in old time won so many nations and countries; and that I hitherunto have done nothing worthy of my self?'

Therefore, when he was come into Spain, he was very careful of his business, and had in few days joined ten new ensigns more of footmen unto the other twenty which he had before. Then, marching forward against the Callaecians and Lusitanians, he conquered all, and went as far as the great sea Oceanus, subduing all the people which before knew not the Romans for their lords. There he took order for pacifying of the war, and did as wisely take order for the establishing of peace. For he did reconcile the cities together and made them friends one with another. But specially he pacified all suits of law and strife betwixt the debtors and creditors, which grew by reason of usury. For he ordained that the creditors should take yearly two parts of the revenue of their debtors, until such time as they had paid themselves; and that the debtors should have the third part to themselves to live withal. He, having won great estimation by this good order taken, returned from his government very rich, and his soldiers also full of rich spoils, who called him *Imperator* (to say, 'sovereign captain').

Now the Romans having a custom that such as demanded honour of Triumph should remain a while without the city, and that they on the other side which sued for the Consulship should of necessity be there in person, Caesar coming unhappily at that very time when the Consuls were chosen, he sent to pray the Senate to do him that favour, that, being absent, he might by his friends sue for the Consulship. Cato at the first did vehemently inveigh against it, vouching an express law forbidding the contrary. But afterwards, perceiving that notwithstanding the reasons he alleged many of the Senators, being won by Caesar, favoured his request, yet he cunningly sought all he could to prevent them, prolonging time, dilating his oration until night. Caesar thereupon determined rather to give over the suit of his Triumph and to make suit for the Consulship; and so came into the city, and had such a device with him as went beyond them all, but Cato only.

His device was this. Pompey and Crassus, two of the greatest personages of the city of Rome, being at jar together, Caesar made them friends, and by that means got unto himself the power of them both. For, by colour of that gentle act and friendship of his, he subtly, unawares to them all, did greatly alter and change the state of the commonwealth. For it was not the private discord between Pompey and Caesar, as many men thought, that caused the civil war. But rather it was their agreement together, who joined all their powers first to overthrow the state of the Senate and nobility; and afterwards they fell at jar one with another. But Cato, that then foresaw and prophesied many times what would follow, was taken but for a vain man. But afterwards they found him a wiser man than happy in his counsel.

Thus Caesar being brought unto the assembly of the election, in the midst of these two noble persons whom he had before reconciled together, he was there chosen Consul, with Calphurnius Bibulus, without gainsaying or contradiction of any man.

Now, when he was entered into his office, he began to put forth laws meeter for a seditious Tribune of the People than for a Consul; because by them he preferred the division of lands, and distributing of corn to every citizen, gratis, to please them withal. But when the noblemen of the Senate were against his device, he, desiring no better occasion, began to cry out and to protest that by the over-hardness and austerity of the Senate they drave him against his will to lean unto the people. And thereupon, having Crassus on the one side of him and Pompey on the other, he asked them openly in the assembly if they did give their consent unto the laws which he had put forth. They both answered, they did. Then he prayed them to stand by him against those that threatened him with force of sword to let him. Crassus gave him his word, he would. Pompey also did the like, and added thereunto that he would come with his sword and target both, against them that would withstand him with their swords. These words offended much the Senate, being far unmeet for his gravity, and undecent for the majesty and honour he carried, and most of all uncomely for the presence of the Senate whom he should have reverenced; and were speeches fitter for a rash light-headed youth than for his person. Howbeit the common people on the other side, they rejoiced.

Then Caesar, because he would be more assured of Pompey's power and friendship, he gave him his daughter Julia in marriage, which was made sure before unto Servilius Caepio, and promised him in exchange Pompey's wife,★ the which was sure also unto Faustus, the son of Sylla. And shortly after, also, Caesar self did marry Calphurnia, the daughter of Piso, whom he caused to be made Consul, to succeed him the next year following. Cato then cried out with open mouth, and called the gods to witness that it was 'a shameful matter, and not to be suffered, that they should in that sort make havoc of the Empire of Rome by such horrible bawdy matches, distributing among themselves through those wicked marriages the governments of the provinces and of great armies'.

Calphurnius Bibulus, fellow Consul with Caesar, perceiving that he did contend in vain, making all the resistance he could to withstand this law, and that oftentimes he was in danger to be slain with

★ Corrected in the 1603 edition to 'Pompey's daughter.' [Ed.]

Cato in the market-place and assembly, he kept close in his house all the rest of his Consulship.

When Pompey had married Julia, he filled all the market-place with soldiers, and by open force authorized the laws which Caesar made in the behalf of the people. Furthermore, he procured that Caesar had Gaul on this side and beyond the Alps, and all Illyria, with four legions granted him for five years. Then Cato standing up to speak against it, Caesar bade his officers lay hold on him and carry him to prison, thinking he would have appealed unto the Tribunes. But Cato said never a word when he went his way. Caesar perceiving then that not only the Senators and nobility were offended but that the common people also, for the reverence they bare unto Cato's virtues, were ashamed and went away with silence, he himself secretly did pray one of the Tribunes that he would take Cato from the officers. But after he had played this part, there were few Senators that would be President of the Senate under him, but left the city, because they could not away with his doings. And of them there was an old man called Considius that on a time boldly told him the rest durst not come to council because they were afraid of his soldiers. Caesar answered him again:

'And why, then, dost not thou keep thee at home, for the same fear?' Considius replied:

'Because my age taketh away fear from me. For, having so short a time to live, I have no care to prolong it further.'

The shamefullest part that Caesar played while he was Consul seemeth to be this: when he chose P. Clodius Tribune of the People, that had offered his wife such dishonour and profaned the holy ancient mysteries of the women which were celebrated in his own house. Clodius sued to be Tribune to no other end but to destroy Cicero; and Caesar self also departed not from Rome to his army before he had set them together by the ears and driven Cicero out of Italy.

All these things they say he did before the wars with the Gauls. But the time of the great armies and conquests he made afterwards, and of the war in the which he subdued all the Gauls (entering into another course of life far contrary unto the first), made him to be known for as valiant a soldier and as excellent a captain to lead men, as those that afore him had been counted the wisest and most valiantest generals that ever were and that by their valiant deeds had achieved great honour. For whosoever would compare the house of the Fabians, of the Scipios, of the Metellians, yea, those also of his own time, or long before him, as Sylla, Marius, the two Lucullians, and Pompey self –

*Whose fame ascendeth up unto the heavens*

– it will appear that Caesar's prowess and deeds of arms did excel them all together. The one, in the hard countries where he made wars; another, in enlarging the realms and countries which he joined unto the Empire of Rome; another, in the multitude and power of his enemies whom he overcame; another, in the rudeness and austere nature of men with whom he had to do, whose manners afterwards he softened and made civil; another, in courtesy and clemency which he used unto them whom he had conquered; another, in great bounty and liberality bestowed upon them that served under him in those wars; and in fine, he excelled them all in the number of battles he had fought and in the multitude of his enemies he had slain in battle. For in less than ten years' war in Gaul he took by force and assault above eight hundred towns; he conquered three hundred several nations; and, having before him in battle thirty hundred thousand soldiers, at sundry times he slew ten hundred thousand of them, and took as many more prisoners.

Furthermore, he was so entirely beloved of his soldiers that, to do him service, where otherwise they were no more than other men in any private quarrel, if Caesar's honour were touched, they were invincible and would so desperately venture themselves, and with such fury, that no man was able to abide them. And this appeareth plainly by the example of Acilius; who, in a battle by sea before the city of Marseilles, boarding one of his enemies' ships, one cut off his right hand with a sword; but yet he forsook not his target which he had in his left hand, but thrust it in his enemies' faces and made them fly, so that he won their ship from them. And Cassius Scaeva also, in a conflict before the city of Dyrrachium, having one of his eyes put out with an arrow, his shoulder stricken through with a dart and his thigh with another, and having received thirty arrows upon his shield, he called to his enemies and made as though he would yield unto them. But when two of them came running to him, he clave one of their shoulders from his body with his sword, and hurt the other in the face; so that he made him turn his back, and at the length saved himself by means of his companions that came to help him. And in Britain also, when the captains of the bands were driven into a marsh or bog full of mire and dirt, and that the enemies did fiercely assail them there, Caesar then standing to view the battle, he saw a private soldier of his thrust in among the captains, and fought so valiantly in their defence that at the length he drave the barbarous people to fly, and by his means saved the captains, which otherwise were in great danger to have been cast away. Then this soldier, being the hindmost man of all the captains, marching with great pain through the mire and dirt, half swimming and half afoot, in the end got to the other side; but left his shield behind him. Caesar, wondering at his noble courage, ran to him with joy to embrace him. But the poor soldier hanging down his head, the water standing in his eyes, fell down at Caesar's feet and besought him to pardon him, for that he had left his target behind him. And in Afric also, Scipio having taken one of Caesar's ships, and Granius Petronius aboard on her amongst other, not long before chosen Treasurer, he put all the rest to the sword but him, and said he would give him his life. But Petronius answered him again: that Caesar's soldiers did not use to have their lives given them, but to give others their lives; and with those words he drew his sword and thrust himself through.

Now Caesar's self did breed this noble courage and life in them. First, for that he gave them bountifully, and did honour them also, showing thereby that he did not heap up riches in the wars to maintain his life afterwards in wantonness and pleasure, but that he did keep it in store, honourably to reward their valiant service; and that by so much he thought himself rich, by how much he was liberal in rewarding of them that had deserved it. Furthermore, they did not wonder so much at his valiantness in putting himself at every instant in such manifest danger, and in taking so extreme pains as he did, knowing that it was his greedy desire of honour that set him afire, and pricked him forward to do it; but that he always continued all labour and hardness, more than his body could bear, that filled them all with admiration. For, concerning the constitution of his body, he was lean, white, and soft skinned, and often subject to headache, and otherwhile to the falling sickness (the which took him the first time, as it is reported, in Corduba, a city of Spain); but yet therefore yielded not to the disease of his body, to make it a cloak to cherish him withal, but, contrarily, took the pains of war as a medicine to cure his sick body, fighting always with his disease, travelling continually, living soberly, and commonly lying abroad in the field. For the most nights he slept in his coach or litter, and thereby bestowed his rest, to make him always able to do something. And in the daytime, he would travel up and down the country to see towns, castles, and strong places.

He had always a secretary with him in his coach, who did still write as he went by the way, and a soldier behind him that carried his sword. He made such speed the first time he came from Rome, when he had his office, that in eight days he came to the river of Rhone. He was so excellent a rider of horse from his youth that, holding his hands behind him, he would gallop his horse upon the spur. In his wars in Gaul he did further exercise himself to indite letters as he rode by the way, and did occupy two secretaries at once with as much as they could write; and (as Oppius writeth) more than two at a time. And it is reported that Caesar was the first that devised friends might talk together by writing ciphers in letters, when he had no leisure to speak with them for his urgent business, and for the great distance besides from Rome.

How little accompt Caesar made of his diet, this example doth prove it. Caesar supping one night in Milan with his friend Valerius Leo, was there served sperage to his board, and oil of perfume put

1 CASSIUS:      He had a fever when he was in Spain,
                And when the fit was on him, I did mark
                How he did shake.          (*Julius Caesar*, I, 2, 119)

See also p. 81 note 11.

into it instead of salad oil. He simply eat it, and found no fault, blaming his friends that were offended; and told them that it had been enough for them to have abstained to eat of that they misliked, and not to shame their friend, and how that he lacked good manner that found fault with his friend.

Another time, as he travelled through the country, he was driven by foul weather on the sudden to take a poor man's cottage, that had but one little cabin in it, and that was so narrow that one man could but scarce lie in it. Then he said to his friends that were about him:
'Greatest rooms are meetest for greatest men, and the most necessary rooms for the sickest persons.'
And thereupon he caused Oppius that was sick to lie there all night; and he himself with the rest of his friends lay without doors under the easing of the house.

The first war that Caesar made with the Gauls was with the Helvetians and Tigurinians, who, having set fire of all their good cities, to the number of twelve, and four hundred villages besides, came to invade that part of Gaul which was subject to the Romans, as the Cimbri and Teutons had done before; unto whom for valiantness they gave no place; and they were also a great number of them, for they were three hundred thousand souls in all, whereof there were a hundred four-score and ten thousand fighting men. Of those, it was not Caesar himself that overcame the Tigurinians, but Labienus, his lieutenant, that overthrew them by the river of Arar. But the Helvetians themselves came suddenly with their army to set upon him as he was going towards a city of his confederates. Caesar, perceiving that, made haste to get him some place of strength, and there did set his men in battle ray. When one brought him his horse to get up on which he used in battle, he said unto them:
'When I have overcome mine enemies, I will then get up on him to follow the chase, but now let us give them charge.'
Therewith he marched forward afoot, and gave charge; and there fought it out a long time, before he could make them fly that were in battle. But the greatest trouble he had was to distress their camp, and to break their strength which they had made with their carts.

For there, they that before had fled from the battle did not only put themselves in force, and valiantly fought it out, but their wives and children also fighting for their lives to the death were all slain; and the battle was scant ended at midnight.

Now if the act of this victory was famous, unto that he also added another as notable, or exceeding it. For, of all the barbarous people that had escaped from this battle, he gathered together again above a hundred thousand of them, and compelled them to return home into their country which they had forsaken and unto their towns also which they had burnt; because he feared the Germans would come over the river of Rhine and occupy that country lying void.

The second war he made was in defence of the Gauls against the Germans; although, before, he himself had caused Ariovistus their king to be received for a confederate of the Romans. Notwithstanding, they were grown very unquiet neighbours; and it appeared plainly that, having any occasion offered them to enlarge their territories, they would not content them with their own, but meant to invade and possess the rest of Gaul.

Caesar perceiving that some of his captains trembled for fear, but specially the young gentlemen of noble houses of Rome who thought to have gone to the wars with him as only for their pleasure and gain, he called them to council and commanded them that were afraid that they should depart home and not put themselves in danger against their wills, sith they had such womanish faint hearts to shrink when he had need of them. And for himself, he said, he would set upon the barbarous people, though he had left him but the Tenth Legion only, saying that the enemies were no valianter than the Cimbri had been, nor that he was a captain inferior unto Marius. This oration being made, the soldiers of the Tenth Legion sent their lieutenants unto him to thank him for the good opinion he had of them. And the other legions also fell out with their captains; and all of them together followed him many days' journey with good will to serve him, until they came within two hundred furlongs of the camp of the enemies.

Ariovistus' courage was well cooled when he saw Caesar was

come and that the Romans came to seek out the Germans, where they thought, and made accompt, that they durst not have abidden them; and therefore, nothing mistrusting it would have come so to pass, he wondered much at Caesar's courage; and the more when he saw his own army in a maze withal. But much more did their courages fall by reason of the foolish women prophesiers they had among them, which did foretell things to come; who, considering the waves and trouble of the rivers, and the terrible noise they made running down the stream, did forewarn them not to fight until the new moon. Caesar, having intelligence thereof and perceiving that the barbarous people thereupon stirred not, thought it best then to set upon them, being discouraged with this superstitious fear, rather than, losing time, he should tarry their leisure. So he did skirmish with them even to their forts and little hills where they lay, and by this means provoked them so that with great fury they came down to fight. There he overcame them in battle, and followed them in chase, with great slaughter, three hundred furlong, even unto the river of Rhine; and he filled all the fields thitherto with dead bodies and spoils. Howbeit Ariovistus, flying with speed, got over the river of Rhine and escaped with a few of his men. It is said that there were slain four-score thousand persons at this battle.

After this exploit Caesar left his army amongst the Sequanes to winter there; and he himself in the meantime, thinking of the affairs at Rome, went over the mountains into Gaul about the river of Po, being part of his province which he had in charge. For there the river called Rubicon divideth the rest of Italy from Gaul on this side the Alps. Caesar, lying there, did practise to make friends in Rome, because many came thither to see him; unto whom he granted their suits they demanded, and sent them home also, partly with liberal rewards and partly with large promises and hope. Now, during all this conquest of the Gauls, Pompey did not consider how Caesar interchangeably did conquer the Gauls with the weapons of the Romans, and won the Romans again with the money of the Gauls.

Caesar being advertised that the Belgae (which were the warlikest men of all the Gauls and that occupied the third part of Gaul) were all up in arms and had raised a great power of men together, he straight made towards them with all possible speed; and found them spoiling and overrunning the country of the Gauls, their neighbours and confederates of the Romans. So he gave them battle; and, they fighting cowardly, he overthrew the most part of them which were in a troop together, and slew such a number of them that the Romans passed over deep rivers and lakes afoot upon their dead bodies, the rivers were so full of them. After this overthrow, they that dwelt nearest unto the sea side, and were next neighbours unto the ocean, did yield themselves without any compulsion or fight.

Whereupon, he led his army against the Nervians, the stoutest warriors of all the Belgae. They, dwelling in the wood country, had conveyed their wives, children, and goods into a marvellous great forest, as far from their enemies as they could; and, being about the number of six-score thousand fighting men and more, they came one day and set upon Caesar, when his army was out of order and fortifying of his camp, little looking to have fought that day. At the first charge they brake the horsemen of the Romans; and compassing in the Twelfth and Seventh Legion, they slew all the centurions and captains of the bands. And had not Caesar self taken his shield on his arm and, flying in amongst the barbarous people, made a lane through them that fought before him, and the Tenth Legion also, seeing him in danger, run unto him from the top of the hill where they stood in battle, and broken the ranks of their enemies, there had not a Roman escaped alive that day. But, taking example of Caesar's valiantness, they fought desperately beyond their power; and yet could not make the Nervians fly, but they fought it out to the death, till they were all in manner slain in the field. It is written that of three-score thousand fighting men there escaped only but five hundred; and of four hundred gentlemen and counsellors of the Romans but three saved. The Senate understanding it at Rome ordained that they should do sacrifice unto the gods, and keep feasts and solemn processions fifteen days together without intermission, having never made the like ordinance at Rome for any victory that ever was obtained; because they saw the danger had been marvellous great, so many nations rising as they did in arms together against him;

and further, the love of the people unto him made his victory much
2 more famous.

For, when Caesar had set his affairs at a stay in Gaul on the other
side of the Alps, he always used to lie about the river of Po in the
winter time, to give direction for the establishing of things at Rome
at his pleasure. For, not only they that made suit for offices at Rome
were chosen magistrates by means of Caesar's money which he gave
them (with the which, bribing the people, they bought their voices,
and when they were in office did all that they could to increase Caesar's
power and greatness), but the greatest and chiefest men also of the
nobility went unto Luke unto him – as Pompey, Crassus, Appius,
Praetor of Sardinia, and Nepos, Proconsul in Spain; insomuch that
there were at one time six-score sergeants carrying rods and axes
before the magistrates, and above two hundred Senators besides.

There they fell in consultation, and determined that Pompey and
Crassus should again be chosen Consuls the next year following.
Furthermore, they did appoint that Caesar should have money again
delivered him to pay his army, and, besides, did prorogue the time
of his government five years further. This was thought a very strange
and an unreasonable matter unto wise men. For they themselves that
had taken so much money of Caesar persuaded the Senate to let
him have money of the common treasure, as though he had had none
before; yea, to speak more plainly, they compelled the Senate unto
it, sighing and lamenting to see the decrees they passed. Cato was not
there then, for they had purposely sent him before into Cyprus.
Howbeit Faonius, that followed Cato's steps, when he saw that he
could not prevail, nor withstand them, he went out of the Senate in
choler, and cried out amongst the people that it was a horrible shame.
But no man did hearken to him, some for the reverence they bare
unto Pompey and Crassus, and others, favouring Caesar's proceedings, did put all their hope and trust in him, and therefore did quiet
themselves and stirred not.

2 ANTONY:   You all do know this mantle: I remember
            The first time ever Caesar put it on;
            'Twas on a summer's evening, in his tent,
            That day he overcame the Nervii. (*Julius Caesar*, III, 2, 174)

Then Caesar, returning into Gaul beyond the Alps unto his army, found there a great war in the country. For two great nations of Germany had not long before passed over the river of Rhine, to conquer new lands; and the one of these people were called Ipes and the other Tenterides. Now touching the battle which Caesar fought with them he himself doth describe it in his *Commentaries* in this sort: that the barbarous people having sent ambassadors unto him to require peace for a certain time, they notwithstanding, against law of arms, came and set upon him as he travelled by the way, insomuch as eight hundred of their men of arms overthrew five thousand of his horsemen, who nothing at all mistrusted their coming. Again, that they sent him other ambassadors to mock him once more; but that he kept them, and therewith caused his whole army to march against them, thinking it a folly and madness to keep faith with such traitorous barbarous breakers of leagues. Canutius writeth that, the Senate appointing again to do new sacrifice, procession, and feasts, to give thanks to the gods for this victory, Cato was of contrary opinion – that Caesar should be delivered into the hands of the barbarous people, for to purge their city and commonwealth of this breach of faith and to turn the curse upon him that was the author of it.

Of these barbarous people which came over the Rhine, being about the number of four hundred thousand persons, they were all in manner slain, saving a very few of them that, flying from the battle, got over the river of Rhine again, who were received by the Sicambrians, another people of the Germans. Caesar taking this occasion against them, lacking no good will of himself besides to have the honour to be counted the first Roman that ever passed over the river of Rhine with an army, he built a bridge over it. This river is marvellous broad and runneth with great fury, and in that place specially where he built his bridge. For there it is of a great breadth from one side to the other, and it hath so strong and swift a stream besides that men, casting down great bodies of trees into the river, which the stream bringeth down with it, did with the great blows and force thereof marvellously shake the posts of the bridge he had set up. But to prevent the blows of those trees, and also to break the fury of the stream, he made a pile of great wood above the bridge a good way and did forcibly ram them into the bottom of the river; so that in ten days' space he had set up and finished his bridge of the goodliest carpenter's work, and most excellent invention to see to, that could be possibly thought or devised. Then, passing over his army upon it, he found none that durst any more fight with him. For the Suevians, which were the warlikest people of all Germany, had gotten themselves with their goods into wonderful great valleys and bogs, full of woods and forests. Now when he had burnt all the country of his enemies and confirmed the league with the confederates of the Romans, he returned back again into Gaul after he had tarried eighteen days at the most in Germany on the other side of the Rhine.

The journey he made also into England was a noble enterprise, and very commendable. For he was the first that sailed the West Ocean with an army by sea, and that passed through the sea Atlanticum with his army, to make war in that so great and famous island – which many ancient writers would not believe that it was so indeed, and did make them vary about it, saying that it was but a fable and a lie – and was the first that enlarged the Roman Empire beyond the earth inhabitable. For twice he passed over the narrow sea against the firm land of Gaul; and, fighting many battles there, did hurt his enemies more than enrich his own men; because, of men hardly brought up and poor, there was nothing to be gotten. Whereupon his war had not such success as he looked for; and therefore, taking pledges only of the king, and imposing a yearly tribute upon him, to be paid unto the people of Rome, he returned
3 again into Gaul.

9 LUCIUS:     When Julius Caesar, whose remembrance yet
               Lives in men's eyes and will to ears and tongues
               Be theme and hearing ever, was in this Britain
               And conquer'd it, Cassibelan, thine uncle, . . .
                                      for him
               And his succession granted Rome a tribute,
               Yearly three thousand pounds, which by thee lately
               Is left untender'd . . .

There he was no sooner landed but he found letters ready to be sent over the sea unto him, in the which he was advertised from Rome of the death of his daughter, that she was dead with child by Pompey; for the which, Pompey and Caesar both were marvellous sorrowful; and their friends mourned also, thinking that this alliance, which maintained the commonwealth (that otherwise was very tickle) in good peace and concord, was now severed and broken asunder; and the rather likely because the child lived not long after the mother. So the common people at Rome took the corpse of Julia, in despite of the Tribunes, and buried it in the field of Mars.

Now Caesar being driven to divide his army, that was very great, into sundry garrisons for the winter time, and returning again into Italy as he was wont, all Gaul rebelled again and had raised great armies in every quarter to set upon the Romans and to assay if they could distress their forts where they lay in garrison. The greatest number and most warlike men of these Gauls that entered into action of rebellion were led by one Ambiorix; and first did set upon the garrisons of Cotta and Titurius, whom they slew and all the soldiers they had about them. Then they went with three-score thousand fighting men to besiege the garrison which Quintus Cicero had in his charge, and had almost taken them by force, because all the soldiers were every man of them hurt. But they were so valiant and courageous that they did more than men (as they say) in defending of themselves.

These news being come to Caesar, who was far from thence at that time, he returned with all possible speed; and, levying seven thousand soldiers, made haste to help Cicero that was in such distress. The Gauls that did besiege Cicero, understanding of Caesar's coming, raised their siege incontinently, to go and meet him,

---

CYMBELINE:
You must know
Till the injurious Romans did extort
This tribute from us, we were free: Caesar's ambition,
Which swell'd so much that it did almost stretch
The sides o' the world, against all colour here
Did put the yoke upon's.          (*Cymbeline*, III, 1, 2; 47)

making account that he was but a handful in their hands, they were so few. Caesar, to deceive them, still drew back, and made as though he fled from them, lodging in places meet for a captain that had but a few to fight with a great number of his enemies, and commanded his men in no wise to stir out to skirmish with them, but compelled them to raise up the ramparts of his camp and to fortify the gates, as men that were afraid, because the enemies should the less esteem of them; until that at length he took opportunity by their disorderly coming to assail the trenches of his camp – they were grown to such a presumptuous boldness and bravery; and then sallying out upon them he put them all to flight with slaughter of a great number of them. This did suppress all the rebellions of the Gauls in those parts; and, furthermore, he himself in person went in the midst of winter thither where he heard they did rebel; for that there was come a new supply out of Italy of three whole legions, in their room which he had lost; of the which, two of them Pompey lent him, and the other legion he himself had levied in Gaul about the river of Po.

During these stirs brake forth the beginning of the greatest and most dangerous war that he had in all Gaul, the which had been secretly practised of long time by the chiefest and most warlike people of that country, who had levied a wonderful great power. For everywhere they levied multitudes of men, and great riches besides, to fortify their strongholds. Furthermore the country where they rose was very ill to come unto, and specially at that time being winter, when the rivers were frozen, the woods and forests covered with snow, the meadows drowned with floods, and the fields so deep of snow that no ways were to be found, neither the marshes nor rivers to be discerned, all was so overflown and drowned with water; all which troubles together were enough, as they thought, to keep Caesar from setting upon the rebels. Many nations of the Gauls were of this conspiracy; but two of the chiefest were the Arvernians and Carnutes; who had chosen Vercingentorix for their lieutenant-general, whose father the Gauls before had put to death, because they thought he aspired to make himself king.

This Vercingentorix, dividing his army into divers parts, and appointing divers captains over them, had gotten to take his part all the people and countries thereabout, even as far as they that dwell towards the sea Adriatic,* having further determined (understanding that Rome did conspire against Caesar) to make all Gaul rise in arms against him; so that, if he had but tarried a little longer, until Caesar had entered into his civil wars, he had put all Italy in as great fear and danger as it was when the Cimbri did come and invade it. But Caesar, that was valiant in all assays and dangers of war and that was very skilful to take time and opportunity, so soon as he understood the news of the rebellion he departed with speed and returned back the self same way which he had gone, making the barbarous people know that they should deal with an army unvincible, and which they could not possibly withstand, considering the great speed he had made with the same in so sharp and hard a winter. For, where they would not possibly have believed that a post or courier could have come in so short a time from the place where he was unto them, they wondered when they saw him burning and destroying the country, the towns, and strong forts where he came with his army, taking all to mercy that yielded unto him; until such time as the Hedui took arms against him, who before were wont to be called the brethren of the Romans and were greatly honoured of them. Wherefore Caesar's men when they understood that they had joined with the rebels, they were marvellous sorry and half discouraged.

Thereupon Caesar, departing from those parties, went through the country of the Lingones to enter the country of the Burgonians (Sequani), who were confederates of the Romans, and the nearest unto Italy on that side, in respect of all the rest of Gaul. Thither the enemies came to set upon him, and to environ him of all sides with an infinite number of thousands of fighting men. Caesar, on the other side, tarried their coming, and fighting with them a long time he made them so afraid of him that at length he overcame the barbarous people. But, at the first, it seemeth notwithstanding that he had received some overthrow. For the Arvernians showed a sword hanged up in one of their temples, which they said they had won from Caesar. Insomuch as Caesar self, coming that way by occasion,

* Some say that in this place is to be read in the Greek *pros ton Ararin*, which is the river Saône.

saw it and fell a-laughing at it. But, some of his friends going about
to take it away, he would not suffer them, but bade them let it alone
and touch it not, for it was a holy thing. Notwithstanding, such as at
first had saved themselves by flying, the most of them were gotten
with their king into the city of Alexia, the which Caesar went and
besieged, although it seemed inexpugnable, both for the height of
the walls, as also for the multitude of soldiers they had to defend it.

But now, during this siege, he fell into a marvellous great danger
without, almost incredible. For an army of three hundred thousand
fighting men of the best men that were among all the nations of the
Gauls came against him, being at the siege of Alexia, besides them
that were within the city, which amounted to the number of three-
score and ten thousand fighting men at the least; so that, perceiving
he was shut in betwixt two so great armies, he was driven to fortify
himself with two walls, the one against them of the city and the
other against them without. For, if those two armies had joined
together, Caesar had been utterly undone. And therefore this siege
of Alexia, and the battle he won before it, did deservedly win him
more honour and fame than any other. For there, in that instant and
extreme danger, he showed more valiantness and wisdom than he
did in any battle he fought before.

But what a wonderful thing was this, that they of the city never
heard anything of them that came to aid them, until Caesar had
overcome them; and furthermore, that the Romans themselves,
which kept watch upon the wall that was built against the city, knew
also no more of it than they, but when it was done and that they
heard the cries and lamentations of men and women in Alexia, when
they perceived on the other side of the city such a number of glistering
shields of gold and silver, such store of bloody corslets and armours,
such a deal of plate and movables, and such a number of tents and
pavilions after the fashion of the Gauls, which the Romans had gotten
of their spoils in their camp. Thus suddenly was this great army
vanished, as a dream or vision; where the most part of them were
slain that day in battle.

Furthermore, after that they within the city of Alexia had done
great hurt to Caesar and themselves also, in the end they all yielded

themselves. And Vercingentorix, he that was their king and captain in all this war, went out of the gates excellently well armed, and his horse furnished with rich caparison accordingly, and rode round about Caesar, who sat in his chair of estate. Then, lighting from his horse, he took off his caparison and furniture, and unarmed himself and laid all on the ground, and went and sat down at Caesar's feet, and said never a word. So Caesar at length committed him as a prisoner taken in the wars, to lead him afterwards in his Triumph at Rome.

Now Caesar had of long time determined to destroy Pompey, and Pompey him also. For Crassus being killed amongst the Parthians (who only did see that one of them two must needs fall), nothing kept Caesar from being the greatest person, but because he destroyed not Pompey, that was the greater; neither did anything let Pompey to withstand that it should not come to pass, but because he did not first overcome Caesar, whom only he feared. For till then Pompey had not long feared him, but always before set light by him, thinking it an easy matter for him to put him down when he would, sith he had brought him to that greatness he was come unto. But Caesar contrarily having had that drift in his head from the beginning, like a wrestler that studieth for tricks to overthrow his adversary, he went far from Rome, to exercise himself in the wars of Gaul, where he did train his army and presently by his valiant deeds did increase his fame and honour.

By these means became Caesar as famous as Pompey in his doings, and lacked no more to put his enterprise in execution but some occasions of colour, which Pompey partly gave him and partly also the time delivered him; but chiefly the hard fortune and ill government at that time of the commonwealth at Rome. For they that made suit for honour and offices bought the voices of the people with ready money, which they gave out openly to usury, without shame or fear. Thereupon the common people that had sold their voices for money came to the market-place at the day of election, to fight for him that had hired them – not with their voices, but with their bows, slings, and swords; so that the assembly seldom time brake up but that the pulpit for orations was defiled and sprinkled with the blood of them that were slain in the market-place, the city remaining all that time without government of magistrate, like a ship left without a pilot; insomuch as men of deep judgment and discretion, seeing such fury and madness of the people, thought themselves happy if the commonwealth were no worse troubled than with the absolute state of a monarchy and sovereign lord to govern them. Furthermore, there were many that were not afraid to speak it openly, that there was no other help to remedy the troubles of the commonwealth but by the authority of one man only that should command them all; and that this medicine must be ministered by the hands of him that was the gentlest physician, meaning covertly Pompey.

Now Pompey used many fine speeches, making semblance as though he would none of it, and yet cunningly underhand did lay all the irons in the fire he could, to bring it to pass that he might be chosen Dictator. Cato finding the mark he shot at, and fearing lest in the end the people should be compelled to make him Dictator, he persuaded the Senate rather to make him sole Consul, that, contenting himself with that more just and lawful government, he should not covet the other unlawful. The Senate, following his counsel, did not only make him Consul, but further did prorogue his government of the provinces he had. For he had two provinces, all Spain and Afric, the which he governed by his lieutenants; and further, he received yearly of the common treasure to pay his soldiers a thousand talents.

Hereupon Caesar took occasion also to send his men to make suit in his name for the Consulship, and also to have the government of his provinces prorogued. Pompey at the first held his peace. But Marcellus and Lentulus, that otherwise hated Caesar, withstood them, and, to shame and dishonour him, had much needless speech in matters of weight. Furthermore, they took away the freedom from the colonies which Caesar had lately brought unto the city of Novum Comum in Gaul towards Italy, where Caesar not long before had lodged them. And, moreover, when Marcellus was Consul, he made one of the Senators in that city to be whipped with rods, who came to Rome about those matters; and said, he gave him those marks that he should know he was no Roman citizen, and bade him go his way and tell Caesar of it.

After Marcellus' Consulship, Caesar, setting open his coffers of the treasure he had gotten among the Gauls, did frankly give it out amongst the magistrates at Rome, without restraint or spare. First, he set Curio, the Tribune, clear out of debt; and gave also unto Paul the Consul a thousand five hundred talents, with which money he built that notable palace by the market-place, called Paul's Basilic in the place of Fulvius' Basilic. Then Pompey, being afraid of this practice, began openly to procure, both by himself and his friends, that they should send Caesar a successor; and moreover, he sent unto Caesar for his two legions of men of war which he had lent him for the conquest of Gaul. Caesar sent him them again, and gave every private soldier two hundred and fifty silver drachmas. Now they that brought these two legions back from Caesar gave out ill and seditious words against him among the people, and did also abuse Pompey with false persuasions and vain hopes, informing him that he was marvellously desired and wished for in Caesar's camp; and that though in Rome, for the malice and secret spite which the governors there did bear him, he could hardly obtain that he desired, yet in Gaul he might assure himself that all the army was at his commandment. They added further also that, if the soldiers there did once return over the mountains again into Italy, they would all straight come to him, they did so hate Caesar, because he wearied them with too much labour and continual fight, and, withal, for that they suspected he aspired to be king. These words, breeding security in Pompey and a vain conceit of himself, made him negligent in his doings, so that he made no preparation for war, as though he had no occasion to be afraid; but only studied to thwart Caesar in speech, and to cross the suits he made.

Howbeit Caesar passed not of all this. For the report went that one of Caesar's captains which was sent to Rome to prosecute his suit, being at the Senate door and hearing that they denied to pro-rogue Caesar's time of government which he sued for, clapping his hand upon his sword he said:

'Sith you will not grant it him, this shall give it him.'

Notwithstanding, the requests that Caesar propounded carried great semblance of reason with them. For he said that he was contented to lay down arms, so that Pompey did the like; and that both of them as private persons should come and make suit of their citizens to obtain honourable recompense; declaring unto them that, taking arms from him and granting them unto Pompey, they did wrongfully accuse him in going about to make himself a tyrant, and in the meantime to grant the other means to be a tyrant.

Curio making these offers and persuasions openly before the people in the name of Caesar, he was heard with great rejoicing and clapping of hands, and there were some that cast flowers and nosegays upon him when he went his way, as they commonly use to do unto any 4 man when he hath obtained victory and won any games. Then Antonius, one of the Tribunes, brought a letter sent from Caesar and made it openly to be read in despite of the Consuls. But Scipio, in the Senate, Pompey's father-in-law, made this motion: that if Caesar did not dismiss his army by a certain day appointed him, the Romans should proclaim him an enemy unto Rome. Then the Consuls openly asked in the presence of the Senators if they thought it good that Pompey should dismiss his army. But few agreed to that demand. After that again, they asked if they liked that Caesar should dismiss his army. Thereto they all in manner answered, 'Yea, yea.' But when Antonius requested again that both of them should lay down arms, then they were all indifferently of his mind. Notwithstanding, because Scipio did insolently behave himself, and Marcellus, also, who cried that they must use force of arms, and not men's opinions, against a thief, the Senate rose straight upon it without further determination: and men changed apparel through the city because of this dissension, as they use to do in a common calamity.

After that, there came other letters from Caesar, which seemed much more reasonable; in the which he requested that they would grant him Gaul, that lieth between the mountains of the Alps and Italy, and Illyria, with two legions only: and then that he would

4 M A R U L L U S: And do you now put on your best attire?
And do you now cull out a holiday?
And do you now strew flowers in his way
That comes in triumph over Pompey's blood?

(*Julius Caesar*, I, I, 53)

request nothing else until he made suit for the second Consulship. Cicero the orator, that was newly come from his government of Cilicia, travailed to reconcile them together, and pacified Pompey the best he could; who told him he would yield to anything he would have him, so he did let him alone with his army. So Cicero persuaded Caesar's friends to be contented to take those two provinces, and six thousand men only, that they might be friends and at peace together. Pompey very willingly yielded unto it, and granted them. But Lentulus the Consul would not agree to it; but shamefully drave Curio and Antonius out of the Senate; whereby they themselves gave Caesar as happy occasion and colour as could be, stirring up his soldiers the more against them when he showed them these two notable men and Tribunes of the People that were driven to fly, disguised like slaves, in a carrier's cart. For they were driven for fear to steal out of Rome disguised in that manner.

Now at that time Caesar had not in all about him above five thousand footmen and three thousand horsemen. For the rest of his army he left on the other side of the mountains, to be brought after him by his lieutenants. So, considering that for the execution of his enterprise he should not need so many men of war at the first, but rather, suddenly stealing upon them, to make them afraid with his valiantness, taking benefit of the opportunity of time, because he should more easily make his enemies afraid of him, coming so suddenly when they looked not for him, than he should otherwise distress them, assailing them with his whole army, in giving them leisure to provide further for him; he commanded his captains and lieutenants to go before, without any other armour than their swords, to take the city of Ariminum (a great city of Gaul, being the first city men come to when they come out of Gaul) with as little bloodshed and tumult as they could possible.

Then, committing that force and army he had with him unto Hortensius, one of his friends, he remained a whole day together, openly in the sight of every man, to see the sword-players handle their weapons before him. At night he went into his lodging, and, bathing his body a little, came afterwards into the hall amongst them and made merry with them a while whom he had bidden to supper. Then, when it was well forward night and very dark, he rose from the table and prayed his company to be merry, and no man to stir, for he would straight come to them again. Howbeit he had secretly before commanded a few of his trustiest friends to follow him, not altogether, but some one way and some another way. He himself in the meantime took a coach he had hired, and made as though he would have gone some other way at the first, but suddenly he turned back again towards the city of Ariminum.

When he was come unto the little river of Rubicon, which divideth Gaul on this side the Alps from Italy, he stayed upon a sudden. For, the nearer he came to execute his purpose, the more remorse he had in his conscience, to think what an enterprise he took in hand; and his thoughts also fell out more doubtful when he entered into consideration of the desperateness of his attempt. So he fell into many thoughts with himself, and spake never a word, waving sometime one way, sometime another way, and oftentimes changed his determination, contrary to himself. So did he talk much also with his friends he had with him, amongst whom was Asinius Pollio, telling them what mischiefs the beginning of this passage over that river would breed in the world, and how much their posterity and them that lived after them would speak of it in time to come. But at length, casting from him with a noble courage all those perilous thoughts to come, and speaking these words, which valiant men commonly say that attempt dangerous and desperate enterprises – 'A desperate man feareth no danger. Come on!' – he passed over the river; and, when he was come over, he ran with his coach and never stayed, so that before daylight he was within the city of Ariminum and took it.

It is said that the night before he passed over this river he dreamed a damnable dream: that he carnally knew his mother.

The city of Ariminum being taken, and the rumour thereof dispersed through all Italy – even as if it had been open war both by sea and land, and as if all the laws of Rome together with the extreme bounds and confines of the same had been broken up – a man would have said that not only the men and women for fear, as experience proved at other times, but whole cities themselves, leaving their habitations, fled from one place to another through all Italy. And Rome itself also was immediately filled with the flowing repair of all the people, their neighbours thereabouts, which came thither from all parties like droves of cattle, that there was neither officer nor magistrate that could any more command them by authority, neither by any persuasion of reason bridle such a confused and disorderly multitude; so that Rome had in manner destroyed itself for lack of rule and order. For in all places men were of contrary opinions; and there were dangerous stirs and tumults everywhere, because they that were glad of this trouble could keep in no certain place; but running up and down the city, when they met with others in divers places that seemed either to be afraid or angry with this tumult (as otherwise it is impossible in so great a city), they flatly fell out with them and boldly threatened them with that that was to come.

Pompey himself, who at that time was not a little amazed, was yet much more troubled with the ill words some gave him on the one side and some on the other. For some of them reproved him, and said that he had done wisely, and had paid for his folly, because he had made Caesar so great and strong against him and the commonwealth. And other again did blame him because he had refused the honest offers and reasonable conditions of peace which Caesar had offered him, suffering Lentulus the Consul to abuse him too much. On the other side, Faonius spake unto him, and bade him stamp on the ground with his foot. For Pompey, being one day in a bravery in the Senate, said openly: let no man take thought for preparation of war; for when he listed, with one stamp of his foot on the ground he would fill all Italy with soldiers. This notwithstanding, Pompey at that time had a greater number of soldiers than Caesar. But they would never let him follow his own determination. For they brought him so many lies, and put so many examples of fear before him, as if Caesar had been already at their heels and had won all; so that in the end he yielded unto them and gave place to their fury and madness, determining (seeing all things in such tumult and garboil) that there was no way but to forsake the city; and thereupon commanded the Senate to follow him, and not a man to tarry there unless he loved tyranny more than his own liberty and the commonwealth.

Thus the Consuls themselves, before they had done their common sacrifices accustomed at their going out of the city, fled every man of them. So did likewise the most part of the Senators, taking their own things in haste, such as came first to hand, as if by stealth they had taken them from another. And there were some of them also that always loved Caesar, whose wits were then so troubled and besides themselves with the fear they had conceived, that they also fled and followed the stream of this tumult, without manifest cause or necessity. But above all things, it was a lamentable sight to see the city itself, that in this fear and trouble was left at all adventure, as a ship tossed in storm of sea, forsaken of her pilots and despairing of her safety. This their departure being thus miserable, yet men esteemed their banishment (for the love they bare unto Pompey) to be their natural country, and reckoned Rome no better than Caesar's camp.

At that time, also, Labienus, who was one of Caesar's greatest friends and had been always used as his lieutenant in the wars of Gaul and had valiantly fought in his cause, he likewise forsook him then and fled unto Pompey. But Caesar sent his money and carriage after him; and then went and encamped before the city of Corfinium, the which Domitius kept with thirty cohorts or ensigns.

When Domitius saw he was besieged, he straight thought himself but undone; and despairing of his success he bade a physician, a slave of his, give him poison. The physician gave him a drink which he drank, thinking to have died. But, shortly after, Domitius, hearing them report what clemency and wonderful courtesy Caesar used unto them he took, repented him then that he had drunk this drink, and began to lament and bewail his desperate resolution taken to die. The physician did comfort him again, and told him that he had taken a drink only to make him sleep, but not to destroy him. Then Domitius rejoiced, and went straight and yielded himself unto Caesar, who gave him his life. (But he notwithstanding stale away immediately, and fled unto Pompey.) When these news were brought to Rome, they did marvellously rejoice and comfort them that still remained there; and moreover there were of them that had forsaken Rome which returned thither again. In the meantime Caesar did put all Domitius' men in pay; and he did the like through all the cities where he had taken any captains that levied men for Pompey.

Now Caesar, having assembled a great and dreadful power together, went straight where he thought to find Pompey himself. But Pompey tarried not his coming, but fled into the city of Brundusium, from whence he had sent the two Consuls before with that army he had unto Dyrrachium; and he himself also went thither afterwards when he understood that Caesar was come, as you shall hear more amply hereafter in his *Life*. Caesar lacked no good will to follow him. But, wanting ships to take the seas, he returned forthwith to Rome; so that in less than three-score days he was lord of all Italy, without any bloodshed; who, when he was come to Rome and found it much quieter than he looked for and many Senators there also, he courteously entreated them, and prayed them to send unto Pompey, to pacify all matters between them upon reasonable conditions. But no man did attempt it, either because they feared Pompey for that they had forsaken him, or else for that they thought Caesar meant not as he spake, but that they were words of course, to colour his purpose withal. And when Metellus also, one of the Tribunes, would not suffer him to take any of the common treasure out of the Temple of Saturn, but told him that it was against the law,

'Tush,' said he, 'time of war and law are two things.* If this that I do,' quoth he, 'do offend thee, then get thee hence for this time; for war cannot abide this frank and bold speech. But when wars are done, and that we are all quiet again, then thou shalt speak in the pulpit what thou wilt. And yet I do tell thee this of favour, impairing so much my right; for thou art mine, both thou and all them that have risen against me and whom I have in my hands.'

When he had spoken thus unto Metellus, he went to the temple door where the treasure lay, and, finding no keys there, he caused smiths to be sent for and made them break open the locks. Metellus thereupon began again to withstand him, and certain men that stood by praised him in his doing. But Caesar at length speaking bigly to him threatened him he would kill him presently, if he troubled him any more; and told him furthermore,

* *Silent leges inter arma.*

'Young man,' quoth he, 'thou knowest it is harder for me to tell it thee than to do it.'

That word made Metellus quake for fear, that he got him away roundly; and ever after that Caesar had all at his commandment for the wars.

From thence he went into Spain, to make war with Petreius and Varro, Pompey's lieutenants; first to get their armies and provinces into his hands which they governed, that afterwards he might follow Pompey the better, leaving never an enemy behind him. In this journey he was oftentimes himself in danger, through the ambushes that were laid for him in divers strange sorts and places, and likely also to have lost all his army for lack of victuals. All this notwithstanding, he never left following of Pompey's lieutenants, provoking them to battle and intrenching them in, until he had gotten their camp and armies into his hands, albeit that the lieutenants themselves fled unto Pompey.

When Caesar returned again to Rome, Piso his father-in-law gave him counsel to send ambassadors unto Pompey, to treat of peace. But Isauricus, to flatter Caesar, was against it. Caesar, being then created Dictator by the Senate, called home again all the banished men, and restored their children to honour whose fathers before had been slain in Sylla's time; and did somewhat cut off the usuries that did oppress them, and, besides, did make some such other ordinances as those, but very few. For he was Dictator but eleven days only, and then did yield it up of himself, and made himself Consul, with Servilius Isauricus; and after that determined to follow the wars. All the rest of his army he left coming on the way behind him, and went himself before with six hundred horse and five legions only of footmen, in the winter quarter, about the month of January (which after the Athenians is called *Posideon*).

Then, having passed over the sea Ionium and landed his men, he won the cities of Oricum and Apollonia. Then he sent his ships back again unto Brundusium, to transport the rest of his soldiers that could not come with that speed he did. They, as they came by the way, like men whose strength of body and lusty youth was decayed, being wearied with so many sundry battles as they had fought with their enemies, complained of Caesar in this sort: 'To what end and purpose doth this man hale us after him, up and down the world, using us like slaves and drudges? It is not our armour but our bodies that bear the blows away; and what, shall we never be without our harness on our backs and our shields on our arms? Should not Caesar think, at the least when he seeth our blood and wounds, that we are all mortal men and that we feel the misery and pains that other men do feel? And now, even in the dead of winter, he putteth us unto the mercy of the sea and tempest, yea, which the gods themselves cannot withstand – as if he fled before his enemies, and pursued them not.'

Thus, spending time with this talk, the soldiers still marching on, by small journeys came at length unto the city of Brundusium. But when they were come and found that Caesar had already passed over the sea, then they straight changed their complaints and minds. For they blamed themselves, and took on also with their captains, because they had not made them make more haste in marching; and, sitting upon the rocks and cliffs of the sea, they looked over the main sea towards the realm of Epirus, to see if they could discern the ships returning back to transport them over.

Caesar in the meantime being in the city of Apollonia, having but a small army to fight with Pompey, it grieved him for that the rest of his army was so long a-coming, not knowing what way to take. In the end he followed a dangerous determination to embark unknown in a little pinnace of twelve oars only, to pass over the sea again unto Brundusium; the which he could not do without great danger, considering that all that sea was full of Pompey's ships and armies. So he took ship in the night apparelled like a slave, and went aboard this little pinnace and said never a word, as if he had been some poor man of mean condition. The pinnace lay in the mouth of the river of Anius, the which commonly was wont to be very calm and quiet, by reason of a little wind that came from the shore, which every morning drave back the waves far into the main sea. But that night, by ill fortune, there came a great wind from the sea that overcame the land wind, insomuch as, the force and strength of the river fighting against the violence of the rage and waves of the sea, the encounter was marvellous dangerous, the water of the river being driven back and rebounding upward, with great noise and danger in turning of the water. Thereupon the master of the pinnace, seeing he could not possibly get out of the mouth of this river, bade the mariners to cast about again and to return against the stream. Caesar, hearing that, straight discovered himself unto the master of the pinnace, who at the first was amazed when he saw him. But Caesar then taking him by the hand said unto him:

'Good fellow, be of good cheer, and forwards hardily; fear not, for thou hast Caesar and his fortune with thee.'

Then the mariners, forgetting the danger of the storm they were in, laid on load with oars and laboured for life what they could against the wind, to get out of the mouth of this river. But at length, perceiving they laboured in vain, and that the pinnace took in abundance of water and was ready to sink, Caesar then to his great grief was driven to return back again; who when he was returned unto his camp, his soldiers came in great companies unto him, and were very sorry that he mistrusted he was not able with them alone to overcome his enemies, but would put his person in danger to go fetch them that were absent, putting no trust in them that were present.

In the meantime Antonius arrived, and brought with him the rest of his army from Brundusium. Then Caesar, finding himself strong enough, went and offered Pompey battle, who was passingly well lodged for victualling of his camp both by sea and land. Caesar on the other side, who had no great plenty of victuals at the first, was in a very hard case; insomuch as his men gathered roots, and mingled them with milk, and eat them. Furthermore they did make bread of it also; and sometime when they skirmished with the enemies, and came alongst by them that watched and warded, they cast of their bread into their trenches, and said that, as long as the earth brought forth such fruits, they would never leave besieging of Pompey. But Pompey straitly commanded them that they should neither carry those words nor bread into their camp, fearing lest his men's hearts would fail them, and that they would be afraid, when they should think of their enemies' hardness, with whom they had to fight, sith they were weary with no pains, no more than brute beasts.

Caesar's men did daily skirmish hard to the trenches of Pompey's camp, in the which Caesar had ever the better, saving once only, at what time his men fled with such fear that all his camp that day was in great hazard to have been cast away. For Pompey came on with his battle upon them; and they were not able to abide it, but were fought with and driven into their camp, and their trenches were filled with dead bodies, which were slain within the very gate and bulwarks of their camp, they were so valiantly pursued. Caesar stood before them that fled, to make them to turn head again. But he could not prevail. For when he would have taken the ensigns to have stayed them, the ensign-bearers threw them down on the ground; so that the enemies took two-and-thirty of them, and Caesar's self also scaped hardly with life. For striking a great big soldier that fled by him, commanding him to stay and turn his face to his enemy, the soldier being afraid lift up his sword to strike at Caesar. But one of Caesar's pages, preventing him, gave him such a blow with his sword, that he strake off his shoulder.

Caesar that day was brought unto so great extremity that (if Pompey had not, either for fear or spiteful fortune, left off to follow his victory and retired into his camp, being contented to have driven his enemies into their camp), returning to his camp with his friends, he said unto them:

'The victory this day had been our enemies', if they had had a captain that could have told how to have overcome.'

So, when he was come to his lodging, he went to bed; and that night troubled him more than any night that ever he had. For still his mind ran with great sorrow of the foul fault he had committed in leading of his army, of self-will to remain there so long by the sea side, his enemies being the stronger by sea; considering that he had before him a goodly country, rich and plentiful of all things, and goodly cities of Macedon and Thessaly, and had not the wit to bring the war from thence, but to lose his time in a place where he was rather besieged of his enemies for lack of victuals, than that he did besiege them by force of arms. Thus, fretting and chafing to see himself so straighted with victuals, and to think of his ill luck, he raised his camp, intending to go set upon Scipio, making account that either he should draw Pompey to battle against his will, when he had not the sea at his back to furnish him with plenty of victuals, or else that he should easily overcome Scipio, finding him alone unless he were aided.

This remove of Caesar's camp did much encourage Pompey's army and his captains, who would needs in any case have followed after him, as though he had been overcome and had fled. But, for Pompey himself, he would in no respect hazard battle, which was a matter of so great importance. For, finding himself so well provided of all things necessary to tarry time, he thought it better to draw this war out in length, by tract of time, the rather to consume this little strength that remained in Caesar's army; of the which, the best men were marvellous well trained and good soldiers, and, for valiantness, at one day's battle were incomparable. But on the other side again, to remove here and there so oft, and to fortify their camp where they came, and to besiege any wall, or to keep watch all night in their armour – the most part of them could not do it, by reason of their age, being then unable to away with that pains, so that the weakness of their bodies did also take away the life and courage of their hearts. Furthermore there fell a pestilent disease among them, that came by ill meats hunger drave them to eat. Yet was not this the worst. For, besides, he had no store of money, neither could tell how to come by victuals, so that it seemed in all likelihood that in very short time he would come to nothing.

For these respects Pompey would in no case fight; and yet had he but Cato only of his mind in that, who stuck in it the rather because he would avoid shedding of his countrymen's blood. For, when Cato had viewed the dead bodies slain in the camp of his enemies, at the last skirmish that was between them the which were no less than a thousand persons, he covered his face and went away weeping. All other but he contrarily fell out with him, and blamed him because he so long refrained from battle; and some pricked him forward, and called him 'Agamemnon' and 'King of Kings', saying, that he delayed this war in this sort because he would not leave his authority to command them all, and that he was glad always to see many captains round about him, which came to his lodging to honour him and wait upon him. And Faonius also, a harebrained fellow, franticly counterfeiting the round and plain speech of Cato, made as though he was marvellous angry and said:

'Is it not great pity that we shall not eat this year of Tusculum figs, and all for Pompey's ambitious mind to reign alone?'

And Afranius, who not long before was but lately come out of Spain (where, because he had but ill success, he was accused of treason – that for money he had sold his army unto Caesar), he went busily asking why they fought not with that merchant unto whom they said he had sold the province of Spain? So that Pompey with these kind of speeches, against his will was driven to follow Caesar, to fight with him.

Then was Caesar at the first marvellously perplexed and troubled by the way, because he found none that would give him any victuals, being despised of every man for the late loss and overthrow he had received. But, after that he had taken the city of Gomphes in Thessaly, he did not only meet with plenty of victuals to relieve his army with, but he strangely also did rid them of their disease. For the soldiers, meeting with plenty of wine, drinking hard and making merry, drave away the infection of the pestilence. For they disposed themselves unto dancing, masking, and playing the Baccherians by the way; insomuch that drinking drunk they overcame their disease and made their bodies new again.

When they both came into the country of Pharsalia and both camps lay before the other, Pompey returned again to his former determination, and the rather because he had ill signs and tokens of misfortune in his sleep. For he thought in his sleep that, when he entered into the theatre, all the Romans received him with great clapping of hands. Whereupon, they that were about him grew to such boldness and security, assuring themselves of victory, that Domitius, Spinther, and Scipio in a bravery contended between themselves for the chief bishopric which Caesar had. Furthermore, there were divers that sent unto Rome to hire the nearest houses unto the market-place, as being the fittest places for the Praetors and Consuls, making their account already that those offices could not scape them, incontinently after the wars. But besides those, the young gentlemen and Roman knights were marvellous desirous to fight, that were bravely mounted and armed with glistering gilt armours, their horses fat and very finely kept, and themselves goodly young men, to the number of seven thousand, where the gentlemen of Caesar's side were but one thousand only. The number of his footmen also were much after the same reckoning. For he had five-and-forty thousand against two-and-twenty thousand.

Wherefore Caesar called his soldiers together, and told them how Cornificius was at hand, who brought two whole legions, and that he had fifteen ensigns led by Calenus, the which he made to stay about Megara and Athens. Then he asked them if they would tarry for that aid or not, or whether they would rather themselves alone venture battle. The soldiers cried out to him, and prayed him not to defer battle, but rather to devise some fetch to make the enemy fight as soon as he could. Then, as he sacrificed unto the gods for the purifying of his army, the first beast was no sooner sacrificed, but his soothsayer assured him that he should fight within three days. Caesar asked him again, if he saw in the sacrifices any lucky sign or token of good luck. The soothsayer answered:

'For that thou shalt answer thyself, better than I can do. For the gods do promise us a marvellous great change and alteration of things that are now, unto another clean contrary. For if thou beest well now, dost thou think to have worse fortune hereafter? And if thou be ill, assure thyself thou shalt have better.'

The night before the battle, as he went about midnight to visit the watch, men saw a great firebrand in the element, all of a light fire, that came over Caesar's camp and fell down in Pompey's. In the morning also, when they relieved the watch, they heard a false alarm in the enemies' camp, without any apparent cause; which they commonly call a 'sudden fear', that makes men besides themselves.

This notwithstanding, Caesar thought not to fight that day, but was determined to have raised his camp from thence, and to have gone towards the city of Scotusa; and his tents in his camp were already overthrown when his scouts came in with great speed to bring him news that his enemies were preparing themselves to fight.

Then he was very glad; and, after he had made his prayers unto the gods to help him that day, he set his men in battle ray, and divided them into three squadrons, giving the middle battle unto Domitius Calvinus, and the left wing unto Antonius, and placed himself in the right wing, choosing his place to fight in the Tenth Legion. But, seeing that against that his enemies had set all their horsemen, he was half afraid when he saw the great number of them, and so brave besides. Wherefore he closely made six ensigns to come from the rearward of his battle, whom he had laid as an ambush behind his right wing, having first appointed his soldiers what they should do when the horsemen of the enemies came to give them charge.

On the other side, Pompey placed himself in the right wing of his battle, gave the left wing unto Domitius, and the middle battle unto Scipio his father-in-law. Now all the Roman knights (as we have told you before) were placed in the left wing, of purpose to environ Caesar's right wing behind, and to give their hottest charge there where the general of their enemies was; making their account that there was no squadron of footmen, how thick soever they were, that could receive the charge of so great a troop of horsemen, and that at the first onset they should overthrow them all and march upon their bellies.

When the trumpets on either side did sound the alarm to the battle, Pompey commanded his footmen that they should stand still without stirring, to receive the charge of their enemies, until they came to throwing of their darts. Wherefore Caesar afterwards said that Pompey had committed a foul fault, not to consider that the charge which is given running with fury, besides that it giveth the more strength also unto their blows, doth set men's hearts also a-fire; for the common hurling of all the soldiers that run together is unto them as a box on the ear that sets men a-fire.

Then Caesar, making his battle march forward to give the onset, saw one of his captains (a valiant man, and very skilful in war, in whom he had also great confidence) speaking to his soldiers that he had under his charge, encouraging them to fight like men that day. So he called him aloud by his name, and said unto him:

'Well, Caius Crassinius, what hope shall we have today? How are we determined? to fight it out manfully?'

Then Crassinius, casting up his hand, answered him aloud:

'This day, O Caesar, we shall have a noble victory; and I promise thee ere night thou shalt praise me alive or dead.'

When he had told him so, he was himself the foremost man that gave charge upon his enemies, with his band following of him, being about six-score men; and, making a lane through the foremost ranks, with great slaughter he entered far into the battle of his enemies; until that, valiantly fighting in this sort, he was thrust in at length in the mouth with a sword, that the point of it came out again at his neck.

Now, the footmen of both battles being come to the sword, the horsemen of the left wing of Pompey did march as fiercely also, spreading out their troops to compass in the right wing of Caesar's battle. But before they began to give charge, the six ensigns of footmen which Caesar had laid in ambush behind him, they began to run full upon them, not throwing away their darts far off as they were wont to do, neither striking their enemies on the thighs nor on the legs, but to seek to hit them full in the eyes and to hurt them in the face, as Caesar had taught them. For he hoped that these lusty young gentlemen, that had not been often in the wars, nor were used to see themselves hurt, and the which being in the prime of their youth and beauty, would be afraid of those hurts, as well for the fear of the present danger to be slain, as also for that their faces should not for ever be deformed. As indeed it came to pass. For they could never abide that they should come so near their faces with the points of their darts, but hung down their heads for fear to be hit with them in their eyes, and turned their backs, covering their face, because they should not be hurt. Then, breaking of themselves, they began at length cowardly to fly, and were occasion also of the loss of all the rest of Pompey's army. For they that had broken them ran immediately to set upon the squadron of the footmen behind, and slew them.

Then Pompey, seeing his horsemen from the other wing of his battle so scattered and dispersed, flying away, forgat that he was any more Pompey the Great which he had been before, but rather was like a man whose wits the gods had taken from him, being afraid and amazed with the slaughter sent from above; and so retired into his tent speaking never a word, and sat there to see the end of this battle; until at length, all his army being overthrown and put to flight, the enemies came and got up upon the ramparts and defence of his camp, and fought hand to hand with them that stood to defend the same. Then, as a man come to himself again, he spake but this only word: 'What, even into our camp?' So, in haste, casting off his coat-armour and apparel of a general, he shifted him and put on such as became his miserable fortune, and so stale out of his camp. Furthermore, what he did after this overthrow, and how he had put himself into the hands of the Egyptians, by whom he was miserably slain, we have set it forth at large in his *Life*.

Then Caesar, entering into Pompey's camp, and seeing the bodies laid on the ground that were slain, and others also that were a-killing, said, fetching a great sigh:

'It was their own doing, and against my will.'

For Caius Caesar, after he had won so many famous conquests and overcome so many great battles, had been utterly condemned notwithstanding, if he had departed from his army. Asinius Pollio writeth that he spake these words then in Latin, which he afterwards wrote in Greek; and saith furthermore that the most part of them which were put to the sword in the camp were slaves and bondsmen, and that there were not slain in all at this battle above six thousand soldiers. As for them that were taken prisoners, Caesar did put many of them amongst his legions, and did pardon also many men of estimation, among whom Brutus was one, that afterwards slew Caesar himself; and it is reported that Caesar was very sorry for him when he could not immediately be found after the battle, and that he rejoiced again when he knew he was alive and that he came to yield himself unto him.

Caesar had many signs and tokens of victory before this battle. But the notablest of all other that happened to him was in the city of Tralles. For in the Temple of Victory within the same city, there was an image of Caesar, and the earth all about it very hard of itself, and was paved besides with hard stone; and yet some say that there

sprang up a palm hard by the base of the same image. In the city of
Padua, Caius Cornelius, an excellent soothsayer – a countryman and
friend of Titus Livius the historiographer – was by chance at that
time set to behold the flying of birds. He (as Livy reporteth) knew the
very time when the battle began, and told them that were present:
'Even now they give the onset on both sides, and both armies do
meet at this instant.'

Then, sitting down again to consider of the birds, after he had
bethought him of the signs he suddenly rose up on his feet, and cried
out as a man possessed with some spirit:

'Oh Caesar, the victory is thine.'

Every man wondering to see him, he took the crown he had on his
head, and made an oath that he would never put it on again till the
event of his prediction had proved his art true. Livy testifieth that
it so came to pass.

Caesar afterwards giving freedom unto the Thessalians, in respect
of the victory which he won in their country, he followed after
Pompey. When he came into Asia, he gave freedom also unto the
Gnidians for Theopompus' sake, who had gathered the *Fables*
together. He did release Asia also the third part of the tribute which
the inhabitants paid unto the Romans. Then he came into Alexandria,
after Pompey was slain; and detested Theodotus that presented him
Pompey's head, and turned his head at the one side because he would
not see it. Notwithstanding, he took his seal and, beholding it, wept.
Furthermore, he courteously used all Pompey's friends and familiars,
who wandering up and down the country were taken of the King of
Egypt, and won them all to be at his commandment.

Continuing these courtesies, he wrote unto his friends at Rome
that the greatest pleasure he took of his victory was that he daily
saved the lives of some of his countrymen that bare arms against him.
And, for the war he made in Alexandria, some say he needed not
have done it, but that he willingly did it for the love of Cleopatra;
wherein he won little honour, and besides did put his person in
great danger. Others do lay the fault upon the King of Egypt's
ministers, but specially on Pothinus the eunuch, who, bearing the
greatest sway of all the King's servants, after he had caused Pompey

to be slain and driven Cleopatra from the court, secretly laid wait
all the ways he could how he might likewise kill Caesar. Wherefore
Caesar, hearing an inkling of it, began thenceforth to spend all the
night long in feasting and banqueting, that his person might be in
the better safety. But, besides all this, Pothinus the eunuch spake
many things openly not to be borne, only to shame Caesar and to
stir up the people to envy him. For he made his soldiers have the
worst and oldest wheat that could be gotten; then, if they did
complain of it, he told them they must be contented, seeing they eat
at another man's cost. And he would serve them also at the table in
treen and earthen dishes, saying that Caesar had away all their gold
and silver, for a debt that the King's father, that then reigned, did
owe unto him – which was a thousand seven hundred and fifty
myriads, whereof Caesar had before forgiven seven hundred and
fifty thousand unto his children. Howbeit then he asked a million
to pay his soldiers withal. Thereto Pothinus answered him that at
that time he should do better to follow his other causes of greater
importance, and afterwards that he should at more leisure recover
his debt, with the King's good will and favour. Caesar replied unto
him, and said that he would not ask counsel of the Egyptians for his
affairs, but would be paid; and thereupon secretly sent for Cleopatra,
which was in the country, to come unto him.

   She, only taking Apollodorus Sicilian of all her friends, took a
little boat, and went away with him in it in the night, and came and
landed hard by the foot of the castle. Then, having no other mean
to come into the court without being known, she laid herself down
upon a mattress or flock-bed which Apollodorus her friend tied and
bound up together like a bundle with a great leather thong, and so
took her up on his back, and brought her thus hampered in this
fardel unto Caesar, in at the castle gate. This was the first occasion,
5 as it is reported, that made Caesar to love her. But afterwards, when

5 POMPEY:      And I have heard, Apollodorus carried –
ENOBARBUS:   No more of that: he did so.
POMPEY:                          What, I pray you?
ENOBARBUS:   A certain Queen to Caesar in a mattress.
                     (*Antony and Cleopatra*, II, 6, 69)

he saw her sweet conversation and pleasant entertainment, he fell then in further liking with her, and did reconcile her again unto her brother the King, with condition that they two jointly should reign together.

Upon this new reconciliation a great feast being prepared, a slave of Caesar's that was his barber, the fearfullest wretch that lived, still busily prying and listening abroad in every corner, being mistrustful by nature, found that Pothinus and Achillas did lie in wait to kill his master Caesar. This being proved unto Caesar, he did set such sure watch about the hall where the feast was made, that, in fine, he slew the eunuch Pothinus himself. Achillas, on the other side, saved himself and fled unto the king's camp, where he raised a marvellous dangerous and difficult war for Caesar, because, he having then but a few men about him as he had, he was to fight against a great and strong city.

The first danger he fell into was for the lack of water he had; for that his enemies had stopped the mouth of the pipes, the which conveyed the water unto the castle. The second danger he had was that, seeing his enemies came to take his ships from him, he was driven to repulse that danger with fire, the which burnt the arsenal where the ships lay and that notable library of Alexandria withal. The third danger was in the battle by sea, that was fought by the tower of Phar, where, meaning to help his men that fought by sea, he leapt from the pier into a boat. Then the Egyptians made towards him with their oars on every side. But he, leaping into the sea, with great hazard saved himself by swimming. It is said that then holding divers books in his hand he did never let them go, but kept them always upon his head above water, and swam with the other hand, notwithstanding that they shot marvellously at him, and was driven sometime to duck into the water; howbeit the boat was drowned presently. In fine, the King coming to his men that made war with Caesar, he went against him and gave him battle, and won it

---

CLEOPATRA:                                        Broad-fronted Caesar,
               When thou wast here above the ground, I was
               A morsel for a monarch.                                   (I, 5, 29)

70

with great slaughter and effusion of blood. But, for the King, no man could ever tell what became of him after.

Thereupon Caesar made Cleopatra his sister Queen of Egypt, who, being great with child by him, was shortly brought to bed of a son, 6 whom the Alexandrians named Caesarion.

From thence he went into Syria; and so going into Asia, there it was told him that Domitius was overthrown in battle by Pharnaces, the son of King Mithridates, and was fled out of the realm of Pont, with a few men with him; and that this King Pharnaces, greedily following his victory, was not contented with the winning of Bithynia and Cappadocia, but further would needs attempt to win Armenia the less, procuring all those kings, princes, and governors of the provinces thereabouts to rebel against the Romans. Thereupon Caesar went thither straight with three legions, and fought a great battle with King Pharnaces by the city of Zela, where he slew his army, and drave him out of all the realm of Pont. And, because he would advertise one of his friends of the suddenness of this victory, he only wrote three words unto Anitius at Rome: *Veni, vidi, vici:* to wit, 'I came, I saw, I overcame.' These three words, ending all with like sound and letters in the Latin, have a certain short grace more pleasant to the ear than can be well expressed in any other 7 tongue.

After this, he returned again into Italy, and came to Rome,

6 AGRIPPA: Royal wench!
She made great Caesar lay his sword to bed;
He plough'd her, and she cropp'd.
(*Antony and Cleopatra*, II, 2, 231)

OCTAVIUS CAESAR: At the feet sat
Caesarion, whom they call my father's son. (III, 6, 5)
See *Life of Antonius*, pp. 242, 285.

7 FALSTAFF: I have foundered nine score and odd posts: and here, travel-tainted as I am, have, in my pure and immaculate valour, taken Sir John Coleville of the dale, a most furious knight and valorous enemy. But what of that? he saw me, and yielded; that I may justly say, with the hook-nosed fellow of Rome, 'I came, saw, and overcame.' (*2 Henry IV*, IV, 3, 39)

ending his year for the which he was made Dictator the second time, which office before was never granted for one whole year but unto him. Then he was chosen Consul for the year following. Afterwards he was very ill spoken of, for that his soldiers in a mutiny having slain two Praetors, Cosconius and Galba, he gave them no other punishment for it, but, instead of calling them soldiers, he named them citizens, and gave unto every one of them a thousand drachmas a man and great possessions in Italy. He was much misliked also for the desperate parts and madness of Dolabella, for the covetousness of Anitius, for the drunkenness of Antonius and Cornificius, which made Pompey's house be pulled down and builded up again, as a thing not big enough for him; wherewith the Romans were marvellously offended. Caesar knew all this well enough, and would have been contented to have redressed them. But to bring his matters to pass, he pretended he was driven to serve his turn by such instruments.

After the battle of Pharsalia, Cato and Scipio being fled into Afric, King Juba joined with them and levied a great puissant army. Wherefore Caesar determined to make war with them, and in the midst of winter he took his journey into Sicily. There, because he would take all hope from his captains and soldiers to make any long abode there, he went and lodged upon the very sands by the sea side, and with the next gale of wind that came he took the sea with three thousand footmen and a few horsemen. Then, having put them a-land, unwares to them he hoisted sail again, to go fetch the rest of his army, being afraid lest they should meet with some danger in passing over, and meeting them midway, he brought them all into his camp; where, when it was told him that his enemies trusted in an

---

ROSALIND:     There was never any thing so sudden [*as the love of Celia and Oliver*], but the fight of two rams and Caesar's thrasonical brag of 'I came, saw, and overcame.'

(*As You Like It*, V, 2, 33)

QUEEN:                         A kind of conquest
Caesar made here [*in Britain*]; but made not here his brag
Of 'came' and 'saw' and 'overcame'.

(*Cymbeline*, III, 1, 22)

ancient oracle, which said that it was predestined unto the family of the Scipios to be conquerors in Afric – either of purpose to mock Scipio the general of his enemies, or otherwise in good earnest to take the benefit of this name, given by the oracle, unto himself – in all the skirmishes and battles fought he gave the charge of his army unto a man of mean quality and account, called Scipio Salutius, who came of the race of Scipio African, and made him always his general when he fought.

For he was eftsoons compelled to weary and harry his enemies; for that neither his men in his camp had corn enough, nor his beasts forage; but the soldiers were driven to take seaweeds, called *alga*, and, washing away the brackishness thereof with fresh water, putting to it a little herb called dog's-tooth, to cast it so to their horse to eat. For the Numidians, which are light horsemen and very ready of service, being a great number together, would be on a sudden in every place and spread all the fields over thereabout, so that no man durst peep out of the camp to go for forage. And one day as the men of arms were staying to behold an African doing notable things in dancing and playing with the flute, they being set down quietly to take their pleasure of the view thereof, having in the meantime given their slaves their horses to hold, the enemies stealing suddenly upon them compassed them in round about, and slew a number of them in the field, and chasing the other also that fled followed them pell-mell into their camp. Furthermore, had not Caesar himself in person, and Asinius Pollio, with him, gone out of the camp to the rescue, and stayed them that fled, the war that day had been ended.

There was also another skirmish where his enemies had the upper hand, in the which it is reported that Caesar, taking the ensign-bearer by the collar that carried the eagle in his hand, stayed him by force and, turning his face, told him: 'See, there be thy enemies.'

These advantages did lift up Scipio's heart aloft, and gave him courage to hazard battle; and, leaving Afranius on the one hand of him and King Juba on the other hand, both their camps lying near to other, he did fortify himself by the city of Thapsacus, above the lake, to be a safe refuge for them all in this battle. But, whilst he was busy entrenching of himself, Caesar having marvellous speedily passed through a great country full of wood, by by-paths which men would never have mistrusted, he stale upon some behind and suddenly assailed the other before, so that he overthrew them all and made them fly. Then, following this first good hap he had, he went forthwith to set upon the camp of Afranius, the which he took at the first onset, and the camp of the Numidians also, King Juba being fled. Thus, in a little piece of the day only, he took three camps, and slew fifty thousand of his enemies, and lost but fifty of his soldiers.

In this sort is set down the effect of this battle by some writers. Yet others do write also that Caesar self was not there in person at the execution of this battle. For, as he did set his men in battle ray, the 8 falling sickness took him, whereunto he was given, and therefore, feeling it coming, before he was overcome withal, he was carried into a castle not far from thence where the battle was fought, and there took his rest till the extremity of his disease had left him.

Now, for the Praetor and Consuls that scaped from this battle, many of them being taken prisoners did kill themselves, and others also Caesar did put to death. But, he being specially desirous of all men else to have Cato alive in his hands, he went with all possible speed unto the city of Utica, whereof Cato was governor, by means whereof he was not at the battle. Notwithstanding, being certified by the way that Cato had slain himself with his own hands, he then made open show that he was very sorry for it, but why or wherefore, no man could tell. But this is true, that Caesar said at that present time:

'O Cato, I envy thy death, because thou didst envy my glory to save thy life.'

This notwithstanding, the book that he wrote afterwards against Cato being dead did show no very great affection nor pitiful heart towards him. For how could he have pardoned him, if living he had had him in his hands, that being dead did speak so vehemently against him? Notwithstanding, men suppose he would have par-

8 See p. 37 note 1 above, and p. 81 note 11 below.

74

doned him, if he had taken him alive, by the clemency he showed unto Cicero, Brutus, and divers others that had borne arms against him. Some report that he wrote that book, not so much for any private malice he had to his death, as for civil ambition, upon this occasion. Cicero had written a book in praise of Cato, which he entitled *Cato*. This book in likelihood was very well liked of, by reason of the eloquence of the orator that made it and of the excellent subject thereof. Caesar therewith was marvellously offended, thinking that to praise him, of whose death he was author, was even as much as to accuse himself; and therefore he wrote a letter against him, and heaped up a number of accusations against Cato, and entitled the book *Anticaton*. Both these books have favourers unto this day, some defending the one for the love they bare to Caesar, and others allowing the other for Cato's sake.

Caesar, being now returned out of Afric, first of all made an oration to the people, wherein he greatly praised and commended this his last victory, declaring unto them that he had conquered so many countries unto the Empire of Rome, that he could furnish the commonwealth yearly with two hundred thousand bushels of wheat and twenty hundred thousand pound weight of oil. Then he made three Triumphs: the one for Egypt; the other for the kingdom of Pont; and the third for Afric – not because he had overcome Scipio there, but King Juba; whose son, being likewise called Juba, being then a young boy, was led captive in the show of this Triumph. (But this his imprisonment fell out happily for him. For, where he was but a barbarous Numidian, by the study he fell unto when he was prisoner he came afterwards to be reckoned one of the wisest historiographers of the Grecians.)

After these three Triumphs ended, he very liberally rewarded his soldiers; and, to curry favour with the people, he made great feasts and common sports. For he feasted all the Romans at one time at two-and-twenty thousand tables, and gave them the pleasure to see divers sword-players to fight at the sharp, and battles also by sea, for the remembrance of his daughter Julia, which was dead long before.

Then, after all these sports, he made the people (as the manner was) to be mustered; and, where there were at the last musters before three hundred and twenty thousand citizens, at this muster only there were but a hundred and fifty thousand. Such misery and destruction had this civil war brought unto the commonwealth of Rome, and had consumed such a number of Romans, not speaking at all of the mischiefs and calamities it had brought unto all the rest of Italy, and to the other provinces pertaining to Rome.

After all these things were ended, he was chosen Consul the fourth time, and went into Spain to make war with the sons of Pompey; who were yet but very young, but had notwithstanding raised a marvellous great army together, and showed to have had manhood and courage worthy to command such an army, insomuch as they put Caesar himself in great danger of his life. The greatest battle that was fought between them in all this war was by the city of Munda. For then Caesar seeing his men sorely distressed, and having their hands full of their enemies, he ran into the press among his men that fought, and cried out unto them:

'What, are ye not ashamed to be beaten and taken prisoners, yielding yourselves with your own hands to these young boys?'

And so, with all the force he could make, having with much ado put his enemies to flight, he slew above thirty thousand of them in the field, and lost of his own men a thousand of the best he had. After this battle he went into his tent, and told his friends that he had often before fought for victory, but, this last time now, that he had fought for the safety of his own life. He won this battle on the very feast day of the Bacchanalians, in the which men say that Pompey the Great went out of Rome, about four years before, to begin this civil war. For his sons, the younger scaped from the battle; but, within few days after, Diddius brought the head of the elder.

This was the last war that Caesar made. But the Triumph he made into Rome for the same did as much offend the Romans, and more, than anything that ever he had done before; because he had not overcome captains that were strangers, nor barbarous kings, but had destroyed the sons of the noblest man in Rome, whom fortune had overthrown. And, because he had plucked up his race by the roots, men did not think it meet for him to triumph so for the calamities of his country, rejoicing at a thing for the which he had but one excuse to allege in his defence unto the gods and men – that he was compelled to do that he did. And the rather they thought it not meet, because he had never before sent letters nor messengers unto the commonwealth at Rome, for any victory that he had ever won in all the civil wars, but did always for shame refuse the glory of it.

This notwithstanding, the Romans inclining to Caesar's prosperity, and taking the bit in the mouth, supposing that, to be ruled by one man alone, it would be a good mean for them to take breath a little after so many troubles and miseries as they had abidden in these civil wars, they chose him perpetual Dictator. This was a plain tyranny. For to this absolute power of Dictator they added this, never to be afraid to be deposed. Cicero propounded before the Senate that they should give him such honours as were meet for a man. Howbeit others afterwards added to honours beyond all reason. For, men striving who should most honour him, they made him hateful and troublesome to themselves that most favoured him, by reason of the unmeasurable greatness and honours which they gave him. Thereupon, it is reported that even they that most hated him were no less

COBBLER:    We make holiday, to see Caesar and to rejoice in his
        triumph.
MARULLUS:    Wherefore rejoice? What conquest brings he home?
        What tributaries follow him to Rome,
        To grace in captive bonds his chariot-wheels?
        You blocks, you stones, you worse than senseless things!
        O you hard hearts, you cruel men of Rome,
        Knew you not Pompey? Many a time and oft
        Have you climb'd up to walls and battlements,
        To towers and windows, yea, to chimney-tops,
        Your infants in your arms, and there have sat
        The live-long day, with patient expectation,
        To see great Pompey pass the streets of Rome ...
        And do you now put on your best attire?
        And do you now cull out a holiday?
        And do you now strew flowers in his way
        That comes in triumph over Pompey's blood?
                          (*Julius Caesar*, I, I, 35; 53)

favourers and furtherers of his honours than they that most flattered him; because they might have greater occasions to rise, and that it might appear they had just cause and colour to attempt that they did against him.

And now for himself, after he had ended his civil wars, he did so honourably behave himself that there was no fault to be found in him; and therefore, methinks, amongst other honours they gave him, he rightly deserved this – that they should build him a Temple of Clemency, to thank him for his courtesy he had used unto them in his victory. For he pardoned many of them that had borne arms against him, and, furthermore, did prefer some of them to honour and office in the commonwealth; as, amongst others, Cassius and Brutus, both the which were made Praetors. And, where Pompey's images had been thrown down, he caused them to be set up again. Whereupon Cicero said then that Caesar setting up Pompey's images again he made his own to stand the surer. And when some of his friends did counsel him to have a guard for the safety of his person, and some also did offer themselves to serve him, he would never consent to it, but said, it was better to die once than always to be afraid 10 of death.

But to win himself the love and good will of the people, as the honourablest guard and best safety he could have, he made common feasts again and general distribution of corn. Furthermore, to gratify the soldiers also, he replenished many cities again with inhabitants, which before had been destroyed, and placed them there that had no place to repair unto; of the which the noblest and chiefest cities were these two, Carthage and Corinth; and it chanced also that, like as aforetime they had been both taken and destroyed together, even so were they both set afoot again, and replenished with people, at one self time.

*10* CAESAR:     Cowards die many times before their deaths;
The valiant never taste of death but once.
Of all the wonders that I yet have heard,
It seems to me most strange that men should fear;
Seeing that death, a necessary end,
Will come when it will come.          ( II, 2, 32)

And, as for great personages, he won them also, promising some of them to make them Praetors and Consuls in time to come, and unto others honours and preferments, but to all men generally good hope, seeking all the ways he could to make every man contented with his reign. Insomuch as, one of the Consuls called Maximus chancing to die a day before his Consulship ended, he declared Caninius Rebilius Consul only for the day that remained. So, divers going to his house (as the manner was) to salute him, and to congratulate with him of his calling and preferment, being newly chosen officer, Cicero pleasantly said:

'Come, let us make haste, and be gone thither before his Consulship come out.'

Furthermore, Caesar being born to attempt all great enterprises and having an ambitious desire besides to covet great honours, the prosperous good success he had of his former conquests bred no desire in him quietly to enjoy the fruits of his labours, but rather gave him hope of things to come, still kindling more and more in him thoughts of greater enterprises and desire of new glory, as if that which he had present were stale and nothing worth. This humour of his was no other but an emulation with himself as with another man, and a certain contention to overcome the things he prepared to attempt. For he was determined, and made preparation also, to make war with the Persians; then, when he had overcome them, to pass through Hyrcania (compassing in the sea Caspium and Mount Caucasus) into the realm of Pontus, and so to invade Scythia; and, overrunning all the countries and people adjoining unto high Germany, and Germany itself, at length to return by Gaul into Italy; and so to enlarge the Roman Empire round, that it might be every way compassed in with the Great Sea, Oceanus. But whilst he was preparing for this voyage, he attempted to cut the bar of the strait of Peloponnesus in the place where the city of Corinth standeth. Then he was minded to bring the rivers of Anienes and Tiber straight from Rome unto the city of Circes with a deep channel and high banks cast up on either side, and so to fall into the sea at Terracina, for the better safety and commodity of the merchants that came to Rome to traffic there. Furthermore, he determined to drain and sew all the water of the marshes betwixt the cities of Nomentum and Setium, to make it firm land, for the benefit of many thousands of people; and on the sea coast next unto Rome to cast great high banks, and to cleanse all the haven about Ostia of rocks and stones hidden under the water, and to take away all other impediments that made the harborough dangerous for ships, and to make new havens and arsenals meet to harbour such ships as did continually traffic thither.

All these things were purposed to be done, but took no effect. But the ordinance of the calendar and reformation of the year, to take away all confusion of time, being exactly calculated by the mathematicians and brought to perfection, was a great commodity unto all men. For the Romans, using then the ancient computation of the year, had not only such incertainty and alteration of the month and times that the sacrifices and yearly feasts came by little and little to seasons contrary for the purpose they were ordained; but also in the revolution of the sun (which is called *annus solaris*) no other nation agreed with them in account; and, of the Romans themselves, only the priests understood it. And therefore, when they listed, they suddenly (no man being able to control them) did thrust in a month above their ordinary number, which they called in old time, *Mercedonius* (*mensis intercalaris*). Some say that Numa Pompilius was the first that devised this way, to put a month between. But it was a weak remedy, and did little help the correction of the errors that were made in the account of the year, to frame them to perfection. But Caesar, committing this matter unto the philosophers and best expert mathematicians at that time, did set forth an excellent and perfect calendar, more exactly calculated than any other that was before; the which the Romans do use until this present day, and do nothing err as others in the difference of time.

But his enemies, notwithstanding, that envied his greatness did not stick to find fault withal. As Cicero the orator, when one said:
'Tomorrow the star Lyra will rise,'
'Yea,' said he, 'at the commandment of Caesar' – as if men were compelled so to say and think by Caesar's edict.

But the chiefest cause that made him mortally hated was the

covetous desire he had to be called king; which first gave the people just cause, and next his secret enemies honest colour, to bear him ill will. This notwithstanding, they that procured him this honour and dignity gave it out among the people that it was written in the Sibylline prophecies how the Romans might overcome the Parthians, if they made war with them and were led by a king, but otherwise that they were unconquerable. And furthermore they were so bold besides that, Caesar returning to Rome from the city of Alba, when they came to salute him, they called him king. But the people being offended, and Caesar also angry, he said he was not called king, but Caesar. Then, every man keeping silence, he went his way heavy and sorrowful.

When they had decreed divers honours for him in the Senate, the Consuls and Praetors accompanied with the whole assembly of the Senate went unto him in the market-place, where he was set by the pulpit for orations, to tell him what honours they had decreed for him in his absence. But he, sitting still in his majesty, disdaining to rise up unto them when they came in, as if they had been private men, answered them: that his honours had more need to be cut off than enlarged. This did not only offend the Senate, but the common people also, to see that he should so lightly esteem of the magistrates of the commonwealth; insomuch as every man that might lawfully go his way departed thence very sorrowfully. Thereupon also Caesar rising departed home to his house, and tearing open his doublet collar, making his neck bare, he cried out aloud to his friends that his throat was ready to offer to any man that would come and cut it. Notwithstanding, it is reported that afterwards, to excuse this folly, he imputed it to his disease, saying that their wits are not perfect which have his disease of the falling evil, when standing on their feet they speak to the common people, but are soon troubled with a trembling of their body and a sudden dimness and giddiness. But

| | |
|---|---|
| CASSIUS: | But soft, I pray you: what, did Caesar swound? |
| CASCA: | He fell down in the market-place, and foamed at the mouth, and was speechless. |
| BRUTUS: | 'Tis very like: he hath the falling sickness . . . What said he when he came unto himself? |

that was not true. For he would have risen up to the Senate; but
Cornelius Balbus one of his friends (but rather a flatterer) would not
let him, saying:
'What, do you not remember that you are Caesar, and will you not
let them reverence you and do their duties?'

Besides these occasions and offences, there followed also his shame
and reproach, abusing the Tribunes of the People in this sort. At that
time the feast *Lupercalia* was celebrated, the which in old time men say
was the feast of shepherds or herdmen and is much like unto the
feast of the Lycaeans in Arcadia. But, howsoever it is, that day there
are divers noblemen's sons, young men – and some of them magistrates themselves that govern then – which run naked through the
city, striking in sport them they meet in their way with leather thongs,
hair and all on, to make them give place. And many noblewomen
and gentlewomen also go of purpose to stand in their way, and do
put forth their hands to be stricken, as scholars hold them out to their
schoolmaster to be stricken with the ferula; persuading themselves
that, being with child, they shall have good delivery, and also, being
12 barren, that it will make them to conceive with child. Caesar sat to
behold that sport upon the pulpit for orations, in a chair of gold,
apparelled in triumphing manner. Antonius, who was Consul at

| | | |
|---|---|---|
| 12 MARULLUS: | You know it is the feast of Lupercal. | (I, 1, 72) |
| CAESAR: | Calpurnia!... | |
| | Stand you directly in Antonius' way, | |
| | When he doth run his course. . . . | |
| | Forget not, in your speed, Antonius, | |
| | To touch Calpurnia; for our elders say, | |
| | The barren, touched in this holy chase, | |
| | Shake off their sterile curse. | (I, 2, 1) |

Compare also *Life of Antonius*, pp. 186–7.

---

CASCA:  Marry before he fell down ... he plucked me ope his
doublet and offered them his throat to cut. ... And so he fell.
When he came to himself again, he said, If he had done or
said any thing amiss, he desired their worships to think it was
his infirmity.                          (*Julius Caesar*, I, 2, 254)

See also pp. 37 and 74 above, and *Life of Antonius*, p. 187.

that time, was one of them that ran this holy course. So, when he came into the market-place, the people made a lane for him to run at liberty; and he came to Caesar and presented him a diadem wreathed about with laurel. Whereupon there rose a certain cry of rejoicing, not very great, done only by a few appointed for the purpose. But when Caesar refused the diadem, then all the people together made an outcry of joy. Then, Antonius offering it him again, there was a a second shout of joy, but yet of a few. But when Caesar refused it again the second time, then all the whole people shouted. Caesar having made this proof found that the people did not like of it, and thereupon rose out of his chair, and commanded the crown to be carried unto Jupiter in the Capitol.

After that, there were set up images of Caesar in the city with diadems upon their heads, like kings. Those the two Tribunes, Flavius and Marullus, went and pulled down; and furthermore, meeting with them that first saluted Caesar as king, they committed them to prison. The people followed them rejoicing at it, and called

CASCA:  I saw Mark Antony offer him a crown; – yet 'twas not a crown neither, 'twas one of these coronets; – and, as I told you, he put it by once: but, for all that, to my thinking, he would fain have had it. Then he offered it to him again; then he put it by again: but, to my thinking, he was very loath to lay his fingers off it. And then he offered it the third time; he put it the third time by: and still as he refused it, the rabblement hooted and clapped their chopped hands and threw up their sweaty nightcaps and uttered such a deal of stinking breath because Caesar refused the crown that it had almost choked Caesar; for he swounded and fell down at it.  (I, 2, 237)

ANTONY:  You all did see that on the Lupercal
I thrice presented him a kingly crown,
Which he did thrice refuse: was this ambition ? (III, 2, 100)

Compare also *Life of Antonius*, p. 187.

FLAVIUS:  Disrobe the images,
If you do find them deck'd with ceremonies . . .
Let no images
Be hung with Caesar's trophies.  (I, 1, 69)

Compare *Life of Brutus*, p. 110.

them 'Brutes', because of Brutus, who had in old time driven the kings out of Rome and that brought the kingdom of one person unto 15 the government of the Senate and people. Caesar was so offended 16 withal, that he deprived Marullus and Flavius of their Tribuneships, and, accusing them, he spake also against the people, and called them *Bruti* and *Cumani* (to wit, 'beasts' and 'fools').

Hereupon the people went straight unto Marcus Brutus, who from his father came of the first Brutus and by his mother of the house of the Servilians, a noble house as any was in Rome, and was also nephew and son-in-law of Marcus Cato. Notwithstanding, the great honours and favour Caesar showed unto him kept him back, that of himself alone he did not conspire nor consent to depose him of his kingdom. For Caesar did not only save his life after the battle of Pharsalia when Pompey fled, and did at his request also save many more of his friends besides. But, furthermore, he put a marvellous confidence in him. For he had already preferred him to the Praetorship for that year, and furthermore was appointed to be Consul, the fourth year after that, having through Caesar's friendship obtained it before Cassius, who likewise made suit for the same. And Caesar also, as it is reported, said in this contention: 'Indeed Cassius hath alleged best reason, but yet shall he not be chosen before Brutus.' Some one day accusing Brutus while he practised this conspiracy, Caesar would not hear of it, but, clapping his hand on his body, told them:

'Brutus will look for this skin';

– meaning thereby that Brutus for his virtue deserved to rule after him, but yet that for ambition's sake he would not show himself unthankful or dishonourable.

Now they that desired change and wished Brutus only their prince and governor above all other, they durst not come to him themselves to tell him what they would have him to do; but in the night did cast sundry papers into the Praetor's seat where he gave audience

15 See also *Life of Brutus*, pp. 103, 110.

16 CASCA:       I could tell you more news too: Marullus and Flavius, for
             pulling scarfs off Caesar's images, are put to silence.   (I, 2, 288)
    See *Life of Antonius*, p. 187.

and the most of them to this effect: 'Thou sleepest, Brutus, and art
_7_ not Brutus indeed.' Cassius, finding Brutus' ambition stirred up the
more by these seditious bills, did prick him forward and egg him
on the more, for a private quarrel he had conceived against Caesar;
the circumstance whereof we have set down more at large in
_18_ Brutus' *Life*.

Caesar also had Cassius in great jealousy and suspected him much.
Whereupon he said on a time to his friends:
'What will Cassius do, think ye? I like not his pale looks.'
Another time, when Caesar's friends complained unto him of Antonius and Dolabella, that they pretended some mischief towards
him, he answered them again:
'As for those fat men and smooth-combed heads', quoth he, 'I never
reckon of them. But these pale-visaged and carrion lean people, I
fear them most'
_19_ – meaning Brutus and Cassius.


_17_ CINNA:           O Cassius, if you could
                    But win the noble Brutus to our party –
    CASSIUS:      Be you content: good Cinna, take this paper,
                    And look you lay it in the praetor's chair,
                    Where Brutus may but find it.            (I, 3, 140)
    CASSIUS:                          I will this night,
                    In several hands, in at his windows throw,
                    As if they came from several citizens,
                    Writings all tending to the great opinion
                    That Rome holds of his name; wherein obscurely
                    Caesar's ambition shall be glanced at.      (I, 2, 319)
    BRUTUS:       'Brutus, thou sleep'st: awake, and see thyself.'   (II, 1, 46)
See also *Life of Brutus*, p. 110.
_18_ See *Life of Brutus*, pp. 108–9.
_19_ CAESAR:        Let me have men about me that are fat;
                    Sleek-headed men and such as sleep o'nights:
                    Yond Cassius has a lean and hungry look;
                    He thinks too much: such men are dangerous.
    ANTONY:       Fear him not, Caesar; he's not dangerous;
                    He is a noble Roman and well given.

Certainly destiny may easier be foreseen than avoided, considering the strange and wonderful signs that were said to be seen before Caesar's death. For, touching the fires in the element and spirits running up and down in the night, and also the solitary birds
20 to be seen at noondays sitting in the great market-place – are not all these signs perhaps worth the noting, in such a wonderful chance as
21 happened? But Strabo the Philosopher writeth that divers men were

20 CASCA:    But never till to-night, never till now,
            Did I go through a tempest dropping fire . . .
            And yesterday the bird of night did sit
            Even at noon-day upon the market-place,
            Hooting and shrieking. When these prodigies
            Do so conjointly meet, let not men say
            'These are their reasons; they are natural;'
            For, I believe, they are portentous things
            Unto the climate that they point upon.        (I, 3, 9; 26)

CALPURNIA:  And ghosts did shriek and squeal about the streets.
            O Caesar! these things are beyond all use,
            And I do fear them.

CAESAR:                      What can be avoided
            Whose end is purposed by the mighty gods?      (II, 2, 24)

Compare *Hamlet*, I, I, 113:
            In the most high and palmy state of Rome,
            A little ere the mightiest Julius fell,
            The graves stood tenantless and the sheeted dead
            Did squeak and gibber in the Roman streets . . .
            As stars with trains of fire and dews of blood,
            Disasters in the sun; and the moist star
            Upon whose influence Neptune's empire stands
            Was sick almost to doomsday with eclipse.

21 CASSIUS:                  You look pale and gaze
            And put on fear and cast yourself in wonder,

CAESAR:     Would he were fatter! But I fear him not:
            Yet if my name were liable to fear,
            I do not know the man I should avoid
            So soon as that spare Cassius.                 (I, 2, 192)

Compare also *Life of Brutus*, p. 109, and *Life of Antonius*, p. 186.

seen going up and down in fire; and, furthermore, that there was a
slave of the soldiers that did cast a marvellous burning flame out of
his hand, insomuch as they that saw it thought he had been burnt,
but, when the fire was out, it was found he had no hurt. Caesar
self also, doing sacrifice unto the gods, found that one of the beasts
which was sacrificed had no heart; and that was a strange thing in
nature – how a beast could live without a heart.

Furthermore, there was a certain soothsayer that had given
Caesar warning long time afore, to take heed of the day of the Ides
of March (which is the fifteenth of the month), for on that day he

CASCA:                          . . . a hundred ghastly women,
                 Transformed with their fear; who swore they saw
                 Men all in fire walk up and down the streets.        (I, 3, 23)

CALPURNIA:     And graves have yawn'd, and yielded up their dead;
                 Fierce fiery warriors fought upon the clouds,
                 In ranks and squadrons and right form of war.      (II, 2, 18)

CASCA:           A common slave – you know him well by sight –
                 Held up his left hand, which did flame and burn
                 Like twenty torches join'd, and yet his hand,
                 Not sensible of fire, remain'd unscorch'd.            (I, 3, 15)

CAESAR:                          What say the augurers?
SERVANT:         They would not have you to stir forth today.
                 Plucking the entrails of an offering forth,
                 They could not find a heart within the beast.        (II, 2, 37)

---

                 To see the strange impatience of the heavens:
                 But if you would consider the true cause
                 Why all these fires, why all these gliding ghosts,
                 Why birds and beasts from quality and kind,
                 Why old men, fools, and children calculate,
                 Why all these things change from their ordinance
                 Their natures and preformed faculties
                 To monstrous quality, – why, you shall find
                 That heaven hath infused them with these spirits,
                 To make them instruments of fear and warning
                 Unto some monstrous state.                          (I, 3, 59)

87

25 should be in great danger. That day being come, Caesar going unto the Senate-house and speaking merrily unto the soothsayer, told him: 'The Ides of March be come.'

'So be they,' softly answered the soothsayer, 'but yet they are not
26 past.'

And the very day before, Caesar, supping with Marcus Lepidus, sealed certain letters as he was wont to do at the board; so, talk falling out amongst them, reasoning what death was best, he preventing their opinions cried out aloud:
27 'Death unlooked for.'

Then going to bed the same night as his manner was and lying with his wife Calpurnia, all the windows and doors of his chamber flying open, the noise awoke him and made him afraid when he saw such light; but more, when he heard his wife Calpurnia, being fast asleep, weep and sigh and put forth many fumbling lamentable speeches. For she dreamed that Caesar was slain, and that she had him in her arms. Others also do deny that she had any such dream; as, amongst other, Titus Livius writeth that it was in this sort: the Senate having set upon the top of Caesar's house, for an ornament and setting forth of the same, a certain pinnacle, Calpurnia dreamed

| | | |
|---|---|---|
| 25 SOOTHSAYER: | Caesar! | |
| CAESAR: | Ha! who calls? . . . | |
| SOOTHSAYER: | Beware the Ides of March. | |
| CAESAR: | What man is that? | |
| BRUTUS: | A soothsayer bids you beware the Ides of March . . . | |
| CAESAR: | He is a dreamer; let us leave him: pass. | (I, 2, 12) |
| 26 CAESAR: | The Ides of March are come. | |
| SOOTHSAYER: | Ay, Caesar; but not gone. | |
| | | (III, I, I) |
| 27 BRUTUS: | That we shall die, we know; 'tis but the time | |
| | And drawing days out, that men stand upon. | |
| CASSIUS: | Why, he that cuts off twenty years of life | |
| | Cuts off so many years of fearing death. | |
| BRUTUS: | Grant that, and then is death a benefit: | |
| | So are we Caesar's friends, that have abridged | |
| | His time of fearing death. | (III, I, 99) |

that she saw it broken down and that she thought she lamented and wept for it. Insomuch that, Caesar rising in the morning, she prayed him if it were possible not to go out of the doors that day, but to adjourn the session of the Senate until another day. And if that he made no reckoning of her dream, yet that he would search further of the soothsayers by their sacrifices, to know what should happen him that day. Thereby it seemed that Caesar likewise did fear and suspect somewhat, because his wife Calpurnia until that time was never given to any fear or superstition, and then, for that he saw her so troubled in mind with this dream she had; but much more afterwards, when the soothsayers, having sacrificed many beasts one after another, told him that none did like them. Then he determined to send Antonius to adjourn the session of the Senate.

But in the meantime came Decius Brutus, surnamed Albinus, in

| | |
|---|---|
| CAESAR: | Nor heaven nor earth have been at peace to-night:<br>Thrice hath Calpurnia in her sleep cried out,<br>'Help, ho! they murder Caesar!'...<br>Calpurnia here, my wife, stays me at home:<br>She dreamt to-night she saw my statue,<br>Which, like a fountain with an hundred spouts,<br>Did run pure blood.           (II, 2, 1; 75) |
| CALPURNIA: | What mean you, Caesar? think you to walk forth?<br>You shall not stir out of your house today.        (II, 2, 8) |
| CAESAR: | Go bid the priests do present sacrifice<br>And bring me their opinions of success.           (II, 2, 5) |
| CALPURNIA: | Caesar, I never stood on ceremonies,<br>Yet now they fright me.           (II, 2, 13) |
| CASSIUS: | But it is doubtful yet,<br>Whether Caesar will come forth today, or no;<br>For he is superstitious grown of late,<br>Quite from the main opinion he held once<br>Of fantasy, of dreams and ceremonies.           (II, 1, 193) |
| CALPURNIA: | We'll send Mark Antony to the senate-house;<br>And he shall say you are not well today.<br>Let me, upon my knee, prevail in this. |
| CAESAR: | Mark Antony shall say I am not well;<br>And, for thy humour, I will stay at home.           (II, 2, 52) |

whom Caesar put such confidence that in his last will and testament
he had appointed him to be his next heir, and yet was of the conspiracy with Cassius and Brutus. He, fearing that if Caesar did
adjourn the session that day the conspiracy would out, laughed the
32 soothsayers to scorn; and reproved Caesar, saying that he gave the
Senate occasion to mislike with him, and that they might think he
mocked them, considering that by his commandment they were
assembled, and that they were ready willingly to grant him all things,
and to proclaim him king of all the provinces of the Empire of Rome
out of Italy, and that he should wear his diadem in all other places
both by sea and land; and furthermore, that if any man should tell
them from him they should depart for that present time, and return
33 again when Calpurnia should have better dreams – what would his

32 CASSIUS:     It may be, these apparent prodigies,
                The unaccustom'd terror of this night,
                And the persuasion of his augurers,
                May hold him from the Capitol today.

DECIUS:     Never fear that: if he be so resolved,
                I can o'ersway him . . .
                For I can give his humour the true bent,
                And I will bring him to the Capitol.    (II, 1, 198; 210)

CAESAR:     Here's Decius Brutus, he shall tell them so.

DECIUS:     Caesar, all hail! good morrow, worthy Caesar:
                I come to fetch you to the senate-house.    (II, 2, 57)

33 DECIUS:              The senate have concluded
                To give this day a crown to mighty Caesar.
                If you shall send them word you will not come,
                Their minds may change.    (II, 2, 93)

CASCA:     Indeed, they say the senators tomorrow
                Mean to establish Caesar as a king;
                And he shall wear his crown by sea and land,
                In every place, save here in Italy.    (I, 3, 85)

DECIUS:              Besides, it were a mock
                Apt to be render'd, for some one to say
                'Break up the senate till another time,
                When Caesar's wife shall meet with better dreams.'
                                              (II, 2, 96)

See also *Life of Brutus*, p. 120.

enemies and ill-willers say, and how could they like of his friends' words? And who could persuade them otherwise, but that they would think his dominion a slavery unto them, and tyrannical in himself? 'And yet, if it be so,' said he, 'that you utterly mislike of this day, it is better that you go yourself in person, and saluting the Senate to dismiss them till another time.'

Therewithal he took Caesar by the hand and brought him out of his house. Caesar was not gone far from his house, but a bondman, a stranger, did what he could to speak with him; and, when he saw he was put back by the great press and multitude of people that followed him, he went straight into his house, and put himself into Calpurnia's hands to be kept till Caesar came back again, telling her that he had great matters to impart unto him. And one Artemidorus also, born in the isle of Gnidos, a doctor of rhetoric in the Greek tongue, who by means of his profession was very familiar with certain of Brutus' confederates and therefore knew the most part of all their practices against Caesar, came and brought him a little bill written with his own hand, of all that he meant to tell him. He, marking how Caesar received all the supplications that were offered him, and that he gave them straight to his men that were about him, pressed nearer to him and said:
'Caesar, read this memorial to yourself, and that quickly, for they be matters of great weight, and touch you nearly.'
Caesar took it of him, but could never read it, though he many times attempted it, for the number of people that did salute him; but holding it still in his hand, keeping it to himself, went on withal 34 into the Senate-house. Howbeit other are of opinion that it was some

34 ARTEMIDORUS: Here will I stand till Caesar pass along,
      And as a suitor will I give him this . . .
      If thou read this, O Caesar, thou mayst live;
      If not, the Fates with traitors do contrive.   (II, 3, 11)
ARTEMIDORUS: Hail, Caesar! read this schedule . . .
      O Caesar, read mine first; for mine's a suit
      That touches Caesar nearer: read it, great Caesar.
CAESAR:     What touches us ourself shall be last served.
ARTEMIDORUS: Delay not, Caesar; read it instantly.   (III, 1, 3)

man else that gave him that memorial, and not Artemidorus, who did what he could all the way as he went to give it Caesar, but he was always repulsed by the people.

For these things, they may seem to come by chance. But the place where the murder was prepared, and where the Senate were assembled, and where also there stood up an image of Pompey dedicated by himself amongst other ornaments which he gave unto the Theatre – all these were manifest proofs that it was the ordinance of some god that made this treason to be executed specially in that
35 very place. It is also reported that Cassius – though otherwise he did favour the doctrine of Epicurus – beholding the image of Pompey
36 before they entered into the action of their traitorous enterprise, he did softly call upon it to aid him. But the instant danger of the present time, taking away his former reason, did suddenly put him
37 into a furious passion and made him like a man half besides himself. Now Antonius, that was a faithful friend to Caesar and a valiant man besides of his hands, him Decius Brutus Albinus entertained out of the
38 Senate-house, having begun a long tale of set purpose.

So, Caesar coming into the house, all the Senate stood up on their feet to do him honour. Then part of Brutus' company and confederates stood round about Caesar's chair, and part of them also came towards him, as though they made suit with Metellus Cimber, to call home his brother again from banishment; and thus, prosecuting still their suit, they followed Caesar till he was set in his chair; who denying their petitions and being offended with them one after another, because the more they were denied, the more they pressed

35 See note 44 below.
36 CASSIUS:      You know that I held Epicurus strong
                  And his opinion: now I change my mind,
                  And partly credit things that do presage.    (v, 1, 77)
   See also *Life of Brutus*, pp. 149–50.
37 CASSIUS:      Brutus, what shall be done? If this be known,
                  Cassius or Caesar never shall turn back,
                  For I will slay myself.
   BRUTUS:                   Cassius, be constant.    (III, 1, 20)
38 See *Life of Brutus*, p. 123 note 32, where Trebonius plays this part, and *Life of Antonius*, p. 188.

39 upon him and were the earnester with him. Metellus at length, taking
his gown with both his hands, pulled it over his neck, which was the
sign given the confederates to set upon him.

40     Then Casca behind him strake him in the neck with his sword.
Howbeit the wound was not great nor mortal, because, it seemed,
the fear of such a devilish attempt did amaze him and take his strength
from him, that he killed him not at the first blow. But, Caesar,
turning straight unto him, caught hold of his sword and held it
hard; and they both cried out, Caesar in Latin:
'O vile traitor Casca, what doest thou?'
And Casca in Greek to his brother:
'Brother, help me.'
At the beginning of this stir, they that were present, not knowing of

39 DECIUS:     Where is Metellus Cimber? Let him go,
              And presently prefer his suit to Caesar.
   BRUTUS:    He is address'd: press near and second him ...
   METELLUS:  Most high, most mighty, and most puissant Caesar,
              Metellus Cimber throws before thy seat
              An humble heart, –
   CAESAR:                   I must prevent thee, Cimber ...
              Thy brother by decree is banished:
              If thou dost bend and pray and fawn for him,
              I spurn thee like a cur out of my way ...
   METELLUS:  Is there no voice more worthy than my own,
              To sound more sweetly in great Caesar's ear
              For the repealing of my banish'd brother?
   BRUTUS:    I kiss thy hand, but not in flattery, Caesar:
              Desiring thee that Publius Cimber may
              Have an immediate freedom of repeal.
   CAESAR:    What, Brutus?
   CASSIUS:               Pardon, Caesar; Caesar, pardon:
              As low as to thy foot doth Cassius fall,
              To beg enfranchisement for Publius Cimber.     (III, I, 27)
See also *Life of Brutus*, p. 123.

40 CINNA:     Casca, you are the first that rears your hand ...
   CASCA:     Speak, hands, for me!      *They stab Caesar.* (III, I, 30; 76)
See also notes 42 and 43 below, and *Life of Brutus*, p. 124.

the conspiracy, were so amazed with the horrible sight they saw, they had no power to fly, neither to help him, not so much as once
41 to make any outcry. They on the other side that had conspired his death compassed him in on every side with their swords drawn in their hands, that Caesar turned him nowhere but he was stricken at by some, and still had naked swords in his face, and was hacked
42 and mangled among them, as a wild beast taken of hunters. For it was agreed among them that every man should give him a wound, because all their parts should be in this murder. And then Brutus himself gave him one wound about his privities.

Men report also that Caesar did still defend himself against the rest, running every way with his body. But when he saw Brutus

| | | |
|---|---|---|
| 41 BRUTUS: | People and senators, be not affrighted; | |
| | Fly not; stand still: ambition's debt is paid. | |
| CASCA: | Go to the pulpit, Brutus . . . | |
| BRUTUS: | Where's Publius? | |
| CINNA: | Here, quite confounded with this mutiny . . . | |
| BRUTUS: | Publius, good cheer; | |
| | There is no harm intended to your person, | |
| | Nor to no Roman else. | (III, I, 82) |
| 42 BRUTUS | And, gentle friends, | |
| | Let's kill him boldly, but not wrathfully; | |
| | Let's carve him as a dish fit for the gods, | |
| | Not hew him as a carcass fit for hounds. | (II, I, 171) |
| ANTONY: | Here wast thou bay'd, brave hart; | |
| | Here didst thou fall; and here thy hunters stand, | |
| | Sign'd in thy spoil, and crimson'd in thy lethe. | |
| | O world, thou wast the forest to this hart; | |
| | And this, indeed, O world, the heart of thee. | |
| | How like a deer, strucken by many princes, | |
| | Dost thou here lie! | (III, I, 204) |
| ANTONY: | Your vile daggers | |
| | Hack'd one another in the sides of Caesar: | |
| | You show'd your teeth like apes, and fawn'd like hounds, | |
| | And bow'd like bondmen, kissing Caesar's feet; | |
| | Whilst damned Casca, like a cur, behind | |
| | Struck Caesar on the neck. | (V, I, 39) |

with his sword drawn in his hand, then he pulled his gown over his
3 head and made no more resistance, and was driven, either casually
or purposely by the counsel of the conspirators, against the base
whereupon Pompey's image stood, which ran all of a gore-blood
till he was slain. Thus it seemed that the image took just revenge of
4 Pompey's enemy, being thrown down on the ground at his feet and
yielding up his ghost there for the number of wounds he had upon
him. For it is reported that he had three-and-twenty wounds upon
5 his body; and divers of the conspirators did hurt themselves, striking
one body with so many blows.

| | | |
|---|---|---|
| 3 CAESAR: | Et tu, Brute! Then fall, Caesar! *Dies.* | (III, I, 77) |
| ANTONY: | Look, in this place ran Cassius' dagger through: | |
| | See what a rent the envious Casca made: | |
| | Through this the well-beloved Brutus stabb'd; | |
| | And as he pluck'd his cursed steel away, | |
| | Mark how the blood of Caesar follow'd it, | |
| | As rushing out of doors, to be resolved | |
| | If Brutus so unkindly knock'd, or no; | |
| | For Brutus, as you know, was Caesar's angel: | |
| | Judge, O you gods, how dearly Caesar loved him! | |
| | This was the most unkindest cut of all; | |
| | For when the noble Caesar saw him stab, | |
| | Ingratitude, more strong than traitors' arms, | |
| | Quite vanquish'd him: then burst his mighty heart. | |
| | | (III, 2, 178) |
| ANTONY: | In your bad strokes, Brutus, you give good words: | |
| | Witness the hole you made in Caesar's heart, | |
| | Crying 'Long live! hail, Caesar!' | (V, I, 30) |
| 4 BRUTUS: | ... Caesar ... | |
| | That now on Pompey's basis lies along | |
| | No worthier than the dust! | (III, I, 114) |
| ANTONY: | And, in his mantle muffling up his face, | |
| | Even at the base of Pompey's statue, | |
| | Which all the while ran blood, great Caesar fell. | (III, 2, 191) |
| 5 OCTAVIUS: | I draw a sword against conspirators; | |
| | When think you that the sword goes up again? | |
| | Never, till Caesar's three and thirty wounds | |
| | Be well avenged. | (V, I, 51) |

When Caesar was slain, the Senate, though Brutus stood in the midst amongst them as though he would have said somewhat touching this fact, presently ran out of the house, and flying filled all 46 the city with marvellous fear and tumult; insomuch as some did shut-to their doors, others forsook their shops and warehouses, and others ran to the place to see what the matter was; and others also that had seen it ran home to their houses again. But Antonius and Lepidus, which were two of Caesar's chiefest friends, secretly conveying themselves away, fled into other men's houses, and forsook 47 their own.

Brutus and his confederates on the other side, being yet hot with this murder they had committed, having their swords drawn in their hands, came all in a troop together out of the Senate, and went into the market-place, not as men that made countenance to fly, but otherwise boldly holding up their heads like men of courage, and called to the people to defend their liberty, and stayed to speak with every great personage whom they met in their 48 way.

Of them, some followed this troop and went amongst them as if

46 See note 41 above.

47 CASSIUS:                    Where is Antony?
    TREBONIUS:   Fled to his house amazed:
                    Men, wives and children stare, cry out and run
                    As it were doomsday.                  (III, 1, 95)
See *Life of Brutus*, p. 125.

48 CINNA:           Liberty! Freedom! Tyranny is dead!
                    Run hence, proclaim, cry it about the streets.
    CASSIUS:      Some to the common pulpits, and cry out,
                    'Liberty, freedom, and enfranchisement!' ...
    BRUTUS:      Then walk we forth, even to the market-place,
                    And, waving our red weapons o'er our heads,
                    Let's all cry 'Peace, freedom and liberty!' ...
    DECIUS:       What, shall we forth?
    CASSIUS:                        Ay, every man away:
                    Brutus shall lead; and we will grace his heels
                    With the most boldest and best hearts of Rome.
                                 (III, 1, 78; 108)

they had been of the conspiracy, and falsely challenged part of the honour with them. Amongst them was Caius Octavius and Lentulus Spinther. But both of them were afterwards put to death, for their vain covetousness of honour, by Antonius and Octavius Caesar the younger; and yet had no part of that honour for the which they were put to death, neither did any man believe that they were any of the confederates or of counsel with them. For they that did put them to death took revenge rather of the will they had to offend, than of any fact they had committed.

The next morning Brutus and his confederates came into the market-place to speak unto the people, who gave them such audience that it seemed they neither greatly reproved nor allowed the fact. For by their great silence they showed that they were sorry for Caesar's death, and also that they did reverence Brutus. Now the Senate granted general pardon for all that was past and, to pacify every man, ordained besides that Caesar's funerals should be honoured as a god, and established all things that he had done, and gave certain provinces also and convenient honours unto Brutus and his confederates, whereby every man thought all things were brought to good peace and quietness again.

But when they had opened Caesar's testament and found a liberal
49 legacy of money bequeathed unto every citizen of Rome, and that they saw his body (which was brought into the market-place) all
50 bemangled with gashes of swords, then there was no order to keep the multitude and common people quiet. But they plucked up forms, tables, and stools, and laid them all about the body, and setting them afire burnt the corpse. Then, when the fire was well kindled, they took the firebrands and went unto their houses that had slain

---

49 See *Life of Brutus*, p. 128 note 44.
50 ANTONY:       Kind souls, what, weep you when you but behold
               Our Caesar's vesture wounded? Look you here,
               Here is himself, marr'd, as you see, with traitors.
1st PLEBEIAN:  O piteous spectacle! . . . O most bloody sight!
(III, 2, 199; 206)

See *Life of Antonius*, p. 189 note 14, and *Life of Brutus*, p. 129.

51 Caesar, to set them afire. Other also ran up and down the city to see if they could meet with any of them to cut them in pieces. Howbeit they could meet with never a man of them, because they had locked themselves up safely in their houses.

There was one of Caesar's friends called Cinna, that had a marvellous strange and terrible dream the night before. He dreamed that Caesar bade him to supper, and that he refused, and would not go; then that Caesar took him by the hand, and led him against his will. Now Cinna hearing at that time that they burnt Caesar's body in the market-place, notwithstanding that he feared his dream and had an ague on him besides, he went into the market-place to honour his funerals. When he came thither, one of the mean sort asked him what his name was? He was straight called by his name. The first man told it to another, and that other unto another, so that it ran straight through them all that he was one of them that murdered Caesar. For indeed one of the traitors to Caesar was also called Cinna as himself. Wherefore, taking him for Cinna the murderer, they fell upon him with such fury that they presently dispatched him
52 in the market-place.

This stir and fury made Brutus and Cassius more afraid than of all that was past; and therefore, within few days after, they departed out of Rome. And touching their doings afterwards, and what calamity they suffered till their deaths, we have written it at large in the
53 *Life of Brutus*.

51 1st PLEBEIAN:                     Come, away, away!
                  We'll burn his body in the holy place,
                  And with the brands fire the traitors' houses.
                  Take up the body.

2nd PLEBEIAN: Go fetch fire.

3rd PLEBEIAN: Pluck down benches.

4th PLEBEIAN: Pluck down forms, windows, any thing.     (III, 2, 258)

3rd PLEBEIAN: Come, brands, ho! fire-brands: to Brutus', to
                  Cassius'; burn all: some to Decius' house, and some to Casca's;
                  some to Ligarius': away, go!                   (III, 3, 40)

See also *Life of Brutus*, p. 129, and *Life of Antonius*, p. 189.

52 See *Life of Brutus*, p. 130 note 48.

53 See pp. 130ff. below.

98

Caesar died at six-and-fifty years of age; and Pompey also lived not passing four years more than he. So he reaped no other fruit of all his reign and dominion, which he had so vehemently desired all his life and pursued with such extreme danger, but a vain name only and a superficial glory that procured him the envy and hatred of his country. But his great prosperity and good fortune, that favoured him all his lifetime, did continue afterwards in the revenge of his death, pursuing the murderers both by sea and land, till they had not left a man more to be executed, of all them that were actors or counsellors in the conspiracy of his death. Furthermore, of all the chances that happen unto men upon the earth, that which came to Cassius above all other is most to be wondered at. For he, being overcome in battle at the journey of Philippes, slew himself with the same
54 sword with the which he strake Caesar. Again, of signs in the element, the great comet, which seven nights together was seen very bright after Caesar's death, the eighth night after was never seen
55 more. Also the brightness of the sun was darkened, the which all that year through rose very pale and shined not out, whereby it gave but small heat; therefore the air being very cloudy and dark, by the weakness of the heat that could not come forth, did cause the earth to bring forth but raw and unripe fruit, which rotted before it
56 could ripe.

But, above all, the ghost that appeared unto Brutus showed plainly that the gods were offended with the murder of Caesar. The vision was thus. Brutus, being ready to pass over his army from the city of

| | |
|---|---|
| 54 BRUTUS: | O Julius Caesar, thou art mighty yet. |
| | Thy spirit walks abroad, and turns our swords |
| | In our own proper entrails. (v, 3, 94) |
| CASSIUS: | With this good sword, |
| | That ran through Caesar's bowels, search this bosom . . . |
| | Caesar, thou art revenged, |
| | Even with the sword that kill'd thee. *Dies.* (v, 3, 41) |
| 55 CALPURNIA: | When beggars die, there are no comets seen; |
| | The heavens themselves blaze forth the death of princes. |
| | (II, 2, 30) |

56 See p. 86 note 20 above (*Hamlet*, I, I, 113).

Abydos to the other coast lying directly against it, slept every night, as his manner was, in his tent; and being yet awake thinking of his affairs – for by report he was as careful a captain and lived with as little sleep as ever man did – he thought he heard a noise at his tent door; and, looking towards the light of the lamp that waxed very dim, he saw a horrible vision of a man, of a wonderful greatness and dreadful look, which at the first made him marvellously afraid. But when he saw that it did him no hurt, but stood by his bedside and said nothing, at length he asked him what he was. The image answered him:

'I am thy ill angel, Brutus, and thou shalt see me by the city of Philippes.'

Then Brutus replied again, and said:

'Well, I shall see thee then.'

57 Therewithal the spirit presently vanished from him.

After that time Brutus being in battle near unto the city of Philippes against Antonius and Octavius Caesar, at the first battle he won the victory, and, overthrowing all them that withstood him, he drave
58 them into young Caesar's camp, which he took. The second battle

57                          *Enter the Ghost of Caesar.*

BRUTUS:      How ill this taper burns! Ha! who comes here?
             I think it is the weakness of mine eyes
             That shapes this monstrous apparition.
             It comes upon me. Art thou any thing?
             Art thou some god, some angel, or some devil
             That makest my blood cold and my hair to stare?
             Speak to me what thou art.
GHOST:       Thy evil spirit, Brutus.
BRUTUS:      Why comest thou?
GHOST:       To tell thee thou shalt see me at Philippi.
BRUTUS:      Well; then I shall see thee again?
GHOST:       Ay, at Philippi.
BRUTUS:      Why, I will see thee at Philippi, then.   *Exit Ghost.*
             Now I have taken heart thou vanishest:
             Ill spirit, I would hold more talk with thee.   (IV, 3, 275)

See also *Life of Brutus*, p. 149.
58 See *Life of Brutus*, p. 158.

being at hand, this spirit appeared again unto him, but spake never
a word. Thereupon Brutus, knowing he should die, did put himself
to all hazard in battle, but yet fighting could not be slain. So, seeing
his men put to flight and overthrown, he ran unto a little rock not
far off; and there setting his sword's point to his breast fell upon it
and slew himself, but yet, as it is reported, with the help of his
friend that dispatched him.

BRUTUS:      The ghost of Caesar hath appear'd to me
              Two several times by night; at Sardis once,
              And, this last night, here at Philippi fields:
              I know my hour is come.             (v, 5, 17)

POMPEY:     [*to Octavius*]  I do not know
              Wherefore my father should revengers want,
              Having a son and friends; since Julius Caesar,
              Who at Philippi the good Brutus ghosted,
              There saw you labouring for him.
                         (*Antony and Cleopatra*, ii, 6, 10)

See also *Life of Brutus*, pp. 165–6.
See *Life of Brutus*, p. 172 note 97.

# THE LIFE OF MARCUS BRUTUS

MARCUS BRUTUS came of that Junius Brutus for whom the ancient Romans made his statue of brass to be set up in the Capitol with the images of the kings, holding a naked sword in his hand, because he 1 had valiantly put down the Tarquins from their kingdom of Rome. But that Junius Brutus, being of a sour stern nature, not softened by reason, being like unto sword blades of too hard a temper, was so subject to his choler and malice he bore unto the tyrants, that for their sakes he caused his own sons to be executed.

But this Marcus Brutus in contrary manner, whose *Life* we presently write, having framed his manners of life by the rules of virtue and study of philosophy, and having employed his wit, which was gentle and constant, in attempting of great things, methinks he was rightly made and framed unto virtue. So that his very enemies which wish him most hurt, because of his conspiracy against Julius Caesar, if there were any noble attempt done in all this conspiracy, they refer it wholly unto Brutus, and all the cruel and violent acts unto Cassius, who was Brutus' familiar friend but not so well given 2 and conditioned as he.

His mother Servilia, it is thought, came of the blood of Servilius

| | | |
|---|---|---|
| *1* CASSIUS: | O, you and I have heard our fathers say, | |
| | There was a Brutus once that would have brook'd | |
| | The eternal devil to keep his state in Rome | |
| | As easily as a king. | (*Julius Caesar*, I, 2, 158) |
| BRUTUS: | My ancestors did from the streets of Rome | |
| | The Tarquin drive, when he was call'd a king. | (II, 1, 53) |
| PLEBEIAN: | Give him a statue with his ancestors. | (III, 2, 55) |
| *2* ANTONY: | [*of Cassius*] He is a noble Roman and well given. | (I, 2, 197) |

Hala, who, when Spurius Melius went about to make himself king, and to bring it to pass had enticed the common people to rebel, took a dagger and hid it close under his arm, and went into the market-place. When he was come thither, he made as though he had somewhat to say unto him, and pressed as near him as he could. Wherefore, Melius stooping down with his head to hear what he would say, Brutus stabbed him in with his dagger, and slew him. Thus much all writers agree for his mother.

Now, touching his father, some for the evil will and malice they bare unto Brutus, because of the death of Julius Caesar, do maintain that he came not of Junius Brutus that drave out the Tarquins – for there were none left of his race, considering that his two sons were executed for conspiracy with the Tarquins – and that Marcus Brutus came of a mean house, the which was raised to honour and office in the commonwealth but of late time. Posidonius the philosopher writeth the contrary: that Junius Brutus indeed slew two of his sons which were men grown, as the histories do declare; howbeit that there was a third son, being but a little child at that time, from whom the house and family afterwards was derived; and furthermore, that there were in his time certain famous men of that family, whose stature and countenance resembled much the image of Junius Brutus. And thus much for this matter.

Marcus Cato the philosopher was brother unto Servilia, M. Brutus' mother; whom Brutus studied most to follow of all the other Romans, because he was his uncle; and afterwards he married his daughter. Now touching the Grecian philosophers, there was no sect nor philosopher of them but he heard and liked it. But above all the rest he loved Plato's sect best, and did not much give himself to the new nor mean Academy as they call it, but altogether to the old Academy. Therefore he did ever greatly esteem the philosopher Antiochus of the city of Ascalon. But he was more familiar with his brother Ariston, who for learning and knowledge was inferior to many other philosophers but for wisdom and courtesy equal with the best and chiefest. Touching Empylus, whom Marcus Brutus himself doth mention in his epistles, and his friends also in many places, he was an orator, and left an excellent book he wrote of the death of Julius Caesar, and titled it *Brutus*.

He was properly learned in the Latin tongue, and was able to make long discourse in it, besides that he could also plead very well in Latin. But, for the Greek tongue, they do note in some of his epistles that he counterfeited that brief compendious manner of speech of the Lacedaemonians. As, when the war was begun, he wrote unto the Pergamenians in this sort:

*I understand you have given Dolabella money: if you have done it willingly, you confess you have offended me; if against your wills, show it then by giving me willingly.*

Another time again unto the Samians:

*Your counsels be long; your doings be slow; consider the end.*

And in another epistle he wrote unto the Patareians:

*The Xanthians, despising my goodwill, have made their country a grave of despair; and the Patareians, that put themselves into my protection, have lost no jot of their liberty. And therefore, whilst you have liberty, either choose the judgement of the Patareians or the fortune of the Xanthians.*

These were Brutus' manner of letters, which were honoured for their briefness.

So Brutus being but a young stripling went into Cyprus with his uncle Cato, who was sent against Ptolemy King of Egypt, who having slain himself, Cato, staying for certain necessary business he had in the isle of Rhodes, had already sent Canidius, one of his friends, before to keep his treasure and goods. But Cato, fearing he would be light-fingered, wrote unto Brutus forthwith to come out of Pamphylia (where he was but newly recovered of a sickness) into Cyprus; the which he did. The which journey he was sorry to take upon him, both for respect of Canidius' shame, whom Cato as he thought wrongfully slandered, as also because he thought this office too mean and unmeet for him, being a young man and given to his book. This notwithstanding, he behaved himself so honestly and carefully, that Cato did greatly commend him; and, after all the goods were sold and converted into ready money, he took the most part of it and returned withal to Rome.

Afterwards, when the Empire of Rome was divided into factions, and that Caesar and Pompey both were in arms one against the other and that all the Empire of Rome was in garboil and uproar, it was thought then that Brutus would take part with Caesar, because Pompey not long before had put his father to death. But Brutus, preferring the respect of his country and commonwealth before private affection, and persuading himself that Pompey had juster cause to enter into arms than Caesar, he then took part with Pompey, though oftentimes, meeting him before, he thought scorn to speak to him, thinking it a great sin and offence in him to speak to the murderer of his father. But then submitting himself unto Pompey, as unto the head of the commonwealth, he sailed into Sicilia, lieutenant under Sestius, that was governor of that province. But when he saw that there was no way to rise nor to do any noble exploits, and that Caesar and Pompey were both camped together and fought for victory, he went of himself unsent for into Macedon, to be partaker of the danger. It is reported that Pompey, being glad and wondering at his coming, when he saw him come to him he rose out of his chair and went and embraced him before them all, and used him as honourably as he could have done the noblest man that took his part. Brutus, being in Pompey's camp, did nothing but study all day long, except he were with Pompey, and not only the days before, but the self same day also before the great battle was fought in the fields of Pharsalia, where Pompey was overthrown. It was in the midst of summer, and the sun was very hot, besides that the camp was lodged near unto marshes; and they that carried his tent tarried long before they came, whereupon, being very weary with travel, scant any meat came into his mouth at dinner-time. Furthermore, when others slept, or thought what would happen the morrow after, he 3 fell to his book, and wrote all day long till night, writing a breviary of Polybius.

It is reported that Caesar did not forget him, and that he gave his captains charge, before the battle, that they should beware they

3 See p. 148 note 63.

killed not Brutus in fight, and, if he yielded willingly unto them, that then they should bring him unto him; but if he resisted, and would not be taken, then that they should let him go and do him no hurt.

Some say he did this for Servilia's sake, Brutus' mother. For, when he was a young man, he had been acquainted with Servilia, who was extremely in love with him. And, because Brutus was born in that time when their love was hottest, he persuaded himself
4 that he begat him. For proof hereof the report goeth that when the weightiest matters were in hand in the Senate about the conspiracy of Catiline, which was likely to have undone the city of Rome, Caesar and Cato sat near together, and were both of contrary minds to each other; and then that in the meantime one delivered Caesar a letter. Caesar took it, and read it softly to himself. But Cato cried out upon Caesar, and said he did not well to receive advertisements from enemies. Whereupon the whole Senate began to murmur at it. Then Caesar gave Cato the letter as it was sent him; who read it, and found that it was a love-letter sent from his sister Servilia. Thereupon he cast it again to Caesar, and said unto him, 'Hold, drunken sop'. When he had done so, he went on with his tale, and maintained his opinion as he did before; so commonly was the love of Servilia known which she bare unto Caesar.

So, after Pompey's overthrow at the battle of Pharsalia, and that he fled to the sea, when Caesar came to besiege his camp, Brutus went out of the camp gates unseen of any man, and leapt into a marsh full of water and reeds. Then when night was come he crept out, and went unto the city of Larissa; from whence he wrote unto Caesar, who was very glad that he had scaped and sent for him to come unto him. When Brutus was come, he did not only pardon him, but also kept him always about him, and did as much honour and esteem him as any man he had in his company.

Now no man could tell whither Pompey was fled, and all were

4 SUFFOLK:    A Roman sworder and banditto slave
               Murder'd sweet Tully; Brutus' bastard hand
               Stabb'd Julius Caesar; savage islanders
               Pompey the Great.        (2 Henry VI, IV, I, 135)

marvellous desirous to know it. Wherefore Caesar walking a good way alone with Brutus, he did ask him which way he thought Pompey took. Caesar perceiving by his talk that Brutus guessed certainly whither Pompey should be fled, he left all other ways, and took his journey directly towards Egypt. Pompey, as Brutus conjectured, was indeed fled into Egypt; but there he was villainously slain. Furthermore, Brutus obtained pardon of Caesar for Cassius; and, defending also the King of Libya's cause, he was overlaid with a world of accusations against him; howbeit, entreating for him, he saved him the best part of his realm and kingdom.*

They say also that Caesar said, when he heard Brutus plead: 'I know not,' said he, 'what this young man would; but, what he would, he willeth it vehemently.' For, as Brutus' gravity and constant mind would not grant all men their requests that sued unto him, but being moved with reason and discretion did always incline to that which was good and honest, even so, when it was moved to follow any matter, he used a kind of forcible and vehement persuasion that calmed not till he had obtained his desire. For, by flattering of him, a man could never obtain anything at his hands, nor make him to do that which was unjust. Further, he thought it not meet for a man of calling and estimation to yield unto the requests and entreaties of a shameless and importunate suitor, requesting things unmeet; the which, notwithstanding, some men do for shame, because they dare deny nothing; and therefore he was wont to say that he thought them evil brought up in their youth, that could deny nothing.

Now when Caesar took sea to go into Afric against Cato and Scipio, he left Brutus governor of Gaul in Italy, on this side of the Alps; which was a great good hap for that province. For, where others were spoiled and polled by the insolency and covetousness of the governors, as if it had been a country conquered, Brutus was a comfort and rest unto their former troubles and miseries they sustained. But he referred it wholly unto Caesar's grace and goodness.

* This King was Juba. Howbeit it is true also that Brutus made intercession for Deïotarus, King of Galatia, who was deprived notwithstanding of the most part of his country by Caesar; and therefore this place were best to be understanded by Deïotarus.

For, when Caesar returned out of Afric and progressed up and down Italy, the things that pleased him best to see were the cities under Brutus' charge and government, and Brutus himself; who honoured Caesar in person, and whose company also Caesar greatly esteemed.

Now there were divers sorts of Praetorships at Rome; and it was looked for that Brutus or Cassius would make suit for the chiefest Praetorship, which they called the Praetorship of the City, because he that had that office was as a judge to minister justice unto the citizens. Therefore they strove one against the other, though some say that there was some little grudge betwixt them for other matters before, and that this contention did set them further out, though they were 5 allied together. For Cassius had married Junia, Brutus' sister. Others say, that this contention betwixt them came by Caesar himself, who secretly gave either of them both hope of his favour. So their suit for the Praetorship was so followed and laboured of either party that one of them put another in suit of law. Brutus with his virtue and good name contended against many noble exploits in arms which Cassius had done against the Parthians. So Caesar, after he had heard both their objections, he told his friends with whom he consulted about this matter:

'Cassius' cause is the juster,' said he, 'but Brutus must be first preferred.'

Thus Brutus had the first Praetorship, and Cassius the second; who thanked not Caesar so much for the Praetorship he had, as he was angry with him for that he had lost. But Brutus in many other things tasted of the benefit of Caesar's favour in anything he requested. For, if he had listed, he might have been one of Caesar's chiefest friends and of greatest authority and credit about him. Howbeit Cassius' friends did dissuade him from it (for Cassius and he were not yet reconciled together sithence their first contention and strife for the Praetorship) and prayed him to beware of Caesar's sweet enticements and to fly his tyrannical favours; the which they said Caesar gave him, not to honour his virtue but to weaken his constant mind, framing it to the bent of his bow.

5 LUCIUS:          Sir, 'tis your brother Cassius at the door.

(*Julius Caesar*, II, I, 70)

Now Caesar on the other side did not trust him overmuch, nor was not without tales brought unto him against him; howbeit he feared his great mind, authority, and friends. Yet, on the other side also, he trusted his good nature and fair conditions. For, intelligence being brought him one day that Antonius and Dolabella did conspire against him, he answered that these fat long-haired men made him not afraid, but the lean and whitely-faced fellows, meaning that by 6 Brutus and Cassius. At another time also when one accused Brutus unto him and bade him beware of him:
'What,' said he again, clapping his hand on his breast, 'think ye that Brutus will not tarry till this body die?'
– meaning that none but Brutus after him was meet to have such power as he had. And surely, in my opinion, I am persuaded that Brutus might indeed have come to have been the chiefest man of Rome, if he could have contented himself for a time to have been next unto Caesar and to have suffered his glory and authority which he had gotten by his great victories to consume with time.

But Cassius being a choleric man and hating Caesar privately, more than he did the tyranny openly, he incensed Brutus against him. It is also reported that Brutus could evil away with the tyranny, and that Cassius hated the tyrant, making many complaints for the injuries he had done him, and, amongst others, for that he had taken away his lions from him. Cassius had provided them for his sports, when he should be Aedile, and they were found in the city of Megara when it was won by Calenus; and Caesar kept them. The rumour went that these lions did marvellous great hurt to the Megarians. For, when the city was taken, they brake their cages where they were tied up, and turned them loose, thinking they would have done great mischief to the enemies, and have kept them from setting upon them. But the lions, contrary to expectation, turned upon themselves that fled unarmed, and did so cruelly tear some in pieces that it pitied their enemies to see them. And this was the cause, as some do report, that made Cassius conspire against Caesar.

But this holdeth no water. For Cassius even from his cradle could

6 See *Life of Caesar*, p. 85 note 19, and *Life of Antonius*, p. 186.

not abide any manner of tyrants, as it appeared when he was but a boy, and went unto the same school that Faustus the son of Sylla did. And Faustus, bragging among other boys, highly boasted of his father's kingdom. Cassius rose up on his feet, and gave him two good whirts on the ear. Faustus' governors would have put this matter in suit against Cassius. But Pompey would not suffer them, but caused the two boys to be brought before him, and asked them how the matter came to pass. Then Cassius, as it is written of him, said unto the other:

'Go to, Faustus, speak again, an thou darest before this nobleman here, the same words that made me angry with thee, that my fists may walk once again about thine ears.'

Such was Cassius' hot stirring nature.

But for Brutus, his friends and countrymen, both by divers procurements and sundry rumours of the city and by many bills also, did openly call and procure him to do that he did. For, under the image of his ancestor Junius Brutus, that drave the kings out of Rome, they wrote:

'Oh that it pleased the gods thou wert now alive, Brutus.'

And again:

7 'That thou wert here among us now.'

His tribunal, or chair, where he gave audience during the time he was Praetor, was full of such bills: 'Brutus, thou art asleep, and art 8 not Brutus indeed.'

And of all this Caesar's flatterers were the cause; who beside many other exceeding and unspeakable honours they daily devised for him, in the night-time they did put diadems upon the heads of his 9 images, supposing thereby to allure the common people to call him King, instead of Dictator. Howbeit it turned to the contrary, as we 10 have written more at large in Julius Caesar's *Life*.

7 See p. 102 and note 1 above; also:
 CASSIUS:            Set this up with wax
            Upon old Brutus' statue.           (I, 3, 145)
8 See *Life of Caesar*, p. 85 note 17.
9 See *Life of Caesar*, pp. 83–4 notes 14 and 16.
10 pp. 83–4 above.

Now when Cassius felt his friends and did stir them up against Caesar, they all agreed and promised to take part with him, so Brutus were the chief of their conspiracy. For they told him that so high an enterprise and attempt as that did not so much require men of manhood and courage to draw their swords, as it stood them upon to have a man of such estimation as Brutus, to make every man boldly think that by his only presence the fact were holy and just: if he took not this course, then that they should go to it with fainter hearts; and when they had done it they should be more fearful, because every man would think that Brutus would not have refused to have made one with them, if the cause had been good and honest. Therefore Cassius, considering this matter with himself, did first of all speak to Brutus since they grew strange together for the suit they had for the Praetorship. So when he was reconciled to him again, and that they had embraced one another, Cassius asked him if he

CASSIUS:    Come, Casca, you and I will yet ere day
    See Brutus at his house: three parts of him
    Is ours already, and the man entire
    Upon the next encounter yields him ours.

CASCA:    O, he sits high in all the people's hearts:
    And that which would appear offence in us,
    His countenance, like richest alchemy,
    Will change to virtue and to worthiness.

CASSIUS:    Him and his worth and our great need of him
    You have right well conceited.        (I, 3, 153)

CASSIUS:    Brutus, I do observe you now of late:
    I have not from your eyes that gentleness
    And show of love as I was wont to have:
    You bear too stubborn and too strange a hand
    Over your friend that loves you.

BRUTUS:                      Cassius,
    Be not deceived: if I have veil'd my look,
    I turn the trouble of my countenance
    Merely upon myself. Vexed I am
    Of late with passions of some difference,
    Conceptions only proper to myself,
    Which give some soil perhaps to my behaviours;

were determined to be in the Senate-house the first day of the month of March, because he heard say that Caesar's friends should move the council that day that Caesar should be called King by the Senate. Brutus answered him, he would not be there.

'But if we be sent for,' said Cassius, 'how then?'

'For myself then,' said Brutus, 'I mean not to hold my peace, but to withstand it, and rather die than lose my liberty.'

Cassius being bold, and taking hold of this word,

'Why,' quoth he, 'what Roman is he alive that will suffer thee to 13 die for the liberty? What, knowest thou not that thou art Brutus? Thinkest thou that they be cobblers, tapsters, or suchlike base

*13* BRUTUS:                I do fear, the people
                Choose Caesar for their king.

CASSIUS:                        Ay, do you fear it?
                Then must I think you would not have it so.

BRUTUS:                I would not, Cassius; yet I love him well.
                But wherefore do you hold me here so long?
                What is it that you would impart to me?
                If it be aught toward the general good,
                Set honour in one eye and death i' the other,
                And I will look on both indifferently,
                For let the gods so speed me as I love
                The name of honour more than I fear death ...

CASSIUS:                I cannot tell what you and other men
                Think of this life; but, for my single self,
                I had as lief not be as live to be
                In awe of such a thing as I myself.
                I was born free as Caesar; so were you.      (I, 2, 79; 93)

                But let not therefore my good friends be grieved –
                Among which number, Cassius, be you one –
                Nor construe any further my neglect,
                Than that poor Brutus, with himself at war,
                Forgets the shows of love to other men.

CASSIUS:                Then, Brutus, I have much mistook your passion;
                By means whereof this breast of mine hath buried
                Thoughts of great value, worthy cogitations.

                                        (I, 2, 32)

mechanical people, that write these bills and scrolls which are found daily in thy Praetor's chair, and not the noblest men and best citizens that do it? No, be thou well assured, that of other Praetors they look for gifts, common distributions amongst the people, and for common plays, and to see fencers fight at the sharp, to show the people pastime. But at thy hands they specially require, as a due debt unto them, the taking away of the tyranny, being fully bent to suffer any extremity for thy sake, so that thou wilt show thyself to be the man thou art taken for, and that they hope thou art.'

Thereupon he kissed Brutus, and embraced him: and so, each taking leave of other, they went both to speak with their friends about it.

Now amongst Pompey's friends there was one called Caius Ligarius, who had been accused unto Caesar for taking part with Pompey, and Caesar discharged him. But Ligarius thanked not Caesar so much for his discharge, as he was offended with him for that he was brought in danger by his tyrannical power. And therefore in his heart he was alway his mortal enemy, and was besides very familiar with Brutus, who went to see him being sick in his bed, and said unto him: 'O Ligarius, in what a time art thou sick!'

Ligarius rising up in his bed and taking him by the right hand, said unto him:

'Brutus,' said he, 'if thou hast any great enterprise in hand worthy of thyself, I am whole.'

Compare the 'mechanical' characters in I, I, especially the cobbler.

CASSIUS:            Good Cinna, take this paper,
            And look you lay it in the praetor's chair,
            Where Brutus may but find it; and throw this
            In at his window.                     (I, 3, 142)

CAESAR:             Caius Ligarius,
            Caesar was ne'er so much your enemy
            As that same ague which has made you lean.   (II, 2, 111)

METELLUS:   Caius Ligarius doth bear Caesar hard,
            Who rated him for speaking well of Pompey:
            I wonder none of you have thought of him.

BRUTUS:     Now, good Metellus, go along by him:
            He loves me well, and I have given him reasons;
            Send him but hither, and I'll fashion him.   (II, 1, 215)

After that time they began to feel all their acquaintance whom they trusted, and laid their heads together consulting upon it, and did not only pick out their friends, but all those also whom they thought stout enough to attempt any desperate matter, and that were not afraid to lose their lives. For this cause they durst not acquaint Cicero with their conspiracy, although he was a man whom they loved dearly and trusted best. For they were afraid that he being a coward by nature, and age also having increased his fear, he would quite turn and alter all their purpose, and quench the heat of their enterprise (the which specially required hot and earnest execution) seeking by persuasion to bring all things to such safety as there should be no peril.

| | |
|---|---|
| **17** CASSIUS: | But what of Cicero? shall we sound him? |
| | I think he will stand very strong with us. |
| CASCA: | Let us not leave him out. |
| CINNA: | No, by no means. |
| METELLUS: | O, let us have him, for his silver hairs |
| | Will purchase us a good opinion |
| | And buy men's voices to commend our deeds: |
| | It shall be said his judgement ruled our hands; |
| | Our youths and wildness shall no whit appear, |
| | But all be buried in his gravity. |
| BRUTUS: | O, name him not: let us not break with him; |
| | For he will never follow any thing |
| | That other men begin. |
| CASSIUS: | Then leave him out. |
| CASCA: | Indeed he is not fit. (II, I, 141) |

| | |
|---|---|
| LIGARIUS: | Vouchsafe good morrow from a feeble tongue. |
| BRUTUS: | O, what a time have you chose out, brave Caius, |
| | To wear a kerchief! Would you were not sick! |
| LIGARIUS: | I am not sick, if Brutus have in hand |
| | Any exploit worthy the name of honour. |
| BRUTUS: | Such an exploit have I in hand, Ligarius, |
| | Had you a healthful ear to hear of it. |
| LIGARIUS: | By all the gods that Romans bow before, |
| | I here discard my sickness! . . . What's to do? |
| BRUTUS: | A piece of work that will make sick men whole. (II, I, 313) |

114

Brutus also did let other of his friends alone, as Statilius Epicurean and Faonius, that made profession to follow Marcus Cato: because that having cast out words afar off, disputing together in philosophy to feel their minds, Faonius answered that civil war was worse than tyrannical government usurped against the law. And Statilius told him also that it were an unwise part of him to put his life in danger for a sight of ignorant fools and asses. Labeo was present at this talk, and maintained the contrary against them both. But Brutus held his peace, as though it had been a doubtful matter and a hard thing to have decided. But afterwards, being out of their company, he made Labeo privy to his intent; who very readily offered himself to make one. And they thought good also to bring in another Brutus to join with him, surnamed Albinus; who was no man of his hands himself, but because he was able to bring good force of a great number of slaves and fencers at the sharp, whom he kept to show the people pastime with their fighting; besides also that Caesar had some trust in him. Cassius and Labeo told Brutus Albinus of it at the first; but he made them no answer. But when he had spoken with Brutus himself alone, and that Brutus had told him he was the chief ringleader of all this conspiracy, then he willingly promised him the best aid he could. Furthermore the only name and great calling of Brutus did bring on the most of them to give consent to this conspiracy; who having never taken oaths together nor taken or given any caution or assurance, nor binding themselves one to another by any religious oaths, they all kept the matter so secret to themselves and could so cunningly handle it that, notwithstanding the gods did reveal it by manifest signs and tokens from above and by predictions of
18 sacrifices, yet all this would not be believed.

| | |
|---|---|
| *18* BRUTUS: | Give me your hands all over, one by one. |
| CASSIUS: | And let us swear our resolution. |
| BRUTUS: | No, not an oath: if not the face of men, |
| | The sufferance of our souls, the time's abuse, – |
| | If these be motives weak, break off betimes, |
| | And every man hence to his idle bed; |
| | So let high-sighted tyranny range on, |
| | Till each man drop by lottery. But if these, |

Now Brutus (who knew very well that for his sake all the noblest, valiantest, and most courageous men of Rome did venture their lives) weighing with himself the greatness of the danger, when he was out of his house he did so frame and fashion his countenance and
19 looks that no man could discern he had anything to trouble his mind. But when night came that he was in his own house, then he was clean changed. For, either care did wake him against his will when he would have slept, or else oftentimes of himself he fell into such deep thoughts of this enterprise, casting in his mind all the dangers that might

19 BRUTUS:      Good gentlemen, look fresh and merrily;
                    Let not our looks put on our purposes . . .    (II, I, 224)

BRUTUS:      O conspiracy,
                    Shamest thou to show thy dangerous brow by night,
                    When evils are most free? O, then by day
                    Where wilt thou find a cavern dark enough
                    To mask thy monstrous visage? Seek none, conspiracy;
                    Hide it in smiles and affability.    (II, I, 77)

                    As I am sure they do, bear fire enough
                    To kindle cowards and to steel with valour
                    The melting spirits of women, then, countrymen,
                    What need we any spur but our own cause,
                    To prick us to redress? what other bond
                    Than secret Romans, that have spoke the word,
                    And will not palter? and what other oath
                    Than honesty to honesty engaged,
                    That this shall be, or we will fall for it?
                    Swear priests and cowards and men cautelous,
                    Old feeble carrions and such suffering souls
                    That welcome wrongs; unto bad causes swear
                    Such creatures as men doubt; but do not stain
                    The even virtue of our enterprise,
                    Nor the insuppressive mettle of our spirits,
                    To think that or our cause or our performance
                    Did need an oath; when every drop of blood
                    That every Roman bears, and nobly bears,
                    Is guilty of a several bastardy,
                    If he do break the smallest particle
                    Of any promise that hath pass'd from him.    (II, I, 112)

0 happen, that his wife, lying by him, found that there was some marvellous great matter that troubled his mind, not being wont to be in
1 that taking, and that he could not well determine with himself. His
2 wife Portia (as we have told you before) was the daughter of Cato,
3 whom Brutus married being his cousin, not a maiden, but a young

0 BRUTUS:      Since Cassius first did whet me against Caesar,
              I have not slept.
              Between the acting of a dreadful thing
              And the first motion, all the interim is
              Like a phantasma, or a hideous dream:
              The Genius and the mortal instruments
              Are then in council; and the state of man,
              Like to a little kingdom, suffers then
              The nature of an insurrection.                    (II, I, 61)

21 PORTIA:                   You've ungently, Brutus,
              Stole from my bed: and yesternight, at supper,
              You suddenly arose, and walk'd about,
              Musing and sighing, with your arms across,
              And when I ask'd you what the matter was,
              You stared upon me with ungentle looks;
              I urged you further; then you scratch'd your head,
              And too impatiently stamp'd with your foot;
              Yet I insisted, yet you answer'd not,
              But, with an angry wafture of your hand,
              Gave sign for me to leave you; so I did;
              Fearing to strengthen that impatience
              Which seem'd too much enkindled, and withal
              Hoping it was but an effect of humour,
              Which sometime hath his hour with every man.
              It will not let you eat, nor talk, nor sleep,
              And could it work so much upon your shape
              As it hath much prevail'd on your condition,
              I should not know you, Brutus. Dear my lord,
              Make me acquainted with your cause of grief.   (II, I, 237)

22 p. 103 above.
23 Compare:
  BASSANIO:   Her name is Portia, nothing undervalued
              To Cato's daughter, Brutus' Portia.
                                    (*The Merchant of Venice*, I, I, 165)

117

widow after the death of her first husband Bibulus – by whom she had also a young son called Bibulus, who afterwards wrote a book *Of the Acts and Gests of Brutus*, extant at this present day.

This young lady being excellently well seen in philosophy, loving her husband well, and being of a noble courage, as she was also wise – because she would not ask her husband what he ailed before she had made some proof by her self – she took a little razor such as barbers occupy to pare men's nails, and, causing her maids and women to go out of her chamber, gave her self a great gash withal in her thigh, that she was straight all of a gore-blood; and, incontinently after, a vehement fever took her, by reason of the pain of her wound. Then perceiving her husband was marvellously out of quiet and that he could take no rest, even in her greatest pain of all she spake in this sort unto him:

'I being, O Brutus,' said she, 'the daughter of Cato, was married unto thee, not to be thy bedfellow and companion in bed and at board only, like a harlot, but to be partaker also with thee of thy 24 good and evil fortune. Now for thyself, I can find no cause of fault in thee touching our match. But for my part, how may I show my duty towards thee and how much I would do for thy sake, if I cannot constantly bear a secret mischance or grief with thee, which requireth secrecy and fidelity? I confess that a woman's wit commonly is too weak to keep a secret safely. But yet, Brutus, good education and the company of virtuous men have some power to reform the defect of nature. And for myself, I have this benefit moreover: that I am the daughter of Cato and wife of Brutus. This notwithstanding, I did not trust to any of these things before, until that now I have found by experience that no pain nor grief whatsoever can overcome me.'

24 PORTIA:     Within the bond of marriage, tell me Brutus,
Is it excepted I should know no secrets
That appertain to you? Am I yourself
But, as it were, in sort or limitation,
To keep with you at meals, comfort your bed,
And talk to you sometimes? Dwell I but in the suburbs
Of your good pleasure? If it be no more,
Portia is Brutus' harlot, not his wife. (*Julius Caesar*, II, 1, 280)

With those words she showed him her wound on her thigh and told
25 him what she had done to prove herself. Brutus was amazed to hear
what she said unto him, and, lifting up his hands to heaven, he
besought the gods to give him the grace he might bring his enterprise
to so good pass, that he might be found a husband worthy of so noble
26 a wife as Portia. So he then did comfort her the best he could.

Now a day being appointed for the meeting of the Senate, at what
time they hoped Caesar would not fail to come, the conspirators
determined then to put their enterprise in execution, because they
might meet safely at that time without suspicion, and the rather, for
that all the noblest and chiefest men of the city would be there; who
when they should see such a great matter executed, would every
man then set-to their hands, for the defence of their liberty. Furthermore, they thought also that the appointment of the place where the
council should be kept was chosen of purpose by divine providence
and made all for them. For it was one of the porches about the
Theatre, in the which there was a certain place full of seats for men to
sit in, where also was set up the image of Pompey which the city had
made and consecrated in honour of him, when he did beautify that

25 PORTIA:   I grant I am a woman; but withal
       A woman that Lord Brutus took to wife:
       I grant I am a woman; but withal
       A woman well-reputed, Cato's daughter.
       Think you I am no stronger than my sex,
       Being so father'd and so husbanded?
       Tell me your counsels, I will not disclose 'em:
       I have made strong proof of my constancy,
       Giving myself a voluntary wound
       Here, in the thigh: can I bear that with patience,
       And not my husband's secrets?   (II, I, 292)

26 BRUTUS:     O ye gods,
       Render me worthy of this noble wife! . . .
          Portia, go in awhile;
       And by and by thy bosom shall partake
       The secrets of my heart.
       All my engagements I will construe to thee,
       All the charactery of my sad brows.  (II, I, 302)

part of the city with the Theatre he built, with divers porches about
27 it. In this place was the assembly of the Senate appointed to be, just
on the fifteenth day of the month of March, which the Romans call
*Idus Martias*. So that it seemed some god of purpose had brought
Caesar thither to be slain, for revenge of Pompey's death.

So, when the day was come, Brutus went out of his house with a
dagger by his side under his long gown, that nobody saw nor
knew, but his wife only. The other conspirators were all assembled at
Cassius' house, to bring his son into the market-place, who on that
day did put on the man's gown, called *toga virilis*; and from thence
they came all in a troop together unto Pompey's porch, looking
that Caesar would straight come thither. But here is to be noted the
wonderful assured constancy of these conspirators in so dangerous
and weighty an enterprise as they had undertaken. For many of
them being Praetors, by reason of their office, whose duty is to
minister justice to everybody, they did not only with great quietness
and courtesy hear them that spake unto them or that pleaded matters
before them, and gave them attentive ear as if they had had no other
matter in their heads; but moreover they gave just sentence and
carefully dispatched the causes before them. So there was one among
them who, being condemned in a certain sum of money, refused to
pay it and cried out that he did appeal unto Caesar. Then Brutus,
casting his eyes upon the conspirators, said:
'Caesar shall not let me to see the law executed.'

Notwithstanding this, by chance there fell out many misfortunes
unto them which was enough to have marred the enterprise. The
first and chiefest was Caesar's long tarrying, who came very late to
the Senate. For, because the signs of the sacrifices appeared unlucky,
his wife Calpurnia kept him at home, and the soothsayers bade him
28 beware he went not abroad. The second cause was when one came
unto Casca being a conspirator, and, taking him by the hand, said
unto him:

'O Casca, thou keptest it close from me; but Brutus hath told me all.'

27 CASSIUS:    Repair to Pompey's porch, where you shall find us . . .
                That done, repair to Pompey's theatre.    (I, 3, 147; 152)
28 See *Life of Caesar*, pp. 88–9 and notes.

Casca being amazed at it, the other went on with his tale and said: 'Why, how now, how cometh it to pass thou art thus rich, that thou dost sue to be Aedile?'

Thus Casca being deceived by the other's doubtful words, he told them it was a thousand to one he blabbed not out all the conspiracy. Another Senator, called Popilius Laena, after he had saluted Brutus and Cassius more friendly than he was wont to do, he rounded softly in their ears and told them:

'I pray the gods you may go through with that you have taken in hand. But withal, dispatch I read you, for your enterprise is bewrayed.' When he had said, he presently departed from them, and left them 29 both afraid that their conspiracy would out.

Now in the meantime there came one of Brutus' men post-haste unto him and told him his wife was a-dying. For Portia being very careful and pensive for that which was to come and being too weak to away with so great and inward grief of mind, she could hardly keep within, but was frighted with every little noise and cry she heard, as those that are taken and possessed with the fury of the Bacchants, asking every man that came from the market-place what Brutus did, and still sent messenger after messenger, to know what news. At length, Caesar's coming being prolonged as you have heard, Portia's weakness was not able to hold out any longer, and thereupon she suddenly swounded, that she had no leisure to go to her chamber, but was taken in the midst of her house, where her speech and senses 30 failed her. Howbeit she soon came to herself again; and so was laid

| 29 POPILIUS: | I wish your enterprise today may thrive. |
| CASSIUS: | What enterprise, Popilius? |
| POPILIUS: | Fare you well. |
| BRUTUS: | What said Popilius Lena? |
| CASSIUS: | He wish'd today our enterprise might thrive. |
| | I fear our purpose is discovered. (III, I, 13) |
| 30 PORTIA: | I prithee, boy, run to the senate-house ... |
| | O constancy, be strong upon my side, |
| | Set a huge mountain 'tween my heart and tongue! |
| | I have a man's mind, but a woman's might. |
| | How hard it is for women to keep counsel! ... |

121

in her bed and tended by her women. When Brutus heard these news, it grieved him, as it is to be presupposed. Yet he left not off the care of his country and commonwealth; neither went home to his house for any news he heard.

Now it was reported that Caesar was coming in his litter; for he determined not to stay in the Senate all that day, because he was afraid of the unlucky signs of the sacrifices, but to adjourn matters of importance unto the next session and council holden, feigning himself not to be well at ease. When Caesar came out of his litter, Popilius Laena, that had talked before with Brutus and Cassius and had prayed the gods they might bring this enterprise to pass, went unto Caesar and kept him a long time with a talk. Caesar gave good ear unto him. Wherefore the conspirators (if so they should be called), not hearing what he said to Caesar, but conjecturing, by that he had told them a little before, that his talk was none other but the very discovery of their conspiracy, they were afraid every man of them; and, one looking in another's face, it was easy to see that they all were of a mind that it was no tarrying for them till they were apprehended, but rather that they should kill themselves with their own hands. And when Cassius and certain other clapped their hands

---

|  | Yes, bring me word, boy, if thy lord look well, |
|---|---|
|  | For he went sickly forth: and take good note |
|  | What Caesar doth, what suitors press to him. |
|  | Hark, boy! what noise is that? |
| LUCIUS: | I hear none, madam. |
| PORTIA: | Prithee, listen well; |
|  | I heard a bustling rumour, like a fray, |
|  | And the wind brings it from the Capitol. |
| LUCIUS: | Sooth, madam, I hear nothing ... |
| PORTIA: | I must go in. Ay me, how weak a thing |
|  | The heart of woman is! O Brutus, |
|  | The heavens speed thee in thine enterprise! ... |
|  | O, I grow faint. |
|  | Run, Lucius, and commend me to my lord; |
|  | Say I am merry: come to me again, |
|  | And bring me word what he doth say to thee. (II, 4, I) |

on their swords under their gowns to draw them, Brutus marking the countenance and gesture of Laena, and considering that he did use himself rather like an humble and earnest suitor than like an accuser, he said nothing to his companion (because there were many amongst them that were not of the conspiracy), but with a pleasant countenance encouraged Cassius. And immediately after, Laena went from Caesar and kissed his hand; which showed plainly that it was for some matter concerning himself that he had held him so
31 long in talk.

Now all the Senators being entered first into this place or chapter house where the council should be kept, all the other conspirators straight stood about Caesar's chair, as if they had had something to have said unto him. And some say that Cassius, casting his eyes upon Pompey's image, made his prayer unto it, as if it had been alive. Trebonius, on the other side, drew Antonius aside as he came into
32 the house where the Senate sat, and held him with a long talk without.

When Caesar was come into the house, all the Senate rose to honour him at his coming in. So, when he was set, the conspirators flocked about him, and amongst them they presented one Tullius Cimber, who made humble suit for the calling home again of his brother that was banished. They all made as though they were intercessors for him, and took him by the hands and kissed his head and breast. Caesar at the first simply refused their kindness and entreaties. But afterwards, perceiving they still pressed on him, he violently thrust

31 BRUTUS:      Look how he makes to Caesar: mark him.
    CASSIUS:    Casca, be sudden, for we fear prevention.
                Brutus, what shall be done? If this be known,
                Cassius or Caesar never shall turn back,
                For I will slay myself.
    BRUTUS:                  Cassius, be constant:
                Popilius Lena speaks not of our purposes;
                For, look, he smiles, and Caesar doth not change.

                                            (III, I, 18)

32 CASSIUS:    Trebonius knows his time; for, look you, Brutus,
                He draws Mark Antony out of the way.    (III, I, 25)
Compare *Life of Caesar*, p. 92, and *Life of Antonius*, p. 188.

them from him. Then Cimber with both his hands plucked Caesar's gown over his shoulders; and Casca that stood behind him drew his dagger first, and strake Caesar upon the shoulder, but gave him no great wound. Caesar, feeling himself hurt, took him straight by the hand he held his dagger in, and cried out in Latin:

33 'O traitor, Casca, what doest thou?'

Casca on the other side cried in Greek and called his brother to help him. So divers running on a heap together to fly upon Caesar, he looking about him to have fled, saw Brutus with a sword drawn in his hand ready to strike at him. Then he let Casca's hand go, and, casting 34 his gown over his face, suffered every man to strike at him that would. Then the conspirators thronging one upon another because every man was desirous to have a cut at him, so many swords and daggers lighting upon one body, one of them hurt another; and among them Brutus caught a blow on his hand, because he would make one in murdering of him, and all the rest also were every man of them bloodied.

Caesar being slain in this manner, Brutus, standing in the midst of the house, would have spoken, and stayed the other Senators that were not of the conspiracy, to have told them the reason why they had done this fact. But they, as men both afraid and amazed, fled one upon another's neck in haste to get out at the door; and no man 35 followed them. For it was set down and agreed between them that they should kill no man but Caesar only, and should entreat all the rest to defend their liberty. All the conspirators but Brutus, determining upon this matter, thought it good also to kill Antonius, because he was a wicked man and that in nature favoured tyranny; besides also, for that he was in great estimation with soldiers, having been conversant of long time amongst them; and specially, having a mind bent to great enterprises, he was also of great authority at that time, being Consul with Caesar. But Brutus would not agree to it. First, for that he said it was not honest. Secondly, because he told them there was hope of change in him; for he did not mistrust but

33 See *Life of Caesar*, pp. 92–3 notes 39 and 40, and p. 95 note 43.
34 See *Life of Caesar*, p. 95 note 44.
35 See *Life of Caesar*, p. 94 note 41.

that Antonius, being a noble-minded and courageous man, when he should know that Caesar was dead, would willingly help his country to recover her liberty, having them an example unto him, to follow their courage and virtue. So Brutus by this means saved Antonius' life, who at that present time disguised himself and stale away.

But Brutus and his consorts, having their swords bloody in their hands, went straight to the Capitol, persuading the Romans, as they went, to take their liberty again. Now at the first time, when the murder was newly done, there were sudden outcries of people that ran up and down the city; the which indeed did the more increase the fear and tumult. But when they saw they slew no man, neither did spoil or make havoc of anything, then certain of the Senators and many of the people, emboldening themselves, went to the Capitol unto them. There a great number of men being assembled together one after another, Brutus made an oration unto them to win the favour of the people and to justify that they had done. All those that were by said they had done well, and cried unto them that they should boldly come down from the Capitol. Whereupon,

CASSIUS:                              I think it is not meet,
                    Mark Antony, so well beloved of Caesar,
                    Should outlive Caesar: we shall find of him
                    A shrewd contriver; and, you know, his means,
                    If he improve them, may well stretch so far
                    As to annoy us all: which to prevent,
                    Let Antony and Caesar fall together.

BRUTUS:         Our course will seem too bloody, Caius Cassius,
                    To cut the head off and then hack the limbs,
                    Like wrath in death and envy afterwards;
                    For Antony is but a limb of Caesar:
                    Let us be sacrificers, but not butchers, Caius ...
                    We shall be call'd purgers, not murderers.
                    And for Mark Antony, think not of him;
                    For he can do no more than Caesar's arm
                    When Caesar's head is off.                    (II, I, 155)

37 See *Life of Caesar*, p. 96 note 48.
38 See *Life of Caesar*, p. 96 note 47.

Brutus and his companions came boldly down into the market-place. The rest followed in troop; but Brutus went foremost, very honourably compassed in round about with the noblest men of the
39 city, which brought him from the Capitol, through the market-place, to the pulpit for orations.

When the people saw him in the pulpit, although they were a multitude of rakehells of all sorts and had a good will to make some stir, yet, being ashamed to do it for the reverence they bare unto Brutus, they kept silence, to hear what he would say. When Brutus
40 began to speak, they gave him quiet audience. Howbeit, immediately after, they showed that they were not all contented with the murder. For when another called Cinna would have spoken and began to accuse Caesar, they fell into a great uproar among them and marvellously reviled him; insomuch that the conspirators returned again into the Capitol. There Brutus, being afraid to be besieged, sent back again the noblemen that came thither with him, thinking it no reason that they, which were no partakers of the
41 murder, should be partakers of the danger.

Then the next morning the Senate being assembled and holden within the Temple of the goddess Tellus (to wit, 'the Earth'), and Antonius, Plancus, and Cicero having made a motion to the Senate

39 CASSIUS:  Brutus shall lead; and we will grace his heels
With the most boldest and best hearts of Rome. (III, 1, 120)

40    *Enter Brutus who goes into the pulpit, and Cassius, with the plebeians.*
PLEBEIANS:  We will be satisfied; let us be satisfied.
BRUTUS:  Then follow me, and give me audience, friends. . . .
And public reasons shall be rendered
Of Caesar's death . . .
PLEBEIAN:  The noble Brutus is ascended: silence!
BRUTUS:  Be patient till the last.
Romans, countrymen, and lovers! hear me for my
cause, and be silent, that you may hear.  (III, 2, 1)

41 CASSIUS:  And leave us, Publius; lest that the people,
Rushing on us, should do your age some mischief.
BRUTUS:  Do so; and let no man abide this deed
But we the doers.  (III, 1, 92)

See *Life of Caesar*, p. 94 note 41.

in that assembly that they should take an order to pardon and forget all that was past and to stablish friendship and peace again, it was decreed that they should not only be pardoned, but also that the Consuls should refer it to the Senate what honours should be appointed unto them. This being agreed upon, the Senate brake up, and Antonius the Consul, to put them in heart that were in the Capitol, sent them his son for a pledge. Upon this assurance, Brutus and his companions came down from the Capitol, where every man saluted and embraced each other; among the which Antonius himself did bid Cassius to supper to him; and Lepidus also bade Brutus; and so one bade another, as they had friendship and acquaintance together.

The next day following, the Senate being called again to council did first of all commend Antonius, for that he had wisely stayed and quenched the beginning of a civil war. Then they also gave Brutus and his consorts great praises; and lastly they appointed them several governments of provinces. For unto Brutus, they appointed Creta: Afric, unto Cassius: Asia, unto Trebonius: Bithynia, unto Cimber; and unto the other Decius Brutus Albinus, Gaul on this side the Alps.

When this was done, they came to talk of Caesar's will and testament, and of his funerals and tomb. Then Antonius thinking good his testament should be read openly, and also that his body should be honourably buried and not in hugger-mugger, lest the people might thereby take occasion to be worse offended if they did otherwise, Cassius stoutly spake against it. But Brutus went with the motion, and agreed unto it. Wherein it seemeth he committed **42** a second fault. For the first fault he did was when he would not

| **42** ANTONY: | I ... am moreover suitor that I may |
| | Produce his body to the market-place; |
| | And in the pulpit, as becomes a friend, |
| | Speak in the order of his funeral. |
| **BRUTUS:** | You shall, Mark Antony. |
| **CASSIUS:** | Brutus, a word with you. |
| | You know not what you do: do not consent |
| | That Antony speak in his funeral: |
| | Know you how much the people may be moved |
| | By that which he will utter? |

consent to his fellow conspirators that Antonius should be slain; and therefore he was justly accused that thereby he had saved and 43 strengthened a strong and grievous enemy of their conspiracy. The second fault was when he agreed that Caesar's funerals should be as Antonius would have them; the which indeed marred all. For first of all, when Caesar's testament was openly read among them, whereby it appeared that he bequeathed unto every citizen of Rome seventy-five drachmas a man, and that he left his gardens and arbours unto the people, which he had on this side of the river of Tiber (in the place where now the Temple of Fortune is built), the people then 44 loved him and were marvellous sorry for him.

Afterwards, when Caesar's body was brought into the market-place, Antonius making his funeral oration in praise of the dead,

43 See p. 125 note 36 above.

44 ANTONY:     But here's a parchment with the seal of Caesar;
                  I found it in his closet, 'tis his will:
                  Let but the commons hear this testament – ...
                  And they would go and kiss dead Caesar's wounds ...
                  'Tis good you know not that you are his heirs ...
                  Here is the will, and under Caesar's seal.
                  To every Roman citizen he gives,
                  To every several man, seventy five drachmas.

PLEBEIAN:    Most noble Caesar! We'll revenge his death ...

ANTONY:     Moreover, he hath left you all his walks,
                  His private arbours and new-planted orchards,
                  On this side Tiber; he hath left them you,
                  And to your heirs for ever, common pleasures,
                  To walk abroad, and recreate yourselves.
                  Here was a Caesar!        (III, 2, 133; 245)

---

BRUTUS:                   By your pardon;
                  I will myself into the pulpit first,
                  And show the reason of our Caesar's death ...
                     We are contented Caesar shall
                  Have all true rites and lawful ceremonies.
                  It shall advantage more than do us wrong.

CASSIUS:    I know not what may fall; I like it not.    (III, 1, 226)

according to the ancient custom of Rome, and perceiving that his words moved the common people to compassion, he framed his
45 eloquence to make their hearts yearn the more; and, taking Caesar's gown all bloody in his hand, he laid it open to the sight of them all, showing what a number of cuts and holes it had upon it. Therewithal the people fell presently into such a rage and mutiny that there was
46 no more order kept amongst the common people. For some of them cried out: 'Kill the murderers'. Others plucked up forms, tables, and stalls about the market-place, as they had done before at the funerals of Clodius; and having laid them all on a heap together, they set them on fire, and thereupon did put the body of Caesar, and burnt it in the middest of the most holy places. And furthermore, when the fire was throughly kindled, some here, some there, took burning fire-brands, and ran with them to the murderers' houses that
47 had killed him, to set them a-fire. Howbeit the conspirators, foreseeing the danger before, had wisely provided for themselves, and fled.

But there was a poet called Cinna, who had been no partaker of the conspiracy but was alway one of Caesar's chiefest friends. He dreamed, the night before, that Caesar bade him to supper with him and that, he refusing to go, Caesar was very importunate with him and compelled him, so that at length he led him by the hand into a great dark place, where, being marvellously afraid, he was driven to follow him in spite of his heart. This dream put him all night into a fever. And yet, notwithstanding, the next morning when he heard that they carried Caesar's body to burial, being ashamed not to accompany his funerals, he went out of his house, and thrust himself into the press of the common people that were in a great uproar. And because some one called him by his name, Cinna, the people thinking he had been that Cinna who in an oration he made had

---

45 See *Julius Caesar* III, 2, 173–234, for the speech which Shakespeare invented for Mark Antony; also *Life of Antonius*, pp. 188–9.

46 ANTONY:  O masters, if I were disposed to stir
  Your hearts and minds to mutiny and rage ... (III, 2, 126)

47 See *Life of Caesar*, p. 98 note 51, and *Life of Antonius*, p. 189.

spoken very evil of Caesar, they falling upon him in their rage slew
48 him outright in the market-place.

This made Brutus and his companions more afraid than any other
thing, next unto the change of Antonius. Wherefore they got them
49 out of Rome, and kept at the first in the city of Antium, hoping to
return again to Rome when the fury of the people were a little
assuaged; the which they hoped would be quickly, considering that
they had to deal with a fickle and unconstant multitude, easy to be
carried, and that the Senate stood for them; who notwithstanding
made no inquiry of them that had torn poor Cinna the poet in pieces,
but caused them to be sought for and apprehended that went with
firebrands to set fire of the conspirators' houses.

The people growing weary now of Antonius' pride and insolency,

48 *Enter Cinna the Poet, and after him the plebeians.*

CINNA:    I dreamt to-night that I did feast with Caesar,
      And things unluckily charge my fantasy:
      I have no will to wander forth of doors,
      Yet something leads me forth.

1st PLEBEIAN: What is your name?

2nd PLEBEIAN: Whither are you going? . . .

CINNA:    I am going to Caesar's funeral . . .

1st PLEBEIAN: As a friend or an enemy?

CINNA:    As a friend . . .

3rd PLEBEIAN: Your name, sir, truly.

CINNA:    Truly, my name is Cinna.

1st PLEBEIAN: Tear him to pieces; he's a conspirator.

CINNA:    I am Cinna the poet, I am Cinna the poet.

4th PLEBEIAN: Tear him for his bad verses, tear him for his bad verses.

CINNA:    I am not Cinna the conspirator.

4th PLEBEIAN: It is no matter, his name's Cinna; pluck but his name out
      of his heart, and turn him going.

3rd PLEBEIAN: Tear him, tear him!          (III, 3, I)

See also *Life of Caesar*, p. 98.

49 SERVANT:        Brutus and Cassius
      Are rid like madmen through the gates of Rome.

ANTONY:    Belike they had some notice of the people,
      How I had moved them.       (III, 2, 273)

who ruled all things in manner with absolute power, they desired that Brutus might return again; and it was also looked for that Brutus would come himself in person to play the plays which were due to the people by reason of his office of Praetorship. But Brutus understanding that many of Caesar's soldiers which served under him in the wars, and that also had lands and houses given them in the cities where they lay, did lie in wait for him to kill him, and that they daily by small companies came by one and by one into Rome, he durst no more return thither. But yet the people had the pleasure and pasttime in his absence to see the games and sports he made them, which were sumptuously set forth and furnished with all things necessary, sparing for no cost. For he had bought a great number of strange beasts, of the which he would not give one of them to any friend he had, but that they should all be employed in his games; and went himself as far as Byzantium to speak to some players of comedies and musicians that were there. And further, he wrote unto his friends for one Canutius an excellent player, that, whatsoever they did, they should entreat him to play in these plays.

'For,' said he, 'it is no reason to compel any Grecian, unless he will come of his own good will.'

Moreover, he wrote also unto Cicero, and earnestly prayed him in any case to be at these plays.

Now the state of Rome standing in these terms, there fell out another change and alteration when the young man Octavius Caesar came to Rome. He was the son of Julius Caesar's niece whom he had adopted for his son and made his heir by his last will and testament. But when Julius Caesar, his adopted father, was slain, he was in the city of Apollonia where he studied, tarrying for him, because he was determined to make war with the Parthians. But when he heard the news of his death, he returned again to Rome, where, to begin to curry favour with the common people, he first of all took upon him his

| | |
|---|---|
| 50 SERVANT: | Sir, Octavius is already come to Rome. |
| ANTONY: | Where is he? |
| SERVANT: | He and Lepidus are at Caesar's house. |
| ANTONY: | And thither will I straight to visit him. |
| | He comes upon a wish. (III, 2, 267) |

adopted father's name, and made distribution among them of the money which his father had bequeathed unto them. By this means he troubled Antonius sorely, and by force of money got a great number of his father's soldiers together that had served in the wars with him. And Cicero himself, for the great malice he bare Antonius, did favour his proceedings. But Brutus marvellously reproved him for it, and wrote unto him that he seemed by his doings not to be sorry to have a master, but only to be afraid to have one that should hate him; and that all his doings in the commonwealth did witness that he chose to be subject to a mild and courteous bondage, sith by his words and writings he did commend this young man Octavius Caesar to be a good and gentle lord.

'For our predecessors,' said he, 'would never abide to be subject to any masters, how gentle or mild soever they were';
– and, for his own part, that he had never resolutely determined with himself to make war or peace, but otherwise that he was certainly minded never to be slave nor subject. And therefore he wondered much at him, how Cicero could be afraid of the danger of civil wars and would not be afraid of a shameful peace; and that, to thrust Antonius out of the usurped tyranny, in recompense he went about to stablish young Octavius Caesar tyrant. These were the contents of Brutus' first letters he wrote unto Cicero.

Now the city of Rome being divided in two factions, some taking part with Antonius, other also leaning unto Octavius Caesar, and the soldiers making port-sale of their service to him that would give most; Brutus seeing the state of Rome would be utterly overthrown, he determined to go out of Italy, and went afoot through the country of Luke unto the city of Elea, standing by the sea. There Portia, being ready to depart from her husband Brutus and to return to Rome, did what she could to dissemble the grief and sorrow she felt at her heart. But a certain painted table bewrayed her in the end, although until that time she always showed a constant and patient mind. The device of the table was taken out of the Greek stories – how Andromache accompanied her husband Hector when he went out of the city of Troy to go to the wars, and how Hector delivered her his little son, and how her eyes were never off him. Portia seeing this picture and likening herself to be in the same case, she fell a-weeping; and, coming thither oftentimes in a day to see it, she wept still. Acilius, one of Brutus' friends, perceiving that, rehearsed the verses Andromache speaketh to this purpose in Homer:

> Thou, Hector, art my father, and my mother, and my brother,
> And husband eke, and all in all: I mind not any other.

Then Brutus, smiling, answered again:
'But yet,' said he, 'I cannot for my part say unto Portia, as Hector answered Andromache in the same place of the poet:

> Tush, meddle thou with weighing duly out
> Thy maids their task, and pricking on a clout.

For indeed the weak constitution of her body doth not suffer her to perform in show the valiant acts that we are able to do. But, for courage and constant mind, she showed herself as stout in the defence of her country as any of us.'
Bibulus, the son of Portia, reporteth this story thus.

Now Brutus embarking at Elea in Luke, he sailed directly towards Athens. When he arrived there, the people of Athens received him with common joys of rejoicing and honourable decrees made for him. He lay with a friend of his, with whom he went daily to hear the lectures of Theomnestus, Academic philosopher, and of Cratippus the Peripatetic; and so would talk with them in philosophy that it seemed he left all other matters and gave himself only unto study. Howbeit secretly, notwithstanding, he made preparation for war. For he sent Herostratus into Macedon to win the captains and soldiers that were upon those marches, and he did also entertain all the young gentlemen of the Romans whom he found in Athens studying philosophy. Amongst them he found Cicero's son, whom he highly praised and commended, saying that whether he waked or slept he found him of a noble mind and disposition, he did in nature so much hate tyrants.

Shortly after, he began to enter openly into arms; and, being advertised that there came out of Asia a certain fleet of Roman ships that had good store of money in them and that the captain of those ships (who was an honest man and his familiar friend) came towards

Athens, he went to meet him as far as the isle of Carystos; and, having spoken with him there, he handled him so that he was contented to leave his ships in his hands. Whereupon he made him a notable banquet at his house, because it was on his birthday. When the feast day came, and that they began to drink lustily one to another, the guests drank to the victory of Brutus and the liberty of the Romans. Brutus, therefore, to encourage them further called for a bigger cup and, holding it in his hand, before he drank spake this aloud:

> My destiny and Phoebus are agreed,
> To bring me to my final end with speed.

And for proof hereof it is reported that, the same day he fought his last battle by the city of Philippes, as he came out of his tent he gave his men for the word and signal of battle 'Phoebus'; so that it was thought ever since that this his sudden crying out at the feast was a prognostication of his misfortune that should happen.

After this, Antistius gave him of the money he carried into Italy fifty myriads. Furthermore, all Pompey's soldiers that straggled up and down Thessaly came with very good will unto him. He took from Cinna also five hundred horsemen, which he carried into Asia unto Dolabella. After that, he went by sea unto the city of Demetriad, and there took a great deal of armour and munition which was going to Antonius, and the which had been made and forced there by Julius Caesar's commandment for the wars against the Parthians. Furthermore, Hortensius, governor of Macedon, did resign the government thereof unto him. Besides, all the princes, kings, and noblemen thereabouts came and joined with him, when it was told him that Caius (Antonius' brother), coming out of Italy, had passed the sea, and came with great speed towards the city of Dyrrachium and Apollonia to get the soldiers into his hands which Gabinius had there. Brutus, therefore, to prevent him, went presently with a few of his men in the midst of winter when it snew hard, and took his way through hard and foul countries, and made such speed, indeed, that he was there long before Antonius' sumpters that carried the victuals; so that, when he came near unto Dyrrachium, a disease took him which the physicians call βουλιμία (to say 'a cormorant and unsatiable appetite to eat'), by reason of the cold and pains he had taken. This sickness chanceth often both to men and beasts that travel when it hath snowen; either because the natural heat being retired into the inward parts of the body, by the coldness of the air hardening the skin, doth straight digest and consume the meat; or else because a sharp subtle wind, coming by reason of the snow when it is molten, doth pierce into the body and driveth out the natural heat which was cast outward. For it seemeth that the heat being quenched with the cold, which it meeteth withal coming out of the skin of the body, causeth the sweats that follow the disease. (But hereof we have spoken at large in other places.)

Brutus being very faint and having nothing in his camp to eat, his soldiers were compelled to go to their enemies and, coming to the gates of the city, they prayed the warders to help them to bread. When they heard in what case Brutus was, they brought him both meat and drink. In requital whereof afterwards, when he won the city, he did not only entreat and use the citizens thereof courteously, but all the inhabitants of the city also for their sakes.

Now when Caius Antonius was arrived in the city of Apollonia, he sent unto the soldiers thereabouts to come unto him. But when he understood that they went all to Brutus, and, furthermore, that the citizens of Apollonia did favour him much, he then forsook that city and went unto the city of Buthrotus. But yet he lost three of his ensigns by the way, that were slain every man of them. Then he sought by force to win certain places of strength about Byllis and to drive Brutus' men from thence, that had taken it before; and therefore, to obtain his purpose, he fought a battle with Cicero, the son of Marcus Tullius Cicero, by whom he was overcome. For Brutus made the younger Cicero a captain and did many notable exploits by his service. Shortly after, having stolen upon Caius Antonius in certain marshes far from the place from whence he fled, he would not set on him with fury; but only rode round about him, commanding his soldiers to spare him and his men, as reckoning them all as his own without stroke striking. And so indeed it happened. For they yielded themselves, and their captain Antonius, unto Brutus; so that Brutus had now a great army about him. Now Brutus kept this Caius Antonius long time in his office, and never took from him the marks and signs of his Consulship, although many of his friends, and Cicero among others, wrote unto him to put him to death. But when he saw Antonius secretly practised with his captains to make some alteration, then he sent him into a ship and made him to be kept there. When the soldiers whom C. Antonius had corrupted were gotten into the city of Apollonia, and sent from thence unto Brutus to come unto them, he made them answer that it was not the manner of Roman captains to come to the soldiers, but the soldiers to come to the captain, and to crave pardon for their offences committed. Thereupon they came to him, and he pardoned them.

So, Brutus preparing to go into Asia, news came unto him of the great change at Rome. For Octavius Caesar was in arms, by commandment and authority from the Senate, against Marcus Antonius. But after that he had driven Antonius out of Italy, the Senate then began to be afraid of him, because he sued to be Consul, which was contrary to the law, and kept a great army about him when the Empire of Rome had no need of them. On the other side, Octavius Caesar perceiving the Senate stayed not there, but turned unto Brutus that was out of Italy, and that they appointed him the government of certain provinces; then he began to be afraid for his part and sent unto Antonius to offer him his friendship. Then, coming on with his army near to Rome, he made himself to be chosen Consul, whether the Senate would or not, when he was yet but a stripling or springal of twenty year old, as himself reporteth in his own *Commentaries*. So, when he was Consul, he presently appointed judges to accuse Brutus and his companions, for killing of the noblest person in Rome and chiefest magistrate, without law or judgement; and made L. Cornificius accuse Brutus, and M. Agrippa, Cassius. So the parties accused were condemned, because the judges were compelled to give such sentence. The voice went that when the herald, according to the custom after sentence given, went up to the chair or pulpit for orations, and proclaimed Brutus with a loud voice, summoning him to appear in person before the judges, the people that stood by sighed openly and the noblemen that were present hung down their heads and durst not speak a word. Among them, the tears fell from Publius Silicius' eyes; who, shortly after, was one of the proscripts or outlaws appointed to be slain.

After that, these three, Octavius Caesar, Antonius, and Lepidus, made an agreement between themselves, and by those articles divided the provinces belonging to the Empire of Rome among themselves, and did set up bills of proscription and outlawry, condemning two hundred of the noblest men of Rome to suffer death; and among that number Cicero was one. News being brought thereof into Macedon, Brutus, being then enforced to it, wrote unto Hortensius that he should put Caius Antonius to death, to be revenged of the death of Cicero and of the other Brutus, of the which the one was his friend and the other his kinsman. For this cause therefore, Antonius afterwards taking Hortensius at the battle of Philippes, he made him to be slain upon his brother's tomb. But then Brutus said that he was more ashamed of the cause for the which Cicero was slain than he was otherwise sorry for his death; and that he could not but greatly reprove his friends he had at Rome who were slaves more through their own fault than through their valiantness or manhood which usurped the tyranny, considering that they were so cowardly and faint-hearted as to suffer the sight of those things before their eyes, the report whereof should only have grieved them to the heart.

Now when Brutus had passed over his army (that was very great) into Asia, he gave order for the gathering of a great number

LEPIDUS: Upon condition Publius shall not live,
Who is your sister's son, Mark Antony.

ANTONY: He shall not live; look, with a spot I damn him. (IV, I, 4)

See *Life of Antonius*, p. 194 note 20. Also:

MESSALA: Myself have letters. . . .
That by proscription and bills of outlawry,
Octavius, Antony, and Lepidus,
Have put to death an hundred senators.

BRUTUS: Therein our letters do not well agree;
Mine speak of seventy senators that died
By their proscriptions, Cicero being one.

CASSIUS: Cicero one!

MESSALA: Cicero is dead,
And by that order of proscription. (IV, 3, 171)

of ships together, as well in the coast of Bithynia, as also in the city of Cyzicum, because he would have an army by sea; and himself in the meantime went unto the cities, taking order for all things and giving audience to princes and noblemen of the country that had to do with him. Afterwards he sent unto Cassius in Syria, to turn him from his journey into Egypt, telling him that it was not for the conquest of any kingdom for themselves that they wandered up and down in that sort, but, contrarily, that it was to restore their country again to their liberty; and that the multitude of soldiers they gathered together was to subdue the tyrants that would keep them in slavery and subjection. Wherefore, regarding their chief purpose and intent, they should not be far from Italy, as near as they could possible, but should rather make all the haste they could to help their countrymen. Cassius believed him and returned. Brutus went to meet him; and they both met at the city of Smyrna, which was the first time that they saw together since they took leave of each other at the haven of Piraea in Athens, the one going into Syria and the other into Macedon. So they were marvellous joyful, and no less courageous when they saw the great
53 armies together which they had both levied; considering that they departed out of Italy like naked and poor banished men, without armour and money, nor having any ship ready, nor soldier about them, nor any one town at their commandment; yet, notwithstanding, in a short time after they were now met together, having ships, money, and soldiers enow, both footmen and horsemen, to fight for the Empire of Rome.

Now Cassius would have done Brutus as much honour as Brutus did unto him. But Brutus most commonly prevented him and
54 went first unto him, both because he was the elder man, as also for

53 ANTONY:           Brutus and Cassius
Are levying powers: we must straight make head.

(IV, I, 41)

54 CASSIUS:           I am a soldier, I,
Older in practice, abler than yourself
To make conditions . . .
I said, an elder soldier, not a better.          (IV, 3, 30; 56)

that he was sickly of body: and men reputed him commonly to be very skilful in wars, but otherwise marvellous choleric and cruel,
55 who sought to rule men by fear rather than with lenity; and on the other side he was too familiar with his friends and would jest too broadly with them. But Brutus in contrary manner, for his virtue and valiantness was well-beloved of the people and his own, esteemed of noblemen, and hated of no man, not so much as of his enemies; because he was a marvellous lowly and gentle person, noble minded,
56 and would never be in any rage, nor carried away with pleasure and covetousness; but had ever an upright mind with him, and would never yield to any wrong or injustice, the which was the chiefest cause of his fame, of his rising, and of the good will that every man bare him; for they were all persuaded that his intent was good. For they did not certainly believe that if Pompey himself had overcome Caesar he would have resigned his authority to the law. But rather they were of opinion that he would still keep the sovereignty and absolute government in his hands, taking only, to please the people, the title of Consul or Dictator, or of some other more civil office. And as for Cassius, a hot, choleric, and cruel man, that would oftentimes be carried away from justice for gain, it was certainly thought that he made war, and put himself into sundry dangers, more to have absolute power and authority than to defend the liberty of his country. For they that will also consider others, that were elder men than they – as Cinna, Marius, and Carbo – it is out of doubt that the end and hope of their victory was to be lords of their country; and in manner they did all confess that they fought for the tyranny and to be lords of the Empire of Rome. And in contrary

55 BRUTUS: Must I give way and room to your rash choler?...
Go show your slaves how choleric you are,
And make your bondmen tremble...
           Must I stand and crouch
Under your testy humour? By the gods,
You shall digest the venom of your spleen.    (IV, 3, 39)

56 ANTONY: His life was gentle, and the elements
So mix'd in him that Nature might stand up
And say to all the world 'This was a man!'    (V, 5, 73)

manner, his enemies themselves did never reprove Brutus for any such change or desire. For it was said that Antonius spake it openly divers times that he thought that of all them that had slain Caesar there was none but Brutus only that was moved to do it as thinking the act commendable of itself; but that all the other conspirators did conspire his death for some private malice or envy that they otherwise

57 did bear unto him.

Hereby it appeareth that Brutus did not trust so much to the power of his army as he did to his own virtue; as is to be seen by his writings. For, approaching near to the instant danger, he wrote unto Pomponius Atticus that his affairs had the best hap that could be. 'For,' said he, 'either I will set my country at liberty by battle, or by honourable death rid me of this bondage.'

And furthermore, that, they being certain and assured of all things else, this one thing only was doubtful to them: whether they should live or die with liberty. He wrote also that Antonius had his due payment for his folly. For, where he might have been a partner equally of the glory of Brutus, Cassius, and Cato, and have made one with them, he liked better to choose to be joined with Octavius Caesar alone;

' – with whom, though now he be not overcome by us, yet shall he shortly after also have war with him.'

And truly he proved a true prophet; for so came it indeed to pass.

Now, whilst Brutus and Cassius were together in the city of Smyrna, Brutus prayed Cassius to let him have some part of his money, whereof he had great store, because all that he could rap and rend of his side he had bestowed it in making so great a number of ships, that by means of them they should keep all the sea at their commandment. Cassius' friends hindered this request and earnestly dissuaded him from it, persuading him that it was no reason that Brutus should have the money which Cassius hath gotten together

57 ANTONY:    This was the noblest Roman of them all:
                   All the conspirators save only he
                   Did that they did in envy of great Caesar;
                   He only, in a general honest thought
                   And common good to all, made one of them.    (v, 5, 68)

by sparing and levied with great evil will of the people their subjects, for him to bestow liberally upon his soldiers and by this means to win their good wills by Cassius' charge. This notwithstanding, 58 Cassius gave him the third part of his total sum.

So Cassius and Brutus then departing from each other, Cassius took the city of Rhodes, where he too dishonestly and cruelly used himself; although, when he came into the city, he answered some of the inhabitants, who called him lord and king, that he was neither lord nor king, but he only that had slain him that would have been lord and king.

Brutus, departing from thence, sent unto the Lycians to require money and men of war. But there was a certain orator called Naucrates that made the cities to rebel against him, insomuch that the countrymen of that country kept the straits and little mountains, thinking by that means to stop Brutus' passage. Wherefore Brutus sent his horsemen against them, who stale upon them as they were at dinner and slew six hundred of them; and, taking all the small towns and villages, he did let all the prisoners he took go without payment of ransom, hoping, by this his great courtesy, to win them to draw

58 BRUTUS:      I did send to you
    For certain sums of gold, which you denied me:
    For I can raise no money by vile means:
    By heaven, I had rather coin my heart,
    And drop my blood for drachmas, than to wring
    From the hard hands of peasants their vile trash
    By any indirection: I did send
    To you for gold to pay my legions,
    Which you denied me: was that done like Cassius?
    Should I have answer'd Caius Cassius so?
    When Marcus Brutus grows so covetous,
    To lock such rascal counters from his friends,
    Be ready, gods, with all your thunderbolts;
    Dash him to pieces!

CASSIUS:      I denied you not.
BRUTUS:  You did.
CASSIUS:  I did not: he was but a fool that brought
    My answer back.        (IV, 3, 69)

all the rest of the country unto him. But they were so fierce and obstinate that they would mutiny for every small hurt they received as they passed by their country, and did despise his courtesy and good nature; until that at length he went to besiege the city of the Xanthians, within the which were shut up the cruellest and most warlikest men of Lycia. There was a river that ran by the walls of the city, in the which many men saved themselves, swimming between two waters, and fled, howbeit they laid nets overthwart the river and tied little bells on the top of them, to sound when any man was taken in the nets. The Xanthians made a sally out by night and came to fire certain engines of battery that beat down their walls. But they were presently driven in again by the Romans, so soon as they were discovered. The wind by chance was marvellous big and increased the flame so sore that it violently carried it into the cranews of the wall of the city, that the next houses unto them were straight set a-fire thereby. Wherefore Brutus being afraid that all the city would take on fire, he presently commanded his men to quench the fire and to save the town if it might be.

But the Lycians at that instant fell into such a frenzy and strange and horrible despair that no man can well express it; and a man cannot more rightly compare or liken it than to a frantic and most desperate desire to die. For all of them together, with their wives and children, masters and servants, and of all sorts of age whatsoever, fought upon the rampart of their walls and did cast down stones and fireworks on the Romans, which were very busy in quenching the flame of the fire to save the city. And in contrary manner also they brought faggots, dry wood, and reeds, to bring the fire further into the city as much as might be, increasing it by such things as they brought. Now when the fire had gotten into all the parts of the city, and that the flame burned bright in every place, Brutus, being sorry to see it, got upon his horse and rode round about the walls of the city to see if it were possible to save it, and held up his hands to the inhabitants, praying them to pardon their city and to save themselves. Howbeit they would not be persuaded; but did all that they could possible to cast themselves away, not only men and women, but also little children. For some of them, weeping and crying out, did cast themselves into the fire. Others headlong throwing themselves down from the walls brake their necks. Others also made their necks bare to the naked swords of their fathers and undid their clothes, praying them to kill them with their own hands. After the city was burnt, they found a woman hanged up by the neck, holding one of her children in her hand dead by her, hanged up also; and in the other hand a burning torch setting fire on her house. Some would have had Brutus to have seen her; but he would not see so horrible and tragical a sight; but when he heard it he fell a-weeping and caused a herald to make proclamation by sound of trumpet that he would give a certain sum of money to every soldier that could save a Xanthian. So there were not, as it is reported, above fifty of them saved; and yet they were saved against their wills. Thus the Xanthians having ended the revolution of their fatal destiny, after a long continuance of time they did through their desperation renew the memory of the lamentable calamities of their ancestors; who in like manner, in the wars of the Persians, did burn their city and destroyed themselves.

Therefore Brutus likewise besieging the city of the Patareians, perceiving that they stoutly resisted him, he was also afraid of that, and could not well tell whether he should give assault to it or not, lest they would fall into the despair and desperation of the Xanthians. Howbeit, having taken certain of their women prisoners, he sent them back again without payment of ransom. Now they that were the wives and daughters of the noblest men of the city, reporting unto their parents that they had found Brutus a merciful, just, and courteous man, they persuaded them to yield themselves and their city unto him; the which they did. So, after they had thus yielded themselves, divers other cities also followed them and did the like; and found Brutus more merciful and courteous than they thought they should have done; but specially far above Cassius. For Cassius, about the self same time, after he had compelled the Rhodians every man to deliver all the ready money they had in gold and silver in their houses, the which being brought together amounted to the sum of eight thousand talents, yet he condemned the city besides to pay the sum of five hundred talents more; where Brutus in contrary manner, after he had levied of all the country of Lycia but a hundred and fifty talents only, he departed thence into the country of Ionia, and did them no more hurt.

Now Brutus in all this journey did many notable acts and worthy of memory, both for rewarding as also in punishing those that had deserved it; wherefore among the rest I will tell you of one thing, of the which he himself and all the noblemen of the Romans were marvellous glad. When Pompey the Great, having lost the battle against Julius Caesar in the fields of Pharsalia, came and fell upon the coast of Egypt, hard by the city of Pelusium, those that were protectors to the young King Ptolemy, being then but a child, sat in council with his servants and friends, what they should determine in that case.

They were not all of one mind in this consultation. For some thought it good to receive Pompey; others also, that they should drive him out of Egypt. But there was a certain rhetorician called Theodotus, that was born in the isle of Chios, who was the king's schoolmaster to teach him rhetoric. He, being called to this council for lack of sufficient men, said that both the one and the other side went awry, as well those that were of opinion to receive Pompey, as the other that would have had him driven away; and that the best way was, considering the present time, that they should lay hold on him and kill him, adding withal this sentence: that 'a dead man biteth not.' The whole council stuck to this opinion. So, for a notable example of incredible misfortune, and unlooked for unto Pompey, Pompey the Great was slain, by the motion and counsel of this wicked rhetorician Theodotus, as Theodotus afterwards did himself boast of it. But when Julius Caesar came afterwards into Egypt, the wicked men that consented to this counsel had their payment according to their deserts. For they died every man of them a wicked death, saving this Theodotus, whom fortune respited a little while longer; and yet in that time he lived a poor and miserable life, never tarrying long in any one place. So, Brutus going up and down Asia, Theodotus could hide himself no longer, but was brought unto Brutus, where he suffered pains of death; so that he won more fame by his death than ever he did in his life.

About that time Brutus sent to pray Cassius to come to the city of Sardis; and so he did. Brutus, understanding of his coming, went to meet him with all his friends. There, both their armies being armed, they called them both emperors. Now as it commonly happeneth in great affairs between two persons, both of them having many friends and so many captains under them, there ran tales and complaints betwixt them. Therefore before they fell in hand with any other matter, they went into a little chamber together, and bade every man avoid, and did shut the doors to them. Then they began to pour out their complaints one to the other, and grew hot and loud, earnestly accusing one another, and at length fell both a-
59 weeping. Their friends that were without the chamber hearing them loud within and angry between themselves, they were both amazed and afraid also lest it would grow to further matter. But yet they

59 BRUTUS:    What now, Lucilius! is Cassius near?

LUCILIUS:   He is at hand; and Pindarus is come
            To do you salutation from his master.

BRUTUS:     He greets me well. Your master, Pindarus,
            In his own change, or by ill officers,
            Hath given me some worthy cause to wish
            Things done, undone . . .
                    *Enter Cassius and his powers.*

CASSIUS:    Most noble brother, you have done me wrong.

BRUTUS:     Judge me, you gods! wrong I mine enemies?
            And if not so, how should I wrong a brother?

CASSIUS:    Brutus, this sober form of yours hides wrongs;
            And when you do them —

BRUTUS:                        Cassius, be content;
            Speak your griefs softly: I do know you well.
            Before the eyes of both our armies here,
            Which should perceive nothing but love from us,
            Let us not wrangle: bid them move away;
            Then in my tent, Cassius, enlarge your griefs,
            And I will give you audience.        (IV, 2, 3; 37)

CASSIUS:            O, I could weep
            My spirit from mine eyes!             (IV, 3, 99)

60 were commanded that no man should come to them. Notwithstanding, one Marcus Faonius, that had been a friend and follower of Cato while he lived, and took upon him to counterfeit a philosopher not with wisdom and discretion but with a certain bedlam and frantic motion, he would needs come into the chamber, though the men offered to keep him out. But it was no boot to let Faonius, when a mad mood or toy took him in the head. For he was a hot hasty man and sudden in all his doings, and cared for never a Senator of them all. Now though he used this bold manner of speech after the profession of the Cynic philosophers (as who would say, 'dogs'), yet this boldness did no hurt many times, because they did but laugh at him to see him so mad. This Faonius at that time, in despite of the doorkeepers, came into the chamber, and, with a certain scoffing and mocking gesture which he counterfeited of purpose, he rehearsed the verses which old Nestor said in Homer:

> *My lords, I pray you hearken both to me,*
> *For I have seen moe years than suchie three.*

Cassius fell a-laughing at him. But Brutus thrust him out of the 61 chamber, and called him dog and counterfeit Cynic. Howbeit his coming in brake their strife at that time; and so they left each other.

The self same night Cassius prepared his supper in his chamber,

60 CASSIUS:                                         Pindarus,
　　　　　Bid our commanders lead their charges off
　　　　　A little from this ground.
BRUTUS:　Lucilius, do you the like; and let no man
　　　　　Come to our tent till we have done our conference.

(IV, 2, 47)

61　　　　　　　　　*Enter a Poet.*
POET:　　Let me go in to see the generals;
　　　　　There is some grudge between 'em, 'tis not meet
　　　　　They be alone.
LUCILIUS:　You shall not come to them.
POET:　　Nothing but death shall stay me.
CASSIUS:　How now! what's the matter?

146

and Brutus brought his friends with him. So when they were set at supper, Faonius came to sit down after he had washed. Brutus told him aloud, no man sent for him; and bade them set him at the upper end, meaning indeed at the lower end of the bed. Faonius made no ceremony, but thrust in amongst the midst of them, and made all the company laugh at him. So they were merry all supper-time and full of their philosophy. The next day after, Brutus, upon complaint of the Sardians, did condemn and noted Lucius Pella for a defamed person, that had been a Praetor of the Romans and whom Brutus had given charge unto; for that he was accused and convicted of robbery and pilfery in his office. This judgement much misliked Cassius, because he himself had secretly, not many days before, warned two of his friends, attainted and convicted of the like offences, and openly had cleared them; but yet he did not therefore leave to employ them in any manner of service as he did before. And therefore he greatly reproved Brutus for that he would show himself so strait and severe, in such a time as was meeter to bear a little than to take things at the worst. Brutus in contrary manner answered that he should remember the Ides of March, at which time they slew Julius Caesar; who neither pilled nor polled the country, but only was a favourer and suborner of all them that did rob and spoil by his countenance and authority. And, if there were any occasion whereby they might honestly set aside justice and equity, they should have had more reason to have suffered Caesar's friends to have robbed and done what wrong and injury they had would, than to bear

---

POET:         For shame, you generals! what do you mean?
                    Love and be friends, as two such men should be;
                    For I have seen more years, I'm sure, than ye.

CASSIUS:  Ha, ha! how vilely doth this cynic rhyme!

BRUTUS:  Get you hence, sirrah; saucy fellow, hence!

CASSIUS:  Bear with him, Brutus; 'tis his fashion.

BRUTUS:  I'll know his humour, when he knows his time;
                    What should the wars do with these jigging fools?
                    Companion, hence!

CASSIUS:                  Away, away, be gone!
                                 *Exit Poet.* (IV, 3, 124)

62 with their own men. For then, said he, they could but have said they
had been cowards:

'And now they may accuse us of injustice, beside the pains we take,
and the danger we put ourselves into.'

And thus may we see what Brutus' intent and purpose was.

But, as they both prepared to pass over again out of Asia into
Europe, there went a rumour that there appeared a wonderful sign
unto him. Brutus was a careful man and slept very little, both for
that his diet was moderate, as also because he was continually occupied. He never slept in the day time, and in the night no longer than
the time he was driven to be alone, and when everybody else took
their rest. But now whilst he was in war and his head ever busily occupied to think of his affairs, and what would happen, after he had
slumbered a little after supper, he spent all the rest of the night in
dispatching of his weightiest causes; and after he had taken order
for them, if he had any leisure left him, he would read some book
63 till the third watch of the night; at what time the captains, petty-
captains, and colonels did use to come to him.

62 CASSIUS:      That you have wrong'd me doth appear in this:
You have condemn'd and noted Lucius Pella
For taking bribes here of the Sardians;
Wherein my letters, praying on his side,
Because I knew the man, were slighted off.

BRUTUS:      You wrong'd yourself to write in such a case.

CASSIUS:      In such a time as this it is not meet
That every nice offence should bear his comment. . . .

BRUTUS:      Remember March, the Ides of March remember:
Did not great Julius bleed for justice' sake?
What villain touch'd his body, that did stab,
And not for justice? What, shall one of us,
That struck the foremost man of all this world
But for supporting robbers, shall we now
Contaminate our fingers with base bribes,
And sell the mighty space of our large honours
For so much trash as may be grasped thus?    (IV, 3, 1; 18)

63 BRUTUS:      Look, Lucius, here's the book I sought for so;
I put it in the pocket of my gown . . .

So, being ready to go into Europe, one night very late, when all the camp took quiet rest, as he was in his tent with a little light, thinking of weighty matters, he thought he heard one come in to him and, casting his eye towards the door of his tent, that he saw a wonderful strange and monstrous shape of a body coming towards him, and said never a word. So Brutus boldly asked what he was, a god or a man, and what cause brought him thither. The spirit answered him:

'I am thy evil spirit, Brutus; and thou shalt see me by the city of Philippes.'

Brutus, being no otherwise afraid, replied again unto it:

'Well, then I shall see thee again.'

64 The spirit presently vanished away; and Brutus called his men unto him, who told him that they heard no noise, nor saw anything

65 at all. Thereupon Brutus returned again to think on his matters as he did before. And when the day brake he went unto Cassius to tell him what vision had appeared unto him in the night.

66 Cassius being in opinion an Epicurean, and reasoning thereon with Brutus, spake to him touching the vision thus:

'In our sect, Brutus, we have an opinion that we do not always feel or see that which we suppose we do both see and feel; but that our

---

64 See *Life of Caesar*, p. 100 note 57.

65 BRUTUS:      Boy, Lucius! Varro! Claudius! Sirs, awake!
                Claudius! . . . didst thou see any thing?

LUCIUS:      Nothing, my lord . . .

BRUTUS:      Fellow thou, awake! . . .
                Why did you so cry out, sirs, in your sleep?

VARRO: ⎱
CLAUDIUS: ⎰  Did we, my lord?

BRUTUS:                      Ay: saw you any thing?

VARRO:      No, my lord, I saw nothing.

CLAUDIUS:                 Nor I, my lord.    (IV, 3, 290)

66 See *Life of Caesar*, p. 92 note 36.

            Let me see, let me see; is not the leaf turn'd down
            Where I left reading? Here it is, I think.    (IV, 3, 252; 273)

Compare p. 105 above.

senses being credulous, and therefore easily abused, when they are idle and unoccupied in their own objects, are induced to imagine they see and conjecture that which they in truth do not. For our mind is quick and cunning to work, without either cause or matter, anything in the imagination whatsoever. And therefore the imagination is resembled to clay, and the mind to the potter, who, without any other cause than his fancy and pleasure, changeth it into what fashion and form he will. And this doth the diversity of our dreams show unto us. For our imagination doth upon a small fancy grow from conceit to conceit, altering both in passions and forms of things imagined. For the mind of man is ever occupied; and that continual moving is nothing but an imagination. But yet there is a further cause of this in you. For, you being by nature given to melancholic discoursing, and of late continually occupied, your wits and senses having been overlaboured do easilier yield to such imaginations. For, to say that there are spirits or angels, and, if there were, that they had the shape of men, or such voices, or any power at all to come unto us, it is a mockery. And for mine own part I would there were such, because that we should not only have soldiers, horses, and ships, but also the aid of the gods, to guide and further our honest and honourable attempts.'

With these words Cassius did somewhat comfort and quiet Brutus.

When they raised their camp, there came two eagles that, flying with a marvellous force, lighted upon two of the foremost ensigns, and always followed the soldiers, which gave them meat, and fed them, until they came near to the city of Philippes; and there, one
67 day only before the battle, they both flew away.

Now Brutus had conquered the most part of all the people and nations of that country. But if there were any other city or captain to overcome, then they made all clear before them; and so drew towards the coasts of Thassos. There Norbanus lying in camp in a

67 CASSIUS:    Coming from Sardis, on our former ensign
               Two mighty eagles fell, and there they perch'd,
               Gorging and feeding from our soldiers' hands;
               Who to Philippi here consorted us:
               This morning are they fled away and gone.     (v, 1, 80)

certain place called the Straits, by another place called Symbolon (which is a port of the sea), Cassius and Brutus compassed him in in such sort that he was driven to forsake the place, which was of great strength for him; and he was also in danger beside to have lost all his army. For Octavius Caesar could not follow him because of his sickness, and therefore stayed behind. Whereupon they had taken his army, had not Antonius' aid been, which made such wonderful speed that Brutus could scant believe it. So Caesar came not thither of ten days after; and Antonius camped against Cassius, and Brutus on the other side against Caesar.

The Romans called the valley between both camps, the Philippian fields; and there were never seen two so great armies of the Romans, one before the other, ready to fight. In truth, Brutus' army was inferior to Octavius Caesar's in number of men. But, for bravery and rich furniture, Brutus' army far excelled Caesar's. For the most part of their armours were silver and gilt, which Brutus had bountifully given them, although in all other things he taught his captains to live in order without excess. But, for the bravery of armour and weapon which soldiers should carry in their hands or otherwise wear upon their backs, he thought that it was an encouragement unto them that by nature are greedy of honour, and that it maketh them also fight like devils, that love to get and to be afraid to lose; because they fight to keep their armour and weapon, as also their goods and lands.

Now when they came to muster their armies, Octavius Caesar took the muster of his army within the trenches of his camp, and gave his men only a little corn, and five silver drachmas to every man to sacrifice to the gods and to pray for victory. But Brutus, scorning this misery and niggardliness, first of all mustered his army and did purify it in the fields, according to the manner of the Romans. And then he gave unto every band a number of wethers to sacrifice, and fifty silver drachmas to every soldier. So that Brutus' and Cassius' soldiers were better pleased, and more courageously bent to fight at the day of battle, than their enemies' soldiers were.

Notwithstanding, being busily occupied about the ceremonies of this purification, it is reported that there chanced certain unlucky

signs unto Cassius. For one of his sergeants that carried the rods before him brought him the garland of flowers turned backwards, the which he should have worn on his head in the time of sacrificing. Moreover it is reported also that another time before, in certain sports and triumph where they carried an image of Cassius' victory of clean gold, it fell by chance, the man stumbling that carried it. And yet further, there were seen a marvellous number of fowls of prey, that
68 feed upon dead carcases. And beehives also were found, where bees were gathered together in a certain place within the trenches of the camp; the which place the soothsayers thought good to shut out of the precinct of the camp, for to take away the superstitious fear and mistrust men would have of it; the which began somewhat to alter
69 Cassius' mind from Epicurus' opinions, and had put the soldiers also in a marvellous fear.

Thereupon Cassius was of opinion not to try this war at one battle, but rather to delay time and to draw it out in length, considering that they were the stronger in money and the weaker in
70 men and armours. But Brutus in contrary manner did alway before, and at that time also, desire nothing more than to put all to the hazard of battle, as soon as might be possible, to the end he might either quickly restore his country to her former liberty, or rid him forthwith of this miserable world, being still troubled in following and maintaining of such great armies together. But perceiving that in the daily skirmishes and bickerings they made his men were alway the

68 CASSIUS:      Ravens, crows, and kites,
    Fly o'er our heads and downward look on us,
    As we were sickly prey.      (v, 1, 85)

69 See *Life of Caesar*, p. 92 note 36 and p. 149 above.

70 BRUTUS:      What do you think
    Of marching to Philippi presently?
 CASSIUS:  I do not think it good.
 BRUTUS:      Your reason?
 CASSIUS:        This it is:
    'Tis better that the enemy seek us:
    So shall he waste his means, weary his soldiers,
    Doing himself offence; whilst we, lying still,
    Are full of rest, defence, and nimbleness.  (IV, 3, 196)

stronger and ever had the better, that yet quickened his spirits again,
71 and did put him in better heart. And furthermore, because that some
of their own men had already yielded themselves to their enemies,
and that it was suspected moreover divers others would do the
like, that made many of Cassius' friends which were of his mind
before (when it came to be debated in council whether the battle
should be fought or not) that they were then of Brutus' mind. But
yet was there one of Brutus' friends called Atellius, that was against
it, and was of opinion that they should tarry the next winter. Brutus
asked him what he should get by tarrying a year longer?
'If I get nothing else,' quoth Atellius again, 'yet have I lived so
much longer.'
Cassius was very angry with this answer; and Atellius was maliced
and esteemed the worse for it of all men. Thereupon it was presently
determined they should fight battle the next day.

So Brutus all supper time looked with a cheerful countenance, like
a man that had good hope, and talked very wisely of philosophy,
and after supper went to bed. But touching Cassius, Messala reporteth
that he supped by himself in his tent with a few of his friends, and that
all supper time he looked very sadly, and was full of thoughts,
although it was against his nature; and that after supper he took him
by the hand, and holding him fast, in token of kindness as his manner
was, told him in Greek:
'Messala, I protest unto thee, and make thee my witness, that I am
compelled against my mind and will, as Pompey the Great was, to

71 BRUTUS:                    We have tried the utmost of our friends,
                    Our legions are brim-full, our cause is ripe:
                    The enemy increaseth every day;
                    We, at the height, are ready to decline.
                    There is a tide in the affairs of men,
                    Which, taken at the flood, leads on to fortune;
                    Omitted, all the voyage of their life
                    Is bound in shallows and in miseries.
                    On such a full sea are we now afloat;
                    And we must take the current when it serves,
                    Or lose our ventures.                    (IV, 3, 214)

jeopard the liberty of our country to the hazard of a battle. And yet we must be lively and of good courage, considering our good fortune, whom we should wrong too much to mistrust her, although we follow evil counsel.'

Messala writeth that Cassius having spoken these last words unto him, he bade him farewell and willed him to come to supper to him 72 the next night following, because it was his birthday.

The next morning, by break of day, the signal of battle was set out 73 in Brutus' and Cassius' camp, which was an arming scarlet coat; and both the chieftains spake together in the midst of their armies. There Cassius began to speak first, and said:

'The gods grant us, O Brutus, that this day we may win the field and ever after to live all the rest of our life quietly one with another. But sith the gods have so ordained it that the greatest and chiefest things amongst men are most uncertain, and that, if the battle fall out otherwise today than we wish or look for, we shall hardly meet 74 again, what art thou then determined to do – to fly, or die?'

Brutus answered him:

72 CASSIUS:    Messala,
This is my birth-day; as this very day
Was Cassius born. Give me thy hand, Messala:
Be thou my witness that against my will
As Pompey was, am I compell'd to set
Upon one battle all our liberties . . .
. . . I am fresh of spirit and resolved
To meet all perils very constantly.    (v, 1, 71; 91)

CASSIUS:    This day I breathed first: time is come round,
And where I did begin, there shall I end;
My life is run his compass.    (v, 3, 23)

73 MESSENGER:    Prepare you, generals:
The enemy comes on in gallant show;
Their bloody sign of battle is hung out.    (v, 1, 12)

74 CASSIUS:    Now, most noble Brutus,
The gods to-day stand friendly, that we may,
Lovers in peace, lead on our days to age!
But since the affairs of men rest still incertain,
Let's reason with the worst that may befall.

'Being yet but a young man and not over greatly experienced in the world, I trust (I know not how) a certain rule of philosophy by the which I did greatly blame and reprove Cato for killing of himself, as being no lawful nor godly act, touching the gods, nor, concerning men, valiant; not to give place and yield to divine providence, and not constantly and patiently to take whatsoever it pleaseth him to send us, but to draw back and fly. But being now in the midst of the danger, I am of a contrary mind. For, if it be not the will of God that this battle fall out fortunate for us, I will look no more for hope, neither seek to make any new supply for war again, but will rid me of this miserable world, and content me with my fortune. For I gave up my life for my country in the Ides of March, 75 for the which I shall live in another more glorious world.'

Cassius fell a-laughing to hear what he said, and embracing him: 'Come on then,' said he, 'let us go and charge our enemies with this mind. For either we shall conquer, or we shall not need to fear the conquerors.'

After this talk, they fell to consultation among their friends for the ordering of the battle. Then Brutus prayed Cassius he might have the leading of the right wing, the which men thought was far meeter

75 BRUTUS: Even by the rule of that philosophy
     By which I did blame Cato for the death
     Which he did give himself, I know not how,
     But I do find it cowardly and vile,
     For fear of what might fall, so to prevent
     The time of life: arming myself with patience
     To stay the providence of some high powers
     That govern us below . . .
         Think not, thou noble Roman,
     That ever Brutus will go bound to Rome;
     He bears too great a mind. But this same day
     Must end that work the Ides of March begun.

               (v, 1, 101; 111)

---

     If we do lose this battle, then is this
     The very last time we shall speak together:
     What are you then determined to do?  (v, 1, 93)

for Cassius, both because he was the elder man, and also for that he
76 had the better experience. But yet Cassius gave it him, and willed
that Messala, who had charge of one of the warlikest legions they had,
should be also in that wing with Brutus. So Brutus presently sent out
his horsemen, who were excellently well appointed; and his footmen
also were as willing and ready to give charge.

Now Antonius' men did cast a trench from the marsh by the which
they lay, to cut off Cassius' way to come to the sea; and Caesar, at
the least, his army stirred not. As for Octavius Caesar himself, he
was not in his camp, because he was sick. And for his people, they
little thought the enemies would have given them battle, but only
have made some light skirmishes to hinder them that wrought in the
trench, and with their darts and slings to have kept them from finish-
ing of their work. But they, taking no heed to them that came full
upon them to give them battle, marvelled much at the great noise
they heard, that came from the place where they were casting their
trench. In the meantime Brutus, that led the right wing, sent little
bills to the colonels and captains of private bands, in the which he
wrote the word of the battle; and he himself, riding a-horseback
by all the troops, did speak to them and encouraged them to stick
77 to it like men. So by this means very few of them understood what
was the word of the battle, and, besides, the most part of them never
tarried to have it told them, but ran with great fury to assail the
enemies; whereby, through this disorder, the legions were marvellously scattered and dispersed one from the other.

---

76 Compare p. 138 note 54: and contrast:

| | |
|---|---|
| ANTONY: | Octavius, lead your battle softly on, |
| | Upon the left hand of the even field. |
| OCTAVIUS: | Upon the right hand I; keep thou the left. |
| ANTONY: | Why do you cross me in this exigent? |
| OCTAVIUS: | I do not cross you; but I will do so. (v, 1, 16) |
| 77 BRUTUS: | Ride, ride, Messala, ride, and give these bills |
| | Unto the legions on the other side. |
| | Let them set on at once; for I perceive |
| | But cold demeanour in Octavius' wing, |
| | And sudden push gives them the overthrow. (v, 2, 1) |

For first of all, Messala's legion, and then the next unto them, went beyond the left wing of the enemies, and did nothing, but glancing by them overthrew some as they went; and so going on further fell right upon Caesar's camp, out of the which (as himself writeth in his *Commentaries*) he had been conveyed away a little before, through the counsel and advice of one of his friends called Marcus Artorius; who, dreaming in the night, had a vision appeared unto him, that commanded Octavius Caesar should be carried out of his camp, insomuch as it was thought he was slain, because his litter, which had nothing in it, was thrust through and through with pikes and darts. There was great slaughter in this camp. For amongst others there were slain two thousand Lacedaemonians, who were arrived but even a little before, coming to aid Caesar. The other also that had not glanced by, but had given a charge full upon Caesar's battle, they easily made them fly, because they were greatly troubled for the loss of their camp; and of them there were slain by hand three legions. Then, being very earnest to follow the chase of them that fled, they ran in amongst them hand over head into their camp, and Brutus among them.

But that which the conquerors thought not of, occasion showed it unto them that were overcome; and that was the left wing of their enemies left naked and unguarded of them of the right wing, who were strayed too far off, in following of them that were overthrown. So they gave a hot charge upon them. But notwithstanding all the force they made, they could not break into the midst of their battle, where they found men that received them and valiantly made head against them. Howbeit they brake and overthrew the left wing where Cassius was, by reason of the great disorder among them, and also because they had no intelligence how the right wing had sped. So they chased them, beating them into their camp, the which they spoiled, none of both the chieftains being present there. For Antonius, as it is reported, to fly the fury of the first charge, was gotten into the next marsh; and no man could tell what became of Octavius Caesar after he was carried out of his camp; insomuch that there were certain soldiers that showed their swords bloodied, and said that they had slain him, and did describe his face and showed what age he was of.

Furthermore, the vaward and the midst of Brutus' battle had already put all their enemies to flight that withstood them, with great slaughter; so that Brutus had conquered all on his side, and Cassius had lost all on the other side. For nothing undid them but that Brutus went not to help Cassius, thinking he had overcome them, as himself had done; and Cassius on the other side tarried not for Brutus, think-
78 ing he had been overthrown, as himself was. And, to prove that the victory fell on Brutus' side, Messala confirmeth it, that they won three eagles and divers other ensigns of their enemies, and their enemies won never a one of theirs.

Now Brutus returning from the chase after he had slain and sacked Caesar's men, he wondered much that he could not see Cassius' tent standing up high as it was wont, neither the other tents of his camp standing as they were before, because all the whole camp had been spoiled and the tents thrown down, at the first coming in of the enemies. But they that were about Brutus, whose sight served them better, told him that they saw a great glistering of harness and a number of silvered targets, that went and came into Cassius' camp and were not, as they took it, the armours nor the number of men that they had left there to guard the camp; and yet that they saw not such a number of dead bodies, and great overthrow, as there should have been if so many legions had been slain.

This made Brutus at the first mistrust that which had happened. So he appointed a number of men to keep the camp of his enemy which he had taken, and caused his men to be sent for that yet followed the chase, and gathered them together, thinking to lead them to aid Cassius, who was in this state as you shall hear. First of all he was marvellous angry to see how Brutus' men ran to give charge upon their enemies and tarried not for the word of the battle nor commandment to give charge; and it grieved him beside that, after he had overcome them, his men fell straight to spoil and were not

78 MESSALA:     It is but change, Titinius; for Octavius
              Is overthrown by noble Brutus' power,
              As Cassius' legions are by Antony.                    (v, 3, 51)

careful to compass in the rest of the enemies behind. But with tarrying too long also, more than through the valiantness or fore-sight of the captains his enemies, Cassius found himself compassed in with the right wing of his enemies' army. Whereupon his horse-men brake immediately, and fled for life towards the sea. Further-more, perceiving his footmen to give ground, he did what he could to keep them from flying, and took an ensign from one of the ensign-bearers that fled, and stuck it fast at his feet; although with much ado he could scant keep his own guard together. So Cassius himself was at length compelled to fly, with a few about him, unto a little hill from whence they might easily see what was done in all the plain; howbeit Cassius himself saw nothing, for his sight was very bad, saving that he saw, and yet with much ado, how the enemies spoiled his camp before his eyes. He saw also a great troop of horsemen whom Brutus sent to aid him, and thought that they were his enemies that followed him. But yet he sent Titinnius, one of them that was with him, to go and know what they were. Brutus' horse-men saw him coming afar off, whom when they knew that he was one of Cassius' chiefest friends, they shouted out for joy; and they that were familiarly acquainted with him lighted from their horses, and went and embraced him. The rest compassed him in round about a-horseback, with songs of victory and great rushing of their harness, so that they made all the field ring again for joy.

TITINIUS:    O Cassius, Brutus gave the word too early;
             Who, having some advantage on Octavius,
             Took it too eagerly: his soldiers fell to spoil,
             Whilst we by Antony are all enclosed.          (v, 3, 5)

CASSIUS:     O, look, Titinius, look, the villains fly!
             Myself have to mine own turn'd enemy:
             This ensign here of mine was turning back;
             I slew the coward, and did take it from him.    (v, 3, 1)

PINDARUS:    Fly further off, my lord, fly further off;
             Mark Antony is in your tents, my lord:
             Fly, therefore, noble Cassius, fly far off.

CASSIUS:     This hill is far enough. Look, look, Titinius;
             Are those my tents where I perceive the fire?

159

But this marred all. For Cassius thinking indeed that Titinnius was taken of the enemies, he then spake these words:

'Desiring too much to live, I have lived to see one of my best
82 friends taken, for my sake, before my face.'

After that, he got into a tent where nobody was, and took Pindarus with him, one of his freed bondmen, whom he reserved ever for such a pinch, since the cursed battle of the Parthians where Crassus was slain, though he notwithstanding scaped from that overthrow. But then casting his cloak over his head and holding out his bare neck unto Pindarus, he gave him his head to be stricken off. So the head was found severed from the body. But after that time Pindarus
83 was never seen more. Whereupon, some took occasion to say that he had slain his master without his commandment.

| | |
|---|---|
| 82 CASSIUS: | Come down, behold no more. |
| | O, coward that I am, to live so long, |
| | To see my best friend ta'en before my face!  (v, 3, 33) |
| 83 CASSIUS: | Come hither, sirrah: |
| | In Parthia did I take thee prisoner; |
| | And then I swore thee, saving of thy life, |
| | That whatsoever I did bid thee do, |

---

| | |
|---|---|
| TITINIUS: | They are, my lord. |
| CASSIUS: | Titinius, if thou lovest me, |
| | Mount thou my horse, and hide thy spurs in him, |
| | Till he have brought thee up to yonder troops, |
| | And here again; that I may rest assured |
| | Whether yond troops are friend or enemy. |
| TITINIUS: | I will be here again, even with a thought. |
| CASSIUS: | Go, Pindarus, get higher on that hill; |
| | My sight was ever thick; regard Titinius, |
| | And tell me what thou notest about the field . . . |
| PINDARUS: | Titinius is enclosed round about |
| | With horsemen, that make to him on the spur; |
| | Yet he spurs on. Now they are almost on him, |
| | Now Titinius! Now some light. O, he lights too. |
| | He's ta'en. And, hark! they shout for joy.  (v, 3, 9; 28) |

By and by they knew the horsemen that came towards them, and might see Titinnius crowned with a garland of triumph, who came before with great speed unto Cassius. But when he perceived, by the cries and tears of his friends which tormented themselves, the misfortune that had chanced to his captain Cassius by mistaking, he drew out his sword, cursing himself a thousand times that he had tarried so long, and so slew himself presently in the field. Brutus in the meantime came forward still, and understood also that Cassius had been overthrown. But he knew nothing of his death, till he came very near to his camp. So when he was come thither, after he had lamented the death of Cassius, calling him the last of all the Romans, being unpossible that Rome should ever breed again so noble and valiant a man as he, he caused his body to be buried and

TITINIUS:    Why didst thou send me forth, brave Cassius?
Did I not meet thy friends? and did not they
Put on my brows this wreath of victory,
And bid me give it thee? Didst thou not hear their shouts?
Alas, thou has misconstrued every thing!
But, hold thee, take this garland on thy brow;
Thy Brutus bid me give it thee, and I
Will do his bidding. Brutus, come apace,
And see how I regarded Caius Cassius.
By your leave, gods: – this is a Roman's part:
Come, Cassius' sword, and find Titinius' heart.   *Dies.*

(v, 3, 80)

---

Thou shouldst attempt it. Come now, keep thine oath;
Now be a freeman: and with this good sword,
That ran through Caesar's bowels, search this bosom.
Stand not to answer: here, take thou the hilts;
And, when my face is cover'd, as 'tis now,
Guide thou the sword. . . .      *Dies.*

PINDARUS:   So, I am free; yet would not so have been,
Durst I have done my will. O Cassius,
Far from this country Pindarus shall run,
Where never Roman shall take note of him.   (v, 3, 36)

sent it to the city of Thassos, fearing lest his funerals within the camp
85 should cause great disorder.

Then he called his soldiers together and did encourage them
again. And when he saw that they had lost all their carriage, which
they could not brook well, he promised every man of them two
thousand drachmas in recompense. After his soldiers had heard his
oration, they were all of them prettily cheered again, wondering
much at his great liberality, and waited upon him with great cries
when he went his way, praising him for that he only of the four
chieftains was not overcome in battle. And, to speak the truth, his
deeds showed that he hoped not in vain to be conqueror. For with
few legions he had slain and driven all them away that made head
against him. And yet if all his people had fought, and that the most
of them had not out-gone their enemies to run to spoil their goods,
surely it was like enough he had slain them all and had left never a
man of them alive.

There were slain of Brutus' side about eight thousand men,
counting the soldiers' slaves, whom Brutus called *Brigas*. And of
the enemies' side, as Messala writeth, there were slain, as he supposeth,
more than twice as many more. Wherefore they were more discouraged than Brutus, until that, very late at night, there was one of
Cassius' men called Demetrius who went unto Antonius and carried
his master's clothes, whereof he was stripped not long before, and his
sword also. This encouraged Brutus' enemies and made them so
brave that, the next morning betimes, they stood in battle ray again
before Brutus. But, on Brutus' side, both his camps stood wavering,
and that in great danger. For his own camp, being full of prisoners,
required a good guard to look unto them: and Cassius' camp on the

85 BRUTUS:    The last of all the Romans, fare thee well!
It is impossible that ever Rome
Should breed thy fellow. Friends, I owe more tears
To this dead man than you shall see me pay.
I shall find time, Cassius, I shall find time.
Come, therefore, and to Thasos send his body:
His funerals shall not be in our camp,
Lest it discomfort us.           (v, 3, 99)

other side took the death of their captain very heavily, and, besides, there was some vile grudge between them that were overcome and those that did overcome. For this cause therefore Brutus did set them in battle ray, but yet kept himself from giving battle.

Now for the slaves that were prisoners, which were a great number of them, and went and came to and fro amongst the armed men, not without suspicion, he commanded they should kill them. But, for the free men, he sent them freely home, and said that they were better prisoners with his enemies than with him. For with them they were slaves and servants; and with him they were free men and citizens. So, when he saw that divers captains and his friends did so cruelly hate some that they would by no means save their lives, Brutus himself hid them and secretly sent them away. Among these prisoners, there was one Volumnius a jester and Sacculio a common player, of whom Brutus made no accompt at all. Howbeit his friends brought them unto him and did accuse them that, though they were prisoners, they did not let to laugh them to scorn and to jest broadly with them. Brutus made no answer to it, because his head was occupied other ways. Whereupon Messala Corvinus said that it were good to whip them on a scaffold, and then to send them naked, well whipped, unto the captains of their enemies, to show them their shame, to keep such mates as those in their camp to play the fools, to make them sport. Some that stood by laughed at his device. But Publius Casca, that gave Julius Caesar the first wound when he was slain, said then:

'It doth not become us to be thus merry at Cassius' funerals. And for thee, Brutus, thou shalt show what estimation thou madest of such a captain thy compeer, by putting to death, or saving the lives of these bloods who hereafter will mock him and defame his memory.'

Brutus answered again in choler:

'Why then do you come to tell me of it, Casca, and do not yourselves what you think good?'

When they heard him say so, they took his answer for a consent against these poor unfortunate men, to suffer them to do what they thought good. And therefore they carried them away and slew them.

Afterwards Brutus performed the promise he had made to the soldiers, and gave them the two thousand drachmas apiece. But yet he first reproved them because they went and gave charge upon the enemies at the first battle, before they had the word of battle given them; and made them a new promise also that, if in the second battle they fought like men, he would give them the sack and spoil of two cities, to wit, Thessalonica and Lacedaemon. In all Brutus' life there is but this only fault to be found, and that is not to be gainsaid; though Antonius and Octavius Caesar did reward their soldiers far worse for their victory. For, when they had driven all the natural Italians out of Italy, they gave their soldiers their lands and towns, to the which they had no right. And, moreover, the only mark they shot at in all this war they made was but to overcome and reign. Where in contrary manner they had so great an opinion of Brutus' virtue, that the common voice and opinion of the world would not suffer him, neither to overcome, nor to save himself, otherwise than justly and honestly, and specially after Cassius' death; whom men burdened that oftentimes he moved Brutus to great cruelty. But now, like as the mariners on the sea after the rudder of their ship is broken by tempest do seek to nail on some other piece of wood in lieu thereof, and do help themselves to keep them from hurt as much as may be upon that instant danger; even so Brutus having such a great army to govern, and his affairs standing very tickle, and having no other captain coequal with him in dignity and authority, he was forced to employ them he had, and likewise to be ruled by them in many things, and was of mind himself also to grant them anything that he thought might make them serve like noble soldiers at time of need. For Cassius' soldiers were very evil to be ruled; and did show themselves very stubborn and lusty in the camp, because they had no chieftain that did command them, but yet rank cowards to their enemies, because they had once overcome them.

On the other side Octavius Caesar and Antonius were not in much better state. For first of all, they lacked victuals. And, because they were lodged in low places, they looked to abide a hard and sharp winter, being camped as they were by the marsh side, and also for that after the battle there had fallen plenty of rain about the autumn, wherethrough all their tents were full of mire and dirt, the which by reason of the cold did freeze incontinently.

But, beside all these discommodities, there came news unto them of the great loss they had of their men by sea. For Brutus' ships met with a great aid and supply of men, which were sent them out of Italy; and they overthrew them in such sort that there scaped but few of them; and yet they were so famished, that they were compelled to eat the tackle and sails of their ships. Thereupon they were very desirous to fight a battle again, before Brutus should have intelligence of this good news for him; for it chanced so, that the battle was fought by sea on the self same day it was fought by land. But by ill fortune, rather than through the malice or negligence of the captains, this victory came not to Brutus' ear till twenty days after. For, had he known of it before, he would not have been brought to have fought a second battle, considering that he had excellent good provision for his army for a long time, and, besides, lay in a place of great strength, so as his camp could not be greatly hurt by the winter, nor also distressed by his enemies; and further, he had been a quiet lord, being a conqueror by sea, as he was also by land. This would have marvellously encouraged him.

Howbeit the state of Rome (in my opinion) being now brought to that pass that it could no more abide to be governed by many lords but required one only absolute governor, God, to prevent Brutus that it should not come to his government, kept this victory from his knowledge, though indeed it came but a little too late. For the day before the last battle was given, very late in the night, came Clodius, one of his enemies, into his camp, who told that Caesar, hearing of the overthrow of his army by sea, desired nothing more than to fight a battle before Brutus understood it. Howbeit they gave no credit to his words, but despised him so much that they would not vouchsafe to bring him unto Brutus, because they thought it was but a lie devised, to be the better welcome for this good news.

The self same night, it is reported that the monstrous spirit, which had appeared before unto Brutus in the city of Sardis, did now appear again unto him in the self same shape and form, and so vanished

86 away, and said never a word. Now Publius Volumnius, a grave and wise philosopher, that had been with Brutus from the beginning of this war, he doth make no mention of this spirit; but saith that the greatest eagle and ensign was covered over with a swarm of bees, and that there was one of the captains whose arm suddenly fell a-sweating, that it dropped oil of roses from him, and that they oftentimes went about to dry him, but all would do no good; and that, before the battle was fought, there were two eagles fought between both armies, and all the time they fought there was a marvellous great silence all the valley over, both the armies, being one before the other, marking this fight between them; and that in the end the eagle towards Brutus gave over and flew away. But this is certain, and a true tale: that, when the gate of the camp was open, the first man the standard-bearer met that carried the eagle was an Ethiopian, whom the soldiers for ill-luck mangled with their swords.

Now after that Brutus had brought his army into the field and had set them in battle ray, directly against the vaward of his enemy, he paused a long time before he gave the signal of battle. For Brutus riding up and down to view the bands and companies, it came in his head to mistrust some of them, besides that some came to tell him so much as he thought. Moreover, he saw his horsemen set forward but faintly, and did not go lustily to give charge, but still stayed to see what the footmen would do. Then suddenly one of the chiefest knights he had in all his army, called Camulatius, and that was alway marvellously esteemed of for his valiantness until that time, he came hard by Brutus on horseback and rode before his face to yield himself unto his enemies. Brutus was marvellous sorry for it, wherefore, partly for anger and partly for fear of greater treason and rebellion, he suddenly caused his army to march, being past three of the clock in the afternoon. So, in that place where he himself fought in person he had the better and brake into the left wing of his enemies, which gave him way, through the help of his horsemen that gave charge with his footmen, when they saw the enemies in a maze and afraid. Howbeit the other also on the right wing, when the captains

86 See *Life of Caesar*, p. 101 note 59.

would have had them to have marched, they were afraid to have been compassed in behind, because they were fewer in number than their enemies; and therefore did spread themselves and leave the midst of their battle. Whereby they having weakened themselves they could not withstand the force of their enemies, but turned tail straight and fled. And those that had put them to flight came in straight upon it to compass Brutus behind, who in the midst of the conflict did all that was possible for a skilful captain and valiant soldier, both for his wisdom as also for his hardiness, for the obtaining of victory. But that which won him the victory at the first battle did now lose it him at the second. For at the first time the enemies that were broken and fled were straight cut in pieces; but at the second battle, of Cassius' men that were put to flight, there were few slain; and they that saved themselves by speed, being afraid because they had been overcome, did discourage the rest of the army when they came to join with them and filled all the army with fear and disorder.

There was the son of M. Cato slain, valiantly fighting amongst the lusty youths. For, notwithstanding that he was very weary and overharried, yet would he not therefore fly, but manfully fighting and laying about him, telling aloud his name and also his father's name, at length he was beaten down amongst many other dead
87 bodies of his enemies which he had slain round about him. So there were slain in the field all the chiefest gentlemen and nobility that were in his army, who valiantly ran into any danger to save Brutus' life.

Amongst them there was one of Brutus' friends called Lucilius, who seeing a troop of barbarous men making no reckoning of all men else they met in their way, but going all together right against Brutus, he determined to stay them with the hazard of his life, and,

87 CATO:       I will proclaim my name about the field:
                 I am the son of Marcus Cato, ho!
                 A foe to tyrants, and my country's friend;
                 I am the son of Marcus Cato, ho! . . .

LUCILIUS:    O young and noble Cato, art thou down?
                 Why, now thou diest as bravely as Titinius;
                 And mayst be honour'd, being Cato's son.    (v, 4, 3; 9)

being left behind, told them that he was Brutus; and, because they should believe him, he prayed them to bring him to Antonius, for he said he was afraid of Caesar, and that he did trust Antonius better. These barbarous men being very glad of this good hap, and thinking themselves happy men, they carried him in the night, and sent some before unto Antonius to tell him of their coming. He was

88 marvellous glad of it, and went out to meet them that brought him. Others also understanding of it that they had brought Brutus prisoner, they came out of all parts of the camp to see him, some pitying his hard fortune and others saying that it was not done like himself, so cowardly to be taken alive of the barbarous people for fear of death. When they came near together, Antonius stayed awhile bethinking himself how he should use Brutus. In the meantime Lucilius was brought to him, who stoutly with a bold countenance said:

'Antonius, I dare assure thee that no enemy hath taken nor shall take Marcus Brutus alive. I beseech God keep him from that fortune. For wheresoever he be found, alive or dead, he will be found like

89 himself. And now for myself, I am come unto thee, having deceived these men of arms here, bearing them down that I was Brutus; and do not refuse to suffer any torment thou wilt put me to.'

Lucilius' words made them all amazed that heard him. Antonius on

| | | |
|---|---|---|
| 88 1st SOLDIER: | Yield, or thou diest. | |
| LUCILIUS: | Only I yield to die: | |
| | There is so much that thou wilt kill me straight; | |
| | Kill Brutus, and be honour'd in his death. | |
| 1st SOLDIER: | We must not. A noble prisoner! | |
| 2nd SOLDIER: | Room ho! Tell Antony, Brutus is ta'en. | |
| 1st SOLDIER: | I'll tell the news. Here comes the general. | (v, 4, 12) |
| 89 SOLDIER: | Brutus is ta'en, Brutus is ta'en, my lord. | |
| ANTONY: | Where is he? | |
| LUCILIUS: | Safe, Antony; Brutus is safe enough: | |
| | I dare assure thee that no enemy | |
| | Shall ever take alive the noble Brutus: | |
| | The gods defend him from so great a shame! | |
| | When you do find him, or alive or dead, | |
| | He will be found like Brutus, like himself. | (v, 4, 18) |

the other side, looking upon all them that had brought him, said unto them:

'My companions, I think ye are sorry you have failed of your purpose, and that you think this man hath done you great wrong. But, I do assure you, you have taken a better booty than that you followed. For, instead of an enemy, you have brought me a friend; and for my part, if you had brought me Brutus alive, truly I cannot tell what I should have done to him. For I had rather have such men my friends as this man here, than enemies.'

Then he embraced Lucilius and at that time delivered him to one of
90 his friends in custody; and Lucilius ever after served him faithfully, even to his death.

Now Brutus having passed a little river walled in on either side with high rocks and shadowed with great trees, being then dark night he went no further, but stayed at the foot of a rock with certain
91 of his captains and friends that followed him. And looking up to the firmament that was full of stars, sighing, he rehearsed two verses, of the which Volumnius wrote the one, to this effect:

> Let not the wight from whom this mischief went,
> O Jove, escape without due punishment.

– and saith that he had forgotten the other. Within a little while after, naming his friends that he had seen slain in battle before his eyes, he fetched a greater sigh than before; specially when he came
92 to name Labio and Flavius, of the which the one was his lieutenant and the other captain of the pioneers of his camp.

In the meantime, one of the company being athirst and seeing Brutus athirst also, he ran to the river for water and brought it in his sallet. At the self same time they heard a noise on the other side of the river. Whereupon Volumnius took Dardanus, Brutus' servant, with him to see what it was; and, returning straight again, asked if

| | | |
|---|---|---|
| 90 ANTONY: | This is not Brutus, friend; but, I assure you, | |
| | A prize no less in worth: keep this man safe; | |
| | Give him all kindness; I had rather have | |
| | Such men my friends than enemies. | (v, 4, 26) |
| 91 BRUTUS: | Come, poor remains of friends, rest on this rock. | (v, 5, 1) |
| 92 BRUTUS: | Labeo and Flavius, set our battles on. | (v, 3, 108) |

there were any water left. Brutus, smiling, gently told them all was drunk; 'but they shall bring you some more.' Thereupon he sent him again that went for water before, who was in great danger of being taken by the enemies, and hardly scaped, being sore hurt. Furthermore, Brutus thought that there was no great number of men slain in battle; and, to know the truth of it, there was one called Statilius that promised to go through his enemies, for otherwise it was impossible to go see their camp, and from thence, if all were well, that he would lift up a torch-light in the air, and then return again with speed to him. The torch-light was lift up as he had promised, for Statilius went thither. Now Brutus seeing Statilius tarry long after that, and that he came not again, he said:

'If Statilius be alive, he will come again.'

But his evil fortune was such that as he came back he lighted in his
93 enemies' hands and was slain.

Now, the night being far spent, Brutus as he sat bowed towards Clitus one of his men and told him somewhat in his ear, the other answered him not, but fell a-weeping. Thereupon he proved Dardanus, and said somewhat also to him. At length he came to Volumnius himself, and, speaking to him in Greek, prayed him, for the study's sake which brought them acquainted together, that he would help him to put his hand to his sword, to thrust it in him to
94 kill him. Volumnius denied his request, and so did many others. And, amongst the rest, one of them said, there was no tarrying for

| | | |
|---|---|---|
| 93 CLITUS: | Statilius show'd the torch-light, but, my lord, | |
| | He came not back: he is or ta'en or slain. | (v, 5, 2) |
| 94 BRUTUS: | Sit thee down, Clitus: slaying is the word; | |
| | It is a deed in fashion. Hark thee, Clitus. | |
| CLITUS: | What I, my lord? No, not for all the world. | |
| BRUTUS: | Peace then! No words. | |
| CLITUS: | I'll rather kill myself. | |
| BRUTUS: | Hark thee, Dardanius. | |
| DARDANIUS: | Shall I do such a deed? | |
| CLITUS: | O Dardanius! | |
| DARDANIUS: | O Clitus! | |
| CLITUS: | What ill request did Brutus make to thee? | |

them there, but that they must needs fly. Then Brutus rising up:
5 'We must fly indeed,' said he, 'but it must be with our hands not
with our feet.'

Then, taking every man by the hand, he said these words unto them
with a cheerful countenance:

'It rejoiceth my heart that not one of my friends hath failed me at
my need, and I do not complain of my fortune, but only for my
country's sake. For, as for me, I think myself happier than they that
have overcome, considering that I leave a perpetual fame of our
courage and manhood, the which our enemies the conquerors shall
never attain unto by force nor money, neither can let their posterity
to say that they, being naughty and unjust men, have slain good
6 men, to usurp tyrannical power not pertaining to them.'

Having said so, he prayed every man to shift for themselves. And
then he went a little aside with two or three only, among the which
Strato was one, with whom he came first acquainted by the study of

| | | |
|---|---|---|
| 95 CLITUS: | Fly, fly, my lord; there is no tarrying here. | (v, 5, 30) |
| 96 BRUTUS: | Farewell to you; and you; and you, Volumnius. . . . | |
| | Farewell to thee too, Strato. Countrymen, | |
| | My heart doth joy that yet in all my life | |
| | I found no man but he was true to me. | |
| | I shall have glory by this losing day | |
| | More than Octavius and Mark Antony | |
| | By this vile conquest shall attain unto. | |
| | So fare you well at once. | (v, 5, 31) |

---

| | | |
|---|---|---|
| DARDANIUS: | To kill him, Clitus. Look, he meditates. | |
| CLITUS: | Now is that noble vessel full of grief. | |
| | That it runs over even at his eyes. | |
| BRUTUS: | Come hither, good Volumnius; list a word. | |
| VOLUMNIUS: | What says my lord? . . . | |
| BRUTUS: | Good Volumnius, | |
| | Thou know'st that we two went to school together: | |
| | Even for that our love of old, I prithee, | |
| | Hold thou my sword-hilts, whilst I run on it. | |
| VOLUMNIUS: | That's not an office for a friend, my lord. | (v, 5, 4) |

rhetoric. He came as near to him as he could, and, taking his sword by the hilts with both his hands and falling down upon the point of it, ran himself through. Others say that not he, but Strato, at his request, held the sword in his hand, and turned his head aside, and that Brutus fell down upon it; and so ran himself through, and died 97 presently.

Messala, that had been Brutus' great friend, became afterwards Octavius Caesar's friend. So, shortly after, Caesar being at good 98 leisure, he brought Strato, Brutus' friend, unto him and weeping said:

99 'Caesar, behold, here is he that did the last service to my Brutus.' Caesar welcomed him at that time, and afterwards he did him as faithful service in all his affairs as any Grecian else he had about him, until the battle of Actium. It is reported also that this Messala himself answered Caesar one day, when he gave him great praise before his face that he had fought valiantly and with great affection for him at the battle of Actium (notwithstanding that he had been his cruel enemy before, at the battle of Philippes, for Brutus' sake): 'I ever loved,' said he, 'to take the best and justest part.'

Now, Antonius having found Brutus' body, he caused it to be wrapped up in one of the richest coat-armours he had. Afterwards

| 97 | BRUTUS: | I prithee, Strato, stay thou by thy lord: |
| | | Thou art a fellow of a good respect; |
| | | Thy life hath had some smatch of honour in it: |
| | | Hold then my sword, and turn away thy face, |
| | | While I do run upon it. Wilt thou, Strato? |
| | STRATO: | Give me your hand first. Fare you well, my lord. |
| | BRUTUS: | Farewell, good Strato. Caesar, now be still: |
| | | I kill'd not thee with half so good a will. *Dies.* (v, 5, 44) |
| 98 | OCTAVIUS: | What man is that? |
| | MESSALA: | My master's man. Strato, where is thy master? |
| | STRATO: | Free from the bondage you are in, Messala. (v, 5, 52) |
| 99 | OCTAVIUS: | All that served Brutus, I will entertain them. |
| | | Fellow, wilt thou bestow thy time with me? |
| | STRATO: | Ay, if Messala will prefer me to you ... |
| | MESSALA: | Octavius, then take him to follow thee, |
| | | That did the latest service to my master. (v, 5, 60; 66) |

also, Antonius understanding that this coat-armour was stolen, he put the thief to death that had stolen it, and sent the ashes of his body unto Servilia his mother. And for Portia, Brutus' wife, Nicolaus the philosopher and Valerius Maximus do write that she, determining to kill herself (her parents and friends carefully looking to her to keep her from it), took hot burning coals and cast them into her mouth, and kept her mouth so close that she choked herself. There was a letter of Brutus found written to his friends, complaining of their negligence, that, his wife being sick, they would not help her but suffered her to kill herself, choosing to die rather than to languish in pain. Thus it appeareth that Nicolaus knew not well that time, sith the letter (at the least if it were Brutus' letter) doth plainly declare the disease and love of this lady and also the manner of her death.

| | | |
|---|---|---|
| STRATO: | The conquerors can but make a fire of him. | (v, 5, 55) |

| | | |
|---|---|---|
| BRUTUS: | Portia is dead ... | |
| CASSIUS: | O insupportable and touching loss! | |
| | Upon what sickness? | |
| BRUTUS: | Impatient of my absence, | |
| | And grief that young Octavius with Mark Antony | |
| | Have made themselves so strong ... | |
| | with this she fell distract, | |
| | And, her attendants absent, swallow'd fire. | |
| CASSIUS: | And died so? | |
| BRUTUS: | Even so. | (IV, 3, 147) |

# THE LIFE OF MARCUS ANTONIUS

ANTONIUS' grandfather was that famous orator whom Marius slew because he took Sylla's part. His father was another Antonius surnamed Cretan (because that by his death he ended the war which he unfortunately made against those of Creta), who was not so famous nor bare any great sway in the commonwealth; howbeit otherwise he was an honest man, and of a very good nature, and specially very liberal in giving, as appeareth by an act he did. He was not very wealthy, and therefore his wife would not let him use his liberality and frank nature. One day a friend of his coming to him to pray him to help him to some money, having great need, Antonius by chance had no money to give him, but he commanded one of his men to bring him some water in a silver basin; and after he had brought it him he washed his beard as though he meant to have shaven it, and then found an errand for his man to send him out, and gave his friend the silver basin, and bade him get him money with that. Shortly after there was a great stir in the house among the servants, seeking out this silver basin; insomuch as Antonius seeing his wife marvellously offended for it, and that she would examine all her servants one after another about it, to know what was become of it, at length he confessed he had given it away, and prayed her to be contented.

His wife was Julia, of the noble house and family of Julius Caesar, who, for her virtue and chastity, was to be compared with the noblest lady of her time. M. Antonius was brought up under her, being married after her first husband's death unto Cornelius Lentulus, whom Cicero put to death with Cethegus and others, for that he was of Catiline's conspiracy against the commonwealth. And this seemeth to be the original cause and beginning of the cruel and mortal hate Antonius bare unto Cicero. For Antonius self saith that he would never give him the body of his father-in-law to bury him, before his mother went first to entreat Cicero's wife; the which undoubtedly was a flat lie. For Cicero denied burial to none of them whom he executed by law.

Now Antonius being a fair young man, and in the prime of his youth, he fell acquainted with Curio, whose friendship and acquaintance (as it is reported) was a plague unto him. For he was a dissolute man, given over to all lust and insolency, who, to have Antonius the better at his commandment, trained him on into great follies and vain expenses upon women, in rioting and banqueting. So that in short time he brought Antonius into a marvellous great debt and too great for one of his years, to wit, of two hundred and fifty talents; for all which sum Curio was his surety. His father hearing of it did put his son from him and forbade him his house.

Then he fell in with Clodius, one of the desperatest and most wicked Tribunes at that time in Rome. Him he followed for a time in his desperate attempts, who bred great stir and mischief in Rome. But at length he forsook him, being weary of his rashness and folly, or else for that he was afraid of them that were bent against Clodius.

Thereupon he left Italy and went into Greece; and there bestowed the most part of his time, sometime in wars and otherwhile in the study of eloquence. He used a manner of phrase in his speech called Asiatic, which carried the best grace and estimation at that time, and was much like to his manners and life; for it was full of ostentation, foolish bravery, and vain ambition. After he had remained there some time, Gabinius, Proconsul, going into Syria, persuaded him to go with him. Antonius told him he would not go as a private man. Wherefore Gabinius gave him charge of his horsemen and so took him with him. So first of all he sent him against Aristobulus, who had made the Jews to rebel; and was the first man himself that got up to the wall of a castle of his, and so drave Aristobulus out of all his holds. And with those few men he had with him he overcame all the Jews in set battle, which were many against one, and put all of them almost to the sword; and furthermore took Aristobulus himself prisoner, with his son.

Afterwards Ptolemy King of Egypt, that had been driven out of his country, went unto Gabinius to entreat him to go with his army with him into Egypt, to put him again into his kingdom; and promised him, if he would go with him, ten thousand talents. The most part of the captains thought it not best to go thither; and Gabinius himself made it dainty to enter into this war, although the covetousness of these ten thousand talents stuck sorely with him. But Antonius, that sought but for opportunity and good occasion to attempt great enterprises, and that desired also to gratify Ptolemy's request, he went about to persuade Gabinius to go this voyage. Now they were more afraid of the way they should go, to come to the city of Pelusium, than they feared any danger of the war besides, because they were to pass through deep sands and desert places, where was no fresh water to be had all the marshes through, which are called the marshes Serbonides (which the Egyptians call the exhalations or fume by the which the giant Typhon breathed – but in truth it appeareth to be the overflowing of the Red Sea, which breaketh out under the ground in that place, where it is divided in the narrowest place from the sea on this side). So Antonius was sent before into Egypt with his horsemen, who did not only win that passage, but also took the city of Pelusium, which is a great city, with all the soldiers in it. And thereby he cleared the way and made it safe for all the rest of the army, and the hope of the victory also certain for his captain. Now did the enemies themselves feel the fruits of Antonius' courtesy and the desire he had to win honour. For when Ptolemy, after he had entered into the city of Pelusium, for the malice he bare unto the city, would have put all the Egyptians in it to the sword, Antonius withstood him, and by no means would suffer him to do it. And in all other great battles and skirmishes which they fought and were many in number, Antonius did many noble acts of a valiant and wise captain; but specially in one battle, where he compassed in the enemies behind, giving them the victory that fought against them; whereby he afterwards had such honourable reward as his valiantness deserved.

So was his great courtesy also much commended of all, the which he showed unto Archelaus. For, having been his very friend, he made war with him against his will while he lived. But after his death he sought for his body and gave it honourable burial. For these respects he won himself great fame of them of Alexandria, and he was also thought a worthy man of all the soldiers in the Romans' camp.

But, besides all this, he had a noble presence and showed a countenance of one of a noble house. He had a goodly thick beard, a broad forehead, crook-nosed; and there appeared such a manly look in his countenance as is commonly seen in Hercules' pictures, stamped or graven in metal. Now it had been a speech of old time that the family of the Antonii were descended from one Anton, the son of Hercules, whereof the family took name. This opinion did Antonius seek to confirm in all his doings, not only resembling him in the likeness of his body, as we have said before, but also in the wearing of his garments. For when he would openly show himself abroad before many people, he would always wear his cassock girt down low upon his hips, with a great sword hanging by his side, and, upon that, 1 some ill-favoured cloak.

Furthermore, things that seem intolerable in other men, as to boast commonly, to jest with one or other, to drink like a good fellow with everybody, to sit with the soldiers when they dine, and to eat and

*1* CLEOPATRA:       Look, prithee, Charmian,
How this Herculean Roman does become
The carriage of his chafe.   (*Antony and Cleopatra*, I, 3, 83)

SOLDIER:    'Tis the god Hercules, whom Antony loved,
Now leaves him.          (IV, 3, 16)

ANTONY:    The shirt of Nessus is upon me: teach me,
Alcides, thou mine ancestor, thy rage:
Let me lodge Lichas on the horns o' the moon;
And with those hands, that grasp'd the heaviest club,
Subdue my worthiest self.     (IV, 12, 43)

ENOBARBUS:    By Jupiter,
Were I the wearer of Antonius' beard,
I would not shave't today.     (II, 2, 6)

2 drink with them soldierlike – it is incredible what wonderful love it won him amongst them. And furthermore, being given to love, that made him the more desired; and by that means he brought many to love him. For he would further every man's love, and also would not be angry that men should merrily tell him of those he loved.

But besides all this, that which most procured his rising and advancement was his liberality, who gave all to the soldiers and kept nothing for himself. And when he was grown to great credit, then was his authority and power also very great, the which notwithstanding himself did overthrow by a thousand other faults he had. In this place I will show you one example only of his wonderful liberality. He commanded one day his cofferer that kept his money to give a friend of his five-and-twenty myriads (which the Romans call in their tongue, *decies*). His cofferer marvelling at it; and, being angry withal in his mind, brought him all this money in a heap together, to show him what a marvellous mass of money it was. Antonius, seeing it as he went by, asked what it was. His cofferer answered him, it was the money he willed him to give unto his friend. Then Antonius perceiving the spite of his man:

'I thought,' said he, 'that *decies* had been a greater sum of money than it is, for this is but a trifle.'

And therefore he gave his friend as much more another time; but that was afterwards.

Now the Romans maintaining two factions at Rome at that time, one against the other; of the which they that took part with the Senate did join with Pompey being then in Rome, and the contrary side taking part with the people sent for Caesar to aid them, who made wars in Gaul. Then Curio, Antonius' friend, that had changed his garments and at that time took part with Caesar, whose enemy he had been before, he won Antonius; and so handled the matter, partly through the great credit and sway he bare amongst the people

2 OCTAVIUS CAESAR: . . . To sit
   And keep the turn of tippling with a slave;
   To reel the streets at noon, and stand the buffet
   With knaves that smell of sweat: say this becomes him.

           (I, 4, 18)

by reason of his eloquent tongue, and partly also by his exceeding expense of money he made which Caesar gave him, that Antonius was chosen Tribune, and afterwards made Augur.

But this was a great help and furtherance to Caesar's practices. For so soon as Antonius became Tribune he did oppose himself against those things which the Consul Marcellus preferred (who ordained that certain legions which had been already levied and billed should be given unto Cneius Pompey, with further commission and authority to levy others unto them); and set down an order that the soldiers which were already levied and assembled should be sent into Syria for a new supply unto Marcus Bibulus, who made war at that time against the Parthians; and, furthermore, prohibition that Pompey should levy no more men, and also that the soldiers should not obey him. Secondly, where Pompey's friends and followers would not suffer Caesar's letters to be received and openly read in the Senate, Antonius, having power and warrant by his person through the holiness of his Tribuneship, did read them openly, and made divers men change their minds; for it appeared to them that Caesar by his letters required no unreasonable matters. At length, when they preferred two matters of consideration unto the Senate, whether they thought good that Pompey or Caesar should leave their army, there were few of the Senators that thought it meet Pompey should leave his army; but they all in manner commanded Caesar to do it. Then Antonius, rising up, asked whether they thought it good that Pompey and Caesar both should leave their armies. Thereunto all the Senators jointly together gave their whole consent; and with a great cry commending Antonius they prayed him to refer it to the judgement of the Senate. But the Consuls would not allow of that. Therefore Caesar's friends preferred other reasonable demands and requests again; but Cato spake against them; and Lentulus, one of the Consuls, drave Antonius by force out of the Senate, who at his going out made grievous curses against him.

After that, he took a slave's gown and speedily fled to Caesar, with Quintus Cassius, in a hired coach. When they came to Caesar, they cried out with open mouth that all went hand over head at Rome; for the Tribunes of the People might not speak their minds, and were driven away in great danger of their lives, as many as stood with law and justice.

Hereupon Caesar incontinently went into Italy with his army, which made Cicero say in his *Philippides* that, as Helen was cause of the war of Troy, so was Antonius the author of the civil wars; which indeed was a stark lie. For Caesar was not so fickle-headed nor so easily carried away with anger that he would so suddenly have gone and made war with his country, upon the sight only of Antonius and Cassius being fled unto him in miserable apparel and in a hired coach, had he not long before determined it with himself. But sith indeed Caesar looked of long time but for some colour, this came as he wished and gave him just occasion of war. But to say truly, nothing else moved him to make war with all the world as he did, but one self cause, which first procured Alexander and Cyrus also before him: to wit, an insatiable desire to reign, with a senseless covetousness to be the best man in the world, the which he could not come unto before he had first put down Pompey and utterly overthrown him.

Now after that Caesar had gotten Rome at his commandment and had driven Pompey out of Italy, he purposed first to go into Spain, against the legions Pompey had there; and in the meantime to make provision for ships and marine preparation, to follow Pompey. In his absence, he left Lepidus, that was Praetor, governor of Rome; and Antonius that was Tribune, he gave him charge of all the soldiers and of Italy. Then was Antonius straight marvellously commended and beloved of the soldiers, because he commonly exercised himself among them, and would oftentimes eat and drink with them, and also be liberal unto them according to his ability. But then in contrary manner he purchased divers other men's evil wills, because that through negligence he would not do them justice that were injured, and dealt very churlishly with them that had any suit unto him; and, besides all this, he had an ill name to entice men's wives. To conclude, Caesar's friends that governed under him were cause why they hated Caesar's government (which indeed in respect of himself was no less than a tyranny) by reason of the great insolencies and outrageous parts that were committed; amongst whom

Antonius, that was of greatest power and that also committed greatest faults, deserved most blame.

But Caesar notwithstanding, when he returned from the wars of Spain, made no reckoning of the complaints that were put up against him. But contrarily, because he found him a hardy man and a valiant captain, he employed him in his chiefest affairs and was no whit deceived in his opinion of him. So he passed over the Ionian Sea unto Brundusium, being but slenderly accompanied; and sent unto Antonius and Gabinius, that they should embark their men as soon as they could and pass them over into Macedon. Gabinius was afraid to take the sea, because it was very rough and in the winter time; and therefore fetched a great compass about by land. But Antonius fearing some danger might come unto Caesar, because he was compassed in with a great number of enemies, first of all he drave away Libo, who rode at anchor with a great army before the haven of Brundusium. For he manned out such a number of pinnaces, barks, and other small boats about every one of his galleys, that he drave him thence. After that, he embarked into ships twenty thousand footmen and eight hundred horsemen, and with this army he hoised sail. When the enemies saw him, they made out to follow him. But the sea rose so high that the billows put back their galleys that they could not come near him; and so he scaped that danger. But withal he fell upon the rocks with his whole fleet, where the sea wrought very high; so that he was out of all hope to save himself. Yet, by good fortune, suddenly the wind turned south-west and blew from the gulf, driving the waves of the river into the main sea. Thus Antonius loofing from the land and sailing with safety at his pleasure, soon after he saw all the coasts full of shipwracks. For the force and boisterousness of the wind did cast away the galleys that followed him; of the which, many of them were broken and splitted, and divers also cast away, and Antonius took a great number of them prisoners, with a great sum of money also. Besides all these, he took the city of Lyssus, and brought Caesar a great supply of men, and made him courageous, coming at a pinch with so great a power to him.

Now there were divers hot skirmishes and encounters, in the which

Antonius fought so valiantly that he carried the praise from them all; but specially at two several times, when Caesar's men turned their backs and fled for life. For he stepped before them and compelled them to return again to fight; so that the victory fell on Caesar's side. For this cause he had the second place in the camp among the soldiers; and they spake of no other man unto Caesar but of him; who showed plainly what opinion he had of him, when at the last battle of Pharsalia (which indeed was the last trial of all, to give the conqueror the whole empire of the world) he himself did lead the right wing of his army and gave Antonius the leading of the left wing as the valiantest man and skilfullest soldier of all those he had about him.

After Caesar had won the victory, and that he was created Dictator, he followed Pompey step by step; howbeit before he named Antonius General of the Horsemen and sent him to Rome. The General of the Horsemen is the second office of dignity when the Dictator is in the city; but, when he is abroad, he is the chiefest man and almost the only man that remaineth; and all the other officers and magistrates are put down after there is a Dictator chosen.

Notwithstanding, Dolabella being at that time Tribune and a young man desirous of change and innovation, he preferred a law which the Romans call *Novas Tabulas* (as much to say as, a cutting off and cancelling of all obligations and specialities; and were called the 'new tables' because they were driven then to make books of daily receipt and expense); and persuaded Antonius his friend, who also gaped for a good occasion to please and gratify the common people, to aid him to pass this law. But Trebellius and Asinius dissuaded from it all they could possible. So by good hap it chanced that Antonius mistrusted Dolabella for keeping of his wife, and took such a conceit of it that he thrust his wife out of his house, being his cousin-german and the daughter of C. Antonius, who was Consul with Cicero; and, joining with Asinius, he resisted Dolabella and fought with him. Dolabella had gotten the market-place where the people do assemble in council, and had filled it full of armed men, intending to have this law of the New Tables to pass by force. Antonius by commandment of the Senate, who had given him authority to levy men, to use force against Dolabella, he went against him, and fought so valiantly, that men were slain on both sides.

But by this means he got the ill will of the common people; and, on the other side, the noblemen (as Cicero saith) did not only mislike him, but also hate him for his naughty life; for they did abhor his banquets and drunken feasts he made at unseasonable times, and his extreme wasteful expenses upon vain light huswives: and then in the day time he would sleep or walk out his drunkenness, thinking to wear away the fume of the abundance of wine which he had taken overnight. In his house they did nothing but feast, dance, and mask. And himself passed away the time in hearing of foolish plays, 3 or in marrying these players, tumblers, jesters, and such sort of people. As for proof hereof it is reported that at Hippias' marriage, one of his jesters, he drank wine so lustily all night that the next morning, when he came to plead before the people assembled in council, who had sent for him, he, being queasy-stomached with his surfeit he had taken, was compelled to lay all before them; and one of his friends held him his gown instead of a basin. He had another pleasant player called Sergius, that was one of the chiefest men about him; and a woman also called Cytheride, of the same profession, whom he loved dearly; he carried her up and down in a litter unto all the towns he went, and had as many men waiting upon her litter, she being but a player, as were attending upon his own mother. It grieved honest men also very much to see that, when he went into the country, he carried with him a great number of cupboards full of silver and gold plate, openly in the face of the world, as it had been the pomp or show of some triumph; and that eftsoons in the midst of his journey he would set up his halls and tents hard by some green grove or pleasant river, and there his cooks should prepare him a sumptuous dinner. And furthermore, lions were harnessed in traces

3 JULIUS CAESAR:  [*Cassius*] loves no plays,
As thou dost, Antony; he hears no music.
(*Julius Caesar*, I, 2, 203)

See! Antony, that revels long o'nights,
Is notwithstanding up. Good morrow, Antony.  (II, 2, 116)

to draw his carts; and besides also, in honest men's houses in the cities where he came he would have common harlots, courtesans, and these tumbling gillots lodged.

Now it grieved men much to see that Caesar should be out of Italy following of his enemies, to end this great war, with such great peril and danger; and that others in the meantime, abusing his name and authority, should commit such insolent and outrageous parts unto their citizens. This methinks was the cause that made the conspiracy against Caesar increase more and more and laid the reins of the bridle upon the soldiers' necks, whereby they durst boldlier commit many extortions, cruelties, and robberies. And therefore Caesar after his return pardoned Dolabella; and, being created Consul the third time, he took not Antonius, but chose Lepidus his colleague and fellow-Consul. Afterwards, when Pomp-
4 ey's house was put to open sale, Antonius bought it. But when they asked him money for it, he made it very strange and was offended with them; and writeth himself that he would not go with Caesar into the wars of Afric, because he was not well recompensed for the service he had done him before.

Yet Caesar did somewhat bridle his madness and insolency, not suffering him to pass his fault so lightly away, making as though he saw them not. And therefore he left his dissolute manner of life, and married Fulvia, that was Clodius' widow, a woman not so basely minded to spend her time in spinning and housewifery, and was not contented to master her husband at home, but would also rule
5 him in his office abroad, and command him that commanded

4 POMPEY:                At land, indeed,
Thou dost o'er-count me of my father's house:
But since the cuckoo builds not for himself,
Remain in't as thou mayst. (*Antony and Cleopatra*, II, 6, 26)
              O Antony,
You have my father's house, – But, what? we are friends.
                        (II, 7, 134)

See also p. 195 and p. 214 note 42.

5 ANTONY:                As for my wife,
I would you had her spirit in such another:

legions and great armies; so that Cleopatra was to give Fulvia thanks for that she had taught Antonius this obedience to women, that learned so well to be at their commandment.

Now, because Fulvia was somewhat sour and crooked of con-
5 dition, Antonius devised to make her pleasanter and somewhat better disposed; and therefore he would play her many pretty youthful parts to make her merry. As he did once, when Caesar returned the last time of all conqueror out of Spain. Every man went out to meet him, and so did Antonius with the rest. But on the sudden there ran a rumour through Italy that Caesar was dead and that his enemies came again with a great army. Thereupon he returned with speed to Rome, and took one of his men's gowns, and so apparelled came home to his house in a dark night, saying that he had brought Fulvia letters from Antonius. So he was let in, and brought to her muffled as he was for being known. But she, taking the matter heavily, asked him if Antonius were well. Antonius gave her the letters, and said never a word. So when she had opened the letters and began to read them, Antonius ramped of her neck and kissed her. We have told you this tale for example's sake only, and so could we also tell you of many suchlike as these.

Now when Caesar was returned from his last war in Spain, all the chiefest nobility of the city rode many days' journey from Rome to meet him, where Caesar made marvellous much of Antonius, above all the men that came unto him. For he always took him into

6 CLEOPATRA: Thou blushest, Antony; and that blood of thine
Is Caesar's homager: else so thy cheek pays shame
When shrill-tongued Fulvia scolds.     (I, 1, 30)

ANTONY:    Rail thou in Fulvia's phrase.     (I, 2, 111)

See also p. 208 note 34.

----

The third o' the world is yours; which with a snaffle
You may pace easy, but not such a wife . . .
So much uncurbable, her garboils, Caesar,
Made out of her impatience, which not wanted
Shrewdness of policy too.     (II, 2, 61; 67)
There's a great spirit gone!     (I, 2, 126)

his coach with him, throughout all Italy; and behind him, Brutus Albinus and Octavius, the son of his niece, who afterwards was called Caesar and became Emperor of Rome long time after.

So, Caesar being afterwards chosen Consul the fifth time, he immediately chose Antonius his colleague and companion; and desired, by deposing himself of his Consulship, to make Dolabella Consul in his room, and had already moved it to the Senate. But Antonius did stoutly withstand it and openly reviled Dolabella in the Senate; and Dolabella also spared him as little. Thereupon Caesar being ashamed of the matter, he let it alone. Another time also, when Caesar attempted again to substitute Dolabella Consul in his place, Antonius cried out that the signs of the birds were against it; so that at length Caesar was compelled to give him place and to let Dolabella alone, who was marvellously offended with him. Now in truth Caesar made no great reckoning of either of them both. For it is reported that Caesar answered one that did accuse Antonius and Dolabella unto him for some matter of conspiracy:

'Tush,' said he, 'they be not those fat fellows and fine combed men that I fear; but I mistrust rather these pale and lean men,'

– meaning by Brutus and Cassius, who afterwards conspired his
7 death and slew him.

Antonius unwares afterwards gave Caesar's enemies just occasion and colour to do as they did; as you shall hear. The Romans by chance celebrated the feast called *Lupercalia*, and Caesar, being apparelled in his triumphing robe, was set in the Tribune where they use to make their orations to the people, and from thence did behold the sport of the runners. The manner of this running was this. On that day there are many young men of noble house, and those specially that be chief officers for that year, who, running naked up and down the city anointed with the oil of olive, for pleasure do strike them they meet in their way with white leather thongs they have
8 in their hands. Antonius being one among the rest that was to run, leaving the ancient ceremonies and old customs of that solemnity, he ran to the tribune where Caesar was set, and carried a laurel

7 See *Life of Caesar*, p. 85 note 19, and *Life of Brutus*, p. 109.
8 See *Life of Caesar*, p. 82 note 12.

crown in his hand, having a royal band or diadem wreathed about it, which in old time was the ancient mark and token of a king. When he was come to Caesar, he made his fellow-runners with him lift him up, and so he did put this laurel crown upon his head, signifying thereby that he deserved to be king. But Caesar, making as though. he refused it, turned away his head. The people were so rejoiced at it that they all clapped their hands for joy. Antonius again did put it on his head. Caesar again refused it; and thus they were striving off and on a great while together. As oft as Antonius did put this laurel crown unto him, a few of his followers rejoiced at it; and as oft also as Caesar refused it, all the people together clapped their hands. And this was a wonderful thing, that they suffered all things subjects should do by commandment of their kings, and yet they could not abide the name of a king, detesting it as the utter destruction
9 of their liberty. Caesar in a rage rose out of his seat and, plucking down the collar of his gown from his neck, he showed it naked,
10 bidding any man strike off his head that would.

This laurel crown was afterwards put upon the head of one of Caesar's statues or images, the which one of the Tribunes plucked off. The people liked his doing therein so well that they waited on him home to his house with great clapping of hands. Howbeit Caesar did
11 turn them out of their offices for it.

This was a good encouragement for Brutus and Cassius to conspire his death, who fell into a consort with their trustiest friends to execute their enterprise, but yet stood doubtful whether they should make Antonius privy to it or not. All the rest liked of it, saving Trebonius only. He told them that, when they rode to meet Caesar at his return out of Spain, Antonius and he always keeping company and lying together by the way, he felt his mind afar off; but Antonius, finding his meaning, would hearken no more unto it; and yet notwithstanding never made Caesar acquainted with this talk, but had faithfully kept it to himself. After that they consulted whether they should kill Antonius with Caesar. But Brutus would in no wise

9 See *Life of Caesar*, p. 83 note 13.
10 See *Life of Caesar*, pp. 81–2 note 11.
11 See *Life of Caesar*, p. 84 note 16.

consent to it, saying that venturing on such an enterprise as that,
12 for the maintenance of law and justice, it ought to be clear from
all villainy. Yet they, fearing Antonius' power and the authority
of his office, appointed certain of the conspiracy, that, when Caesar
were gone into the Senate, and while others should execute their
enterprise, they should keep Antonius in a talk out of the Senate-
13 house.

Even as they had devised these matters, so were they executed; and
Caesar was slain in the midst of the Senate. Antonius, being put in
a fear withal, cast a slave's gown upon him and hid himself. But
afterwards, when it was told him that the murderers slew no man else
and that they went only into the Capitol, he sent his son unto them
for a pledge and bade them boldly come down upon his word. The
selfsame day he did bid Cassius to supper, and Lepidus also bade
Brutus. The next morning the Senate was assembled; and Antonius
himself preferred a law that all things past should be forgotten, and
that they should appoint provinces unto Cassius and Brutus; the
which the Senate confirmed; and further ordained that they should
cancel none of Caesar's laws. Thus went Antonius out of the Senate
more praised and better esteemed than ever man was, because it
seemed to every man that he had cut off all occasion of civil wars,
and that he had showed himself a marvellous wise governor of the
commonwealth, for the appeasing of these matters of so great weight
and importance.

But now the opinion he conceived of himself after he had a little
felt the good will of the people towards him, hoping thereby to
make himself the chiefest man if he might overcome Brutus, did easily
make him alter his first mind. And therefore when Caesar's body
was brought to the place where it should be buried, he made a
funeral oration in commendation of Caesar, according to the ancient
custom of praising noblemen at their funerals. When he saw that
the people were very glad and desirous also to hear Caesar spoken of
and his praises uttered, he mingled his oration with lamentable words,
and by amplifying of matters did greatly move their hearts and affec-

12 See *Life of Brutus*, p. 125 note 36.
13 See *Life of Caesar*, p. 92, and *Life of Brutus*, p. 123 note 32.

tions unto pity and compassion. In fine, to conclude his oration, he unfolded before the whole assembly the bloody garments of the dead, thrust through in many places with their swords, and called 14 the malefactors cruel and cursed murderers. With these words he put the people into such a fury that they presently took Caesar's body and burnt it in the market-place with such tables and forms as they could get together. Then, when the fire was kindled, they took firebrands, and ran to the murderers' houses to set them a-fire 15 and to make them come out to fight. Brutus therefore and his

14 ANTONY:     If you have tears, prepare to shed them now.
              You all do know this mantle: I remember
              The first time ever Caesar put it on;
              'Twas on a summer's evening, in his tent,
              That day he overcame the Nervii:
              Look, in this place ran Cassius' dagger through:
              See what a rent the envious Casca made:
              Through this the well-beloved Brutus stabb'd;
              And as he pluck'd his cursed steel away,
              Mark how the blood of Caesar follow'd it,
              As rushing out of doors, to be resolved
              If Brutus so unkindly knock'd, or no:
              For Brutus, as you know, was Caesar's angel:
              Judge, O you gods, how dearly Caesar loved him!
              This was the most unkindest cut of all;
              For when the noble Caesar saw him stab,
              Ingratitude, more strong than traitors' arms,
              Quite vanquish'd him: then burst his mighty heart;
              And, in his mantle muffling up his face,
              Even at the base of Pompey's statue,
              Which all the while ran blood, great Caesar fell ...
              O, now you weep; and, I perceive, you feel
              The dint of pity: these are gracious drops.
              Kind souls, what, weep you when you but behold
              Our Caesar's vesture wounded? Look you here,
              Here is himself, marr'd, as you see, with traitors.

PLEBEIAN:     O piteous spectacle!          (*Julius Caesar*, III, 2, 173)
See also *Life of Brutus*, p. 129.
15 See *Life of Caesar*, p. 98 note 51, and *Life of Brutus*, p. 129.

16 accomplices, for safety of their persons, were driven to fly the city.

Then came all Caesar's friends unto Antonius; and specially his wife Calpurnia putting her trust in him, she brought the most part of her money into his house, which amounted to the sum of four thousand talents; and furthermore brought him all Caesar's books and writings, in the which were his memorials of all that he had done and ordained. Antonius did daily mingle with them such as he thought good, and by that means he created new officers, made new Senators, called home some that were banished, and delivered those that were prisoners; and then he said that all those things were so appointed and ordained by Caesar. Therefore the Romans mocking them that were so moved, they called them *Charonites*; because that, when they were overcome, they had no other help but to say that thus they were found in Caesar's memorials, who had sailed in Charon's boat and was departed. Thus Antonius ruled absolutely also in all other matters, because he was Consul; and Caius, one of his brethren, Praetor; and Lucius, the other, Tribune.

Now things remaining in this state at Rome, Octavius Caesar the younger came to Rome, who was the son of Julius Caesar's niece, as you have heard before, and was left his lawful heir by will, remaining, at the time of the death of his great uncle that was slain, in the city of Apollonia. This young man at his first arrival went to salute Antonius, as one of his late dead father Caesar's friends, who by his last will and testament had made him his heir. And withal, he was presently in hand with him for money and other things which were left of trust in his hands, because Caesar had by will bequeathed unto the people of Rome three-score and fifteen silver drachmas to be given to every man, the which he as heir stood

17 charged withal.

Antonius at the first made no reckoning of him, because he was very young; and said he lacked wit and good friends to advise him, if he looked to take such a charge in hand as to undertake to be Caesar's heir. But when Antonius saw that he could not shake him off with those words, and that he was still in hand with him for his father's

16 See *Life of Brutus*, p. 130 note 49, and *Life of Caesar*, p. 98.
17 See *Life of Brutus*, p. 128 note 44, and *Life of Caesar*, p. 97.

goods, but specially for the ready money, then he spake and did what he could against him. And first of all it was he that did keep him from being Tribune of the People; and also, when Octavius Caesar began to meddle with the dedicating of the chair of gold which was prepared by the Senate to honour Caesar with, he threatened to send him to prison, and moreover desisted not to put the people in an uproar. This young Caesar, seeing his doings, went unto Cicero and others, which were Antonius' enemies, and by them crept into favour with the Senate; and he himself sought the people's good will every manner of way, gathering together the old soldiers of the late deceased Caesar, which were dispersed in divers cities and colonies. Antonius being afraid of it talked with Octavius in the Capitol and became his friend.

But the very same night Antonius had a strange dream, who thought that lightning fell upon him and burnt his right hand. Shortly after word was brought him that Caesar lay in wait to kill him. Caesar cleared himself unto him and told him there was no such matter. But he could not make Antonius believe the contrary. Whereupon they became further enemies than ever they were; insomuch that both of them made friends of either side to gather together all the old soldiers through Italy, that were dispersed in divers towns, and made them large promises, and sought also to win the legions on their side, which were already in arms.

Cicero on the other side being at that time the chiefest man of authority and estimation in the city, he stirred up all men against Antonius; so that in the end he made the Senate pronounce him an enemy to his country, and appointed young Caesar's sergeants to carry axes before him and such other signs as were incident to the dignity of a Consul or Praetor; and moreover sent Hircius and Pansa, then Consuls, to drive Antonius out of Italy. These two Consuls together with Caesar, who also had an army, went against Antonius that besieged the city of Modena, and there overthrew him in
18 battle. But both the Consuls were slain there.

18 OCTAVIUS CAESAR:  Antony,
Leave thy lascivious wassails. When thou once
Wast beaten from Modena, where thou slew'st
Hirtius and Pansa, consuls . . . (*Antony and Cleopatra*, 1, 4, 55)

Antonius, flying upon this overthrow, fell into great misery all at once; but the chiefest want of all other, and that pinched him most, was famine. Howbeit he was of such a strong nature that by patience he would overcome any adversity; and the heavier fortune lay upon him, the more constant showed he himself. Every man that feeleth want or adversity knoweth by virtue and discretion what he should do. But when indeed they are overlaid with extremity and be sore oppressed, few have the hearts to follow that which they praise and commend, and much less to avoid that they reprove and mislike. But rather, to the contrary, they yield to their accustomed easy life, and through faint heart and lack of courage do change their first mind and purpose. And therefore it was a wonderful example to the soldiers to see Antonius, that was brought up in all fineness and superfluity, so easily to drink puddle water and to eat wild fruits and roots. And moreover it is reported that, even as they passed the Alps, they did eat the barks of trees and such beasts as never man tasted of their 19 flesh before.

Now their intent was to join with the legions that was on the other side of the mountains under Lepidus' charge; whom Antonius took to be his friend, because he had holpen him to many things at Caesar's hand through his means. When he was come to the place where Lepidus was, he camped hard by him; and when he saw that no man came to him to put him in any hope, he determined to

*19* OCTAVIUS CAESAR:                    ... at thy heel
>                     Did famine follow; whom thou fought'st against,
>                     Though daintily brought up, with patience more
>                     Than savages could suffer: thou didst drink
>                     The stale of horses, and the gilded puddle
>                     Which beasts would cough at: thy palate then did deign
>                     The roughest berry on the rudest hedge;
>                     Yea, like the stag, when snow the pasture sheets,
>                     The barks of trees thou browsed'st; on the Alps
>                     It is reported thou didst eat strange flesh,
>                     Which some did die to look on: and all this –
>                     It wounds thine honour that I speak it now –
>                     Was borne so like a soldier, that thy cheek
>                     So much as lank'd not.                    (I, 4, 58)

venture himself and to go unto Lepidus. Since the overthrow he had at Modena, he suffered his beard to grow at length and never clipped it, that it was marvellous long, and the hair of his head also without combing; and, besides all this, he went in a mourning gown; and after this sort came hard to the trenches of Lepidus' camp. Then he began to speak unto the soldiers; and many of them their hearts yearned for pity to see him so poorly arrayed, and some also through his words began to pity him; insomuch that Lepidus began to be afraid, and therefore commanded all the trumpets to sound together to stop the soldiers' ears, that they should not hearken to Antonius. This notwithstanding, the soldiers took the more pity of him, and spake secretly with him by Clodius' and Laelius' means, whom they sent unto him disguised in women's apparel; and gave him counsel that he should not be afraid to enter into their camp, for there were a great number of soldiers that would receive him and kill Lepidus, if he would say the word. Antonius would not suffer them to hurt him. But the next morning he went with his army to wade a ford, at a little river that ran between them; and himself was the foremost man that took the river to get over, seeing a number of Lepidus' camp that gave him their hands, plucked up the stakes, and laid flat the bank of their trench to let him into their camp. When he was come into their camp, and that he had all the army at his commandment, he used Lepidus very courteously, embraced him, and called him father; and though indeed Antonius did all and ruled the whole army, yet he alway gave Lepidus the name and honour of the captain. Munatius Plancus, lying also in camp hard by with an army, understanding the report of Antonius' courtesy, he also came and joined with him.

Thus Antonius being afoot again and grown of great power, repassed over the Alps, leading into Italy with him seventeen legions and ten thousand horsemen, besides six legions he left in garrison among the Gauls under the charge of one Varius, a companion of his that would drink lustily with him and therefore in mockery was surnamed *Cotylon*: to wit, 'a bibber'.

So Octavius Caesar would not lean to Cicero, when he saw that his whole travail and endeavour was only to restore the commonwealth to her former liberty. Therefore he sent certain of his friends

to Antonius, to make them friends again. And thereupon all three met together (to wit, Caesar, Antonius, and Lepidus) in an island environed round about with a little river; and there remained three days together. Now, as touching all other matters, they were easily agreed and did divide all the Empire of Rome between them, as if it had been their own inheritance. But yet they could hardly agree whom they would put to death; for every one of them would kill their enemies, and save their kinsmen and friends. Yet at length, giving place to their greedy desire to be revenged of their enemies, they spurned all reverence of blood and holiness of friendship at their feet. For Caesar left Cicero to Antonius' will; Antonius also forsook Lucius Caesar, who was his uncle by his mother; and both of them together suffered Lepidus to kill his own brother Paulus. Yet some writers affirm that Caesar and Antonius requested Paulus
20 might be slain, and that Lepidus was contented with it.

In my opinion there was never a more horrible, unnatural, and crueller change than this was. For, thus changing murder for murder, they did as well kill those whom they did forsake and leave unto others, as those also which others left unto them to kill; but so much more was their wickedness and cruelty great unto their friends, for that they put them to death being innocents and having no cause to hate them.

After this plot was agreed upon between them, the soldiers that were thereabouts would have this friendship and league betwixt them confirmed by marriage, and that Caesar should marry Claudia, the daughter of Fulvia, Antonius' wife. This marriage also being agreed upon, they condemned three hundred of the chiefest citizens
21 of Rome to be put to death by proscription. And Antonius also

20 ANTONY:      These many, then, shall die; their names are prick'd.
OCTAVIUS CAESAR: Your brother too must die; consent you, Lepidus?
LEPIDUS:      I do consent, –
OCTAVIUS CAESAR:      Prick him down, Antony.
LEPIDUS:      Upon condition Publius shall not live,
      Who is your sister's son, Mark Antony.
ANTONY:      He shall not live; look, with a spot I damn him.
                    (*Julius Caesar*, IV, I, I)

21 See *Life of Brutus*, p. 137 note 52.

commanded them to whom he had given commission to kill Cicero, that they should strike off his head and right hand, with the which he had written the invective orations, called *Philippides*, against Antonius. So, when the murderers brought him Cicero's head and hand cut off, he beheld them a long time with great joy and laughed heartily, and that oftentimes, for the great joy he felt. Then, when he had taken his pleasure of the sight of them, he caused them to be set up in an open place, over the pulpit for orations (where when he was alive he had often spoken to the people), as if he had done the dead man hurt and not blemished his own fortune, showing himself (to his great shame and infamy) a cruel man and unworthy the office and authority he bare. His uncle Lucius Caesar also, as they sought for him to kill him and followed him hard, fled unto his sister. The murderers coming thither, forcing to break into her chamber, she stood at her chamber door with her arms abroad, crying out still: 'You shall not kill Lucius Caesar, before you first kill me that bare your captain in my womb.'
By this means she saved her brother's life.

Now the government of these Triumviri grew odious and hateful to the Romans, for divers respects. But they most blamed Antonius, because he, being elder than Caesar and of more power and force than Lepidus, gave himself again to his former riot and excess when he left to deal in the affairs of the commonwealth. But, setting aside the ill name he had for his insolency, he was yet much more hated in respect of the house he dwelt in, the which was the house of Pompey the Great, a man as famous for his temperance, modesty, and civil life, as for his three Triumphs. For it grieved them to see the gates commonly shut against the captains, magistrates of the city, and also ambassadors of strange nations, which were sometimes thrust from the gate with violence; and that the house within was full of tumblers, antic dancers, jugglers, players, jesters, and drunkards, quaffing and guzzling, and that on them he spent and bestowed the most part of his money he got by all kind of possible extortions, bribery, and policy. For they did not only sell by the crier the goods of those whom they had outlawed and appointed to murder, slanderously deceived

22 See above, p. 184 note 4.

the poor widows and young orphans, and also raised all kind of imposts, subsidies, and taxes; but, understanding also that the holy Vestal nuns had certain goods and money put in their custody to keep, both of men's in the city and those also that were abroad, they went thither and took them away by force.

Octavius Caesar perceiving that no money would serve Antonius' turn, he prayed that they might divide the money between them; and so did they also divide the army, for them both to go into Macedon to make war against Brutus and Cassius; and in the meantime they left the government of the city of Rome unto Lepidus. When they had passed over the seas, and that they began to make war, they being both camped by their enemies, to wit, Antonius against Cassius, and Caesar against Brutus, Caesar did no great matter, but Antonius had alway the upper hand and did all. For at the first battle Caesar was overthrown by Brutus and lost his camp, and very hardly saved himself by flying from them that followed him. Howbeit he writeth himself in his *Commentaries* that he fled before the charge was given, because of a dream one of his friends had. Antonius on the other side overthrew Cassius in battle, though some write that he was not there himself at the battle, but that he came after the overthrow whilst his men had the enemies in chase. So Cassius at his earnest request was slain by a faithful servant of his own called Pindarus, whom he had enfranchised, because he knew not in time that Brutus had overcome Caesar. Shortly after they fought another battle again, in the which Brutus was overthrown, who afterwards also slew himself.

Thus Antonius had the chiefest glory of all this victory, specially because Caesar was sick at that time. Antonius having found Brutus' body after this battle, blaming him much for the murder of his brother Caius, whom he had put to death in Macedon for revenge of Cicero's cruel death, and yet laying the fault more in Hortensius than in him, he made Hortensius to be slain on his brother's tomb. Furthermore, he cast his coat armour (which was wonderful rich and sumptuous) upon Brutus' body and gave commandment to one of his slaves enfranchised to defray the charge of his burial. But afterwards, Antonius hearing that his enfranchised bondman had not burnt his coat armour with his body, because it was very rich and worth a great sum of money, and that he had also kept back much of the ready money appointed for his funeral and tomb, he also put him to death.

After that Caesar was conveyed to Rome; and it was thought he would not live long, nor escape the sickness he had. Antonius on the other side went towards the east provinces and regions, to levy money; and first of all he went into Greece, and carried an infinite number of soldiers with him. Now because every soldier was promised five thousand silver drachmas, he was driven of necessity to impose extreme tallages and taxations. At his first coming into Greece he was not hard nor bitter unto the Grecians, but gave himself only to hear wise men dispute, to see plays, and also to note the ceremonies and sacrifices of Greece, ministering justice to every man; and it pleased him marvellously to hear them call him *Philhellene* (as much to say, 'a lover of the Grecians'), and specially the Athenians, to whom he did many great pleasures. Wherefore the Megarians, to exceed the Athenians, thinking to show Antonius a goodly sight, they prayed him to come and see their Senate-house and Council-hall. Antonius went thither to see it. So when he had seen it at his pleasure, they asked him:

'My lord, how like you our hall?'

'Methinks,' quoth he, 'it is little, old, and ready to fall down.' Furthermore he took measure of the Temple of Apollo Pythias, and promised the Senate to finish it.

But when he was once come into Asia (having left Lucius Censorinus governor in Greece), and that he had felt the riches and pleasures of the east parts, and that princes, great lords, and kings came to wait at his gate for his coming out, and that queens and princesses to excel one another gave him very rich presents and came to see him, curiously setting forth themselves and using all art that might be to show their beauty, to win his favour the more – Caesar in the mean space turmoiling his wits and body in civil wars at home – Antonius living merrily and quietly abroad, he easily fell again to his old licentious life. For straight one Anaxenor a player of the cithern, Xoutus a player of the flutes, Metrodorus a tumbler, and such a rabble of minstrels and fit ministers for the pleasures of Asia (who in fineness and flattery passed all the other plagues he brought with him out of Italy), all these flocked in his court and bare the whole sway; and, after that, all went awry. For every one gave themselves to riot and excess, when they saw he delighted in it; and all Asia was like to the city Sophocles speaketh of in one of his tragedies:

> *Was full of sweet perfumes and pleasant songs,*
> *With woeful weeping mingled there amongs.*

For, in the city of Ephesus, women attired as they go in the feasts and sacrifice of Bacchus came out to meet him with such solemnities and ceremonies as are then used, with men and children disguised like fauns and satyrs. Moreover, the city was full of ivy, and darts wreathed about with ivy, psalterions, flutes, and howboys; and in their songs they called him Bacchus, father of mirth, courteous, and gentle; and so was he unto some, but, to the most part of men, cruel and extreme. For he robbed noblemen and gentlemen of their goods, to give it unto vile flatterers, who oftentimes begged men's goods living, as though they had been dead, and would enter their houses by force; as, he gave a citizen's house of Magnesia unto a cook, because, as it is reported, he dressed him a fine supper.

In the end he doubled the taxation and imposed a second upon Asia. But then Hybraeas the orator, sent from the estates of Asia to tell him the state of their country, boldly said unto him:

'If thou wilt have power to lay two tributes in one year upon us, thou shouldst also have power to give us two summers, two autumns, and two harvests.'

This was gallantly and pleasantly spoken unto Antonius by the orator, and it pleased him well to hear it. But afterwards, amplifying his speech, he spake more boldly and to better purpose:

'Asia hath paid the two hundred thousand talents. If all this money be not come to thy coffers, then ask account of them that levied it. But, if thou have received it and nothing be left of it, then are we utterly undone.'

Hybraeas' words nettled Antonius roundly. For he understood not many of the thefts and robberies his officers committed by his authority in his treasure and affairs; not so much because he was careless, as for that he over-simply trusted his men in all things.

For he was a plain man, without subtilty, and therefore over-late found out the foul faults they committed against him. But when he heard of them he was much offended, and would plainly confess it unto them whom his officers had done injury unto by countenance of his authority. He had a noble mind, as well to punish offenders, as to reward well-doers; and yet he did exceed more in giving, than in punishing. Now for his outrageous manner of railing he commonly used, mocking and flouting of every man, that was remedied by itself. For a man might as boldly exchange a mock with him, and he was as well contented to be mocked as to mock others. But yet it oftentimes marred all. For he thought that those which told him so plainly and truly in mirth would never flatter him in good earnest in any matter of weight. But thus he was easily abused by the praises they gave him, not finding how these flatterers mingled their flattery, under this familiar and plain manner of speech unto him, as a fine device to make difference of meats with sharp and tart sauce, and also to keep him, by this frank jesting and bourding with him at the table, that their common flattery should not be troublesome unto him, as men do easily mislike to have too much of one thing; and that they handled him finely thereby, when they would give him place in any matter of weight and follow his counsel, that it might not appear to him they did it so much to please him, but because they were ignorant and understood not so much as he did.

Antonius being thus inclined, the last and extremest mischief of all other (to wit, the love of Cleopatra) lighted on him, who did waken and stir up many vices yet hidden in him, and were never seen to any; and, if any spark of goodness or hope of rising were left him, Cleopatra quenched it straight and made it worse than before.

The manner how he fell in love with her was this. Antonius, going to make war with the Parthians, sent to command Cleopatra to appear personally before him when he came into Cilicia, to answer unto such accusations as were laid against her, being this: that she had aided Cassius and Brutus in their war against him. The messenger sent unto Cleopatra to make this summons unto her was called Dellius; who when he had throughly considered her beauty, the excellent grace and sweetness of her tongue, he nothing mistrusted that Antonius would do any hurt to so noble a lady, but rather assured himself that within few days she should be in great favour with him. Thereupon he did her great honour and persuaded her to come into Cilicia as honourably furnished as she could possible, and bade her not to be afraid at all of Antonius, for he was a more courteous lord than any that she had ever seen.

Cleopatra, on the other side, believing Dellius' words and guessing by the former access and credit she had with Julius Caesar and Cneius Pompey, the son of Pompey the Great, only for her beauty, she began to have good hope that she might more easily win Antonius. For Caesar and Pompey knew her when she was but a young thing, and knew not then what the world meant. But now she went to Antonius at the age when a woman's beauty is at the prime, and she also of best
23 judgement. So she furnished herself with a world of gifts, store of gold and silver, and of riches and other sumptuous ornaments, as is credible enough she might bring from so great a house and from so wealthy and rich a realm as Egypt was. But yet she carried nothing with her wherein she trusted more than in herself and in the charms and enchantment of her passing beauty and grace.

Therefore when she was sent unto by divers letters, both from

---

23 CLEOPATRA:  Broad-fronted Caesar,
When thou wast here above the ground, I was
A morsel for a monarch; and great Pompey
Would stand and make his eyes grow in my brow.
                              (*Antony and Cleopatra*, I, 5, 29)
                    My salad days,
When I was green in judgement, cold in blood.   (I, 5, 73)
ANTONY:  I found you as a morsel cold upon
Dead Caesar's trencher; nay, you were a fragment
Of Cneius Pompey's: besides what hotter hours,
Unregister'd in vulgar fame, you have
Luxuriously pick'd out.                         (III, 13, 116)

Antonius himself and also from his friends, she made so light of it
and mocked Antonius so much that she disdained to set forward
otherwise but to take her barge in the river of Cydnus, the poop
whereof was of gold, the sails of purple, and the oars of silver, which
kept stroke in rowing after the sound of the music of flutes, howboys,
citherns, viols, and such other instruments as they played upon in
the barge. And now for the person of herself: she was laid under a
pavilion of cloth of gold of tissue, apparelled and attired like the
goddess Venus commonly drawn in picture; and hard by her, on
either hand of her, pretty fair boys apparelled as painters do set forth
god Cupid, with little fans in their hands, with the which they fanned
wind upon her. Her ladies and gentlewomen also, the fairest of them
were apparelled like the nymphs Nereides (which are the mermaids
of the waters) and like the Graces, some steering the helm, others
tending the tackle and ropes of the barge, out of the which there
came a wonderful passing sweet savour of perfumes, that perfumed
the wharf's side, pestered with innumerable multitudes of people.
Some of them followed the barge all alongst the river's side; others
also ran out of the city to see her coming in; so that in the end there
ran such multitudes of people one after another to see her that Antonius was left post-alone in the market-place in his imperial seat
to give audience. And there went a rumour in the people's mouths

ENOBARBUS:    The barge she sat in, like a burnish'd throne,
               Burn'd on the water: the poop was beaten gold;
               Purple the sails, and so perfumed that
               The winds were love-sick with them; the oars were silver,
               Which to the tune of flutes kept stroke, and made
               The water which they beat to follow faster,
               As amorous of their strokes. For her own person,
               It beggar'd all description: she did lie
               In her pavilion – cloth-of-gold of tissue –
               O'er picturing that Venus where we see
               The fancy outwork nature: on each side her
               Stood pretty dimpled boys, like smiling Cupids,
               With divers colour'd fans, whose wind did seem
               To glow the delicate cheeks which they did cool,
               And what they undid did.

that the goddess Venus was come to play with the god Bacchus, for the general good of all Asia.

When Cleopatra landed, Antonius sent to invite her to supper to him. But she sent him word again, he should do better rather to come and sup with her. Antonius therefore, to show himself courteous unto her at her arrival, was contented to obey her, and went to 25 supper to her; where he found such passing sumptuous fare, that no tongue can express it. But, amongst all other things, he most wondered at the infinite number of lights and torches hanged on the top of the house, giving light in every place, so artificially set and ordered by devices, some round, some square, that it was the rarest thing to behold that eye could discern or that ever books could mention. The next night, Antonius feasting her contended to pass her in magnificence and fineness; but she overcame him in both.

25 ENOBARBUS:   Upon her landing, Antony sent to her,
              Invited her to supper: she replied,
              It should be better he became her guest;
              Which she entreated: our courteous Antony,
              Whom ne'er the word of 'No' woman heard speak,
              Being barber'd ten times o'er, goes to the feast,
              And for his ordinary pays his heart
              For what his eyes eat only.         (II, 2, 224)

AGRIPPA:                        O rare for Antony!
ENOBARBUS:   Her gentlewomen, like the Nereides,
              So many mermaids, tended her i' the eyes,
              And made their bends adornings: at the helm
              A seeming mermaid steers: the silken tackle
              Swell with the touches of those flower-soft hands,
              That yarely frame the office. From the barge
              A strange invisible perfume hits the sense
              Of the adjacent wharfs. The city cast
              Her people out upon her; and Antony,
              Enthroned i' the market-place, did sit alone,
              Whistling to the air; which, but for vacancy,
              Had gone to gaze on Cleopatra too
              And made a gap in nature.

                                             (II, 2, 196)

So that he himself began to scorn the gross service of his house, in respect of Cleopatra's sumptuousness and fineness. And, when Cleopatra found Antonius' jests and slents to be but gross and soldierlike in plain manner, she gave it him finely and without fear taunted him throughly.

Now her beauty, as it is reported, was not so passing as unmatchable of other women, nor yet such as upon present view did enamour men with her; but so sweet was her company and conversation that a man could not possibly but be taken. And, besides her beauty, the good grace she had to talk and discourse, her courteous nature that tempered her words and deeds, was a spur that pricked to the quick. Furthermore, besides all these, her voice and words were marvellous pleasant; for her tongue was an instrument of music to divers sports and pastimes, the which she easily turned to any language that pleased her. She spake unto few barbarous people by interpreter, but made them answer herself, or at the least the most part of them: as, the Ethiopians, the Arabians, the Troglodytes, the Hebrews, the Syrians, the Medes, and the Parthians, and to many others also, whose languages she had learned. Whereas divers of her progenitors, the Kings of Egypt, could scarce learn the Egyptian tongue only; and many of them forgot to speak the Macedonian.

Now Antonius was so ravished with the love of Cleopatra that though his wife Fulvia had great wars and much ado with Caesar for his affairs, and that the army of the Parthians (the which the king's lieutenants had given to the only leading of Labienus) was now assembled in Mesopotamia ready to invade Syria; yet, as though all this had nothing touched him, he yielded himself to go with Cleopatra into Alexandria, where he spent and lost in childish sports (as a man might say) and idle pastimes the most precious thing a man can 26 spend, as Antiphon saith: and that is, time.

26 OCTAVIUS CAESAR:     From Alexandria
This is the news: he fishes, drinks, and wastes
The lamps of night in revel; is not more manlike
Than Cleopatra; nor the queen of Ptolemy
More womanly than he; hardly gave audience, or
Vouchsafed to think he had partners.    (I, 4, 3)

For they made an order between them which they called *Amime-tobion* (as much to say, 'no life comparable and matchable with it'), one feasting each other by turns, and in cost exceeding all measure and reason. And, for proof hereof, I have heard my grandfather Lampryas report that one Philotas a physician, born in the city of Amphissa, told him that he was at that present time in Alexandria and studied physic; and that, having acquaintance with one of Antonius' cooks, he took him with him to Antonius' house (being a young man desirous to see things), to show him the wonderful sumptuous charge and preparation of one only supper. When he was in the kitchen and saw a world of diversities of meats and, amongst others, eight wild boars roasted whole, he began to wonder at it and said:

'Sure you have a great number of guests to supper.'

The cook fell a-laughing, and answered him:

'No,' quoth he, 'not many guests, nor above twelve in all; but yet all that is boiled or roasted must be served in whole, or else it would 27 be marred straight. For Antonius peradventure will sup presently; or it may be a pretty while hence; or likely enough he will defer it longer, for that he hath drunk well today or else hath had some other great matters in hand; and therefore we do not dress one supper only, but many suppers, because we are uncertain of the hour he will sup in.'

Philotas the physician told my grandfather this tale, and said moreover that it was his chance shortly after to serve the eldest son of the said Antonius, whom he had by his wife Fulvia; and that he sat commonly at his table with his other friends, when he did not dine nor sup with his father. It chanced one day there came a physician that was so full of words that he made every man weary of him at the board. But Philotas, to stop his mouth, put out a subtle proposition to him:

27 MAECENAS:     Eight wild-boars roasted whole at a breakfast, and but twelve persons there; is this true?

ENOBARBUS:     This was but as a fly by an eagle; we had much more monstrous matter of feast, which worthily deserved noting.

(II, 2, 183)

'It is good in some sort to let a man drink cold water that hath an ague: every man that hath an ague hath it in some sort: *ergo*, it is good for a man that hath an ague to drink cold water.'

The physician was so gravelled and a-mated withal that he had not a word more to say. Young Antonius burst out in such a laughing at him and was so glad of it that he said unto him:

'Philotas, take all that; I give it thee'

– showing him his cupboard full of plate, with great pots of gold and silver. Philotas thanked him and told him he thought himself greatly bound to him for this liberality; but he would never have thought that he had had power to have given so many things and of so great value. But much more he marvelled when, shortly after, one of young Antonius' men brought him home all the pots in a basket, bidding him set his mark and stamp upon them and to lock them up. Philotas returned the bringer of them, fearing to be reproved if he took them. Then the young gentleman Antonius said unto him:

'Alas, poor man, why dost thou make it nice to take them? Knowest thou not that it is the son of Antonius that gives them thee, and is able to do it? If thou wilt not believe me, take rather the ready money they come to; because my father peradventure may ask for some of the plate, for the antique and excellent workmanship of them.'

This I have heard my grandfather tell oftentimes.

But now again to Cleopatra. Plato writeth that there are four kinds of flattery; but Cleopatra divided it into many kinds. For she, were it in sport or in matters of earnest, still devised sundry new delights to have Antonius at commandment, never leaving him night nor day, nor once letting him go out of her sight. For she would play at dice with him, drink with him, and hunt commonly with him, and also be with him when he went to any exercise or activity of body. And sometime also when he would go up and down the city disguised like a slave in the night, and would peer into poor men's windows and their shops, and scold and brawl with them within the house, Cleopatra would be also in a chambermaid's array, and amble up and down the streets with him, so that

28 oftentimes Antonius bare away both mocks and blows. Now, though most men misliked this manner, yet the Alexandrians were commonly glad of this jollity and liked it well, saying very gallantly and wisely that Antonius showed them a comical face, to wit, a 29 merry countenance; and the Romans a tragical face, to say, a grim look.

But to reckon up all the foolish sports they made, revelling in this sort, it were too fond a part of me; and therefore I will only tell you one among the rest. On a time he went to angle for fish; and when he could take none he was as angry as could be, because Cleopatra stood by. Wherefore he secretly commanded the fishermen that when he cast in his line they should straight dive under the water and put a fish on his hook which they had taken before; and so snatched up his angling rod and brought up fish twice or thrice. Cleopatra found it straight; yet she seemed not to see it, but wondered at his excellent fishing. But when she was alone by herself among her own people, she told them how it was and bade them the next morning to be on the water to see the fishing. A number of people came to the haven and got into the fisher-boats to see this fishing. Antonius then threw in his line; and Cleopatra straight commanded one of her men to dive under water before Antonius' men and to put some old salt fish upon his bait, like unto those that are brought out of the country of Pont. When he had hung the

28 ANTONY:                              All alone
　　　　　　　Tonight we'll wander through the streets and note
　　　　　　　The qualities of people. Come, my queen;
　　　　　　　Last night you did desire it.　　　　　　(I, 1, 52)
　OCTAVIUS CAESAR:　　　Let us grant, it is not
　　　　　　　Amiss to tumble on the bed of Ptolemy;
　　　　　　　To give a kingdom for a mirth; to sit
　　　　　　　And keep the turn of tippling with a slave;
　　　　　　　To reel the streets at noon, and stand the buffet
　　　　　　　With knaves that smell of sweat: say this becomes him.
　　　　　　　　　　　　　　　　　　　　　　(I, 4, 16)
29 CLEOPATRA:　He was disposed to mirth; but on the sudden
　　　　　　　A Roman thought hath struck him.　　　(I, 2, 86)

fish on his hook, Antonius, thinking he had taken a fish indeed,
snatched up his line presently. Then they all fell a-laughing. Cleopatra,
laughing also, said unto him:

'Leave us, my lord, Egyptians, which dwell in the country of Pharus
and Canobus, your angling rod. This is not thy profession. Thou
must hunt after conquering of realms and countries.'

Now Antonius delighting in these fond and childish pastimes,
very ill news were brought him from two places. The first from
Rome: that his brother Lucius and Fulvia his wife fell out first
between themselves, and afterwards fell to open war with Caesar,
and had brought all to nought, that they were both driven to fly out
of Italy. The second news, as bad as the first: that Labienus conquered
all Asia with the army of the Parthians, from the river of Euphrates

CLEOPATRA: Give me mine angle; we'll to the river: there,
My music playing far off, I will betray
Tawny-finn'd fishes; my bended hook shall pierce
Their slimy jaws; and, as I draw them up,
I'll think them every one an Antony,
And say 'Ah, ha! you're caught'.

CHARMIAN:                              'Twas merry when
You wager'd on your angling; when your diver
Did hang a salt-fish on his hook, which he
With fervency drew up.

CLEOPATRA:                    That time, – O times! –
I laugh'd him out of patience; and that night
I laugh'd him into patience: and next morn,
Ere the ninth hour, I drunk him to his bed.     (II, 5, 10)

See also p. 203 note 26.

MESSENGER: Fulvia thy wife first came into the field.

ANTONY: Against my brother Lucius?

MESSENGER: Ay:
But soon that war had end, and the time's state
Made friends of them, jointing their force 'gainst Caesar;
Whose better issue in the war, from Italy,
Upon the first encounter, drave them.     (I, 2, 92)

32 and from Syria unto the countries of Lydia and Ionia. Then began Antonius with much ado a little to rouse himself, as if he had been wakened out of a deep sleep and, as a man may say, coming out of a 33 great drunkenness.

So first of all he bent himself against the Parthians, and went as far as the country of Phoenicia. But there he received lamentable letters from his wife Fulvia. Whereupon he straight returned towards Italy with two hundred sail; and, as he went, took up his friends by the way that fled out of Italy to come to him. By them he was informed that his wife Fulvia was the only cause of this war; who, being of a peevish, crooked, and troublesome nature, had purposely raised this 34 uproar in Italy, in hope thereby to withdraw him from Cleopatra.

But by good fortune his wife Fulvia, going to meet with Antonius,

| | | |
|---|---|---|
| 32 MESSENGER: | Labienus – | |
| | This is stiff news – hath, with his Parthian force, | |
| | Extended Asia from Euphrates; | |
| | His conquering banner shook from Syria | |
| | To Lydia and to Ionia. | (I, 2, 103) |
| 33 ANTONY: | These strong Egyptian fetters I must break, | |
| | Or lose myself in dotage . . . | |
| | I must from this enchanting queen break off: | |
| | Ten thousand harms, more than the ills I know, | |
| | My idleness doth hatch. | (I, 2, 120; 132) |
| ANTONY: | O, then we bring forth weeds, | |
| | When our quick minds lie still; and our ills told us | |
| | Is as our earing. | (I, 2, 113) |
| POMPEY: | Tie up the libertine in a field of feasts, | |
| | Keep his brain fuming; Epicurean cooks | |
| | Sharpen with cloyless sauce his appetite; | |
| | That sleep and feeding may prorogue his honour | |
| | Even till a Lethe'd dulness! | (II, 1, 23) |
| 34 ANTONY: | Truth is, that Fulvia, | |
| | To have me out of Egypt, made wars here; | |
| | For which myself, the ignorant motive, do | |
| | So far ask pardon as befits mine honour | |
| | To stoop in such a case. | (II, 2, 94) |

See also pp. 184–5 notes 5 and 6.

sickened by the way, and died in the city of Sicyon. And therefore
Octavius Caesar and he were the easilier made friends together. For
when Antonius landed in Italy, and that men saw Caesar asked nothing of him, and that Antonius on the other side laid all the fault and
burden on his wife Fulvia, the friends of both parties would not suffer
them to unrip any old matters, and to prove or defend who had the
wrong or right, and who was the first procurer of this war, fearing
to make matters worse between them; but they made them friends
together, and divided the Empire of Rome between them, making
the sea Ionium the bounds of their division. For they gave all the
provinces eastward unto Antonius; and the countries westward,

ANTONY:　　　From Sicyon, ho, the news! Speak there!
1st ATTENDANT: The man from Sicyon, – is there such an one?
2nd ATTENDANT: He stays upon your will.
ANTONY:　　　　　　　　　　Let him appear. . . .
　　　　　　*Enter another Messenger with a letter.*
　　　　　　　　　　What are you?
MESSENGER:　Fulvia thy wife is dead.
ANTONY:　　　　　　　　　Where died she?
MESSENGER:　In Sicyon:
　　　　　　Her length of sickness, with what else more serious
　　　　　　Importeth thee to know, this bears.
　　　　　　　　　　　*Gives a letter.*　　　(I, 2, 117)

See note 34 above; and
ANTONY:　　　　　　　I grieving grant
　　　　　　Did you too much disquiet: for that you must
　　　　　　But say, I could not help it.　　　(II, 2, 69)
LEPIDUS:　　　　　　　'Tis not a time
　　　　　　For private stomaching. . . . Noble friends,
　　　　　　That which combined us was most great, and let not
　　　　　　A leaner action rend us. What's amiss,
　　　　　　May it be gently heard: when we debate
　　　　　　Our trivial difference loud, we do commit
　　　　　　Murder in healing wounds: then, noble partners,
　　　　　　The rather, for I earnestly beseech
　　　　　　Touch you the sourest points with sweetest terms,
　　　　　　Nor curstness grow to the matter . . .

unto Caesar; and left Afric unto Lepidus; and made a law that they three one after another should make their friends Consuls, when they would not be themselves.

This seemed to be a sound counsel, but yet it was to be confirmed with a straiter bond, which fortune offered thus. There was Octavia the eldest sister of Caesar – not by one mother, for she came of Ancharia, and Caesar himself afterwards of Accia. It is reported that he dearly loved his sister Octavia; for indeed she was a noble lady, and left the widow of her first husband Caius Marcellus, who died not long before; and it seemed also that Antonius had been widower ever since the death of his wife Fulvia. For he denied not that he kept Cleopatra; but so did he not confess that he had her as his wife; and so with reason he did defend the love he bare unto this Egyptian Cleopatra.

Thereupon every man did set forward this marriage, hoping thereby that this lady Octavia, having an excellent grace, wisdom, and honesty joined unto so rare a beauty, that when she were with Antonius (he loving her as so worthy a lady deserveth) she should be a good mean to keep good love and amity betwixt her brother and him. So, when Caesar and he had made the match between **38** them, they both went to Rome about this marriage, although it was

**38** OCTAVIUS CAESAR:　　　　'T cannot be
　　　　　　　　　　　We shall remain in friendship, our conditions
　　　　　　　　　　　So differing in their acts. Yet, if I knew
　　　　　　　　　　　What hoop should hold us stanch, from edge to edge
　　　　　　　　　　　O' the world I would pursue it.
AGRIPPA:　　　　　　　　　　　　　　　　Give me leave, Caesar, –
OCTAVIUS CAESAR: Speak Agrippa.
AGRIPPA:　　　　　　Thou hast a sister by the mother's side,
　　　　　　　　　　　Admired Octavia: great Mark Antony
　　　　　　　　　　　Is now a widower.

———————

MAECENAS:　　　　If it might please you, to enforce no further
　　　　　　　　　　　The griefs between ye: to forget them quite
　　　　　　　　　　　Were to remember that the present need
　　　　　　　　　　　Speaks to atone you.　　　　　(II, 2, 8; 17; 99)

OCTAVIUS CAESAR:          Say not so, Agrippa:
        If Cleopatra heard you, your reproof
        Were well deserved of rashness.

ANTONY:         I am not married, Caesar: let me hear
        Agrippa further speak.

AGRIPPA:         To hold you in perpetual amity,
        To make you brothers, and to knit your hearts
        With an unslipping knot, take Antony
        Octavia to his wife; whose beauty claims
        No worse a husband than the best of men;
        Whose virtue and whose general graces speak
        That which none else can utter. By this marriage,
        All little jealousies, which now seem great,
        And all great fears, which now import their dangers,
        Would then be nothing: truths would be tales,
        Where now half tales be truths: her love to both
        Would, each to other and all loves to both,
        Draw after her. . . .

ANTONY:               . . . Let me have thy hand:
        Further this act of grace; and from this hour
        The heart of brothers govern in our loves
        And sway our great designs!

OCTAVIUS CAESAR:         There is my hand.
        A sister I bequeath you, whom no brother
        Did ever love so dearly: let her live
        To join our kingdoms and our hearts; and never
        Fly off our loves again!

LEPIDUS:         Happily, amen!     (II, 2, 114; 148)

MAECENAS:         If beauty, wisdom, modesty, can settle
        The heart of Antony, Octavia is
        A blessed lottery to him.       (II, 2, 246)

MENAS:         We looked not for Mark Antony here: pray you, is he
married to Cleopatra?

ENOBARBUS:         Caesar's sister is called Octavia.

MENAS:         True, sir; she was the wife of Caius Marcellus.

ENOBARBUS:         But she is now the wife of Marcus Antonius . . .

MENAS:         Then is Caesar and he for ever knit together.

ENOBARBUS:         If I were bound to divine of this unity, I would not prophesy
so.

against the law that a widow should be married within ten months after her husband's death. Howbeit the Senate dispensed with the law, and so the marriage proceeded accordingly.

Sextus Pompeius at that time kept in Sicilia, and so made many an inroad into Italy with a great number of pinnaces and other pirates' ships, of the which were captains two notable pirates, Menas and Menecrates, who so scoured all the sea thereabouts that none durst peep out with a sail. Furthermore, Sextus Pompeius had dealt very
39 friendly with Antonius, for he had courteously received his mother

39 ANTONY:            Sextus Pompeius
                Hath given the dare to Caesar, and commands
                The empire of the sea: our slippery people,
                Whose love is never link'd to the deserver
                Till his deserts are past, begin to throw
                Pompey the Great and all his dignities
                Upon his son; who, high in name and power,
                Higher than both in blood and life, stands up
                For the main soldier: whose quality, going on,
                The sides o' the world may danger. (I, 2, 190)
                    Sextus Pompeius
                Makes his approaches to the port of Rome ...
                        the condemn'd Pompey,
                Rich in his father's honour, creeps apace
                Into the hearts of such as have not thriv'd
                Upon the present state.                    (I, 3, 45)

MESSENGER:            Pompey is strong at sea;
                And it appears he is beloved of those
                That only have fear'd Caesar: to the ports
                The discontents repair, and men's reports
                Give him much wrong'd. . . . Caesar, I bring thee word,
                Menecrates and Menas, famous pirates,
                Make the sea serve them, which they ear and wound

MENAS:        I think the policy of that purpose made more in the marriage
                than the love of the parties.

ENOBARBUS:    I think so too. But you shall find, the band that seems to
                tie their friendship together will be the very strangler of their
                amity: Octavia is of a holy, cold, and still conversation.
                                            (II, 6, 112)

212

when she fled out of Italy with Fulvia; and therefore they thought good to make peace with him. So they met all three together by the mount of Misena, upon a hill that runneth far into the sea, Pompey having his ships riding hard by at anchor, and Antonius and Caesar their armies upon the shore side, directly over against him.

ANTONY: I did not think to draw my sword 'gainst Pompey;
For he hath laid strange courtesies and great
Of late upon me: I must thank him only,
Lest my remembrance suffer ill report;
At heel of that, defy him.

LEPIDUS:                Time calls upon's:
Of us must Pompey presently be sought,
Or else he seeks out us.

ANTONY:              Where lies he?

OCTAVIUS CAESAR: About the mount Misenum.

ANTONY: What is his strength by land?

OCTAVIUS CAESAR: Great and increasing: but by sea
He is an absolute master.

ANTONY:            So is the fame.
Would we had spoke together!         (II, 2, 156)

POMPEY:            Though I lose
The praise of it by telling, you must know,
When Caesar and your brother were at blows,
Your mother came to Sicily and did find
Her welcome friendly.

ANTONY:           I have heard it, Pompey;
And am well studied for a liberal thanks
Which I do owe you.

POMPEY:         Let me have your hand.    (II, 6, 43)

---

With keels of every kind: many hot inroads
They make in Italy; the borders maritime
Lack blood to think on't, and flush youth revolt:
No vessel can peep forth, but 'tis as soon
Taken as seen; for Pompey's name strikes more
Than could his war resisted.      (I, 4, 36; 47)

Now after they had agreed that Sextus Pompeius should have Sicilia and Sardinia, with this condition, that he should rid the sea of all thieves and pirates and make it safe for passengers, and withal that
41 he should send a certain of wheat to Rome, one of them did feast another, and drew cuts who should begin. It was Pompeius' chance to invite them first. Whereupon Antonius asked him:

'And where shall we sup?'

'There,' said Pompey, and showed him his admiral galley which had six banks of oars. 'That,' said he, 'is my father's house they have left me.'

He spake it to taunt Antonius, because he had his father's house, that
42 was Pompey the Great. So he cast anchors enow into the sea to make his galley fast, and then built a bridge of wood to convey them to his galley from the head of Mount Misena; and there he welcomed them, and made them great cheer.

Now in the midst of the feast, when they fell to be merry with Antonius' love unto Cleopatra, Menas the pirate came to Pompey and, whispering in his ear, said unto him:

'Shall I cut the gables of the anchors, and make thee lord not only of Sicilia and Sardinia, but of the whole Empire of Rome besides?'

Pompey, having paused awhile upon it, at length answered him:

'Thou shouldst have done it and never have told it me; but now we

| | | |
|---|---|---|
| *41* POMPEY: | You have made me offer Of Sicily, Sardinia; and I must Rid all the sea of pirates; then, to send Measures of wheat to Rome. | (II, 6, 34) |
| *42* POMPEY: | We'll feast each other ere we part; and let's Draw lots who shall begin. | |
| ANTONY: | That will I, Pompey. | |
| POMPEY: | No, Antony, take the lot. | (II, 6, 61) |
| POMPEY: | Aboard my galley I invite you all . . . O Antony, You have my father's house, – But, what? we are friends. Come, down into the boat. | (II, 6, 82; 7, 134) |

See also p. 184 note 4.

must content us with that we have. As for myself, I was never taught to break my faith nor to be counted a traitor.'

The other two also did likewise feast him in their camp, and then he returned into Sicilia.

Antonius, after this agreement made, sent Ventidius before into Asia to stay the Parthians and to keep them they should come no further; and he himself in the meantime, to gratify Caesar, was contented to be chosen Julius Caesar's priest and sacrificer; and so they jointly together dispatched all great matters concerning the state of the Empire. But in all other manner of sports and exercises wherein they passed the time away the one with the other, Antonius was ever inferior unto Caesar, and alway lost; which grieved him much.

With Antonius there was a soothsayer or astronomer of Egypt, that could cast a figure and judge of men's nativities, to tell them what should happen to them. He, either to please Cleopatra or else for that he found it so by his art, told Antonius plainly that his fortune, which of itself was excellent good and very great, was altogether blemished and obscured by Caesar's fortune; and therefore he counselled him utterly to leave his company and to get him as far from him as he could.

'For thy Demon,' said he, '(that is to say, the good angel and spirit

| | |
|---|---|
| MENAS: | Wilt thou be lord of all the world? . . . |
| | Thou art, if thou darest be, the earthly Jove: |
| | Whate'er the ocean pales, or sky inclips, |
| | Is thine, if thou wilt ha't. . . . |
| | These three world-sharers, these competitors, |
| | Are in thy vessel: let me cut the cable; |
| | And, when we are put off, fall to their throats; |
| | All there is thine. |
| POMPEY: |         Ah, this thou shouldst have done, |
| | And not have spoke on't! In me 'tis villainy; |
| | In thee't had been good service. Thou must know, |
| | 'Tis not my profit that does lead mine honour; |
| | Mine honour, it. Repent that e'er thy tongue |
| | Hath so betray'd thine act: being done unknown, |
| | I should have found it afterwards well done; |
| | But must condemn it now. Desist. (II, 7, 67) |

that keepeth thee) is afraid of his, and, being courageous and high when he is alone, becometh fearful and timorous when he cometh near unto the other.'

Howsoever it was, the events ensuing proved the Egyptian's words true. For it is said that as often as they two drew cuts for pastime who should have anything, or whether they played at dice, Antonius alway lost. Oftentimes when they were disposed to see cock-fight, or quails that were taught to fight one with another, Caesar's cocks or quails did ever overcome; the which spited Antonius in his mind, although he made no outward show of it; and therefore he believed 44 the Egyptian the better.

In fine, he recommended the affairs of his house unto Caesar, and went out of Italy with Octavia his wife, whom he carried into

44 ANTONY: Now, sirrah; you do wish yourself in Egypt?
SOOTHSAYER: Would I had never come from thence, nor you
    Thither!
ANTONY: If you can, your reason?
SOOTHSAYER:         I see it in
    My motion, have it not in my tongue: but yet
    Hie you to Egypt again.
ANTONY:             Say to me,
    Whose fortunes shall rise higher, Caesar's or mine?
SOOTHSAYER: Caesar's.
    Therefore, O Antony, stay not by his side:
    Thy demon, that's thy spirit which keeps thee, is
    Noble, courageous, high, unmatchable,
    Where Caesar's is not; but, near him, thy angel
    Becomes a fear, as being o'erpower'd: therefore
    Make space enough between you.
ANTONY:               Speak this no more.
SOOTHSAYER: To none but thee; no more, but when to thee.
    If thou dost play with him at any game,
    Thou art sure to lose; and, of that natural luck,
    He beats thee 'gainst the odds: thy lustre thickens,
    When he shines by: I say again, thy spirit
    Is all afraid to govern thee near him;
    But, he away, 'tis noble.

Greece, after he had had a daughter by her. So Antonius lying all the winter at Athens, news came unto him of the victories of Ventidius, who had overcome the Parthians in battle, in the which also were slain Labienus and Pharnabates, the chiefest captain King Orodes had. For these good news he feasted all Athens, and kept open house for all the Grecians; and many games of price were played at Athens, of the which he himself would be judge. Wherefore, leaving his guard, his axes, and tokens of his empire at his house, he came into the show place, or lists, where these games were played, in a long gown and slippers after the Grecian fashion; and they carried tip-staves before him, as marshals' men do carry before the judges to make place; and he himself in person was a stickler to part the young men, when they had fought enough. After that, preparing to go to the wars, he made him a garland of the holy olive and carried a vessel with him of the water of the fountain Clepsydra, because of an oracle he had received that so commanded him.

In the meantime, Ventidius once again overcame Pacorus (Orodes' son, King of Parthia) in a battle fought in the country of Cyrrestica, he being come again with a great army to invade Syria; at which battle was slain a great number of the Parthians, and among them Pacorus the King's own son slain. This noble exploit, as famous as ever any was, was a full revenge to the Romans of the shame and

---

ANTONY:                          Get thee gone ...   *Exit Soothsayer.*
                                   Be it art or hap,
He hath spoken true: the very dice obey him;
And in our sports my better cunning faints
Under his chance: if we draw lots, he speeds;
His cocks do win the battle still of mine,
When it is all to nought; and his quails ever
Beat mine, inhoop'd, at odds. I will to Egypt:
And though I make this marriage for my peace,
I' the east my pleasure lies.                (II, 3, 10)

MACBETH: [*of Banquo*]     There is none but he
Whose being I do fear; and under him
My Genius is rebuked, as it is said
Mark Antony's was by Caesar.    (*Macbeth*, III, 1, 54)

loss they had received before by the death of Marcus Crassus. And
45 he made the Parthians fly, and glad to keep themselves within the
confines and territories of Mesopotamia and Media, after they had
thrice together been overcome in several battles. Howbeit Ventidius
durst not undertake to follow them any farther, fearing lest he should
have gotten Antonius' displeasure by it. Notwithstanding, he led his
army against them that had rebelled, and conquered them again;
amongst whom he besieged Antiochus, king of Commagena, who
offered him to give a thousand talents to be pardoned his rebellion,
and promised ever after to be at Antonius' commandment. But
Ventidius made him answer that he should send unto Antonius,
who was not far off and would not suffer Ventidius to make any
peace with Antiochus, to the end that yet this little exploit should
pass in his name and that they should not think he did anything but
46 by his lieutenant Ventidius. The siege grew very long, because

45 *Enter Ventidius as it were in triumph, the dead body of Pacorus borne before him.*

VENTIDIUS:    Now, darting Parthia, art thou struck; and now
                Pleased fortune does of Marcus Crassus' death
                Make me revenger. Bear the king's son's body
                Before our army. Thy Pacorus, Orodes,
                Pays this for Marcus Crassus.

                                    (*Antony and Cleopatra*, III, I, I)

46 SILIUS:                Noble Ventidius,
                Whilst yet with Parthian blood thy sword is warm,
                The fugitive Parthians follow; spur through Media,
                Mesopotamia, and the shelters whither
                The routed fly: so thy grand captain Antony
                Shall set thee on triumphant chariots and
                Put garlands on thy head.

VENTIDIUS:                  O Silius, Silius,
                I have done enough; a lower place, note well,
                May make too great an act: for learn this, Silius;
                Better to leave undone, than by our deed
                Acquire too high a fame when him we serve's away.
                Caesar and Antony have ever won
                More in their officer than person: Sossius,
                One of my place in Syria, his lieutenant,

they that were in the town, seeing they could not be received upon
no reasonable composition, determined valiantly to defend themselves to the last man. Thus Antonius did nothing, and yet received
great shame, repenting him much that he took not their first offer.
And yet at last he was glad to make truce with Antiochus and to
take three hundred talents for composition.

Thus, after he had set order for the state and affairs of Syria, he
returned again to Athens; and, having given Ventidius such honours
as he deserved, he sent him to Rome, to triumph for the Parthians.
Ventidius was the only man that ever triumphed of the Parthians
until this present day; a mean man born, and of no noble house nor
family, who only came to that he attained unto through Antonius'
friendship, the which delivered him happy occasion to achieve to
great matters. And yet, to say truly, he did so well quit himself in all
his enterprises, that he confirmed that which was spoken of Antonius
and Caesar: to wit, that they were alway more fortunate when they
made war by their lieutenants than by themselves. For Sossius, one
of Antonius' lieutenants in Syria, did notable good service; and
47 Canidius, whom he had also left his lieutenant in the borders of

47 See note 46 above (lines 17–20).

---

                    For quick accumulation of renown,
                    Which he achieved by the minute, lost his favour.
                    Who does i' the wars more than his captain can
                    Becomes his captain's captain: and ambition,
                    The soldier's virtue, rather makes choice of loss,
                    Than gain which darkens him.
                    I could do more to do Antonius good,
                    But 'twould offend him; and in his offence
                    Should my performance perish.
SILIUS:                                      Thou hast, Ventidius, that
                    Without the which a soldier, and his sword,
                    Grants scarce distinction. Thou wilt write to Antony?
VENTIDIUS:          I'll humbly signify what in his name,
                    That magical word of war, we have effected;
                    How, with his banners and his well-paid ranks,
                    The ne'er-yet-beaten horse of Parthia
                    We have jaded out o' the field.                    (III, I, 5)

Armenia, did conquer it all. So did he also overcome the kings of
the Iberians and Albanians, and went on with his conquests unto
Mount Caucasus.

By these conquests the fame of Antonius' power increased more
and more, and grew dreadful unto all the barbarous nations. But
Antonius, notwithstanding, grew to be marvellously offended
48 with Caesar, upon certain reports that had been brought unto him.
49 And so took sea to go towards Italy with three hundred sail. And,
because those of Brundusium would not receive his army into their
haven, he went farther unto Tarentum. There his wife Octavia,
that came out of Greece with him, besought him to send her unto her
50 brother; the which he did. Octavia at that time was great with child,
and moreover had a second daughter by him; and yet she put herself
in journey, and met with her brother Octavius Caesar by the way,

| | | |
|---|---|---|
| *48* ANTONY: | Nay, nay, Octavia, not only that, – | |
| | That were excusable, that, and thousands more | |
| | Of semblable import, – but he hath waged | |
| | New wars 'gainst Pompey; made his will, and read it | |
| | To public ear: | |
| | Spoke scantly of me: when perforce he could not | |
| | But pay me terms of honour, cold and sickly | |
| | He vented them; most narrow measure lent me: | |
| | When the best hint was given him, he not took't, | |
| | Or did it from his teeth. | (III, 4, 1) |
| *49* ENOBARBUS: | Our great navy's rigg'd. | |
| EROS: | For Italy and Caesar. | (III, 5, 20) |
| *50* ANTONY: | Gentle Octavia . . . as you requested, | |
| | Yourself shall go between's: the mean time, lady, | |
| | I'll raise the preparation of a war | |
| | Shall stain your brother: make your soonest haste; | |
| | So your desires are yours. | (III, 4, 20) |
| OCTAVIA: [*to Octavius Caesar*] | Good my lord, | |
| | To come thus was I not constrain'd, but did it | |
| | On my free will. My lord, Mark Antony, | |
| | Hearing that you were prepared for war, acquainted | |
| | My grieved ear withal; whereon, I begg'd | |
| | His pardon for return. | (III, 6, 55) |

who brought his two chief friends, Maecenas and Agrippa, with him. She took them aside and, with all the instance she could possible, entreated them they would not suffer her, that was the happiest woman of the world, to become now the most wretched and unfortunatest creature of all other.

'For now,' said she, 'every man's eyes do gaze on me, that am the sister of one of the Emperors and wife of the other. And if the worst counsel take place (which the gods forbid!) and that they grow to wars, for yourselves it is uncertain to which of them two the gods have assigned the victory or overthrow. But for me, on which side soever victory fall, my state can be but most miserable still.'

These words of Octavia so softened Caesar's heart that he went quickly unto Tarentum. But it was a noble sight for them that were present, to see so great an army by land not to stir, and so many ships afloat in the road quietly and safe; and, furthermore, the meeting and kindness of friends, lovingly embracing one another. First, Antonius feasted Caesar, which he granted unto for his sister's sake. Afterwards they agreed together that Caesar should give Antonius two legions to go against the Parthians, and that Antonius should let Caesar have a hundred galleys armed with brazen spurs at the prows. Besides all this, Octavia obtained of her husband twenty brigantines for her brother, and of her brother for her husband a thousand armed men. After they had taken leave of each other, Caesar went immediately to make war with Sextus Pompeius, to get Sicilia into his hands. Antonius also, leaving his wife Octavia and little children begotten of her with Caesar, and his other children which he had by Fulvia, he went directly into Asia.

1 OCTAVIA: [to Antony]    A more unhappy lady,
    If this division chance, ne'er stood between,
    Praying for both parts:
    The good gods will mock me presently,
    When I shall pray, 'O, bless my lord and husband!'
    Undo that prayer, by crying out as loud,
    'O, bless my brother!' Husband win, win brother,
    Prays, and destroys the prayer; no midway
    'Twixt these extremes at all.    (III, 4, 12)

Then began this pestilent plague and mischief of Cleopatra's love – which had slept a long time, and seemed to have been utterly forgotten, and that Antonius had given place to better counsel – again to kindle and to be in force, so soon as Antonius came near unto Syria. And in the end, 'the horse of the mind', as Plato termeth it, that is so hard of rein (I mean the unreined lust of concupiscence), did put out of Antonius' head all honest and commendable thoughts. For he sent Fonteius Capito to bring Cleopatra into Syria. Unto whom, to welcome her, he gave no trifling things. But unto that she had already he added the provinces of Phoenicia, those of the 52 nethermost Syria, the isle of Cyprus, and a great part of Cilicia, and that country of Jewry where the true balm is, and that part of Arabia where the Nabatheians do dwell, which stretcheth out towards the Ocean.

These great gifts much misliked the Romans. But now, though Antonius did easily give away great seigniories, realms, and mighty 53 nations unto some private men, and that also he took from other kings their lawful realms (as from Antigonus King of the Jews, whom he 54 openly beheaded, where never king before had suffered like death), yet all this did not so much offend the Romans as the unmeasurable honours which he did unto Cleopatra. But yet he did much more aggravate their malice and ill will towards him, because that, Cleopatra having brought him two twins, a son and a daughter, he named his son Alexander and his daughter Cleopatra, and gave

52 See p. 242 note 58 below.

53 CLEOPATRA:          For his bounty,
There was no winter in't; an autumn 'twas
That grew the more by reaping . . . in his livery
Walk'd crowns and crownets; realms and islands were
As plates dropp'd from his pocket.      (V, 2, 86)

54 ALEXAS:          Good majesty,
Herod of Jewry dare not look upon you
But when you are well pleased.

CLEOPATRA:          That Herod's head
I'll have: but how, when Antony is gone
Through whom I might command it?      (III, 3, 2)

them to their surnames, the Sun to the one and the Moon to the other. This notwithstanding, he that could finely cloak his shameful deeds with fine words said that the greatness and magnificence of the Empire of Rome appeared most, not where the Romans took, but where they gave much; and nobility was multiplied amongst men by the posterity of kings when they left of their seed in divers places; and that by this means his first ancestor was begotten of Hercules, who had not left the hope and continuance of his line and posterity in the womb of one only woman, fearing Solon's laws or regarding the ordinances of men touching the procreation of children; but that he gave it unto nature, and established the foundation of many noble races and families in divers places.

Now, when Phraortes had slain his father Orodes and possessed the kingdom, many gentlemen of Parthia forsook him and fled from him. Amongst them was Monaezes, a nobleman and of great authority among his countrymen, who came unto Antonius, that received him, and compared his fortune unto Themistocles and his own riches and magnificence unto the Kings of Persia. For he gave Monaezes three cities, Larissa, Arethusa, and Hierapolis, which was called before Bombyce. Howbeit the King of Parthia shortly after called him home again, upon his faith and word. Antonius was glad to let him go, hoping thereby to steal upon Phraortes unprovided. For he sent unto him and told him that they would remain good friends and have peace together, so he would but only redeliver the standards and ensigns of the Romans, which the Parthians had won in the battle where Marcus Crassus was slain, and the men also that remained yet prisoners of this overthrow.

In the meantime he sent Cleopatra back into Egypt, and took his way towards Arabia and Armenia; and there took a general muster of all his army he had together and of the kings his confederates that were come by his commandment to aid him, being a marvellous number; of the which the chiefest was Artavasdes, King of Armenia, who did furnish him with six thousand horsemen and seven thousand footmen. There were also of the Romans about three-score thousand footmen, and of horsemen (Spaniards and Gauls reckoned for

Romans) to the number of ten thousand, and of other nations thirty thousand men, reckoning together the horsemen and light-armed footmen.

This so great and puissant army, which made the Indians quake for fear dwelling about the country of the Bactrians, and all Asia also to tremble, served him to no purpose; and all for the love he bare to Cleopatra. For the earnest great desire he had to lie all winter with her made him begin his war out of due time; and for haste to put all in hazard, being so ravished and enchanted with the sweet poison of her love that he had no other thought but of her, and how he might quickly return again, more than how he might overcome his enemies. For first of all, where he should have wintered in Armenia to refresh his men, wearied with the long journey they had made, having come eight thousand furlongs, and then at the beginning of the spring to go and invade Media, before the Parthians should stir out of their houses and garrisons; he could tarry no longer, but led them forthwith unto the province of Atropatene, leaving Armenia on the left hand, and foraged all the country.

Furthermore, making all the haste he could, he left behind him engines of battery which were carried with him in three hundred carts (among the which also there was a ram four-score foot long), being things most necessary for him and the which he could not get again for money if they were once lost or marred. For the high provinces of Asia have no trees growing of such height and length, neither strong nor straight enough, to make suchlike engines of battery. This notwithstanding, he left them all behind him, as a hindrance to bring his matters and intent speedily to pass; and left a certain number of men to keep them, and gave them in charge unto one Tatianus.

Then he went to besiege the city of Phraata, being the chiefest and greatest city the King of Media had, where his wife and children were. Then he straight found his own fault and the want of his artillery he left behind him, by the work he had in hand. For he was fain, for lack of a breach where his men might come to the sword with their enemies that defended the wall, to force a mount of earth hard to the walls of the city, the which by little and little with great labour rose to some height. In the meantime King Phraortes came down with a great army; who understanding that Antonius had left his engines of battery behind him, he sent a great number of horsemen before, which environed Tatianus with all his carriage and slew him and ten thousand men he had with him. After this the barbarous people took these engines of battery and burnt them, and got many prisoners, amongst whom they took also King Polemon.

This discomfiture marvellously troubled all Antonius' army, to receive so great an overthrow, beyond their expectation, at the beginning of their journey; insomuch that Artabazus, King of the Armenians, despairing of the good success of the Romans, departed with his men, notwithstanding that he was himself the first procurer of this war and journey. On the other side, the Parthians came courageously unto Antonius' camp, who lay at the siege of their chiefest city, and cruelly reviled and threatened him.

Antonius therefore fearing that, if he lay still and did nothing, his men's hearts would fail them, he took ten legions, with three cohorts or ensigns of the Praetors (which are companies appointed for the guard of the general), and all his horsemen, and carried them out to forage, hoping thereby he should easily allure the Parthians to fight a battle. But when he had marched about a day's journey from his camp, he saw the Parthians wheeling round about him to give him the onset and to skirmish with him, when he would think to march his way. Therefore he set out his signal of battle, and yet caused his tents and fardels to be trussed up, as though he meant not to fight but only to lead his men back again. Then he marched before the army of the barbarous people, the which was marshalled like a crescent or half moon; and commanded his horsemen that as soon as they thought the legions were near enough unto their enemies to set upon the voward, that then they should set spurs to their horses and begin the charge. The Parthians standing in battle ray, beholding the countenance of the Romans as they marched, they appeared to be soldiers indeed, to see them march in so good array as was possible. For in their march they kept the ranks a little space one from another, not straggling out of order, and shaking their pikes, speaking never a word. But so soon as the alarm was given, the horsemen suddenly turned head upon the Parthians and with great cries gave charge on them; who at the first received their charge courageously, for they were joined nearer them within an arrow's shoot. But when the legions also came to join with them, shouting out aloud and rattling of their armours, the Parthians' horses and themselves were so afraid and amazed withal that they all turned tail and fled, before the Romans could come to the sword with them.

Then Antonius followed them hard in chase, being in great good hope by this conflict to have brought to end all, or the most part, of this war. But after that his footmen had chased them fifty furlongs off and the horsemen also thrice as far, they found in all but thirty prisoners taken and about four-score men only slain. But this did much discourage them, when they considered with themselves that, obtaining the victory, they had slain so few of their enemies; and where they were overcome they lost as many of their men as they had done at the overthrow when the carriage was taken.

The next morning, Antonius' army trussed up their carriage and marched back towards their camp; and by the way in their return they met at the first a few of the Parthians; then going further they met a few more. So at length, when they all came together, they reviled them and troubled them on every side, as freshly and courageously as if they had not been overthrown; so that the Romans very hardly got to their camp with safety. The Medes on the other side, that were besieged in their chief city of Phraata, made a sally out upon them that kept the mount, which they had forced and cast against the wall of the city, and drave them for fear from the mount they kept. Antonius was so offended withal that he executed the decimation. For he divided his men by ten legions, and then of them he put the tenth legion to death, on whom the lot fell; and, to the other nine, he caused them to have barley given them instead of wheat.

Thus this war fell out troublesome unto both parties, and the end thereof much more fearful. For Antonius could look for no other of his side but famine, because he could forage no more, nor fetch in any victuals, without great loss of his men. Phraortes on the other side, he knew well enough that he could bring the Parthians to anything else but to lie in camp abroad in the winter. Therefore he was afraid that, if the Romans continued their siege all winter long and made war with him still, that his men would forsake him, and specially because the time of the year went away apace and the air waxed cloudy and cold in the equinoctial autumn.

Thereupon he called to mind this device. He gave the chiefest of his gentlemen of the Parthians charge that, when they met the Romans out of their camp, going to forage or to water their horse or for some other provision, that they should not distress them too much but should suffer them to carry somewhat away and greatly commend their valiantness and hardiness, for the which their King did esteem them the more and not without cause. After these first baits and allurements they began by little and little to come nearer unto them and to talk with them a-horseback, greatly blaming Antonius' self-will that did not give their King Phraortes occasion to make a good peace, who desired nothing more than to save the lives of so goodly a company of valiant men; but that he was too fondly bent to abide two of the greatest and most dreadful enemies he could have, to wit, winter and famine, the which they should hardly away withal, though the Parthians did the best they could to aid and accompany them. These words being oftentimes brought to Antonius, they made him a little pliant, for the good hope he had of his return. But yet he would not send unto the King of Parthia before they had first asked these barbarous people that spake so courteously unto his men, whether they spake it of themselves or that they were their master's words. When they told them the King himself said so, and did persuade them further not to fear or mistrust them, then Antonius sent some of his friends unto the King to make demand for the delivery of the ensigns and prisoners he had of the Romans since the overthrow of Crassus; to the end it should not appear that, if he asked nothing, they should think he were glad that he might only scape with safety out of the danger he was in. The King of Parthia answered him: that, for the ensigns and prisoners he demanded, he should not break his head about it; notwithstanding, that, if he would presently depart without delay, he might depart in peaceable manner and without danger.

Wherefore Antonius, after he had given his men some time to truss up their carriage, he raised his camp and took his way to depart. But though he had an excellent tongue at will, and very gallant to entertain his soldiers and men of war and that he could passingly well do it, as well or better than any captain in his time, yet, being ashamed for respects, he would not speak unto them at his removing, but willed Domitius Aenobarbus to do it. Many of them took this in very ill part and thought that he did it in disdain of them. But the most part of them presently understood the truth of it and were also ashamed. Therefore they thought it their duties to carry the like respect unto their captain that their captain did unto them; and so they became the more obedient unto him. So Antonius was minded to return the same way he came, being a plain barren country without wood.

But there came a soldier to him born in the country of the Mardians, who, by oft frequenting the Parthians of long time, knew their fashions very well, and had also showed himself very true and faithful to the Romans in the battle where Antonius' engines of battery and carriage were taken away. This man came unto Antonius to counsel him to beware how he went that way and to make his army a prey, being heavily armed, unto so great a number of horsemen, all archers in the open field, where they should have nothing to let them to compass him round about; and that this was Phraortes' fetch, to offer him so friendly conditions and courteous words to make him raise his siege, that he might afterwards meet him as he would in the plains; howbeit, that he would guide him, if he thought good, another way on the right hand through woods and mountains, a far nearer way and where he should find great plenty of all things needful for his army.

Antonius, hearing what he said, called his council together to consult upon it. For, after he had made peace with the Parthians, he was loath to give them cause to think he mistrusted them; and on the other side also he would gladly shorten his way, and pass by places well inhabited, where he might be provided of all things necessary. Therefore he asked the Mardian what pledge he would put in to perform that he promised. The Mardian gave himself to be bound hand and foot till he had brought his army into the country of Armenia. So he guided the army thus bound, two days together, without any trouble or sight of enemy.

But the third day, Antonius thinking the Parthians would no more follow him and trusting therein, suffered the soldiers to march in disorder as every man listed. The Mardian perceiving that the dams of a river were newly broken up, which they should have passed over, and that the river had overflown the banks and drowned all the way they should have gone, he guessed straight that the Parthians had done it and had thus broken it open to stay the Romans for getting too far before them. Thereupon he bade Antonius look to himself, and told him that his enemies were not far from thence. Antonius having set his men in order, as he was placing of his archers and slingmen to resist the enemies and to drive them back, they descried the Parthians that wheeled round about the army to compass them in on every side and to break their ranks; and their light-armed men gave charge upon them. So, after they had hurt many of the Romans with their arrows and that they themselves were also hurt by them with their darts and plummets of lead, they retired a little and then came again and gave charge; until that the horsemen of the Gauls turned their horses and fiercely galloped towards them, that they dispersed them so as all that day they gathered no more together.

Thereby Antonius knew what to do, and did not only strengthen the rearward of his army, but both the flanks also, with darts and slingmen, and made his army march in a square battle, commanding the horsemen that, when the enemies should come to assail them, they should drive them back but not follow them too far. Thus the Parthians four days after, seeing they did no more hurt to the Romans than they also received of them, they were not so hot upon them as they were commanded; but, excusing themselves by the winter that troubled them, they determined to return back again.

The fifth day Flavius Gallus, a valiant man of his hands that had charge in the army, came unto Antonius to pray him to let him have some more of his light-armed men than were already in the rearward, and some of the horsemen that were in the vaward hoping thereby to do some notable exploit. Antonius granting them unto him, when the enemies came according to their manner to set upon the tail of the army and to skirmish with them, Flavius courageously made them retire, but not, as they were wont to do before, to retire and join presently with their army, for he over-rashly thrust in among them to fight it out at the sword. The captains that had the leading of the rearward, seeing Flavius stray too far from the army, they sent unto him to will him to retire; but he would not hearken to it. And it is reported also that Titius himself the treasurer took the ensigns and did what he could to make the ensign-bearers return back, reviling Flavius Gallus because that through his folly and desperateness he caused many honest and valiant men to be both hurt and slain to no purpose. Gallus also fell out with him and commanded his men to stay. Wherefore Titius returned again into the army, and Gallus still overthrowing and driving the enemies back whom he met in the vaward, he was not ware that he was compassed in. Then seeing himself environed of all sides he sent unto the army that they should come and aid him.

But there the captains that led the legions (among the which Canidius, a man of great estimation about Antonius, made one) committed many faults. For, where they should have made head with the whole army upon the Parthians, they sent him aid by small companies; and, when they were slain, they sent him others also. So that by their beastliness and lack of consideration they had like to have made all the army fly, if Antonius himself had not come from the front of the battle with the third legion, the which came through the midst of them that fled, until they came to the front of the enemies, and that they stayed them from chasing any farther. Howbeit at this last conflict there were slain no less than three thousand men, and five thousand besides brought sore hurt into the camp, and amongst them also Flavius Gallus, whose body was shot through in four places, whereof he died.

Antonius went to the tents to visit and comfort the sick and wounded, and for pity's sake he could not refrain from weeping; and they also, showing him the best countenance they could, took him by the hand and prayed him to go and be dressed, and not to trouble himself for them, most reverently calling him their emperor and captain; and that, for themselves, they were whole and safe, so that he had his health.

For indeed, to say truly, there was not at that time any emperor or captain that had so great and puissant an army as his together, both for lusty youths and courage of the soldiers, as also for their patience to away with so great pains and trouble. Furthermore, the obedience and reverence they showed unto their captain, with a marvellous earnest love and good will, was so great, and all were indifferently (as well great as small, the noblemen as mean men, the captains and soldiers) so earnestly bent to esteem Antonius' good will and favour above their own life and safety, that, in this point of martial discipline, the ancient Romans could not have done any more. But divers things were cause thereof, as we have told you before: Antonius' nobility and ancient house, his eloquence, his plain nature, his liberality and magnificence, and his familiarity to sport and to be merry in company; but specially the care he took at that time to help, visit, and lament those that were sick and wounded, seeing every man to have that which was meet for him; that was of such force and effect as it made them that were sick and wounded to love him better, and were more desirous to do him service than those that were whole and sound.

This victory so encouraged the enemies (who otherwise were weary to follow Antonius any farther) that all night long they kept the fields and hovered about the Romans' camp, thinking that they would presently fly and then that they should take the spoil of their camp. So the next morning, by break of day, there were gathered together a far greater number of the Parthians than they were before. For the rumour was that there were not much fewer than forty thousand horse, because their King sent thither even the very guard about his person, as unto a most certain and assured victory, that they might be partners of the spoil and booty they hoped to have had – for, as touching the King himself, he was never in any conflict or battle.

Then Antonius, desirous to speak to his soldiers, called for a black gown, to appear the more pitiful to them. But his friends did dissuade him from it. Therefore he put on his coat armour, and being so apparelled made an oration to his army; in the which he highly commended them that had overcome and driven back their enemies, and greatly rebuked them that had cowardly turned their backs. So that those which had overcome prayed him to be of good cheer; the other also to clear themselves willingly offered to take the lots of decimation if he thought good, or otherwise to receive what kind of punishment it should please him to lay upon them, so that he would forget any more to mislike or to be offended with them. Antonius, seeing that, did lift up his hands to heaven and made his prayer to the gods that, if in exchange of his former victories they would now send him some bitter adversity, then that all might light on himself alone and that they would give the victory to the rest of his army.

The next morning they gave better order on every side of the army and so marched forward; so that, when the Parthians thought to return again to assail them, they came far short of the reckoning. For, where they thought to come not to fight but to spoil and make havoc of all, when they came near them, they were sore hurt with their slings and darts and such other javelins as the Romans darted at them; and the Parthians found them as rough and desperate in fight as if they had been fresh men they had dealt withal. Whereupon their hearts began again to fail them. But yet, when the Romans came to go down any steep hills or mountains, then they would set on them with their arrows, because the Romans could go down but fair and softly. But then again, the soldiers of the legion that carried great shields returned back, and enclosed them that were naked or light-armed in the midst amongst them; and did kneel of one knee on the ground, and so set down their shields before them; and they of the second rank also covered them of the first rank, and the third also covered the second; and so from rank to rank all were covered; insomuch that this manner of covering and shading themselves with shields was devised after the fashion of laying tiles upon houses, and, to sight, was like the degrees of a theatre, and is a most strong defence and bulwark against all arrows and shot that falleth upon it.

When the Parthians saw this countenance of the Roman soldiers of the legion, which kneeled on the ground in that sort upon one knee, supposing that they had been wearied with travel they laid down their bows, and took their spears and lances, and came to fight with them man for man. Then the Romans suddenly rose upon their feet, and with the darts that they threw from them they slew the foremost, and put the rest to flight; and so did they the next days that followed.

But by means of these dangers and lets Antonius' army could win no way in a day, by reason whereof they suffered great famine. For they could have but little corn; and yet were they driven daily to fight for it, and, besides that, they had no instruments to grind it, to make bread of it. For the most part of them had been left behind, because the beasts that carried them were either dead or else employed to carry them that were sore and wounded. For the famine was so extreme great that the eighth part of a bushel of wheat was sold for fifty drachmas; and they sold barley bread by the weight of silver.

In the end they were compelled to live off herbs and roots. But they found few of them that men do commonly eat of, and were enforced to taste of them that were never eaten before; among the which there was one that killed them and made them out of their wits. For he that had once eaten of it, his memory was gone from him, and he knew no manner of thing, but only busied himself in digging and hurling of stones from one place to another, as though it had been a matter of great weight and to be done with all possible speed. All the camp over, men were busily stooping to the ground, digging and carrying of stones from one place to another. But at the last they cast up a great deal of choler, and died suddenly, because they lacked wine, which was the only sovereign remedy to cure that disease.

It is reported that Antonius seeing such a number of his men die daily, and that the Parthians left them not, neither would suffer them to be at rest, he oftentimes cried out sighing, and said: 'O, ten thousand!' He had the valiantness of ten thousand Grecians in such admiration, whom Xenophon brought away after the overthrow

BANQUO:        Were such things here as we do speak about?
               Or have we eaten on the insane root
               That takes the reason prisoner?        (*Macbeth*, I, 3, 83)

233

of Cyrus because they had come a farther journey from Babylon, and had also fought against much more enemies many times told than themselves, and yet came home with safety.

The Parthians, therefore, seeing that they could not break the good order of the army of the Romans, and contrarily that they themselves were oftentimes put to flight and well-favouredly beaten, they fell again to their old crafty subtilties. For, when they found any of the Romans scattered from the army to go forage, to seek some corn, or other victuals, they would come to them as if they had been their friends and showed them their bows unbent, saying that themselves also did return home to their country as they did, and that they would follow them no farther, howbeit that they should yet have certain Medes that would follow them a day's journey or two, to keep them that they should do no hurt to the villages from the highways; and so, holding them with this talk, they gently took their leave of them and bade them farewell, so that the Romans began again to think themselves safe. Antonius also understanding this, being very glad of it, determined to take his way through the plain country, because also they should find no water in the mountains, as it was reported unto him.

So, as he was determined to take this course, there came into his host one Mithridates, a gentleman from the enemies' camp, who was cousin unto Monaezes that fled unto Antonius and unto whom he had given three cities. When he came to Antonius' camp, he prayed them to bring him one that could speak the Parthian or Syrian tongue. So one Alexander Antiochian, a familiar of Antonius, was brought unto him. Then the gentleman told him what he was; and said that Monaezes had sent him to Antonius to requite the honour and courtesy he had showed unto him. After he had used this ceremonious speech, he asked Alexander if he saw those high mountains afar off, which he pointed unto him with his finger. Alexander answered, he did.

'The Parthians,' said he, 'do lie in ambush at the foot of those mountains, under the which lieth a goodly plain champion country; and they think that you, being deceived with their crafty subtile words, will leave the way of the mountains and turn into the plain. For the other way, it is very hard and painful, and you shall abide great thirst, the which you are well acquainted withal. But, if Antonius take the lower way, let him assure himself to run the same fortune that Marcus Crassus did.'

So Mithridates having said, he departed. Antonius was marvellously troubled in his mind when he heard thus much, and therefore called for his friends, to hear what they would say to it. The Mardian also that was their guide, being asked his opinion, answered that he thought as much as the gentleman Mithridates had said.

'For,' said he, 'admit that there were no ambush of enemies in the valley, yet is it a long crooked way and ill to hit; where, taking the mountain way, though it be stony and painful, yet there is no other danger but a whole day's travelling without any water.'

So Antonius, changing his first mind and determination, removed that night and took the mountain way, commanding every man to provide himself of water. But the most part of them lacking vessels to carry water in, some were driven to fill their sallets and murrions with water, and others also filled goats' skins to carry water in.

Now they marching forward, word was brought unto the Parthians that they were removed. Whereupon, contrary to their manner, they presently followed them the self same night, so that by break of day they overtook the rearward of the Romans, who were so lame and wearied with going and lack of sleep that they were even done. For, beyond expectation, they had gone that night two hundred and forty furlong; and, further, to see their enemies so suddenly at their backs, that made them utterly despair; but most of all, the fighting with them increased their thirst, because they were forced to fight as they marched, to drive their enemies back, yet creeping on still. The vaward of the army by chance met with a river that was very clear and cold water, but it was salt and venomous to drink; for straight it did gnaw the guts of those that had drunk it, and made them marvellous dry, and put them into a terrible ache and pricking. And, notwithstanding that the Mardian had told them of it before, yet they would not be ruled, but violently thrust them back that would have kept them from drinking; and so drank. But

Antonius going up and down amongst them prayed them to take a little patience for a while, for hard by there was another river that the water was excellent good to drink, and that from thenceforth the way was so stony and ill for horsemen that the enemies could follow them no further. So he caused the retreat to be sounded to call them back that fought, and commanded the tents to be set up, that the soldiers might yet have shadow to refresh them with.

So when the tents were set up and the Parthians also retired according to their manner, the gentleman Mithridates before named returned again as before, and Alexander in like manner again brought unto him for interpreter. Then Mithridates advised him that, after the army had reposed a little, the Romans should remove forthwith and with all possible speed get to the river; because the Parthians would go no further, but yet were cruelly bent to follow them thither. Alexander carried the report thereof unto Antonius, who gave him a great deal of gold plate to bestow upon Mithridates. Mithridates took as much of him as he could well carry away in his gown, and so departed with speed.

So Antonius raised his camp, being yet daylight, and caused all his army to march; and the Parthians never troubled any of them by the way. But amongst themselves it was as ill and dreadful a night as ever they had. For there were villains of their own company who cut their fellows' throats for the money they had and, besides that, robbed the sumpters and carriage of such money as they carried; and at length they set upon Antonius' slaves that drave his own sumpters and carriage, they brake goodly tables and rich plate in pieces, and divided it among themselves. Thereupon all the camp was straight in tumult and uproar; for the residue of them were afraid it had been the Parthians that had given them this alarm and had put all the army out of order; insomuch that Antonius called for one Rhamnus, one of his slaves enfranchised that was of his guard, and made him give his faith that he would thrust his sword through him when he would bid him, and cut off his head; because he might not be taken alive of his enemies, nor known when he were dead. This grieved his friends to the heart, that they burst out a-weeping for sorrow. The Mardian also did comfort him, and assured him that the river he sought for was hard by, and that he did guess it by a sweet moist wind that breathed upon them, and by the air which they found fresher than they were wont, and also for that they fetched their wind more at liberty; and moreover, because that since they did set forward he thought they were near their journey's end, not lacking much of day. On the other side, also, Antonius was informed that this great tumult and trouble came not through the enemies, but through the vile covetousness and villainy of certain of his soldiers. Therefore Antonius, to set his army again in order and to pacify this uproar, sounded the trumpet that every man should lodge.

Now day began to break, and the army to fall again into good order, and all the hurly-burly to cease, when the Parthians drew near and that their arrows lighted among them of the rearward of his army. Thereupon the signal of battle was given to the light-armed men; and the legioners did cover themselves as they had done before with their shields, with the which they received and defended the force of the Parthians' arrows, who never durst any more come to handy-strokes with them; and thus they that were in the voward went down by little and little, till at length they spied the river. There Antonius placed his armed men upon the sands to receive and drive back the enemies, and first of all got over his men that were sick and hurt, and afterwards all the rest. And those also that were left to resist the enemies had leisure enough to drink safely and at their pleasure. For, when the Parthians saw the river, they unbent their bows, and bade the Romans pass over without any fear, and greatly commended their valiantness. When they had all passed over the river at their ease, they took a little breath, and so marched forward again, not greatly trusting the Parthians.

The sixth day after this last battle, they came to the river of Araxes, which divideth the country of Armenia from Media; the which appeared unto them very dangerous to pass, for the depth and swiftness of the stream. And furthermore, there ran a rumour through the camp that the Parthians lay in ambush thereabouts and that they would come and set upon them whilst they were troubled in passing over the river. But now, after they were all come safely over without any danger and that they had gotten to the other side, into the province of Armenia, then they worshipped that land, as if it had been the first land they had seen after a long and dangerous voyage by sea, being now arrived in a safe and happy haven; and the tears ran down their cheeks, and every man embraced each other for the great joy they had.

But now, keeping the fields in this fruitful country so plentiful of all things, after so great a famine and want of all things, they so crammed themselves with such plenty of victuals that many of them were cast into fluxes and dropsies. There Antonius, mustering his whole army, found that he had lost twenty thousand footmen and four thousand horsemen, which had not all been slain by their enemies; for the most part of them died of sickness, making seven-and-twenty days' journey, coming from the city of Phraata into Armenia, and having overcome the Parthians in eighteen several battles.

But these victories were not throughly performed nor accomplished, because they followed no long chase; and thereby it easily appeared that Artabazus King of Armenia had reserved Antonius to end this war. For, if the sixteen thousand horsemen which he brought with him out of Media had been at these battles (considering that they were armed and apparelled much after the Parthians' manner and acquainted also with their fight) when the Romans had put them to flight that fought a battle with them and that these Armenians had followed the chase of them that fled – they had not gathered themselves again in force, neither durst they also have returned to fight with them so often after they had been so many times overthrown. Therefore all those that were of any credit and countenance in the army did persuade and egg Antonius to be revenged of this Armenian king. But Antonius wisely dissembling his anger, he told him not of his treachery, nor gave him the worse countenance, nor did him less honour than he did before, because he knew his army was weak and lacked things necessary.

Howbeit afterwards he returned again into Armenia with a great army, and so with fair words and sweet promises of messengers, he allured Artabazus to come unto him; whom he then kept prisoner, and led in triumph in the city of Alexandria. This greatly offended the Romans, and made them much to mislike it when they saw that for Cleopatra's sake he deprived his country of her due honour and glory, only to gratify the Egyptians. But this was a pretty while after.

Howbeit then the great haste he made to return unto Cleopatra caused him to put his men to so great pains, forcing them to lie in the field all winter long when it snew unreasonably, that by the way he lost eight thousand of his men; and so came down to the sea side with a small company, unto a certain place called Blancbourg, which standeth betwixt the cities of Berytus and Sidon; and there tarried for Cleopatra. And, because she tarried longer than he would have had her, he pined away for love and sorrow; so that he was at such a strait that he wist not what to do, and therefore, to wear it out, he gave himself to quaffing and feasting. But he was so drowned with the love of her that he could not abide to sit at the table till the feast were ended; but many times, while others banqueted, he ran to the sea side to see if she were coming. At length she came, and brought with her a world of apparel and money to give unto the soldiers. But some say, notwithstanding, that she brought apparel but no money, and that she took of Antonius' money and caused it to be given amongst the soldiers in her own name, as if she had given it them.

In the meantime it chanced that the King of the Medes and Phraortes King of the Parthians fell at great wars together, the which began (as it is reported) for the spoils of the Romans, and grew to be so hot between them that the King of Medes was no less afraid, than also in danger, to lose his whole realm. Thereupon he sent unto Antonius to pray him to come and make war with the Parthians, promising him that he would aid him to his uttermost power. This put Antonius again in good comfort, considering that, unlooked for, the only thing he lacked (which made him he could not overcome the Parthians, meaning that he had not brought horsemen and men with darts and slings enough) was offered him in that sort that he did him more pleasure to accept it than it was pleasure to the other to offer it. Hereupon, after he had spoken with the King of Medes at the river of Araxes, he prepared himself once more to go through Armenia and to make more cruel war with the Parthians than he had done before.

Now, whilst Antonius was busy in this preparation, Octavia his wife, whom he had left at Rome, would needs take sea to come unto him. Her brother Octavius Caesar was willing unto it, not for his respect at all (as most authors do report), as for that he might have an honest colour to make war with Antonius if he did misuse her and not esteem of her as she ought to be. But, when she was come to Athens, she received letters from Antonius willing her to stay there until his coming, and did advertise her of his journey and determination; the which though it grieved her much and that she knew it was but an excuse, yet by her letters to him of answer she asked him whether he would have those things sent unto him which she had brought him, being great store of apparel for soldiers, a great number of horse, sum of money and gifts to bestow on his friends and captains he had about him; and, besides all those, she had two thousand soldiers, chosen men, all well armed like unto the Praetors' bands.

When Niger, one of Antonius' friends whom he had sent unto Athens, had brought these news from his wife Octavia, and withal did greatly praise her, as she was worthy and well deserved, Cleopatra knowing that Octavia would have Antonius from her and fearing also that, if with her virtue and honest behaviour (besides the great power of her brother Caesar) she did add thereunto her modest kind love to please her husband, that she would then be too strong for her and in the end win him away, she subtilly seemed to languish for the love of Antonius, pining her body for lack of meat. Furthermore, she every way so framed her countenance that, when Antonius came to see her, she cast her eyes upon him like a woman ravished for joy. Straight again, when he went from her, she fell a weeping and blubbering, looked ruefully of the matter, and still found the means that Antonius should oftentimes find her weeping; and then, when he came suddenly upon her, she made as though she dried her eyes, and turned her face away, as if she were unwilling that he should see her weep. All these tricks she used, Antonius being in readiness to go into Syria to speak with the King of Medes.

Then the flatterers that furthered Cleopatra's mind blamed Antonius and told him that he was a hard-natured man and that he had small love in him, that would see a poor lady in such torment for his sake, whose life depended only upon him alone. For Octavia, said they, that was married unto him as it were of necessity, because her brother Caesar's affairs so required it, hath the honour to be called Antonius' lawful spouse and wife; and Cleopatra, being born a queen of so many thousands of men, is only named Antonius' leman; and yet that she disdained not so to be called, if it might please him she might enjoy his company and live with him; but, if he once leave her, that then it is unpossible she should live. To be short, by these their flatteries and enticements they so wrought Antonius' effeminate mind that, fearing lest she would make herself away, he returned again unto Alexandria and referred the King of Medes to the next year following, although he received news that the Parthians at that time were at civil wars among themselves. This notwithstanding, he went afterwards and made peace with him. For he married his daughter, which was very young, unto one of the sons that Cleopatra had by him; and then returned, being fully bent to make war with Caesar.

When Octavia was returned to Rome from Athens, Caesar commanded her to go out of Antonius' house and to dwell by herself, because he had abused her. Octavia answered him again that she would not forsake her husband's house and that, if he had no other occasion to make war with him, she prayed him then to take no thought for her.

'For,' said she, 'it were too shameful a thing that two so famous captains should bring in civil wars among the Romans, the one for the love of a woman and the other for the jealousy betwixt one another.'

Now, as she spake the word, so did she also perform the deed. For she kept still in Antonius' house, as if he had been there, and very honestly and honourably kept his children, not those only she had by him, but the other which her husband had by Fulvia. Furthermore when Antonius sent any of his men to Rome to sue for any office in the commonwealth, she received him very courteously, and so used herself unto her brother that she obtained the thing she requested. Howbeit thereby, thinking no hurt, she did Antonius great hurt. For her honest love and regard to her husband made every man hate him when they saw he did so unkindly use so noble a lady.

But yet the greatest cause of their malice unto him was for the division of lands he made amongst his children in the city of Alexandria. And, to confess a troth, it was too arrogant and insolent a part, and done (as a man would say) in derision and contempt of the Romans. For he assembled all the people in the show-place where young men do exercise themselves; and there upon a high tribunal silvered he set two chairs of gold, the one for himself and the other for Cleopatra, and lower chairs for his children. Then he openly published before the assembly that, first of all, he did establish Cleopatra Queen of Egypt, of Cyprus, of Lydia, and of the lower Syria, and, at that time also, Caesarion King of the same realms. (This Caesarion was supposed to be the son of Julius Caesar, who had left
57 Cleopatra great with child.) Secondly he called the sons he had by her 'the Kings of Kings': and gave Alexander for his portion, Armenia, Media, and Parthia (when he had conquered the country);
58 and unto Ptolemy for his portion, Phoenicia, Syria, and Cilicia. And therewithal he brought out Alexander in a long gown after

57 See *Life of Caesar*, p. 71 note 6.
58 OCTAVIUS CAESAR: Contemning Rome, he has done all this, and more,
> In Alexandria: here's the manner of 't:
> I' the market-place, on a tribunal silver'd,
> Cleopatra and himself in chairs of gold
> Were publicly enthroned: at the feet sat
> Caesarion, whom they call my father's son,
> And all the unlawful issue that their lust
> Since then hath made between them. Unto her
> He gave the stablishment of Egypt; made her
> Of lower Syria, Cyprus, Lydia,
> Absolute queen.

MAECENAS:  This in the public eye?

OCTAVIUS CAESAR: I' the common show-place, where they exercise.
> His sons he there proclaim'd the kings of kings:
> Great Media, Parthia, and Armenia,
> He gave to Alexander; to Ptolemy he assign'd
> Syria, Cilicia, and Phoenicia.

(*Antony and Cleopatra*, III, 6, 1)

the fashion of the Medes, with a high copped-tank hat on his head, narrow in the top, as the Kings of the Medes and Armenians do use to wear them; and Ptolemy apparelled in a cloak after the Macedonian manner, with slippers on his feet, and a broad hat with a royal band or diadem – such was the apparel and old attire of the ancient kings and successors of Alexander the Great. So, after his sons had done their humble duties and kissed their father and mother, presently a company of Armenian soldiers set there of purpose, compassed the one about, and a like company of the Macedonians the other. Now, for Cleopatra, she did not only wear at that time, but at all other times else when she came abroad, the apparel of the goddess Isis, and so gave audience unto all her subjects as a new Isis.

Octavius Caesar reporting all these things unto the Senate and oftentimes accusing him to the whole people and assembly in Rome, he thereby stirred up all the Romans against him. Antonius on the other side sent to Rome likewise to accuse him; and the chiefest points of his accusations he charged him with were these: first, that having spoiled Sextus Pompeius in Sicilia he did not give him his part of the isle; secondly, that he did detain in his hands the ships he lent him to make that war; thirdly, that, having put Lepidus their companion and triumvirate out of his part of the Empire and having deprived him of all honours, he retained for himself the lands and revenues thereof which had been assigned unto him for his part; and last of all, that he had in manner divided all Italy amongst his own soldiers and had left no part of it for his soldiers. Octavius Caesar

OCTAVIUS CAESAR:           She
         In the habiliments of the goddess Isis
         That day appear'd; and oft before gave audience,
         As 'tis reported, so.

MAECENAS:             Let Rome be thus
         Inform'd.

AGRIPPA:         Who, queasy with his insolence
         Already, will their good thoughts call from him.

                           (III, 6, 16)

OCTAVIUS CAESAR: The people . . . have now received
         His accusations.

answered him again that, for Lepidus, he had indeed deposed him and taken his part of the Empire from him, because he did over-cruelly use his authority; and secondly, for the conquests he had made by force of arms, he was contented Antonius should have his part of
61 them, so that he would likewise let him have his part of Armenia; and thirdly, that, for his soldiers, they should seek for nothing in Italy, because they possessed Media and Parthia, the which provinces they had added to the Empire of Rome, valiantly fighting with their emperor and captain.

Antonius hearing these news, being yet in Armenia, commanded Canidius to go presently to the sea side with his sixteen legions he had; and he himself with Cleopatra went unto the city of Ephesus, and there gathered together his galleys and ships out of all parts, which came to the number of eight hundred, reckoning the great ships of burden; and of those Cleopatra furnished him with two hundred, and twenty thousand talents besides, and provision of victuals also to maintain all the whole army in this war. So Antonius through the persuasions of Domitius, commanded Cleopatra to return again into Egypt, and there to understand the success of this war. But Cleopatra fearing lest Antonius should again be made

61 AGRIPPA:　　　　　　　Sir, this should be answer'd.
OCTAVIUS CAESAR: 'Tis done already, and the messenger gone.
　　　　　　　　I have told him, Lepidus was grown too cruel;
　　　　　　　　That he his high authority abused,
　　　　　　　　And did deserve his change: for what I have conquer'd,
　　　　　　　　I grant him part; but then, in his Armenia,
　　　　　　　　And other of his conquer'd kingdoms, I
　　　　　　　　Demand the like.　　　　　　　　　　(III, 6, 30)

---

AGRIPPA:　　　　　　　Who does he accuse?
OCTAVIUS CAESAR: Caesar: and that, having in Sicily
　　　　　　　　Sextus Pompeius spoil'd, we had not rated him
　　　　　　　　His part o' the isle: then does he say, he lent me
　　　　　　　　Some shipping unrestored: lastly, he frets
　　　　　　　　That Lepidus of the triumvirate
　　　　　　　　Should be deposed; and, being, that we detain
　　　　　　　　All his revenue.　　　　　　　　　　(III, 6, 22)

friends with Octavius Caesar by the means of his wife Octavia, she so plied Canidius with money, and filled his purse, that he became her spokesman unto Antonius, and told him there was no reason to send her from this war, who defrayed so great a charge; neither that it was for his profit, because that thereby the Egyptians would then be utterly discouraged, which were the chiefest strength of the army by sea; considering that he could see no king of all the kings their confederates that Cleopatra was inferior unto, either for wisdom or judgement, seeing that long before she had wisely governed so great a realm as Egypt, and besides that she had been so long acquainted with him, by whom she had learned to manage great affairs. These fair persuasions won him; for it was predestined that the government of all the world should fall into Octavius Caesar's hands.

Thus, all their forces being joined together, they hoised sail towards the isle of Samos, and there gave themselves to feasts and solace. For as all the kings, princes, and commonalties, peoples, and cities, from Syria unto the marshes Maeotides, and from the Armenians to the Illyrians, were sent unto, to send and bring all munition and warlike preparation they could; even so all players, minstrels, tumblers, fools, and jesters were commanded to assemble in the isle of Samos; so that, where in manner all the world in every place was full of lamentations, sighs and tears, only in this isle of Samos there was nothing for many days' space but singing and piping, and all the theatre full of these common players, minstrels, and singing men. Besides all this, every city sent an ox thither to sacrifice; and kings did strive one with another who should make the noblest feasts and give the richest gifts; so that every man said:

'What can they do more for joy of victory if they win the battle, when they make already such sumptuous feasts at the beginning of the war?' When this was done, he gave the whole rabble of these minstrels, and such kind of people, the city of Priene to keep them withal, during this war.

62 CLEOPATRA:    A charge we bear i' the war,
    And, as the president of my kingdom, will
    Appear there for a man. Speak not against it;
    I will not stay behind.     (III, 7, 17)

Then he went unto the city of Athens, and there gave himself again to see plays and pastimes and to keep the theatres. Cleopatra, on the other side, being jealous of the honours which Octavia had received in this city (where indeed she was marvellously honoured and beloved of the Athenians), to win the people's good will also at Athens, she gave them great gifts; and they likewise gave her many great honours, and appointed certain ambassadors to carry the decree to her house, among the which Antonius was one, who as a citizen of Athens reported the matter unto her and made an oration in the behalf of the city. Afterwards he sent to Rome to put his wife Octavia out of his house, who, as it was reported, went out of his house with all Antonius' children (saving the eldest of them he had by Fulvia, who was with his father), bewailing and lamenting her cursed hap that had brought her to this, that she was accompted one of the chiefest causes of this civil war. The Romans did pity her, but much more Antonius, and those specially that had seen Cleopatra, who neither excelled Octavia in beauty, nor yet in young years.

Octavius Caesar understanding the sudden and wonderful great preparation of Antonius, he was not a little astonied at it (fearing he should be driven to fight that summer), because he wanted many things, and the great and grievous exactions of money did sorely oppress the people. For all manner of men else were driven to pay the fourth part of their goods and revenue; but the libertines (to wit, those whose fathers or other predecessors had sometime been bondmen) they were sessed to pay the eighth part of all their goods at one payment. Hereupon there rose a wonderful exclamation and great uproar all Italy over; so that, among the greatest faults that ever Antonius committed, they blamed him most for that he delayed to give Caesar battle. For he gave Caesar leisure to make his preparations and also to appease the complaints of the people. When such a great sum of money was demanded of them, they grudged at it, and grew to mutiny upon it; but, when they had once paid it, they remembered it no more.

Furthermore, Titius and Plancus (two of Antonius' chiefest friends and that had been both of them Consuls), for the great injuries Cleopatra did them, because they hindered all they could that she should not come to this war, they went and yielded themselves unto Caesar, and told him where the testament was that Antonius had made, knowing perfectly what was in it. The will was in the custody of the Vestal nuns; of whom Caesar demanded for it. They answered him that they would not give it him; but if he would go and take it, they would not hinder him. Thereupon Caesar went thither; and having read it first to himself he noted certain places worthy of reproach. So, assembling all the Senate, he read it before them all. Whereupon divers were marvellously offended, and thought it a strange matter that he, being alive, should be punished for that he had appointed by his will to be done after his death. Caesar chiefly took hold of this that he ordained touching his burial; for he willed that his body, though he died at Rome, should be brought in funeral pomp through the midst of the market-place and that it should be sent into Alexandria unto Cleopatra.

Furthermore, among divers other faults wherewith Antonius was to be charged for Cleopatra's sake, Calvisius, one of Caesar's friends, reproved him because he had frankly given Cleopatra all the libraries of the royal city of Pergamum, in the which she had above two hundred thousand several books; again also that, being on a time set at the table, he suddenly rose from the board and trod upon Cleopatra's foot, which was a sign given between them that they were agreed of; that he had also suffered the Ephesians in his presence to call Cleopatra their sovereign lady; that divers times sitting in his tribunal and chair of state, giving audience to all kings and princes, he had received love-letters from Cleopatra, written in tables of onyx or crystal, and that he had read them, sitting in his imperial seat; that one day when Furnius, a man of great account and the eloquentest man of all the Romans, pleaded a matter before him, Cleopatra by chance coming through the market-place in her litter where Furnius was a-pleading, Antonius straight rose out of his seat and left his audience, to follow her litter. This notwithstanding, it was thought Calvisius devised the most part of all these accusations of his own head.

Nevertheless they that loved Antonius were intercessors to the people for him; and amongst them they sent one Geminius unto

Antonius to pray him he would take heed that, through his negligence, his Empire were not taken from him, and that he should be counted an enemy to the people of Rome. This Geminius being arrived in Greece made Cleopatra jealous straight of his coming; because she surmised that he came not but to speak for Octavia. Therefore she spared not to taunt him all supper-time; and moreover, to spite him the more, she made him to be set lowest of all at the board; the which he took patiently, expecting occasion to speak with Antonius. Now Antonius commanding him at the table to tell him what wind brought him thither; he answered him that it was no table-talk, and that he would tell him tomorrow morning fasting; but drunk or fasting, howsoever it were, he was sure of one thing, that all would not go well on his side, unless Cleopatra were sent back into Egypt. Antonius took these words in very ill part. Cleopatra on the other side answered him:

'Thou doest well, Geminius,' said she, 'to tell the truth before thou be compelled by torments.'

But, within few days after, Geminius stale away, and fled to Rome.

The flatterers also, to please Cleopatra, did make her drive many other of Antonius' faithful servants and friends from him, who could not abide the injuries done unto them; among the which these two were chief, Marcus Syllanus, and Dellius the historiographer, who wrote that he fled, because her physician Glaucus told him that Cleopatra had set some secretly to kill him. Furthermore he had Cleopatra's displeasure, because he said one night at supper that they made them drink sour wine, where Sarmentus at Rome drank good wine of Falerna. (This Sarmentus was a pleasant young boy, such as the lords of Rome are wont to have about them to make them pastime, which they call their 'joys'; and he was Octavius Caesar's boy.)

Now after that Caesar had made sufficient preparation, he proclaimed open war against Cleopatra, and made the people to abolish the power and empire of Antonius because he had before given it up unto a woman. And Caesar said furthermore that Antonius was not master of himself, but that Cleopatra had brought him beside himself by her charms and amorous poisons, and that they

that should make war with them should be Mardian the eunuch,
Photinus, and Iras, a woman of Cleopatra's bed-chamber that
frizzled her hair and dressed her head, and Charmion, the which
63 were those that ruled all the affairs of Antonius' empire.

Before this war, as it is reported, many signs and wonders fell out.
First of all, the city of Pisaurum, which was made a colony to
Rome and replenished with people by Antonius, standing upon the
shore side of the sea Adriatic, was by a terrible earthquake sunk into
the ground. One of the images of stone which was set up in the
honour of Antonius in the city of Alba did sweat many days together,
and, though some wiped it away, yet it left not sweating still. In the
city of Patras, whilst Antonius was there, the Temple of Hercules was
burnt with lightning. And at the city of Athens also, in a place where
the war of the giants against the gods is set out in imagery, the
statue of Bacchus with a terrible wind was thrown down in the
theatre. (It was said that Antonius came of the race of Hercules, as
64 you have heard before, and in the manner of his life he followed
Bacchus; and therefore he was called the new Bacchus.) Furthermore,
the same blustering storm of wind overthrew the great monstrous
images at Athens, that were made in the honour of Eumenes and
Attalus, the which men had named and entitled 'the Antonians';
and yet they did hurt none of the other images which were many
65 besides. The admiral galley of Cleopatra was called Antoniad, in the
which there chanced a marvellous ill sign. Swallows had bred under
the poop of her ship; and there came others after them that drave
66 away the first and plucked down their nests.

63 ENOBARBUS: [to Cleopatra]   He is already
                    Traduced for levity; and 'tis said in Rome
                    That Photinus an eunuch and your maids
                    Manage this war.                     (III, 7, 13)
64 See p. 177 note 1 above.
65                 The Antoniad, the Egyptian admiral ...      (III, 10, 2)
66 SCARUS:                  Swallows have built
                    In Cleopatra's sails their nests: the augurers
                    Say they know not, they cannot tell; look grimly,
                    And dare not speak their knowledge.      (IV, 12, 3)

Now when all things were ready and that they drew near to fight, it was found that Antonius had no less than five hundred good ships of war, among which there were many galleys that had eight and ten banks of oars, the which were sumptuously furnished, not so meet for fight as for triumph, a hundred thousand footmen and twelve thousand horsemen; and had with him to aid him these kings and subjects following: Bocchus King of Libya, Tarcondemus King of High Cilicia, Archelaus King of Cappadocia, Philadelphus King of Paphlagonia, Mithridates King of Comagena, and Adallas King of Thracia; all which were there every man in person. The residue that were absent sent their armies; as Polemon King of Pont, Manchus King of Arabia, Herodes King of Jewry; and furthermore, Amyntas King of Lycaonia and of the Galatians; and, besides all 67 these, he had all the aid the King of Medes sent unto him. Now for Caesar, he had two hundred and fifty ships of war, fourscore thousand footmen, and well near as many horsemen as his enemy Antonius. Antonius for his part had all under his dominion from Armenia and the river of Euphrates unto the sea Ionium and Illyricum. Octavius Caesar had also for his part all that which was in our hemisphere, or half part of the world, from Illyria unto the Ocean sea upon the west; then all from the Ocean unto Mare Siculum; and from Afric all that which is against Italy, as Gaul and Spain. Furthermore, all from the province of Cyrenia to Ethiopia was subject unto Antonius.

Now Antonius was made so subject to a woman's will that, though he was a great deal the stronger by land, yet for Cleopatra's

67 OCTAVIUS CAESAR:     He hath given his empire
Up to a whore: who now are levying
The kings o' the earth for war: he hath assembled
Bocchus, the king of Libya; Archelaus,
Of Cappadocia; Philadelphos, king
Of Paphlagonia; the Thracian king, Adallas;
King Malchus of Arabia; King of Pont;
Herod of Jewry; Mithridates, king
Of Comagene; Polemon and Amyntas,
The kings of Mede and Lycaonia,
With a more larger list of sceptres.     (III, 6, 66)

58 sake he would needs have this battle tried by sea; though he saw before his eyes that, for lack of watermen, his captains did prest by force all sorts of men out of Greece that they could take up in the field, as travellers, muleteers, reapers, harvest men, and young boys, and yet could they not sufficiently furnish his galleys; so that the most part of them were empty, and could scant row, because they lacked watermen enow. But on the contrary side Caesar's ships were not built for pomp, high and great, only for a sight and bravery; but they were light of yarage, armed and furnished with 69 watermen as many as they needed, and had them all in readiness in the havens of Tarentum and Brundusium.

So Octavius Caesar sent unto Antonius to will him to delay no more time, but to come on with his army into Italy; and that for his own part he would give him safe harbour, to land without any trouble and that he would withdraw his army from the sea as far as one horse could run, until he had put his army ashore and had lodged his men. Antonius on the other side bravely sent him word again, and challenged the combat of him man to man, though he were the elder; and that, if he refused him so, he would then fight a battle with him in the fields of Pharsalia, as Julius Caesar and Pompey 70 had done before.

| | | |
|---|---|---|
| 68 ANTONY: | Canidius, we | |
| | Will fight with him by sea. | |
| CLEOPATRA: | By sea! what else? | |
| CANIDIUS: | Why will my lord do so? | |
| ANTONY: | For that he dares us to't. | |
| | | (III, 7, 28) |

| | | |
|---|---|---|
| 69 ENOBARBUS: | Your ships are not well mann'd; | |
| | Your mariners are muleters, reapers, people | |
| | Ingross'd by swift impress; in Caesar's fleet | |
| | Are those that often have 'gainst Pompey fought: | |
| | Their ships are yare; yours, heavy: no disgrace | |
| | Shall fall you for refusing him at sea, | |
| | Being prepared for land. | (III, 7, 35) |

| | | |
|---|---|---|
| 70 ENOBARBUS: | So hath my lord dared him to single fight. | |
| CANIDIUS: | Ay, and to wage this battle at Pharsalia, | |
| | Where Caesar fought with Pompey. | (III, 7, 31) |

Now, whilst Antonius rode at anchor, lying idly in harbour at the head of Actium, in the place where the city of Nicopolis standeth at this present, Caesar had quickly passed the sea Ionium and taken a

71 place called Toryne, before Antonius understood that he had taken ship. Then began his men to be afraid, because his army by land was left behind. But Cleopatra making light of it:

'And what danger, I pray you,' said she, 'if Caesar keep at Toryne?'*

The next morning by break of day, his enemies coming with full force of oars in battle against him, Antonius was afraid that if they came to join they would take and carry away his ships that had no men of war in them. So he armed all his watermen, and set them in order of battle upon the fore-castle of their ships, and then lift up all his ranks of oars towards the element, as well on the one side as on the other, with the prows against the enemies, at the entry and mouth of the gulf which beginneth at the point of Actium; and so kept them in order of battle, as if they had been armed and furnished with watermen and soldiers. Thus Octavius Caesar, being finely deceived by this stratagem, retired presently and therewithal Antonius very wisely and suddenly did cut him off from fresh water. For, understanding that the places where Octavius Caesar landed had very little store of water, and yet very bad, he shut them in with strong ditches and trenches he cast, to keep them from sallying out at their pleasure, and so to go seek water farther off.

Furthermore, he dealt very friendly and courteously with

71 ANTONY:                          Is it not strange, Canidius,
                  That from Tarentum and Brundusium
                  He could so quickly cut the Ionian sea,
                  And take in Toryne? . . .

MESSENGER:   The news is true, my lord; he is descried;
                  Caesar has taken Toryne.

ANTONY:       Can he be there in person? 'tis impossible;
                  Strange that his power should be.     (III, 7, 21; 55)

* The grace of this taunt cannot properly be expressed in any other tongue because of the equivocation of this word *Toryne*, which signifieth a city of Albania, and also a ladle to skim the pot with: as if she meant, Caesar sat by the fire side, skimming of the pot.

Domitius, and against Cleopatra's mind. For, he being sick of an
ague when he went and took a little boat to go unto Caesar's camp,
Antonius was very sorry for it, but yet he sent after him all his carriage, train, and men; and the same Domitius, as though he gave
him to understand that he repented his open treason, he died imme-
72 diately after. There were certain kings also that forsook him, and
73 turned on Caesar's side; as Amyntas and Deiotarus.

Furthermore his fleet and navy that was unfortunate in all things
and unready for service compelled him to change his mind and to

72 ANTONY:                        Who's gone this morning?
SOLDIER:                                              Who!
          One ever near thee: call for Enobarbus,
          He shall not hear thee; or from Caesar's camp
          Say 'I am none of thine.'
ANTONY:                            What say'st thou?
SOLDIER:                                          Sir,
          He is with Caesar.
EROS:                        Sir, his chests and treasure
          He has not with him.
ANTONY:                      Is he gone?
SOLDIER:                                Most certain.
ANTONY:   Go, Eros, send his treasure after; do it;
          Detain no jot, I charge thee: write to him –
          I will subscribe – gentle adieus and greetings,
          Say that I wish he never find more cause
          To change a master. O, my fortunes have
          Corrupted honest men! Dispatch. – Enobarbus!   (IV, 5, 6)

See also IV, 6, 12–39, and IV, 9, 5–23, especially:
ENOBARBUS:               O Antony,
          Nobler than my revolt is infamous,
          Forgive me in thine own particular;
          But let the world rank me in register
          A master-leaver and a fugitive:
          O Antony! O Antony!                    Dies. (IV, 9, 18)
73 CANIDIUS:             To Caesar will I render
          My legions and my horse: six kings already
          Show me the way of yielding.            (III, 10, 33)

hazard battle by land. And Canidius also, who had charge of his army by land, when time came to follow Antonius' determination, he turned him clean contrary, and counselled him to send Cleopatra back again, and himself to retire into Macedon, to fight there on the mainland. And furthermore told him that Dicomes King of the Getes promised him to aid him with a great power; and that it should be no shame nor dishonour to him to let Caesar have the sea, because himself and his men both had been well practised and exercised in battles by sea, in the war of Sicilia against Sextus
74 Pompeius; but rather that he should do against all reason, he having so great skill and experience of battles by land as he had, if he should not employ the force and valiantness of so many lusty armed footmen as he had ready, but would weaken his army by dividing them into
75 ships. But now, notwithstanding all these good persuasions, Cleopatra forced him to put all to the hazard of battle by sea; considering with herself how she might fly and provide for her safety, not to help him to win the victory, but to fly more easily after the battle lost.

Betwixt Antonius' camp and his fleet of ships there was a great high point of firm land that ran a good way into the sea, the which Antonius used often for a walk, without mistrust of fear or danger. One of Caesar's men perceived it, and told his master that he would laugh if they could take up Antonius in the midst of his walk. Thereupon Caesar sent some of his men to lie in ambush for him, and they missed not much of taking of him; for they took him that came be-

74 ENOBARBUS:               In Caesar's fleet
Are those that often have 'gainst Pompey fought.

(III, 7, 37)

75 ENOBARBUS:   Most worthy sir, you therein throw away
The absolute soldiership you have by land;
Distract your army, which doth most consist
Of war-mark'd footmen; leave unexecuted
Your own renowned knowledge; quite forego
The way which promises assurance; and
Give up yourself merely to chance and hazard,
From firm security.                          (III, 7, 42)

fore him, because they discovered too soon; and so Antonius scaped very hardly.

So, when Antonius had determined to fight by sea, he set all the other ships on fire but three-score ships of Egypt, and reserved only but the best and greatest galleys, from three banks unto ten banks of oars. Into them he put two-and-twenty thousand fighting men, with two thousand darters and slingers. Now, as he was setting his men in order of battle, there was a captain (and a valiant man that had served Antonius in many battles and conflicts and had all his body hacked and cut) who, as Antonius passed by him, cried out unto him and said:

'O noble Emperor, how cometh it to pass that you trust to these vile brittle ships? What, do you mistrust these wounds of mine and this sword? Let the Egyptians and Phoenicians fight by sea, and set us on the mainland, where we use to conquer, or to be slain on our feet.'

Antonius passed by him and said never a word, but only beckoned to him with his hand and head, as though he willed him to be of good courage, although indeed he had no great courage himself. For, when the masters of the galleys and pilots would have let their sails alone, he made them clap them on, saying, to colour the matter withal, that not one of his enemies should scape.

All that day, and the three days following, the sea rose so high and

| | |
|---|---|
| ANTONY: | I'll fight at sea. |
| CLEOPATRA: | I have sixty sails, Caesar none better. |
| ANTONY: | Our overplus of shipping will we burn; |
| | And, with the rest full-mann'd, from the head of Actium |
| | Beat the approaching Caesar. But, if we fail, |
| | We then can do't at land. (III, 7, 49) |
| ANTONY: | How now, worthy soldier! |
| SOLDIER: | O noble emperor, do not fight by sea; |
| | Trust not to rotten planks: do you misdoubt |
| | This sword and these my wounds? Let the Egyptians |
| | And the Phoenicians go a-ducking: we |
| | Have used to conquer, standing on the earth, |
| | And fighting foot to foot. |
| ANTONY: | Well, well; away! (III, 7, 61) |

was so boisterous that the battle was put off. The fifth day the storm
ceased and the sea calmed again; and then they rowed with force of
oars in battle one against the other, Antonius leading the right wing
with Publicola, and Caelius the left and Marcus Octavius and Marcus
Justeius the midst. Octavius Caesar on the other side, had placed
Agrippa in the left wing of his army, and had kept the right wing
for himself. For the armies by land Canidius was general of Antonius'
side, and Taurus of Caesar's side; who kept their men in battle ray
the one before the other, upon the sea side, without stirring one
78 against the other.

Further, touching both the chieftains: Antonius, being in a swift
pinnace, was carried up and down by force of oars through his
army, and spake to his people to encourage them to fight valiantly,
as if they were on mainland, because of the steadiness and heaviness
of their ships; and commanded the pilots and masters of the galleys
that they should not stir, none otherwise than if they were at anchor,
and so to receive the first charge of their enemies, and that they should
not go out of the strait of the gulf. Caesar betimes in the morning,
going out of his tent to see his ships throughout met a man by chance
that drave an ass before him. Caesar asked the man what his name was.
The poor man told him that his name was Eutychus (to say, 'Fortunate') and his ass's name Nicon (to say, 'Conqueror'). Therefore
Caesar after he had won the battle setting out the market-place with
the spurs of the galleys he had taken, for a sign of his victory, he
caused also the man and his ass to be set up in brass. When he had
visited the order of his army throughout, he took a little pinnace,
and went to the right wing, and wondered when he saw his enemies
lie still in the strait and stirred not. For, discerning them afar off,

78 SOLDIER:                    You keep by land
        The legions and the horse whole, do you not?
CANIDIUS:    Marcus Octavius, Marcus Justeius,
        Publicola, and Caelius, are for sea:
        But we keep whole by land. This speed of Caesar's
        Carries beyond belief. . . . Who's his lieutenant, hear you?
SOLDIER:     They say, one Taurus.
CANIDIUS:                         Well I know the man.     (III, 7, 71)

men would have thought they had been ships riding at anchor; and a good while he was so persuaded. So he kept his galleys eight furlong from his enemies.

About noon there rose a little gale of wind from the sea; and then Antonius' men waxing angry with tarrying so long; and trusting to the greatness and height of their ships, as if they had been invincible, they began to march forward with their left wing. Caesar seeing that was a glad man, and began a little to give back from the right wing, to allure them to come farther out of the strait and gulf, to the end that he might with his light ships well manned with watermen turn and environ the galleys of the enemies, the which were heavy of yarage, both for their bigness as also for lack of watermen to row them. When the skirmish began and that they came to join, there was no great hurt at the first meeting, neither did the ships vehemently hit one against the other, as they do commonly in fight by sea. For, on the one side, Antonius' ships for their heaviness could not have the strength and swiftness to make their blows of any force; and Caesar's ships, on the other side, took great heed not to rush and shock with the forecastles of Antonius' ships, whose prows were armed with great brazen spurs. Furthermore they durst not flank them, because their points were easily broken, which way so ever they came to set upon his ships, that were made of great main square pieces of timber, bound together with great iron pins. So that the battle was much like to a battle by land, or, to speak more properly, to the assault of a city. For there were always three or four of Caesar's ships about one of Antonius' ships, and the soldiers fought with their pikes, halberds, and darts, and threw pots and darts with fire. Antonius' ships on the other side bestowed among them, with their cross-bows and engines of battery, great store of shot from their high towers of wood that were upon their ships.

Now Publicola seeing Agrippa put forth his left wing of Caesar's army, to compass in Antonius' ships that fought, he was driven also to loof off to have more room, and, going a little at one side, to put those farther off that were afraid, and in the midst of the battle. For they were sore distressed by Aruntius.

Howbeit the battle was yet of even hand, and the victory doubtful, being indifferent to both; when suddenly they saw the three-score ships of Cleopatra busy about their yard-masts, and hoising sail to fly. So they fled through the midst of them that were in fight, for they had been placed behind the great ships, and did marvellously disorder the other ships. For the enemies themselves wondered much to see
79 them sail in that sort with full sail towards Peloponnesus. There Antonius showed plainly that he had not only lost the courage and heart of an Emperor but also of a valiant man, and that he was not his own man, proving that true which an old man spake in mirth: that the soul of a lover lived in another body, and not in his own. He was so carried away with the vain love of this woman, as if he had been glued unto her and that she could not have removed without moving of him also. For, when he saw Cleopatra's ship under sail, he forgot, forsook, and betrayed them that fought for him, and embarked upon a galley with five banks of oars, to follow her that was already begun to overthrow him, and would in the end be his utter
80 destruction. When she knew his galley afar off, she lift up a sign in

| | |
|---|---|
| 79 ENOBARBUS: | Naught, naught, all naught! I can behold no longer: |
| | The Antoniad, the Egyptian admiral, |
| | With all their sixty, fly and turn the rudder: |
| | To see't mine eyes are blasted.... |
| | How appears the fight? |
| SCARUS: | On our side like the token'd pestilence, |
| | Where death is sure. Yon ribaudred nag of Egypt – |
| | Whom leprosy o'ertake! – i' the midst o'the fight, |
| | When vantage like a pair of twins appear'd. |
| | Both as the same, or rather ours the elder, |
| | The breese upon her, like a cow in June, |
| | Hoists sails and flies . . . |
| CANIDIUS: | Toward Peloponnesus are they fled.     (III, 10, 1; 8; 31) |
| 80 SCARUS: | We have kiss'd away |
| | Kingdoms and provinces . . . She once being loof'd, |
| | The noble ruin of her magic, Antony, |
| | Claps on his sea-wing, and, like a doting mallard, |
| | Leaving the fight in height, flies after her: |
| | I never saw an action of such shame; |

the poop of her ship, and so Antonius coming to it was plucked up where Cleopatra was; howbeit he saw her not at his first coming, nor she him, but went and sat down alone in the prow of his ship, and said never a word, clapping his head between both his hands.

In the meantime, came certain light brigantines of Caesar's that followed him hard. So Antonius straight turned the prow of his ship, and presently put the rest to flight, saving one Eurycles Lacedaemonian, that followed him near and pressed upon him with great courage, shaking a dart in his hand over the prow as though he would have thrown it unto Antonius. Antonius seeing him, came to the forecastle of his ship, and asked him what he was that durst follow Antonius so near?

'I am,' answered he, 'Eurycles the son of Lachares, who through Caesar's good fortune seeketh to revenge the death of my father.' This Lachares was condemned of felony and beheaded by Antonius. But yet Eurycles durst not venture upon Antonius' ship, but set upon the other admiral galley (for there were two), and fell upon him with such a blow of his brazen spur, that was so heavy and big that he

---

ANTONY:     Experience, manhood, honour, ne'er before
                Did violate so itself.         (III, 10, 7; 18)
                I have lost command. . . .
                O, whither hast thou led me, Egypt? See,
                How I convey my shame out of thine eyes
                By looking back what I have left behind
                'Stroy'd in dishonour.

CLEOPATRA:              O my lord, my lord.
                Forgive my fearful sails! I little thought
                You would have follow'd.

ANTONY:             Egypt, thou knew'st too well
                My heart was to thy rudder tied by the strings,
                And thou shouldst tow me after: o'er my spirit
                Thy full supremacy thou knew'st, and that
                Thy beck might from the bidding of the gods
                Command me.         (III, 11, 23; 51)

turned her round and took her, with another that was loaden with very rich stuff and carriage.

After Eurycles had left Antonius, he returned again to his place and sat down, speaking never a word as he did before; and so lived three days alone, without speaking to any man. But, when he arrived at the head of Taenarus, there Cleopatra's women first brought Antonius and Cleopatra to speak together and afterwards 31 to sup and lie together.

Then began there again a great number of merchants' ships to gather about them, and some of their friends that had escaped from this overthrow; who brought news that his army by sea was overthrown, but that they thought the army by land was yet whole. Then Antonius sent unto Canidius to return with his army into Asia by Macedon. Now for himself, he determined to cross over into Afric; and took one of his carects or hulks loaden with gold and silver and other rich carriage, and gave it unto his friends, commanding them to depart and to seek to save themselves. They answered him weeping that they would neither do it nor yet forsake him. Then Antonius very courteously and lovingly did comfort them, and prayed them to depart; and wrote unto Theophilus, governor of Corinth, that he would see them safe and help to hide them in some

| | |
|---|---|
| 81 EROS: | Nay, gentle madam, to him, comfort him. |
| IRAS: | Do, most dear queen. |
| CHARMIAN: | Do! why: what else? . . . |
| EROS: | Sir, sir . . . The queen, my lord, the queen. |
| IRAS: | Go to him, madam, speak to him. |
| | He is unqualitied with very shame. |
| CLEOPATRA: | Well then, sustain me: O! |
| EROS: | Most noble sir, arise; the queen approaches: |
| | Her head's declined, and death will seize her, but |
| | Your comfort makes the rescue . . . |
| CLEOPATRA: | Pardon, pardon! |
| ANTONY: | Fall not a tear, I say; one of them rates |
| | All that is won and lost: give me a kiss; |
| | Even this repays me . . . Love, I am full of lead. |
| | Some wine, within there, and our viands! |

(III, 11, 25; 42; 68)

82 secret place until they had made their way and peace with Caesar. This Theophilus was the father of Hipparchus, who was had in great estimation about Antonius. He was the first of all his enfranchised
83 bondmen that revolted from him and yielded unto Caesar, and afterwards went and dwelt at Corinth. And thus it stood with Antonius.

Now, for his army by sea, that fought before the head or foreland of Actium, they held out a long time; and nothing troubled them more than a great boisterous wind that rose full in the prows of their ships, and yet with much ado his navy was at length overthrown, five hours within night. There were not slain above five thousand men; but yet there were three hundred ships taken, as Octavius Caesar writeth himself in his *Commentaries*. Many plainly saw Antonius fly, and yet could very hardly believe it, that he, that had nineteen legions whole by land and twelve thousand horsemen upon the
84 sea side, would so have forsaken them, and have fled so cowardly; as

82 ANTONY:      Friends, come hither:
I am so lated in the world, that I
Have lost my way for ever: I have a ship
Laden with gold; take that, divide it; fly,
And make your peace with Caesar.

ALL:             Fly! not we.

ANTONY:  I have fled myself; and have instructed cowards
To run and show their shoulders. Friends, be gone;
I have myself resolved upon a course
Which has no need of you; be gone:
My treasure's in the harbour, take it . . .
    . . . Friends, be gone: you shall
Have letters from me to some friends that will
Sweep your way for you. Pray you, look not sad,
Nor make replies of loathness: take the hint
Which my despair proclaims; let that be left
Which leaves itself: to the sea-side straightway:
I will possess you of that ship and treasure.  (III, 11, 2; 15)

83 See p. 271 note 100.

84 ANTONY:      Canidius,
Our nineteen legions thou shalt hold by land,
And our twelve thousand horse.     (III, 7, 58)

if he had not oftentimes proved both the one and the other fortune, and that he had not been throughly acquainted with the diverse changes and fortunes of battles. And yet his soldiers still wished for him, and ever hoped that he would come by some means or other unto them. Furthermore they showed themselves so valiant and faithful unto him that after they certainly knew he was fled they kept themselves whole together seven days. In the end Canidius, Antonius' lieutenant, flying by night and forsaking his camp, when they saw themselves thus destitute of their heads and leaders
85 they yielded themselves unto the stronger.

This done, Caesar sailed towards Athens, and there made peace with the Grecians, and divided the rest of the corn that was taken up for Antonius' army unto the towns and cities of Greece, the which had been brought to extreme misery and poverty, clean without money, slaves, horse, and other beasts of carriage; so that my grandfather Nicarchus told that all the citizens of our city of Chaeronea (not one excepted) were driven themselves to carry a certain measure of corn on their shoulders to the sea side, that lieth directly over against the isle of Anticyra, and yet were they driven thither with whips. They carried it thus but once. For the second time that they were charged again to make the like carriage, all the corn being ready to be carried, news came that Antonius had lost the battle. And so scaped our poor city. For Antonius' soldiers and deputies fled immediately; and the citizens divided the corn amongst them.

Antonius being arrived in Libya, he sent Cleopatra before into Egypt from the city of Paraetonium; and he himself remained very solitary, having only two of his friends with him, with whom he wandered up and down; both of them orators: the one Aristocrates a Grecian; and the other Lucilius a Roman, of whom we have
86 written in another place that, at the battle where Brutus was over-

85 See page 253 note 73 above, and
   ENOBARBUS:              Canidius and the rest
                    That fell away have entertainment, but
                    No honourable trust.                (IV, 6, 16)
86 See *Life of Brutus*, pp. 167–9 and notes.

thrown by the city of Philippes, he came and willingly put himself into the hands of those that followed Brutus, saying that it was he; because Brutus in the meantime might have liberty to save himself; and, afterwards, because Antonius saved his life, he still remained with him, and was very faithful and friendly unto him till his death.

But when Antonius heard that he whom he had trusted with the government of Libya, and unto whom he had given the charge of his army there, had yielded unto Caesar, he was so mad withal, that he would have slain himself for anger, had not his friends about him withstood him, and kept him from it.

So he went unto Alexandria, and there found Cleopatra about a wonderful enterprise, and of great attempt. Betwixt the Red Sea and the sea between the lands that point upon the coast of Egypt there is a little piece of land that divideth both the seas and separateth Afric from Asia; the which strait is so narrow at the end where the two seas are narrowest that it is not above three hundred furlongs over. Cleopatra went about to lift her ships out of the one sea, and to hale them over the strait into the other sea; that, when her ships were come into the Gulf of Arabia, she might then carry all her gold and silver away, and so with a great company of men go and dwell in some place about the Ocean sea far from the sea Mediterranean, to scape the danger and bondage of this war. But now, because the Arabians dwelling about the city of Petra did burn the first ships that were brought to land, and that Antonius thought that his army by land, which he left at Actium, was yet whole, she left off her enterprise and determined to keep all the ports and passages of her realm.

Antonius, he forsook the city and company of his friends, and built him a house in the sea, by the isle of Pharos, upon certain forced mounts which he caused to be cast into the sea, and dwelt there, as a man that banished himself from all men's company, saying that he would lead Timon's life, because he had the like wrong offered him that was before offered unto Timon; and that for the unthankfulness of those he had done good unto and whom he took to be his friends he was angry with all men and would trust no man.

This Timon was a citizen of Athens that lived about the war of

Peloponnesus, as appeareth by Plato and Aristophanes' comedies, in the which they mocked him, calling him a viper and malicious man unto mankind, to shun all other men's companies but the company of young Alcibiades, a bold and insolent youth, whom he would greatly feast and make much of, and kissed him very gladly. Apemantus, wondering at it, asked him the cause what he meant to make so much of that young man alone and to hate all others. Timon answered him:

'I do it,' said he, 'because I know that one day he shall do great
87 mischief unto the Athenians.'

This Timon sometimes would have Apemantus in his company, because he was much like of his nature and conditions, and also followed him in manner of life. On a time when they solemnly celebrated the feasts called *Choae* at Athens (to wit, the feasts of the dead, where they make sprinklings and sacrifices for the dead) and that they two then feasted together by themselves, Apemantus said unto the other:

'Oh, here is a trim banquet, Timon.'

87 ALCIBIADES:  When I have laid proud Athens on a heap, –
   TIMON:  Warr'st thou 'gainst Athens?
  ALCIBIADES:                    Ay, Timon, and have cause.
   TIMON:  The gods confound them all in thy conquest;
             And thee after, when thou hast conquer'd!
  ALCIBIADES:  Why me, Timon?
   TIMON:                That, by killing of villains,
             Thou wast born to conquer my country.

                                      (*Timon of Athens*, IV, 3, 101)

   TIMON:  If Alcibiades kill my countrymen,
             Let Alcibiades know this of Timon,
             That Timon cares not. But if he sack fair Athens,
             And take our goodly aged men by the beards,
             Giving our holy virgins to the stain
             Of contumelious, beastly, mad-brain'd war
             Then let him know, and tell him Timon speaks it,
             In pity of our aged and our youth,
             I cannot choose but tell him, that I care not.

                                        (V, 1, 172)

Timon answered again:

88 'Yea,' said he, 'so thou wert not here.'

It is reported of him also that this Timon on a time, the people being assembled in the market-place about dispatch of some affairs, got up into the pulpit for orations, where the orators commonly use to speak unto the people; and silence being made, every man listening to hear what he would say, because it was a wonder to see him in that place, at length he began to speak in this manner:

'My Lords of Athens, I have a little yard in my house, where there groweth a fig tree, on the which many citizens have hanged themselves; and because I mean to make some building on the place, I thought good to let you all understand it that, before the fig tree be cut down, if any of you be desperate, you may there in time go 89 hang yourselves.'

He died in the city of Hales, and was buried upon the sea side. Now it chanced so, that, the sea getting in, it compassed his tomb round about, that no man could come to it; and upon the same was 90 written this epitaph:

> *Here lies a wretched corse, of wretched soul bereft.*
> *Seek not my name. A plague consume you wicked wretches left!*

88 See the characterization of Apemantus in *Timon of Athens*, especially:

APEMANTUS:     Here; I will mend thy feast.

TIMON:  First mend my company, take away thyself.

APEMANTUS: So I shall mend mine own, by the lack of thine. (IV, 3, 282)

89 TIMON:  I have a tree, which grows here in my close,

     That mine own use invites me to cut down,

     And shortly must I fell it: tell my friends,

     Tell Athens, in the sequence of degree

     From high to low throughout, that whoso please

     To stop affliction, let him take his haste,

     Come hither, ere my tree hath felt the axe,

     And hang himself.     (V, 1, 208)

90 TIMON:  Timon hath made his everlasting mansion

     Upon the beached verge of the salt flood;

     Who once a day with his embossed froth

     The turbulent surge shall cover: thither come,

     And let my grave-stone be your oracle. (V, 1, 218)

It is reported that Timon himself when he lived made this epitaph. For that which is commonly rehearsed was not his, but made by the poet Callimachus:

> *Here lie I, Timon, who alive all living men did hate.*
> 91 *Pass by, and curse thy fill. But pass, and stay not here thy gait.*

Many other things could we tell you of this Timon, but this little shall suffice at this present.

But now to return to Antonius again. Canidius himself came to bring him news that he had lost all his army by land at Actium. On the other side he was advertised also that Herodes King of Jewry, who had also certain legions and bands with him, was revolted unto 92 Caesar, and all the other kings in like manner; so that, saving those that were about him, he had none left him.

All this notwithstanding did nothing trouble him; and it seemed that he was contented to forgo all his hope, and so to be rid of all his care and troubles. Thereupon he left his solitary house he had built by the sea, which he called *Timoneon*; and Cleopatra received him into her royal palace. He was no sooner come thither, but he straight set all the city on rioting and banqueting again, and himself to liberality and gifts. He caused the son of Julius Caesar and Cleopatra to be enrolled, according to the manner of the Romans, amongst the number of young men; and gave Antyllus, his eldest son he had by Fulvia, the man's gown (the which was a plain gown without guard or embroidery of purple). For these things there was kept great feasting, banqueting, and dancing in Alexandria many days together.

*91* SOLDIER:    My noble general, Timon is dead;
                    Entomb'd upon the very hem o'the sea;
                    And on his grave-stone this insculpture, which
                    With wax I brought away, whose soft impression
                    Interprets for my poor ignorance.

ALCIBIADES:   *Here lies a wretched corse, of wretched soul bereft:*
                    *Seek not my name. A plague consume you wicked caitiffs left!*
                    *Here lie I, Timon, who alive all living men did hate.*
                    *Pass by, and curse thy fill. But pass, and stay not here thy gait.*
                                      (v, 4, 65)

*92* See note 96 below.

Indeed, they did break their first order they had set down, which they call *Amimetobion* (as much to say 'no life comparable'), and did set up another, which they called *Synapothanumenon* (signifying 'the order and agreement of those that will die together'), the which in exceeding sumptuousness and cost was not inferior to the first. For their friends made themselves to be enrolled in this order of those that would die together, and so made great feasts one to another; for every man, when it came to his turn, feasted their whole company and fraternity.

Cleopatra in the meantime was very careful in gathering all sorts of poisons together, to destroy men. Now, to make proof of those 3 poisons which made men die with least pain, she tried it upon condemned men in prison. For, when she saw the poisons that were sudden and vehement and brought speedy death with grievous torments, and, in contrary manner, that such as were more mild and gentle had not that quick speed and force to make one die suddenly, she afterwards went about to prove the stinging of snakes and adders, and made some to be applied unto men in her sight, some in one sort and some in another. So, when she had daily made divers and sundry proofs, she found none of them all she had proved so fit as the biting of an aspic, the which causeth only a heaviness of the head, without swounding or complaining, and bringeth a great desire also to sleep, with a little sweat in the face, and so by little and little taketh away the senses and vital powers, no living creature perceiving that the patients feel any pain. For they are so sorry when anybody awaketh them, and taketh them up, as those that being 4 taken out of a sound sleep are very heavy and desirous to sleep.

3 OCTAVIUS CAESAR:      Her physician tells me
                    She hath pursued conclusions infinite
                    Of easy ways to die.      (*Antony and Cleopatra*, v, 2, 357)

4 CLEOPATRA:      Hast thou the pretty worm of Nilus there,
                    That kills and pains not?              (v, 2, 243)
                          Peace, peace!
                    Dost thou not see my baby at my breast,
                    That sucks the nurse asleep? . . .
                    As sweet as balm, as soft as air, as gentle . . .

This notwithstanding, they sent ambassadors unto Octavius Caesar in Asia, Cleopatra requesting the realm of Egypt for their children, and Antonius praying that he might be suffered to live at Athens like a private man, if Caesar would not let him remain in Egypt. And, because they had no other men of estimation about them (for that some were fled, and, those that remained, they did not greatly trust them), they were enforced to send Euphronius the
95 schoolmaster of their children. For Alexas Laodician, who was brought into Antonius' house and favour by means of Timagenes and afterwards was in greater credit with him than any other

95 ANTONY:                  We sent our schoolmaster;
Is he come back?               (III, 11, 71)

OCTAVIUS CAESAR: Let him appear that's come from Antony.
Know you him?

DOLABELLA:                 Caesar, 'tis his schoolmaster:
An argument that he is pluck'd, when hither
He sends so poor a pinion of his wing,
Which had superfluous kings for messengers
Not many moons gone by.
*Enter ambassador from Antony.*

OCTAVIUS CAESAR:             Approach, and speak.

AMBASSADOR: Such as I am, I come from Antony:
I was of late as petty to his ends
As is the morn-dew on the myrtle-leaf
To his grand sea.

OCTAVIUS CAESAR:       Be't so: declare thine office.

AMBASSADOR: Lord of his fortunes he salutes thee, and
Requires to live in Egypt: which not granted,
He lessens his requests; and to thee sues
To let him breathe between the heavens and earth,
A private man in Athens: this for him.
Next, Cleopatra does confess thy greatness;
Submits her to thy might; and of thee craves
The circle of the Ptolemies for her heirs,
Now hazarded to thy grace.       (III, 12, 1)

CHARMIAN:              Downy windows, close; ...
Speak softly, wake her not.   (V, 2, 311; 314; 319; 323)

Grecian (for that he had alway been one of Cleopatra's ministers to
win Antonius and to overthrow all his good determinations to use his
wife Octavia well), him Antonius had sent unto Herodes King of
Jewry, hoping still to keep him his friend, that he should not revolt
from him. But he remained there, and betrayed Antonius. For,
where he should have kept Herodes from revolting from him, he
persuaded him to turn to Caesar; and, trusting King Herodes, he
presumed to come in Caesar's presence. Howbeit Herodes did him
no pleasure; for he was presently taken prisoner, and sent in chains
to his own country; and there by Caesar's commandment put to
death. Thus was Alexas in Antonius' lifetime put to death for betray-
6 ing of him.

Furthermore, Caesar would not grant unto Antonius' requests.
But, for Cleopatra, he made her answer that he would deny her
nothing reasonable, so that she would either put Antonius to death
7 or drive him out of her country. Therewithal he sent Thyreus one of
his men unto her, a very wise and discreet man, who, bringing letters
of credit from a young lord unto a noble lady, and that besides greatly
8 liked her beauty, might easily by his eloquence have persuaded her.

6 ENOBARBUS:    Alexas did revolt; and went to Jewry on
                Affairs of Antony; there did persuade
                Great Herod to incline himself to Caesar,
                And leave his master Antony: for this pains
                Caesar hath hang'd him.          (IV, 6, 12)

7 OCTAVIUS CAESAR:        For Antony,
                I have no ears to his request. The queen
                Of audience nor desire shall fail, so she
                From Egypt drive her all-disgraced friend,
                Or take his life there: this if she perform,
                She shall not sue unheard. So to them both.   (III, 12, 19)

8 OCTAVIUS CAESAR: [to Thidias]  To try thy eloquence, now 'tis time:
                        dispatch;
                From Antony win Cleopatra: promise,
                And in our name, what she requires; add more,
                From thine invention, offers: women are not
                In their best fortunes strong; but want will perjure

He was longer in talk with her than any man else was, and the Queen herself also did him great honour; insomuch as he made Antonius jealous of him. Whereupon Antonius caused him to be
99 taken and well-favouredly whipped, and so sent him unto Caesar;

99 CLEOPATRA:                                What's your name?
THIDIAS:          My name is Thidias.
CLEOPATRA:                          Most kind messenger,
                 Say to great Caesar this: in deputation
                 I kiss his conquering hand: tell him, I am prompt
                 To lay my crown at's feet, and there to kneel:
                 Tell him, from his all-obeying breath I hear
                 The doom of Egypt.
THIDIAS:                            'Tis your noblest course.
                 Wisdom and fortune combating together,
                 If that the former dare but what it can,
                 No chance may shake it. Give me grace to lay
                 My duty on your hand.
CLEOPATRA:                          Your Caesar's father oft,
                 When he hath mused of taking kingdoms in,
                 Bestow'd his lips on that unworthy place,
                 As it rain'd kisses.
                           *Enter Antony and Enobarbus.*
ANTONY:                            Favours, by Jove that thunders!
                 What art thou, fellow? . . .
                 Approach, there! Ah, you kite! . . .
                 Take hence this Jack, and whip him . . . Moon and
                      stars!
                 Whip him. Were't twenty of the greatest tributaries
                 That do acknowledge Caesar, should I find them
                 So saucy with the hand of she here, – what's her name,
                 Since she was Cleopatra? Whip him, fellows,
                 Till, like a boy, you see him cringe his face,
                 And whine aloud for mercy: take him hence.

                 ─────

                 The ne'er touch'd vestal: try thy cunning, Thidias;
                 Make thine own edict for thy pains, which we
                 Will answer as a law.                    (III, 12, 26)

and bade him tell him that he made him angry with him, because
he showed himself proud and disdainful towards him, and now
specially when he was easy to be angered, by reason of his present
misery.

'To be short, if this mislike thee,' said he, 'thou hast Hipparchus
one of my enfranchised bondmen with thee. Hang him if thou wilt,
or whip him at thy pleasure, that we may cry quittance.'

From thenceforth Cleopatra, to clear herself of the suspicion he
had of her, she made more of him than ever she did. For first of all,
where she did solemnize the day of her birth very meanly and
sparingly, fit for her present misfortune, she now in contrary manner
did keep it with such solemnity, that she exceeded all measure of

ANTONY:                    Get thee back to Caesar,
            Tell him thy entertainment; look, thou say
            He makes me angry with him; for he seems
            Proud and disdainful, harping on what I am,
            Not what he knew I was: he makes me angry;
            And at this time most easy 'tis to do't,
            When my good stars, that were my former guides,
            Have empty left their orbs, and shot their fires
            Into the abysm of hell. If he mislike
            My speech and what is done, tell him he has
            Hipparchus, my enfranchised bondman, whom
            He may at pleasure whip, or hang, or torture,
            As he shall like, to quit me: urge it thou:
            Hence with thy stripes, begone!          (III, 13, 139)

THIDIAS:    Mark Antony!
ANTONY:     Tug him away: being whipp'd,
            Bring him again: this Jack of Caesar's shall
            Bear us an errand to him.
                    *Exeunt Attendants with Thidias.*
            You were half blasted ere I knew you: ha!
            Have I my pillow left unpress'd in Rome,
            Forborne the getting of a lawful race,
            And by a gem of women, to be abused
            By one that looks on feeders?          (III, 13, 72; 89)

271

sumptuousness and magnificence, so that the guests that were
101 bidden to the feasts and came poor, went away rich.

Now, things passing thus, Agrippa by divers letters sent one after
another unto Caesar prayed him to return to Rome, because the
affairs there did of necessity require his person and presence. Thereupon he did defer the war till the next year following. But, when
winter was done, he returned again through Syria by the coast of
Afric, to make wars against Antonius and his other captains.

When the city of Pelusium was taken, there ran a rumour in the
city that Seleucus, by Cleopatra's consent, had surrendered the same.
But, to clear herself that she did not, Cleopatra brought Seleucus'
wife and children unto Antonius, to be revenged of them at his
pleasure. Furthermore Cleopatra had long before made many
sumptuous tombs and monuments, as well for excellency of workmanship as for height and greatness of building, joining hard to the
Temple of Isis. Thither she caused to be brought all the treasure and
precious things she had of the ancient Kings her predecessors: as
gold, silver, emeralds, pearls, ebony, ivory, and cinnamon; and
besides all that, a marvellous number of torches, faggots, and flax.
So Octavius Caesar being afraid to lose such a treasure and mass of
riches, and that this woman for spite would set it afire, and burn it
every whit, he always sent some one or other unto her from him,
to put her in good comfort, whilst he in the meantime drew near the
city with his army.

So Caesar came, and pitched his camp hard by the city, in the
place where they run and manage their horses. Antonius made a
sally upon him, and fought very valiantly, so that he drave Caesar's
horsemen back, fighting with his men even into their camp. Then he

101 CLEOPATRA:              It is my birthday:
                  I had thought to have held it poor; but, since my lord
                  Is Antony again, I will be Cleopatra.
       ANTONY:    We will yet do well.
       CLEOPATRA: Call all his noble captains to my lord.
       ANTONY:    Do so, we'll speak to them; and tonight I'll force
                  The wine peep through their scars. Come on, my queen;
                  There's sap in't yet.                    (III, 13, 185)

came again to the palace greatly boasting of this victory, and sweetly kissed Cleopatra, armed as he was when he came from the fight, recommending one of his men of arms unto her, that had valiantly fought in this skirmish. Cleopatra to reward his manliness gave him an armour and head-piece of clean gold; howbeit the man at arms, when he had received this rich gift, stale away by night and went to Caesar.

Antonius sent again to challenge Caesar to fight with him hand to hand. Caesar answered him that he had many other ways to die than so. Then Antonius, seeing there was no way more honourable for him to die than fighting valiantly, he determined to set up his rest, both by sea and land. So, being at supper as it is reported, he commanded his officers and household servants, that waited on him at his board, that they should fill his cups full, and make as much of him as they could.

ANTONY:  We have beat him to his camp: run one before,
    And let the queen know of our gests . . . *Enter Cleopatra.*
      [*To Scarus*] Give me thy hand;
    To this great fairy I'll commend thy acts,
    Make her thanks bless thee.
      [*To Cleopatra*] O thou day o' the world,
    Chain mine arm'd neck; leap thou, attire and all,
    Through proof of harness to my heart, and there
    Ride on the pants triumphing! . . . Behold this man:
    Commend unto his lips thy favouring hand;
    Kiss it, my warrior: he hath fought to-day
    As if a god, in hate of mankind, had
    Destroy'd in such a shape.

CLEOPATRA:      I'll give thee, friend,
    An armour all of gold; it was a king's.  (IV, 8, 1; 11; 22)

OCTAVIUS CAESAR: He calls me boy, . . . dares me to personal combat,
    Caesar to Antony: let the old ruffian know
    I have many other ways to die; meantime
    Laugh at his challenge.      (IV, 1, 1)

ANTONY:    Tomorrow, soldier,
    By sea and land I'll fight: or I will live,
    Or bathe my dying honour in the blood
    Shall make it live again.    (IV, 2, 4)

'For,' said he, 'you know not whether you shall do so much for me tomorrow or not, or whether you shall serve another master; and
105 it may be you shall see me no more, but a dead body.'

This notwithstanding, perceiving that his friends and men fell a-weeping to hear him say so, to salve that he had spoken he added this more unto it: that he would not lead them to battle where he thought not rather safely to return with victory than valiantly to
106 die with honour.

Furthermore, the self same night within little of midnight, when all the city was quiet, full of fear and sorrow, thinking what would be the issue and end of this war, it is said that suddenly they heard a

*105* ANTONY:     Call forth my household servants: let's to-night
    Be bounteous at our meal . . .
    Well, my good fellows, wait on me to-night:
    Scant not my cups; and make as much of me
    As when mine empire was your fellow too,
    And suffer'd my command.

CLEOPATRA: [*Aside to Enobarbus*]   What does he mean?

ENOBARBUS: [*Aside to Cleopatra*]   To make his followers weep.

ANTONY:     Tend me to-night;
    May be it is the period of your duty:
    Haply you shall not see me more; or if,
    A mangled shadow: perchance to-morrow
    You'll serve another master. I look on you
    As one that takes his leave.     (IV, 2, 9; 20)

*106* ENOBARBUS:         What mean you, sir,
    To give them this discomfort? Look, they weep;
    And I, an ass, am onion-eyed: for shame,
    Transform us not to women.

ANTONY:              Ho, ho, ho!
    Now the witch take me, if I meant it thus!
    Grace grow where those drops fall! My hearty friends
    You take me in too dolorous a sense;
    For I spake to you for your comfort; did desire you
    To burn this night with torches: know, my hearts,
    I hope well of tomorrow; and will lead you
    Where rather I'll expect victorious life
    Than death and honour.     (IV, 2, 33)

marvellous sweet harmony of sundry sorts of instruments of music, with the cry of a multitude of people, as they had been dancing and had sung as they use in Bacchus' feasts, with movings and turnings after the manner of the Satyrs. And it seemed that this dance went through the city unto the gate that opened to the enemies, and that all the troop that made this noise they heard went out of the city at that gate. Now such as in reason sought the depth of the interpretation of this wonder thought that it was the god unto whom Antonius bare singular devotion to counterfeit and resemble him, that did for-sake them.

The next morning by break of day he went to set those few footmen he had in order upon the hills adjoining unto the city; and there he stood to behold his galleys which departed from the haven and rowed against the galleys of his enemies; and so stood still, looking what exploit his soldiers in them would do. But when by force of rowing they were come near unto them, they first saluted

*Music of the hautboys is under the stage.*

| | |
|---|---|
| A SOLDIER: | Peace! what noise? |
| ANOTHER SOLDIER: | List, list! |
| 1st SOLDIER: | Hark! |
| 2nd SOLDIER: | Music i'the air. |
| 3rd SOLDIER: | Under the earth. |
| 4th SOLDIER: | It signs well, does it not? |
| 3rd SOLDIER: | No. |
| 1st SOLDIER: | Peace, I say! What should this mean? |
| 2nd SOLDIER: | 'Tis the god Hercules, whom Antony loved, |
| | Now leaves him. (IV, 3, 12) |
| ANTONY: | Their preparation is to-day by sea . . . |

      Our foot
Upon the hills adjoining to the city
Shall stay with us: order for sea is given;
They have put forth the haven,
Where their appointment we may best discover,
And look on their endeavour . . .

      Where yond pine does stand,
I shall discover all: I'll bring thee word
Straight, how 'tis like to go.    (IV, 10, 1; 12, 1)

Caesar's men, and then Caesar's men re-saluted them also, and of
two armies made but one, and then did all together row toward the
city. When Antonius saw that his men did forsake him and yielded
unto Caesar, and that his footmen were broken and overthrown he
then fled into the city, crying out that Cleopatra had betrayed him
109 unto them with whom he had made war for her sake. Then she,
being afraid of his fury, fled into the tomb which she had caused to
be made; and there locked the doors unto her, and shut all the
springs of the locks with great bolts; and in the meantime sent unto

| | |
|---|---|
| *109* ANTONY: | All is lost; |

        This foul Egyptian hath betrayed me:
        My fleet hath yielded to the foe; and yonder
        They cast their caps up and carouse together
        Like friends long lost. Triple-turn'd whore! 'Tis thou
        Hast sold me to this novice; and my heart
        Makes only wars on thee. Bid them all fly;
        For when I am revenged upon my charm,
        I have done all ... Betray'd I am:
        O this false soul of Egypt! this grave charm, –
        Whose eye beck'd forth my wars, and call'd them
            home;
        Whose bosom was my crownet, my chief end, –
        Like a right gipsy, hath, at fast and loose,
        Beguiled me to the very heart of loss ...

                *Enter Cleopatra.*
                Ah, thou spell! Avaunt!

| | |
|---|---|
| CLEOPATRA: | Why is my lord enraged against his love? |
| ANTONY: | Vanish, or I shall give thee thy deserving ... |

                *Exit Cleopatra.*
                'Tis well thou'rt gone,

        If it be well to live: but better 'twere
        Thou fell'st into my fury, for one death
        Might have prevented many.       (IV, 12, 9; 24; 39)

| | |
|---|---|
| ANTONY: | I made these wars for Egypt; and the queen, – |

        Whose heart I thought I had, for she had mine ...
        Pack'd cards with Caesar, and false-play'd my glory ...
                            (IV, 14, 15)

10 Antonius to tell him that she was dead. Antonius, believing it, said
unto himself:

'What dost thou look for further, Antonius, sith spiteful fortune
hath taken from thee the only joy thou hadst, for whom thou yet
reservedst thy life?'

When he had said these words, he went into a chamber and un-
11 armed himself; and being naked said thus:

'O Cleopatra, it grieveth me not that I have lost thy company,
12 for I will not be long from thee. But I am sorry that, having been so
great a captain and Emperor, I am indeed condemned to be judged
13 of less courage and noble mind than a woman.'

Now he had a man of his called Eros, whom he loved and trusted
much and whom he had long before caused to swear unto him that
he should kill him when he did command him; and then he willed
14 him to keep his promise. His man drawing his sword lift it up as

| | | |
|---|---|---|
| 10 CHARMIAN: | To the monument! | |
| | There lock yourself, and send him word you are dead. | |
| | The soul and body rive not more in parting | |
| | Than greatness going off. | |
| CLEOPATRA: | To the monument! | (IV, 13, 3) |
| 11 ANTONY: | Unarm, Eros; the long day's task is done, | |
| | And we must sleep . . . Off, pluck off . . . | |
| | No more a soldier. | (IV, 14, 35) |
| 12 ANTONY: | I will o'ertake thee, Cleopatra, and | |
| | Weep for my pardon . . . I come, my queen. | |
| | | (IV, 14, 44; 50) |
| 13 ANTONY: | Since Cleopatra died, | |
| | I have lived in such dishonour, that the gods | |
| | Detest my baseness. I, that with my sword | |
| | Quarter'd the world, and o'er green Neptune's back | |
| | With ships made cities, condemn myself to lack | |
| | The courage of a woman; less noble mind | |
| | Than she which by her death our Caesar tells | |
| | 'I am conqueror of myself.' | (IV, 14, 55) |
| 14 ANTONY: | Thou art sworn, Eros, | |
| | That, when the exigent should come, which now | |
| | Is come indeed, when I should see behind me | |

though he had meant to have stricken his master. But turning his head at one side, he thrust his sword into himself and fell down
115 dead at his master's foot. Then said Antonius:

'O noble Eros, I thank thee for this; and it is valiantly done of thee, to show me what I should do to myself, which thou couldst not
116 do for me.'

Therewithal he took his sword and thrust it into his belly; and so fell down upon a little bed. The wound he had killed him not presently, for the blood stinted a little when he was laid; and when he came somewhat to himself again, he prayed them that were about him to dispatch him. But they all fled out of the chamber, and left
117 him crying out and tormenting himself; until at last there came a

| | |
|---|---|
| *115* EROS: | Turn from me, then, that noble countenance, |
| | Wherein the worship of the whole world lies . . . |
| | My sword is drawn. |
| ANTONY: |                Then let it do at once |
| | The thing why thou hast drawn it . . . |
| EROS: | Why, there then: thus I do escape the sorrow |
| | Of Antony's death.         *Kills himself.* (IV, 14, 85; 95) |
| *116* ANTONY: |              Thrice nobler than myself! |
| | Thou teachest me, O valiant Eros, what |
| | I should, and thou couldst not. My queen and Eros |
| | Have by their brave instruction got upon me |
| | A nobleness in record . . . Come then; and, Eros, |
| | Thy master dies thy scholar: to do thus *Falling on his sword.* |
| | I learn'd of thee.                  (IV, 14, 95) |
| *117* ANTONY: |           How! not dead? not dead? |
| | The guard, ho! O, dispatch me! . . . |
| 1st GUARD: | Not I. |
| 2nd GUARD: | Nor I. |

---

The inevitable prosecution of
Disgrace and horror, that, on my command,
Thou then wouldst kill me: do't; the time is come . . .
When I did make thee free, sworest thou not then
To do this when I bade thee? Do it at once,
Or thy precedent services are all
But accidents unpurposed.         (IV, 14, 62; 81)

secretary unto him called Diomedes, who was commanded to
bring him into the tomb or monument where Cleopatra was.

When he heard that she was alive, he very earnestly prayed his
men to carry his body thither; and so he was carried in his men's
arms into the entry of the monument. Notwithstanding, Cleopatra
would not open the gates, but came to the high windows, and cast
out certain chains and ropes, in the which Antonius was trussed; and
Cleopatra her own self, with two women only which she had
suffered to come with her into these monuments, triced Antonius
up.

They that were present to behold it said they never saw so pitiful
a sight. For they plucked up poor Antonius, all bloody as he was and
drawing on with pangs of death, who holding up his hands to
Cleopatra raised up himself as well as he could. It was a hard thing
for these women to do, to lift him up. But Cleopatra stooping down
with her head, putting to all her strength to her uttermost power,

ANTONY: Art thou there, Diomed? Draw thy sword, and give me
Sufficing strokes for death.

DIOMEDES:                      Most absolute lord,
My mistress Cleopatra sent me to thee.

ANTONY: When did she send thee?

DIOMEDES:                  Now, my lord.

ANTONY:                     Where is she?

DIOMEDES: Lock'd in her monument. She had a prophesying fear
Of what hath come to pass . . .
              She sent you word she was dead;
But, fearing since how it might work, hath sent
Me to proclaim the truth; and I am come,
I dread, too late.

ANTONY: Too late, good Diomed: call my guard, I prithee . . .
Bear me, good friends, where Cleopatra bides . . .
            Take me up:
I have led you oft: carry me now, good friends.

                                (IV, 14, 116; 131; 139)

---

3rd GUARD: Nor any one.

DERCETAS: Thy death and fortunes bid thy followers fly.    (IV, 14, 103) did lift him up with much ado and never let go her hold, with the help of the women beneath that bade her be of good courage, and 119 were as sorry to see her labour so, as she herself. So when she had gotten him in after that sort and laid him on a bed, she rent her garments upon him, clapping her breast and scratching her face and stomach. Then she dried up his blood that had berayed his face, and called him her lord, her husband, and Emperor, forgetting her own misery and calamity, for the pity and compassion she took of him.

Antonius made her cease her lamenting, and called for wine, either because he was athirst, or else for that he thought thereby to hasten his death. When he had drunk, he earnestly prayed her and persuaded her that she would seek to save her life, if she could possible without reproach and dishonour; and that chiefly she should trust Proculeius 120 above any man else about Caesar; and, as for himself, that she should

| | | |
|---|---|---|
| *119* DIOMEDES: | His guard have brought him thither ... | |
| CLEOPATRA: |           O Antony! | |
| | ... Help, Charmian, help, Iras, help; | |
| | Help, friends, below; let's draw him hither ... | |
| ANTONY: | I am dying, Egypt, dying; only | |
| | I here importune death awhile, until | |
| | Of many thousand kisses the poor last | |
| | I lay upon thy lips. | |
| CLEOPATRA: |           I dare not, dear, – | |
| | Dear my lord, pardon, – I dare not, | |
| | Lest I be taken ... But come, come, Antony, – | |
| | Help me, my women, – we must draw thee up: | |
| | Assist, good friends. | |
| ANTONY: |           O, quick, or I am gone. ... | |
| |   *They heave Antony aloft to Cleopatra.* | (IV, 15, 9; 29) |
| *120* ANTONY: | I am dying, Egypt, dying: | |
| | Give me some wine, and let me speak a little ... | |
| |       One word, sweet queen: | |
| | Of Caesar seek your honour, with your safety. O! | |
| CLEOPATRA: | They do not go together. | |
| ANTONY: |          Gentle, hear me. | |
| | None about Caesar trust but Proculeius. | (IV, 15, 41; 45) |

not lament nor sorrow for the miserable change of his fortune at the end of his days; but rather that she should think him the more fortunate for the former triumphs and honours he had received, considering that while he lived he was the noblest and greatest prince of the world, and that now he was overcome not cowardly, but valiantly, a Roman by another Roman.

As Antonius gave the last gasp, Proculeius came that was sent from Caesar. For, after Antonius had thrust his sword in himself, as they carried him into the tombs and monuments of Cleopatra, one of his guard called Dercetaeus took his sword with the which he had stricken himself and hid it; then he secretly stale away, and brought Octavius Caesar the first news of his death, and showed him his sword that was bloodied. Caesar hearing these news straight withdrew himself into a secret place of his tent, and there burst out

ANTONY:        The miserable change now at my end
               Lament nor sorrow at; but please your thoughts
               In feeding them with those my former fortunes
               Wherein I lived, the greatest prince o' the world,
               The noblest; and do now not basely die,
               Not cowardly put off my helmet to
               My countryman, – a Roman by a Roman
               Valiantly vanquish'd.                    (IV, 15,51)

DERCETAS:      This sword but shown to Caesar, with this tidings,
               Shall enter me with him.                 (IV, 14, 112)

DERCETAS:              I am call'd Dercetas;
               Mark Antony I served, who best was worthy
               Best to be served . . .
               I say, O Caesar, Antony is dead . . .
                       This is his sword;
               I robb'd his wound of it; behold it stain'd
               With his most noble blood.          (V, 1, 5; 13; 24)

CLEOPATRA:                 What's thy name?
PROCULEIUS: My name is Proculeius.
CLEOPATRA:                     Antony
               Did tell me of you, bade me trust you; but
               I do not greatly care to be deceived,
               That have no use for trusting.           (V, 2, 11)

with tears, lamenting his hard and miserable fortune that had been his friend and brother-in-law, his equal in the Empire, and companion
123 with him in sundry great exploits and battles. Then he called for all his friends, and showed them the letters Antonius had written to him, and his answers also sent him again, during their quarrel and strife; and how fiercely and proudly the other answered him to all
124 just and reasonable matters he wrote unto him. After this he sent Proculeius, and commanded him to do what he could possible to get Cleopatra alive, fearing lest otherwise all the treasure would be lost; and furthermore, he thought that if he could take Cleopatra and bring her alive to Rome, she would marvellously beautify and set
125 out his triumph.

123 OCTAVIUS CAESAR:   Look you sad, friends?
    The gods rebuke me, but it is tidings
    To wash the eyes of kings . . .

          O Antony!
    I have follow'd thee to this . . .

          yet let me lament,
    With tears as sovereign as the blood of hearts,
    That thou, my brother, my competitor
    In top of all design, my mate in empire,
    Friend and companion in the front of war,
    The arm of mine own body, and the heart
    Where mine his thoughts did kindle, – that our stars,
    Unreconciliable, should divide
    Our equalness to this.    (v, 1, 26; 35; 40)
124 OCTAVIUS CAESAR: Go with me to my tent; where you shall see
    How hardly I was drawn into this war;
    How calm and gentle I proceeded still
    In all my writings: go with me, and see
    What I can show in this.    (v, 1, 73)
125 OCTAVIUS CAESAR: Come hither, Proculeius. Go and say,
    We purpose her no shame: give her what comforts
    The quality of her passion shall require,
    Lest, in her greatness, by some mortal stroke
    She do defeat us; for her life in Rome
    Would be eternal in our triumph.    (v, 1, 61)

But Cleopatra would never put herself into Proculeius' hands, although they spake together. For Proculeius came to the gates that were very thick and strong, and surely barred, but yet there were some cranews through the which her voice might be heard. And so they without understood that Cleopatra demanded the kingdom of Egypt for her sons, and that Proculeius answered her that she should be of good cheer and not be afraid to refer all unto Caesar. After he had viewed the place very well, he came and reported her answer unto Caesar; who immediately sent Gallus to speak once again with her, and bade him purposely hold her with talk whilst Proculeius did set up a ladder against that high window by the which Antonius was triced up, and came down into the monument with two of his men, hard by the gate where Cleopatra stood to hear what Gallus said unto her. One of her women which was shut in her monuments with her saw Proculeius by chance as he came down, and shrieked out:

'O poor Cleopatra, thou art taken.'

Then, when she saw Proculeius behind her as she came from the gate, she thought to have stabbed herself in with a short dagger she wore of purpose by her side. But Proculeius came suddenly upon her, and taking her by both the hands said unto her:

'Cleopatra, first thou shalt do thyself great wrong, and secondly

CLEOPATRA:                If your master
Would have a queen his beggar, you must tell him,
That majesty, to keep decorum, must
No less beg than a kingdom: if he please
To give me conquer'd Egypt for my son,
He gives me so much of mine own, as I
Will kneel to him with thanks.

PROCULEIUS:                         Be of good cheer;
You're fall'n into a princely hand, fear nothing:
Make your full reference freely to my lord.      (V, 2, 15)

GALLUS:      You see how easily she may be surprised:
Guard her till Caesar come.

IRAS:      Royal queen!

CHARMIAN:      O Cleopatra! thou art taken, queen.

CLEOPATRA:      Quick, quick, good hands.      (V, 2, 35)

unto Caesar, to deprive him of the occasion and opportunity openly to show his bounty and mercy, and to give his enemies cause to accuse the most courteous and noble prince that ever was, and to appeach him, as though he were a cruel and merciless man that were 128 not to be trusted.'

So even as he spake the word he took her dagger from her, and shook her clothes for fear of any poison hidden about her. Afterwards Caesar sent one of his enfranchised men called Epaphroditus, whom he straitly charged to look well unto her, and to beware in any case that she made not herself away; and for the rest, to use her with all the courtesy possible.

And for himself, he in the meantime entered the city of Alexandria and, as he went, talked with the philosopher Arrius, and held him by the hand, to the end that his countrymen should reverence him the more because they saw Caesar so highly esteem and honour him. Then he went into the show-place of exercises, and so up to his chair of state which was prepared for him of a great height; and there according to his commandment all the people of Alexandria were assembled, who, quaking for fear, fell down on their knees before him, and craved mercy. Caesar bade them all stand up, and told them openly that he forgave the people, and pardoned the felonies and offences they had committed against him in this war; first, for the founder's sake of the same city, which was Alexander the Great; secondly, for the beauty of the city, which he much esteemed and wondered at; thirdly, for the love he bare unto his very friend Arrius. Thus did Caesar honour Arrius, who craved pardon for himself and many others, and specially for Philostratus, the eloquentest man of all the sophisters and orators of his time for present and sudden speech. Howbeit he falsely named himself an academic

*128* PROCULEIUS:             Hold, worthy lady, hold:
Do not yourself such wrong, who are in this
Relieved, but not betray'd . . . Cleopatra,
Do not abuse my master's bounty by
The undoing of yourself: let the world see
His nobleness well acted, which your death
Will never let come forth.             (v, 2, 39)

philosopher. Therefore Caesar, that hated his nature and conditions, would not hear his suit. Thereupon he let his grey beard grow long, and followed Arrius step by step in a long mourning gown, still buzzing in his ears this Greek verse:

> *A wise man if that he be wise indeed,*
> *May by a wise man have the better speed.*

Caesar understanding this, not for the desire he had to deliver Philostratus of his fear, as to rid Arrius of malice and envy that might have fallen out against him, he pardoned him.

Now, touching Antonius' sons, Antyllus his eldest son by Fulvia was slain, because his schoolmaster Theodorus did betray him unto the soldiers, who strake off his head. And the villain took a precious stone of great value from his neck, the which he did sew in his girdle, and afterwards denied that he had it. But it was found about him; and so Caesar trussed him up for it.

For Cleopatra's children, they were very honourably kept, with their governors and train that waited on them. But, for Caesarion, who was said to be Julius Caesar's son, his mother Cleopatra had sent him unto the Indians through Ethiopia, with a great sum of money. But one of his governors also called Rhodon, even such another as Theodorus, persuaded him to return into his country, and told him that Caesar sent for him to give him his mother's kingdom. So, as Caesar was determining with himself what he should do, Arrius said unto him:

> *Too many Caesars is not good,*

alluding unto a certain verse of Homer that saith:

> *Too many lords doth not well.*

Therefore Caesar did put Caesarion to death, after the death of his mother Cleopatra.

Many princes, great kings, and captains did crave Antonius' body of Octavius Caesar, to give him honourable burial. But Caesar would never take it from Cleopatra, who did sumptuously and royally bury him with her own hands, whom Caesar suffered to take as much as she would to bestow upon his funerals.

Now was she altogether overcome with sorrow and passion of mind, for she had knocked her breast so pitifully, that she had martyred it and in divers places had raised ulcers and inflammations, so that she fell into a fever withal; whereof she was very glad, hoping thereby to have good colour to abstain from meat, and that so she 129 might have died easily without any trouble. She had a physician called Olympus, whom she made privy of her intent, to the end he 130 should help her to rid her out of her life, as Olympus writeth himself, who wrote a book of all these things. But Caesar mistrusted the matter by many conjectures he had, and therefore did put her in fear, and 131 threatened her to put her children to shameful death. With these threats Cleopatra for fear yielded straight as she would have yielded unto strokes; and afterwards suffered herself to be cured and dieted as they listed.

Shortly after, Caesar came himself in person to see her and to comfort her. Cleopatra being laid upon a little low bed in poor estate, when she saw Caesar come into her chamber, she suddenly 132 rose up, naked in her smock, and fell down at his feet marvellously disfigured; both for that she had plucked her hair from her head, as also for that she had martyred all her face with her nails; and besides, her voice was small and trembling, her eyes sunk into her head with continual blubbering, and moreover they might see the

*129* CLEOPATRA:    Sir, I will eat no meat, I'll not drink, sir;
                If idle talk will once be necessary,
                I'll not sleep neither: this mortal house I'll ruin,
                Do Caesar what he can.         (v, 2, 49)

*130* See p. 267 note 93.

*131* OCTAVIUS CAESAR:           If you seek
                To lay on me a cruelty, by taking
                Antony's course, you shall bereave yourself
                Of my good purposes, and put your children
                To that destruction which I'll guard them from
                If thereon you rely.         (v, 2, 128)

*132* OCTAVIUS CAESAR: Which is the Queen of Egypt? . . . *Cleopatra kneels.*
                Arise, you shall not kneel:
                I pray you, rise; rise, Egypt.         (v, 2, 112)

most part of her stomach torn in sunder. To be short, her body was not much better than her mind. Yet her good grace and comeliness and the force of her beauty was not altogether defaced. But, notwithstanding this ugly and pitiful state of hers, yet she showed herself within by her outward looks and countenance. When Caesar had made her lie down again, and sat by her bed's side, Cleopatra began to clear and excuse herself for that she had done, laying all to the 33 fear she had of Antonius. Caesar, in contrary manner, reproved her in every point. Then she suddenly altered her speech, and prayed him to pardon her, as though she were afraid to die and desirous to live. At length, she gave him a brief and memorial of all the ready money and treasure she had. But by chance there stood Seleucus by, one of her treasurers, who to seem a good servant, came straight to Caesar to disprove Cleopatra, that she had not set in all but kept many things back of purpose. Cleopatra was in such a rage with him that she flew upon him, and took him by the hair of the head, and boxed him well-favouredly. Caesar fell a-laughing and parted the 34 fray.

| | |
|---|---|
| 33 THIDIAS: | He knows that you embrace not Antony<br>As you did love, but as you fear'd him. |
| CLEOPATRA: | O! |
| THIDIAS: | The scars upon your honour, therefore, he<br>Does pity, as constrained blemishes,<br>Not as deserved. |
| CLEOPATRA: | He is a god, and knows<br>What is most right: mine honour was not yielded,<br>But conquer'd merely. (III, 13, 56) |
| 34 CLEOPATRA: | This is the brief of money, plate, and jewels,<br>I am possess'd of: 'tis exactly valued;<br>Not petty things admitted. Where's Seleucus? |
| SELEUCUS: | Here, madam. |
| CLEOPATRA: | This is my treasurer: let him speak, my lord,<br>Upon his peril, that I have reserved<br>To myself nothing. Speak the truth, Seleucus. |
| SELEUCUS: | Madam,<br>I had rather seal my lips, than, to my peril,<br>Speak that which is not. |

'Alas,' said she, 'O Caesar, is not this a great shame and reproach, that thou having vouchsafed to take the pains to come unto me, and hast done me this honour, poor wretch and caitiff creature brought into this pitiful and miserable estate, and that mine own servants should come now to accuse me; though it may be I have reserved some jewels and trifles meet for women, but not for me, poor soul, to set out myself withal, but meaning to give some pretty presents and gifts unto Octavia and Livia, that, they making means and intercession for me to thee, thou mightest yet extend thy favour and
135 mercy upon me?'

135 CLEOPATRA:　O Caesar, what a wounding shame is this,
　　　　　　　That thou, vouchsafing here to visit me,
　　　　　　　Doing the honour of thy lordliness
　　　　　　　To one so meek, that mine own servant should
　　　　　　　Parcel the sum of my disgraces by
　　　　　　　Addition of his envy! Say, good Caesar,
　　　　　　　That I some lady trifles have reserved,

---

CLEOPATRA:　　　　　　　　　What have I kept back?
SELEUCUS:　Enough to purchase what you have made known.
OCTAVIUS CAESAR: Nay, blush not, Cleopatra; I approve
　　　　　　　Your wisdom in the deed.
CLEOPATRA:　　　　　　　　　See, Caesar! O, behold,
　　　　　　　How pomp is follow'd! mine will now be yours;
　　　　　　　And, should we shift estates, yours would be mine.
　　　　　　　The ingratitude of this Seleucus does
　　　　　　　Even make me wild: O slave, of no more trust
　　　　　　　Than love that's hired! What, goest thou back? thou shalt
　　　　　　　Go back, I warrant thee; but I'll catch thine eyes,
　　　　　　　Though they had wings: slave, soulless villain, dog!
　　　　　　　O rarely base!
OCTAVIUS CAESAR:　　Good queen, let us entreat you.

　　　　　　　　　　　　　　　　　(v, 2, 139)

Compare also:
CLEOPATRA:　Horrible villain! or I'll spurn thine eyes
　　　　　　　Like balls before me: I'll unhair thy head...
　　　　　　　　　　　　　　　　*She hales him up and down.*
　　　　　　　　　　　　　　　　(II, 4, 63)

Caesar was glad to hear her say so, persuading himself thereby that she had yet a desire to save her life. So he made her answer that he did not only give her that to dispose of at her pleasure which she had kept back, but further promised to use her more honourably and bountifully than she would think for. And so he took his leave of her, supposing he had deceived her. But indeed he was deceived

136 himself.

There was a young gentleman, Cornelius Dolabella, that was one of Caesar's very great familiars, and besides did bear no evil will unto Cleopatra. He sent her word secretly, as she had requested him, that Caesar determined to take his journey through Syria, and that within

136 OCTAVIUS CAESAR:                                    Cleopatra,
          Not what you have reserved, nor what acknowledged,
          Put we i' the roll of conquest: still be't yours,
          Bestow it at your pleasure; and believe,
          Caesar's no merchant, to make prize with you
          Of things that merchants sold. Therefore be cheer'd;
          Make not your thoughts your prisons: no, dear queen;
          For we intend so to dispose you as
          Yourself shall give us counsel. Feed, and sleep:
          Our care and pity is so much upon you,
          That we remain your friend; and so, adieu.

CLEOPATRA:   My master, and my lord!
OCTAVIUS CAESAR:                  Not so. Adieu.
          *Exeunt Caesar and his Train.*

CLEOPATRA:   He words me, girls, he words me, that I should not
          Be noble to myself.                         (v, 2, 179)

          Immoment toys, things of such dignity
          As we greet modern friends withal; and say,
          Some nobler token I have kept apart
          For Livia and Octavia, to induce
          Their mediation; must I be unfolded
          With one that I have bred? The gods! it smites me
          Beneath the fall I have. [*To Seleucus*] Prithee, go hence;
          Or I shall show the cinders of my spirits
          Through the ashes of my chance: wert thou a man,
          Thou wouldst have mercy on me.          (v, 2, 159)

137 three days he would send her away before with her children. When this was told Cleopatra, she requested Caesar that it would please him to suffer her to offer the last oblations of the dead unto the soul of Antonius. This being granted her, she was carried to the place where his tomb was; and there, falling down on her knees, embracing the tomb with her women, the tears running down her cheeks, she began to speak in this sort:

'O my dear lord Antonius, not long sithence I buried thee here, being a free woman; and now I offer unto thee the funeral sprinklings and oblations, being a captive and prisoner; and yet I am forbidden and kept from tearing and murdering this captive body of mine with blows, which they carefully guard and keep, only to triumph of thee. Look therefore henceforth for no other honours, offerings, nor sacrifices from me, for these are the last which Cleopatra can give thee, sith now they carry her away. Whilst we lived together, nothing could sever our companies. But now at our death I fear me they will make us change our countries. For as thou being a Roman hast been buried in Egypt, even so wretched creature I, an Egyptian, shall be buried in Italy, which shall be all the good that I have received by thy country. If therefore the gods where thou art now have any power and authority, sith our gods here have forsaken us, suffer not thy true friend and lover to be carried away alive, that in me they triumph of thee. But receive me with thee, and let me be buried in one self tomb with thee. For though my griefs and miseries be infinite, yet none hath grieved me more, nor that I could less bear withal, than this small time which I have been driven to live alone without thee.'

Then, having ended these doleful plaints, and crowned the tomb with garlands and sundry nosegays, and marvellous lovingly em-

137 DOLABELLA:  Madam, as thereto sworn by your command,
Which my love makes religion to obey,
I tell you this: Caesar through Syria
Intends his journey; and within three days
You with your children will he send before:
Make your best use of this: I have perform'd
Your pleasure and my promise.          (v, 2, 198)

braced the same, she commanded they should prepare her bath; and when she had bathed and washed herself she fell to her meat, and was sumptuously served.

Now whilst she was at dinner there came a countryman, and brought her a basket. The soldiers that warded at the gates asked him straight what he had in his basket. He opened the basket and took out the leaves that covered the figs, and showed them that they were figs he brought. They all of them marvelled to see so goodly figs. The countryman laughed to hear them, and bade them take some if they would. They believed he told them truly, and so bade him carry them in. After Cleopatra had dined, she sent a certain table written and sealed unto Caesar, and commanded them all to go out of the tombs where she was, but the two women. Then she shut the doors to her. Caesar, when he received this table and began to read her lamentation and petition, requesting him that he would let her be buried with Antonius, found straight what she meant, and thought to have gone thither himself; howbeit he sent one before in all haste that might be, to see what it was.

Her death was very sudden. For those whom Caesar sent unto her ran thither in all haste possible, and found the soldiers standing at the gate, mistrusting nothing, nor understanding of her death. But when they had opened the doors they found Cleopatra stark dead,

| | |
|---|---|
| 8 GUARDSMAN: | Here is a rural fellow<br>That will not be denied your highness' presence:<br>He brings you figs. |
| CLEOPATRA: | Let him come in. (v, 2, 233) |
| 9 GUARD: | Caesar hath sent – . . .<br>Approach ho! All's not well: Caesar's beguiled. |
| 2nd GUARD: | There's Dolabella sent from Caesar; call him . . . |
| DOLABELLA: | Caesar, thy thoughts<br>Touch their effects in this: thyself art coming<br>To see perform'd the dreaded act which thou<br>So sought'st to hinder . . .<br>   *Enter Caesar and all his train, marching.*<br>O sir, you are too sure an augurer;<br>That you did fear is done. (v, 2, 324; 332) |

140 laid upon a bed of gold, attired and arrayed in her royal robes, and one of her two women, which was called Iras, dead at her feet; and her other woman called Charmion half dead and trembling, trimming the diadem which Cleopatra ware upon her head. One of the soldiers, seeing her, angrily said unto her:

'Is that well done, Charmion?'

'Very well,' said she again, 'and meet for a princess descended from the race of so many noble kings.'

141 She said no more, but fell down dead hard by the bed.

Some report that this aspic was brought unto her in the basket with figs, and that she had commanded them to hide it under the fig
142 leaves, that, when she should think to take out the figs, the aspic should bite her before she should see her; howbeit that, when she would have taken away the leaves for the figs, she perceived it, and said:

'Art thou here then?'

And so, her arm being naked, she put it to the aspic to be bitten. Others say again, she kept it in a box, and that she did prick and thrust it with a spindle of gold, so that the aspic, being angered withal,

---

*140* CLEOPATRA:  Show me, my women, like a queen: go fetch
My best attires . . . Bring our crown and all . . .
Give me my robe, put on my crown; I have
Immortal longings in me.  (v, 2, 227; 232; 282)

*141* CHARMIAN:  Your crown's awry;
I'll mend it, and then play . . .

GUARD:  What work is here! Charmian, is this well done?

CHARMIAN:  It is well done, and fitting for a princess
Descended of so many royal kings.
Ah, soldier!  *Charmian dies.*

GUARD:  This Charmian lived but now; she stood and spake:
I found her trimming up the diadem
On her dead mistress; tremblingly she stood
And on a sudden dropp'd.  (v, 2, 321; 344)

*142* See note 138 above and:

DOLABELLA:  Who was last with them?

GUARD:  A simple countryman, that brought her figs:
This was his basket.  (v, 2, 341)

43 leapt out with great fury, and bit her in the arm. Howbeit few can tell the troth. For they report also that she had hidden poison in a hollow razor which she carried in the hair of her head. And yet was there no mark seen of her body, or any sign discerned that she was poisoned; neither also did they find this serpent in her tomb. But it was reported only that there were seen certain fresh steps or tracks where it had gone, on the tomb side toward the sea and specially by the door side. Some say also that they found two little pretty bitings in her arm, scant to be discerned; the which it seemeth Caesar himself gave credit unto, because in his Triumph he carried Cleopatra's image, with an aspic biting of her arm. And 44 thus goeth the report of her death.

Now Caesar, though he was marvellous sorry for the death of Cleopatra, yet he wondered at her noble mind and courage; and therefore commanded she should be nobly buried and laid by Antonius; and willed also that her two women should have honourable 45 burial.

43 CLEOPATRA:                    Come, thou mortal wretch,
                     With thy sharp teeth this knot intrinsicate
                     Of life at once untie: poor venomous fool,
                     Be angry, and dispatch.                    (v, 2, 306)

44 OCTAVIUS CAESAR: If they had swallow'd poison, 'twould appear
                     By external swelling: but she looks like sleep,
                     As she would catch another Antony
                     In her strong toil of grace.

DOLABELLA:                         Here, on her breast,
                     There is a vent of blood and something blown:
                     The like is on her arm.

GUARD:               This is an aspic's trail: and these fig-leaves
                     Have slime upon them, such as the aspic leaves
                     Upon the caves of Nile.

OCTAVIUS CAESAR:               Most probable
                     That so she died.                    (v, 2, 348

45 OCTAVIUS CAESAR:          Take up her bed;
                     And bear her women from the monument:
                     She shall be buried by her Antony:
                     No grave upon the earth shall clip in it

Cleopatra died being eight-and-thirty year old, after she had reigned two-and-twenty years and governed above fourteen of them with Antonius. And for Antonius, some say that he lived three-and-fifty years, and others say, six-and-fifty. All his statues, images, and metals were plucked down and overthrown, saving those of Cleopatra which stood still in their places, by means of Archibius, one of her friends, who gave Caesar a thousand talents that they should not be handled as those of Antonius were.

Antonius left seven children by three wives; of the which Caesar did put Antyllus, the eldest son he had by Fulvia, to death. Octavia his wife took all the rest, and brought them up with hers, and married Cleopatra, Antonius' daughter, unto King Juba, a marvellous courteous and goodly prince. And Antonius the son of Fulvia came to be so great that, next unto Agrippa, who was in greatest estimation about Caesar, and next unto the children of Livia, which were the second in estimation, he had the third place. Furthermore, Octavia, having had two daughters by her first husband Marcellus and a son also called Marcellus, Caesar married his daughter unto that Marcellus, and so did adopt him for his son. And Octavia also married one of her daughters unto Agrippa. But when Marcellus was dead, after he had been married a while, Octavia perceiving that her brother Caesar was very busy to choose some one among his friends whom he trusted best to make his son-in-law, she persuaded him that Agrippa should marry his daughter (Marcellus' widow) and leave her own daughter. Caesar first was contented withal, and then Agrippa; and so she afterwards took away her daughter and married her unto Antonius; and Agrippa married Julia, Caesar's daughter.

Now there remained two daughters more of Octavia and Antonius. Domitius Aenobarbus married one; and the other, which was Antonia, so fair and virtuous a young lady, was married unto Drusus, the son of Livia and son-in-law of Caesar. Of this marriage

---

A pair so famous . . . Our army shall
In solemn show attend this funeral . . .
Come, Dolabella, see
High order in this great solemnity. (v, 2, 359)

came Germanicus and Claudius; of the which, Claudius afterwards came to be Emperor. And of the sons of Germanicus, the one whose name was Caius came also to be Emperor; who, after he had licentiously reigned a time, was slain, with his wife and daughter. Agrippina also, having a son by her first husband Aenobarbus called Lucius Domitius, was afterwards married unto Claudius, who adopted her son and called him Nero Germanicus.

This Nero was Emperor in our time, and slew his own mother; had almost destroyed the Empire of Rome through his madness and wicked life, being the fifth Emperor of Rome after Antonius.

# THE LIFE OF MARTIUS CORIOLANUS

THE house of the Martians at Rome was of the number of the patricians, out of the which hath sprung many noble personages; whereof Ancus Martius was one, King Numa's daughter's son, who was King of Rome after Tullus Hostilius. Of the same house were Publius and Quintus, who brought to Rome their best water they had by conduits. Censorinus also came of that family, that was so surnamed because the people had chosen him Censor twice; through whose persuasion they made a law that no man from thenceforth might 1 require or enjoy the Censorship twice.

Caius Martius, whose life we intend now to write, being left an orphan by his father, was brought up under his mother, a widow, who taught us by experience that orphanage bringeth many discommodities to a child, but doth not hinder him to become an honest man and to excel in virtue above the common sort; as they that are meanly born wrongfully do complain that it is the occasion of their casting away, for that no man in their youth taketh any care of them to see them well brought up and taught that were meet.

This man also is a good proof to confirm some men's opinions that

1 JUNIUS BRUTUS:          What stock he springs of –
The noble house o' the Martians, from whence came
That Ancus Martius, Numa's daughter's son,
Who, after great Hostilius, here was king;
Of the same house Publius and Quintus were,
That our best water brought by conduits hither;
[And Censorinus that was so surnamed]
And nobly named so, twice being censor,
Was his great ancestor.        (*Coriolanus*, II, 3, 245)

a rare and excellent wit, untaught, doth bring forth many good and evil things together, like a fat soil bringeth forth herbs and weeds that lieth unmanured. For this Martius' natural wit and great heart did marvellously stir up his courage to do and attempt notable acts. But on the other side, for lack of education, he was so choleric and impatient that he would yield to no living creature; which made him churlish, uncivil, and altogether unfit for any man's conversation. Yet men marvelling much at this constancy – that he was never overcome with pleasure nor money, and how he would endure easily all manner of pains and travails – thereupon they well liked and commended his stoutness and temperancy. But, for all that, they could not be acquainted with him, as one citizen useth to be with another in the city. His behaviour was so unpleasant to them, by reason of a certain insolent and stern manner he had, which, because it was too lordly, was disliked. And, to say truly, the greatest benefit that learning bringeth men unto is this: that it teacheth men that be rude and rough of nature, by compass and rule of reason to be civil and courteous and to like better the mean state than the higher.

Now in those days valiantness was honoured in Rome above 2 all other virtues; which they call *virtus*, by the name of virtue itself, as including in that general name all other special virtues besides. So that *virtus* in the Latin was as much as valiantness. But Martius, being more inclined to the wars than any other gentleman of his time, began from his childhood to give himself to handle weapons and daily did exercise himself therein; and outward he esteemed armour to no purpose, unless one were naturally armed within. Moreover he did so exercise his body to hardness and all kind of activity that he was very swift in running, strong in wrestling, and mighty in griping, so that no man could ever cast him; insomuch as those that would try masteries with him for strength and nimbleness would say, when they were overcome, that all was by reason of his natural strength and hardness of ward, that never yielded to any pain or toil he took upon him.

2 COMINIUS:                              It is held
          That valour is the chiefest virtue, and
          Most dignifies the haver.                    (II, 2, 87)

The first time he went to the wars, being but a stripling, was when Tarquin surnamed the Proud (that had been King of Rome, and was driven out for his pride) – after many attempts made by sundry battles to come in again, wherein he was ever overcome – did come to Rome, with all the aid of the Latins and many other people of Italy; even as it were to set up his whole rest upon a battle by them, who with a great and mighty army had undertaken to put him into his kingdom again, not so much to pleasure him as to overthrow the power of the Romans, whose greatness they both feared and envied.

In this battle, wherein were many hot and sharp encounters of either party, Martius valiantly fought in the sight of the Dictator; and, a Roman soldier being thrown to the ground even hard by him, Martius straight bestrid him and slew the enemy with his own hands that had before overthrown the Roman. Hereupon, after the battle was won, the Dictator did not forget so noble an act; and therefore
3 first of all he crowned Martius with a garland of oaken boughs.

For whosoever saveth the life of a Roman, it is a manner among them to honour him with such a garland. This was either because

3 COMINIUS:                    At sixteen years,
> When Tarquin made a head for Rome, he fought
> Beyond the mark of others: our then dictator,
> Whom with all praise I point at, saw him fight,
> When with his Amazonian chin he drove
> The bristled lips before him: he bestrid
> An o'er-press'd Roman and i' the consul's view
> Slew three opposers: Tarquin's self he met,
> And struck him on his knee: in that day's feats,
> When he might act the woman in the scene,
> He proved best man i' the field, and for his meed
> Was brow-bound with the oak. His pupil age
> Man-enter'd thus, he waxed like a sea,
> And in the brunt of seventeen battles since
> He lurch'd all swords of the garland. (II, 2, 91)

VOLUMNIA: To a cruel war I sent him: from whence he returned, his
brows bound with oak. (I, 3, 14)

the law did this honour to the oak in favour of the Arcadians, who by the oracle of Apollo were in old time called eaters of acorns; or else because the soldiers might easily in every place come by oaken boughs; or, lastly, because they thought it very necessary to give him that had saved a citizen's life a crown of this tree to honour him, being properly dedicated unto Jupiter, the patron and protector of their cities, and thought amongst other wild trees to bring forth a profitable fruit and of plants to be the strongest. Moreover, men at the first beginning did use acorns for their bread and honey for their drink; and further, the oak did feed their beasts and give them birds by taking glue from the oaks, with the which they made bird-lime to catch silly birds.

They say that Castor and Pollux appeared in this battle, and how, incontinently after the battle, men saw them in the market-place at Rome, all their horses being on a white foam; and they were the first that brought news of the victory, even in the same place where remaineth at this present a temple built in the honour of them, near unto the fountain. And this is the cause why the day of this victory (which was the fifteenth of July) is consecrated yet to this day unto Castor and Pollux.

Moreover it is daily seen that, honour and reputation lighting on young men before their time and before they have no great courage by nature, the desire to win more dieth straight in them; which easily happeneth, the same having no deep root in them before. Where, contrariwise, the first honour that valiant minds do come unto doth quicken up their appetite, hasting them forward as with force of wind, to enterprise things of high deserving praise. For they esteem not to receive reward for service done, but rather take it for a remembrance and encouragement to make them do better in time to come; and be ashamed also to cast their honour at their heels, not seeking to increase it still by like desert of worthy valiant deeds. This desire being bred in Martius, he strained still to pass himself in manliness; and being desirous to show a daily increase of his valiantness, his noble service did still advance his fame, bringing in spoils upon spoils from the enemy. Whereupon, the captains that came afterwards (for envy of them that went before) did contend who should most honour him and who should bear most honourable testimony of his valiantness; insomuch, the Romans having many wars and battles in those days, Coriolanus was at them all; and there was not a battle fought from whence he returned not without some reward of honour. And as for other, the only respect that made them valiant was they hoped to have honour. But touching Martius, the only thing that made him to love honour was the joy he saw his 4 mother did take of him.

For he thought nothing made him so happy and honourable as that his mother might hear everybody praise and commend him; that she might always see him return with a crown upon his head; and that she might still embrace him with tears running down her cheeks for joy. Which desire, they say, Epaminondas did avow and confess to have been in him: as to think himself a most happy and blessed man that his father and mother in their lifetime had seen the victory he won in the plain of Leuctres. Now as for Epaminondas, he had this good hap, to have his father and mother living, to be partakers of his joy and prosperity. But Martius thinking all due to his mother that had been also due to his father if he had lived, did not only content himself to rejoice and honour her, but at her desire took a wife also, by whom he had two children; and yet never left 5 his mother's house therefore.

Now, he being grown to great credit and authority in Rome for his valiantness, it fortuned there grew sedition in the city because the

4 CITIZEN:    I say unto you, what he hath done famously, he did it to that end: though soft-conscienced men can be content to say it was for his country, he did it to please his mother, and to be partly proud: which he is, even to the altitude of his virtue.

(I, I, 36)

VOLUMNIA:    I prithee now, sweet son, as thou hast said
My praises made thee first a soldier, so,
To have my praise for this, perform a part
Thou hast not done before.          (III, 2, 107)

5 VALERIA:     How does your little son?
VIRGILIA:    I thank your ladyship: well, good madam.
VOLUMNIA:    He had rather see the swords, and hear a drum than look upon his schoolmaster.

300

Senate did favour the rich against the people, who did complain of the sore oppression of usurers, of whom they borrowed money. For those that had little were yet spoiled of that little they had by their creditors (for lack of ability to pay the usury), who offered their goods to be sold to them that would give most. And such as had nothing left, their bodies were laid hold on, and they were made their bondmen, notwithstanding all the wounds and cuts they showed, which they had received in many battles, fighting for defence of their country and commonwealth; of the which the last war they made was against the Sabines, wherein they fought upon the promise the rich men had made them that from thenceforth they would entreat them more gently, and also upon the word of Marcus Valerius, chief of the Senate, who, by authority of the Council, and in the behalf of the rich, said they should perform that they had promised. But after that they had faithfully served in this last battle of all, where they overcame their enemies, seeing they were never a whit the better nor more gently entreated, and that the Senate would give no ear to them, but made as though they had forgotten their former promise and suffered them to be made slaves and bondmen to their creditors and, besides, to be turned out of all that ever they had; they fell then even to flat rebellion and mutiny, and to stir
6 up dangerous tumults within the city.

6    *Enter a company of mutinous Citizens, with staves, clubs, and other weapons.*

(I, I; stage direction)

MENENIUS:                     Alack,
You are transported by calamity
Thither where more attends you, and you slander
The helms o' the state, who care for you like fathers,
When you curse them as enemies.

---

VALERIA:       O' my word, the father's son: I'll swear, 'tis a very pretty boy. O' my troth, I looked upon him o' Wednesday half an hour together: has such a confirmed countenance. I saw him run after a gilded butterfly; and when he caught it, he let it go again; and after it again; and over and over he comes, and up again; catched it again; or whether his fall enraged him, or how 'twas, he did so set his teeth and tear it; O, I warrant, how he mammocked it!               (I, 3, 56)

The Romans' enemies, hearing of this rebellion, did straight enter the territories of Rome with a marvellous great power, spoiling and burning all as they came. Whereupon the Senate immediately made open proclamation by sound of trumpet that all those that were of lawful age to carry weapon should come and enter their names into the muster-master's book, to go to the wars. But no man obeyed their commandment. Whereupon their chief magistrates and many of the Senate began to be of divers opinions among themselves. For some thought it was reason they should somewhat yield to the poor people's request and that they should a little qualify the severity of the law. Other held hard against that opinion; and that was Martius for one. For he alleged that the creditors losing their money they had lent was not the worst thing that was thereby; but that the lenity that was favoured was a beginning of disobedience, and that the proud attempt of the commonalty was to abolish law and to bring all to confusion. Therefore he said, if the Senate were wise, they should betimes prevent and quench this ill-favoured and worse meant beginning.

The Senate met many days in consultation about it; but in the end they concluded nothing. The poor common people, seeing no redress, gathered themselves one day together; and, one encouraging another, they all forsook the city, and encamped themselves upon a hill, called at that day the Holy Hill, alongst the river of Tiber, offering no creature any hurt or violence or making any show of

7 CITIZEN:       Our business is not unknown to the senate; they have had inkling this fortnight what we intend to do, which now we'll show 'em in deeds. They say poor suitors have strong breaths: they shall know we have strong arms too.       (I, I, 59)

---

CITIZEN:       Care for us! True, indeed! They ne'er cared for us yet: suffer us to famish, and their store-houses crammed with grain; make edicts for usury, to support usurers; repeal daily any wholesome act established against the rich, and provide more piercing statutes daily, to chain up and restrain the poor. If the wars eat us not up, they will; and there's all the love they bear us.       (I, I, 76) actual rebellion; saving that they cried, as they went up and down, that the rich men had driven them out of the city and that all Italy through they should find air, water, and ground to bury them in. Moreover, they said, to dwell at Rome was nothing else but to be slain, or hurt with continual wars and fighting for defence of the rich men's goods.

The Senate, being afeared of their departure, did send unto them certain of the pleasantest old men and the most acceptable to the people among them. Of those Menenius Agrippa was he who was sent for chief man of the message from the Senate. He, after many good persuasions and gentle requests made to the people on the behalf of the Senate, knit up his oration in the end with a notable tale, in this manner:

That on a time all the members of man's body did rebel against the belly, complaining of it that it only remained in the midst of the body, without doing anything, neither did bear any labour to the maintenance of the rest; whereas all other parts and members did labour painfully and were very careful to satisfy the appetites and desires of the body. And so the belly, all this notwithstanding, laughed at their folly and said:

'It is true, I first receive all meats that nourish man's body; but afterwards I send it again to the nourishment of other parts of the same.'

'Even so,' quoth he, 'O you, my masters and citizens of Rome, the reason is alike between the Senate and you. For matters being well digested, and their counsels throughly examined, touching the benefit of the commonwealth, the Senators are cause of the common commodity that cometh unto every one of you.'

CITIZEN: Worthy Menenius Agrippa, one that hath always loved the people. (I, I, 52)

MENENIUS:    I shall tell you
A pretty tale: it may be you have heard it;
But, since it serves my purpose, I will venture
To stale't a little more . . .
There was a time when all the body's members
Rebell'd against the belly, thus accused it:
That only like a gulf it did remain

I' the midst o' the body, idle and unactive,
Still cupboarding the viand, never bearing
Like labour with the rest, where the other instruments
Did see and hear, devise, instruct, walk, feel,
And, mutually participate, did minister
Unto the appetite and affection common
Of the whole body. The belly answer'd . . .
                with a kind of smile,
Which ne'er came from the lungs, but even thus –
For look you, I may make the belly smile
As well as speak – it tauntingly replied
To the discontented members, the mutinous parts
That envied his receipt; even so most fitly
As you malign our senators for that
They are not such as you.

CITIZEN:                Your belly's answer? What!
The kingly-crowned head, the vigilant eye,
The counsellor heart, the arm our soldier,
Our steed the leg, the tongue our trumpeter,
With other muniments and petty helps
In this our fabric, if that they . . .
Should by the cormorant belly be restrain'd,
Who is the sink o' the body . . .
The former agents, if they did complain,
What could the belly answer? . . .

MENENIUS:     Your most grave belly was deliberate,
Not rash like his accusers, and thus answer'd:
'True is it, my incorporate friends,' quoth he,
'That I receive the general food at first,
Which you do live upon; and fit it is,
Because I am the store-house and the shop
Of the whole body: but, if you do remember,
I send it through the rivers of your blood,
Even to the court, the heart, to the seat o' the brain;
And, through the cranks and offices of man,
The strongest nerves and small inferior veins
From me receive that natural competency
Whereby they live; and though that all at once,
You, my good friends,' – this says the belly, mark me, –

These persuasions pacified the people, conditionally that the Senate would grant there should be yearly chosen five magistrates, which they now call *Tribuni plebis*, whose office should be to defend the poor people from violence and oppression. So Junius Brutus and Sicinius Vellutus were the first Tribunes of the People that were chosen, who had only been the causers and procurers of this sedition.

Hereupon, the city being grown again to good quiet and unity, the people immediately went to the wars, showing that they had a good will to do better than ever they did and to be very willing to obey the magistrates in that they would command concerning the wars. Martius also, though it liked him nothing to see the greatness of the people thus increased, considering it was to the prejudice and embasing of the nobility, and also saw that other noble patricians were troubled as well as himself, he did persuade the patricians to show themselves no less forward and willing to fight for their country than the common people were, and to let them know,

MENENIUS:     What is granted them?

MARTIUS:     Five tribunes to defend their vulgar wisdoms,
               Of their own choice: one's Junius Brutus,
               Sicinius Velutus, and I know not – 'Sdeath!
               The rabble should have first unroof'd the city,
               Ere so prevail'd with me: it will in time
               Win upon power and throw forth greater themes
               For insurrection's arguing.        (I, I, 218)

---

'Though all at once cannot
See what I do deliver out to each,
Yet I can make my audit up, that all
From me do back receive the flour of all
And leave me but the bran.' . . .
The senators of Rome are this good belly,
And you the mutinous members; for examine
Their counsels and their cares, digest things rightly
Touching the weal o' the common, you shall find
No public benefit which you receive
But it proceeds or comes from them to you
And no way from yourselves.        (I, I, 92)

by their deeds and acts, that they did not so much pass the people in power and riches, as they did exceed them in true nobility and valiantness.

In the country of the Volsces, against whom the Romans made war at that time, there was a principal city, and of most fame, that was called Corioles, before the which the Consul Cominius did lay siege. Wherefore all the other Volsces fearing lest that city should be taken by assault, they came from all parts of the country to save it, intending to give the Romans battle before the city and to give an onset on them in two several places. The Consul Cominius, understanding this, divided his army also into two parts; and, taking the one part with himself, he marched towards them that were drawing to the city out of the country; and the other part of his army he left in the camp with Titus Lartius (one of the valiantest men the Romans had at that time) to resist those that would make any sally out of the 11 city upon them.

So the Coriolans, making small accompt of them that lay in camp 12 before the city, made a sally out upon them, in the which at the first the Coriolans had the better, and drave the Romans back again into the trenches of their camp. But Martius being there at that time, running out of the camp with a few men with him, he slew the first enemies he met withal and made the rest of them stay upon the sudden, crying out to the Romans that had turned their backs, and 13 calling them again to fight with a loud voice. For he was even such

---

*11* VALERIA:    There came news. . . . last night. . . . I heard a
senator speak it. Thus it is: the Volsces have an army forth; against whom Cominius the general is gone, with one part of our Roman power: your lord and Titus Lartius are set down before their city Corioli; they nothing doubt prevailing and to make it brief wars.    (I, 3, 103)

*12*                    *Enter the army of the Volsces.*

MARTIUS:    They fear us not, but issue forth their city . . .
They do disdain us much beyond our thoughts.    (I, 4, 23)

*13*    *The Romans are beat back to their trenches. Enter Martius, cursing.*

MARTIUS:    All the contagion of the south light on you,
You shames of Rome! You herd of – Boils and plagues

another as Cato would have a soldier and a captain to be, not only
terrible and fierce to lay about him, but to make the enemy afeared
with the sound of his voice and grimness of his countenance. Then
there flocked about him immediately a great number of Romans;
whereat the enemies were so afeared that they gave back presently.
But Martius, not staying so, did chase and follow them to their own
gates, that fled for life. And there perceiving that the Romans
retired back, for the great number of darts and arrows which flew
about their ears from the walls of the city, and that there was not
one man amongst them that durst venture himself to follow the
flying enemies into the city, for that it was full of men of war, very
well armed and appointed; he did encourage his fellows with
words and deeds, crying out to them that fortune had opened the
gates of the city more for the followers than the fliers. But all this not-
5 withstanding, few had the hearts to follow him. Howbeit Martius,

4 TITUS LARTIUS:        Thou wast a soldier
                    Even to Cato's wish, not fierce and terrible
                    Only in strokes; but, with thy grim looks and
                    The thunder-like percussion of thy sounds,
                    Thou madest thine enemies shake, as if the world
                    Were feverous and did tremble.      (I, 4, 56)

5          *The Volsces fly, and Martius follows them to the gates.*

MARTIUS:      So, now the gates are ope: now prove good seconds:
                    'Tis for the followers fortune widens them,
                    Not for the fliers: mark me, and do the like.
                          *Enters the gates.*

                    Plaster you o'er, that you may be abhorr'd
                    Further than seen and one infect another
                    Against the wind a mile! You souls of geese,
                    That bear the shapes of men, how have you run
                    From slaves that apes would beat! Pluto and hell!
                    All hurt behind; backs red and faces pale
                    With flight and agued fear! Mend and charge home,
                    Or, by the fires of heaven, I'll leave the foe,
                    And make my wars on you: look to't; come on:
                    If you'll stand fast, we'll beat them to their wives,
                    As they us to our trenches followed.      (I, 4, 29)

being in the throng among the enemies, thrust himself into the gates of the city and entered the same among them that fled, without that any one of them durst at the first turn their face upon him or else offer to stay him. But he looking about him, and seeing he was entered the city with very few men to help him, and perceiving he was environed by his enemies that gathered round about to set upon him, did things then, as it is written, wonderful and incredible, as well for the force of his hand as also for the agility of his body; and with a wonderful courage and valiantness he made a lane through the midst of them and overthrew also those he laid at, that some he made run to the furthest part of the city, and other for fear he made yield themselves and to let fall their weapons before him. By this means Martius that was gotten out had some leisure to bring the Romans with more safety into the city.

The city being taken in this sort, the most part of the soldiers began incontinently to spoil, to carry away, and to lock up the booty they had won. But Martius was marvellous angry with them, and cried out on them that it was no time now to look after spoil and to run straggling here and there to enrich themselves, whilst the other Consul and their fellow-citizens peradventure were fighting with their enemies; and how that, leaving the spoil, they should
16 seek to wind themselves out of danger and peril. Howbeit, cry and

16                       *Enter certain Romans, with spoils.*

1st ROMAN:    This will I carry to Rome.
2nd ROMAN:    And I this.
3rd ROMAN:    A murrain on't! I took this for silver....
MARTIUS:      See here these movers that do prize their hours
              At a crack'd drachma! Cushions, leaden spoons,
              Irons of a doit, doublets that hangmen would
              Bury with those that wore them, these base slaves,
              Ere yet the fight be done, pack up: down with them!
              And hark, what noise the general makes! To him!...
              Whilst I, with those that have the spirit, will haste
              To help Cominius.                                    (I, 5, 1)

1st SOLDIER:   Fool-hardiness; not I.
2nd SOLDIER:                    Nor I.
                               *Martius is shut in.*    (I, 4, 43)

say to them what he could, very few of them would hearken to him. Wherefore, taking those that willingly offered themselves to follow him, he went out of the city and took his way towards that part where he understood the rest of the army was, exhorting and entreating them by the way that followed him not to be faint-hearted; and oft holding up his hands to heaven, he besought the gods to be gracious and favourable unto him, that he might come in time to the battle and in good hour to hazard his life in defence of his countrymen.

Now the Romans, when they were put in battle ray and ready to take their targets on their arms and to gird them upon their arming coats, had a custom to make their wills at that very instant, without any manner of writing, naming him only whom they would make their heir in the presence of three or four witnesses. Martius came just to that reckoning, whilst the soldiers were doing after that sort, and that the enemies were approached so near as one stood in view of the other.

17    When they saw him at his first coming, all bloody and in a sweat, and but with a few men following him, some thereupon began to be afeared. But soon after, when they saw him run with a lively cheer to the Consul and to take him by the hand, declaring how he had taken the city of Corioles, and that they saw the Consul Cominius also kiss and embrace him, then there was not a man but took heart again to him and began to be of a good courage, some hearing him report from point to point the happy success of this exploit and other also conjecturing it by seeing their gestures afar off. Then they all began to call upon the Consul to march forward and to delay no longer, but to give charge upon the enemy.

*17* COMINIUS:                    Who's yonder,
                      That does appear as he were flay'd? O gods!
                      He has the stamp of Martius; and I have
                      Before-time seen him thus . . .
MARTIUS:       Come I too late?
COMINIUS:     Ay, if you come not in the blood of others,
                      But mantled in your own.              (I, 6, 21; 27)

Martius asked him how the order of their enemies' battle was, and on which side they had placed their best fighting men. The Consul made him answer that he thought the bands which were in the vaward of their battle were those of the Antiates, whom they esteemed to be the warlikest men and which for valiant courage would give no place to any of the host of their enemies. Then prayed Martius to be set directly against them. The Consul granted him, greatly praising his courage.

Then Martius, when both armies came almost to join, advanced himself a good space before his company and went so fiercely to give charge on the vaward that came right against him that they could stand no longer in his hands; he made such a lane through them and opened a passage into the battle of the enemies. But the two wings of either side turned one to the other, to compass him in between them; which the Consul Cominius perceiving, he sent thither straight of the best soldiers he had about him. So the battle was marvellous bloody about Martius, and in a very short space many were slain in the place. But in the end the Romans were so strong that they distressed the enemies and brake their array and, scattering them, made them fly. Then they prayed Martius that he would retire to the camp, because they saw he was able to do no more, he was already so wearied with the great pain he had taken and so faint with the great wounds he had upon him. But Martius answered them that it was not for conquerors to yield, nor to be faint-hearted; and thereupon began afresh to chase those that fled, until such time as the army of

18 MARTIUS:     How lies their battle? know you on which side
                They have placed their men of trust?
COMINIUS:                 As I guess, Martius,
                Their bands i' the vaward are the Antiates,
                Of their best trust; o'er them Aufidius,
                Their very heart of hope.
MARTIUS:                       I do beseech you,
                By all the battles wherein we have fought,
                By the blood we have shed together, by the vows
                We have made to endure friends, that you directly
                Set me against Aufidius and his Antiates.     (I, 6, 51)

the enemies was utterly overthrown and numbers of them slain and
19 taken prisoners.

The next morning, betimes, Martius went to the Consul, and the
other Romans with him. There the Consul Cominius, going up to
his chair of state, in the presence of the whole army, gave thanks to
the gods for so great, glorious, and prosperous a victory. Then
he spake to Martius, whose valiantness he commended beyond the
moon, both for that he himself saw him do with his eyes, as also
for that Martius had reported unto him. So in the end he willed
Martius that he should choose out of all the horses they had taken
of their enemies, and of all their goods they had won (whereof there
was great store), ten of every sort which he liked best, before any
20 distribution should be made to other. Besides this great honourable
offer he had made him, he gave him, in testimony that he had won
that day the price of prowess above all other, a goodly horse with
21 a caparison and all furniture to him; which the whole army beholding did marvellously praise and commend.

But Martius, stepping forth, told the Consul he most thankfully
accepted the gift of his horse, and was a glad man besides that his

19 COMINIUS:              Then straight his doubled spirit
              Re-quicken'd what in flesh was fatigate,
              And to the battle came he; where he did
              Run reeking o'er the lives of men, as if
              'Twere a perpetual spoil; and till we call'd
              Both field and city ours, he never stood
              To ease his breast with panting.          (II, 2, 120)

20 COMINIUS:              Of all the horses,
              Whereof we have ta'en good and good store, of all
              The treasure in this field achieved and city,
              We render you the tenth, to be ta'en forth,
              Before the common distribution, at
              Your only choice.                          (I, 9, 31)

21 COMINIUS:              Be it known,
              As to us, to all the world, that Caius Martius
              Wears this war's garland: in token of the which,
              My noble steed, known to the camp, I give him,
              With all his trim belonging.               (I, 9, 58)

311

service had deserved his general's commendation; and as for his other offer, which was rather a mercenary reward than an honourable recompense, he would have none of it; but was contented to have 22 his equal part with other soldiers.

'Only this grace,' said he, 'I crave and beseech you to grant me. Among the Volsces there is an old friend and host of mine, an honest wealthy man, and now a prisoner, who, living before in great wealth in his own country, liveth now a poor prisoner in the hands of his enemies; and yet, notwithstanding all this his misery and misfortune, it would do me great pleasure if I could save him from 23 this one danger, to keep him from being sold as a slave.'

The soldiers, hearing Martius' words, made a marvellous great shout among them; and they were more that wondered at his great contentation and abstinence, when they saw so little covetousness in him, than they were that highly praised and extolled his valiantness. For even they themselves that did somewhat malice and envy his glory, to see him thus honoured and passingly praised, did think him so much the more worthy of an honourable recompense for his valiant service, as the more carelessly he refused the great offer

22 MARTIUS:      I thank you, general;
But cannot make my heart consent to take
A bribe to pay my sword: I do refuse it;
And stand upon my common part with those
That have beheld the doing.            (I, 9, 36)

23 CORIOLANUS:        I, that now
Refused most princely gifts, am bound to beg
Of my lord general.

COMINIUS:                Take't; 'tis yours. What is't?

CORIOLANUS: I sometime lay here in Corioli
At a poor man's house; he used me kindly:
He cried to me; I saw him prisoner;
But then Aufidius was within my view,
And wrath o'erwhelm'd my pity: I request you
To give my poor host freedom. . . .

LARTIUS:   Martius, his name?

CORIOLANUS:          By Jupiter! forgot.
I am weary; yea, my memory is tired.        (I, 9, 79)

24 made him for his profit; and they esteemed more the virtue that was in him, that made him refuse such rewards, than that which made them to be offered him, as unto a worthy person. For it is far more commendable to use riches well than to be valiant; and yet it is better not to desire them than to use them well.

After this shout and noise of the assembly was somewhat appeased the Consul Cominius began to speak in this sort:
'We cannot compel Martius to take these gifts we offer him, if he will not receive them. But we will give him such a reward for the noble service he hath done, as he cannot refuse. Therefore we do order and decree that henceforth he be called *Coriolanus*, unless his 25 valiant acts have won him that name before our nomination.'
And so, ever since, he still bare the third name of Coriolanus.

And thereby it appeareth, that the first name the Romans have, as *Caius*, was our Christian name now. The second, as *Martius*, was the name of the house and family they came of. The third was some addition given, either for some act or notable service, or for some mark on their face, or of some shape of their body, or else for some special virtue they had. Even so did the Grecians in old time give additions to princes, by reason of some notable act worthy memory. As when they have called some *Soter* and *Callinicos*: as much to say, 'saviour' and 'conqueror'. Or else for some notable apparent mark on one's face or on his body, they have called him *Phiscon* and *Grypos*, as ye would say, 'gorbelly' and 'hook-nosed'. Or else for some virtue, as *Euergetes* and *Philadelphos*: to wit, a 'benefactor' and 'lover of his brethren'. Or otherwise for one's great felicity, as *Eudaemon*: as much to say as, 'fortunate'; for so was the second of the Battes surnamed (these were the princes that built the city of

24 COMINIUS:            Our spoils he kick'd at,
And look'd upon things precious as they were
The common muck of the world.          (II, 2, 128)

25 COMINIUS:                       From this time,
For what he did before Corioli, call him,
With all the applause and clamour of the host,
CAIUS MARTIUS CORIOLANUS!  Bear
The addition nobly ever!          (I, 9, 62)

313

Cyrene). And some kings have had surnames of jest and mockery. As one of the Antigones that was called *Doson*, to say, the 'Giver'; who was ever promising and never giving. And one of the Ptolemies was called *Lamyros*, to say, 'conceitive'. The Romans use more than any other nation to give names of mockery in this sort. As there was one Metellus surnamed *Diadematus*, the 'banded'; because he carried a band about his head of long time, by reason of a sore he had in his forehead. One other of his own family was called *Celer*, the 'quick-fly'; because, a few days after the death of his father, he showed the people the cruel fight of fencers at unrebated swords, which they found wonderful for the shortness of time. Other had their surnames derived of some accident of their birth. As to this day they call him *Proculeius* that is born his father being in some far voyage; and him *Posthumius* that is born after the death of his father. And when of two brethren twins the one doth die and the other surviveth, they call the survivor *Vopiscus*. Sometimes also they give surnames derived of some mark or misfortune of the body. As *Sylla*, to say, 'crooked-nose'; *Niger*, 'black'; *Rufus*, 'red'; *Caecus*, 'blind'; *Claudus*, 'lame'. They did wisely in this thing to accustom men to think that neither the loss of their sight nor other such misfortunes as may chance to men are any shame or disgrace unto them; but the manner was to answer boldly to such names, as if they were called by their proper names. Howbeit these matters would be better amplified in other stories than this.

Now when this war was ended, the flatterers of the people began to stir up sedition again, without any new occasion or just matter offered of complaint. For they did ground this second insurrection against the nobility and patricians upon the people's misery and misfortune, that could not but fall out, by reason of the former discord and sedition between them and the nobility; because the most part of the arable land within the territory of Rome was become heathy and barren for lack of ploughing, for that they had no time nor mean to cause corn to be brought them out of other countries to sow, by reason of their wars which made the extreme dearth they had among them. Now those busy prattlers that sought the people's good will by such flattering words, perceiving great scarcity of corn to be within the city, and, though there had been plenty enough, yet the common people had no money to buy it; they spread abroad false tales and rumours against the nobility: that they, in revenge of the people, had practised and procured the extreme dearth among them.

Furthermore, in the midst of this stir, there came ambassadors to Rome from the city of Velitres, that offered up their city to the Romans and prayed them they would send new inhabitants to replenish the same, because the plague had been so extreme among them and had killed such a number of them as there was not left alive the tenth person of the people that had been there before. So the wise men of Rome began to think that the necessity of the Velitrians fell out in a most happy hour, and how by this occasion it was very meet, in so great a scarcity of victuals, to disburden Rome of a great number of citizens; and by this means as well to take away this new sedition and utterly to rid it out of the city, as also to clear the same of many mutinous and seditious persons, being the superfluous ill humours that grievously fed this disease. Hereupon the Consuls pricked out all those by a bill whom they intended to send to Velitres, to go dwell there as in form of a colony; and they levied, out of all the rest that remained in the city of Rome, a great number to go against the Volsces, hoping by the means of foreign war to pacify their sedition at home. Moreover they imagined, when the poor with the rich, and the mean sort with the nobility, should by this

| MENENIUS: | For the dearth, |
| | The gods, not the patricians, make it ... |
| MARTIUS: | What's the matter, |
| | That in these several places of the city |
| | You cry against the noble senate, who, |
| | Under the gods, keep you in awe, which else |
| | Would feed on one another? What's their seeking? |
| MENENIUS: | For corn at their own rates; whereof, they say, |
| | The city is well stored. (I, I, 74; 188) |
| MESSENGER: | The news is, sir, the Volsces are in arms. |
| MARTIUS: | I am glad on't: then we shall ha' means to vent |
| | Our musty superfluity. (I, I, 228) |

device be abroad in the wars, and in one camp and in one service and in one like danger, that then they would be more quiet and loving together.

But Sicinius and Brutus, two seditious Tribunes, spake against either of these devices, and cried out upon the noblemen that under the gentle name of a colony they would cloak and colour the most cruel and unnatural fact as might be: because they sent their poor citizens into a sore infected city and pestilent air, full of dead bodies unburied; and there also to dwell under the tuition of a strange god that had so cruelly persecuted his people. This were, said they, even as much as if the Senate should headlong cast down the people into a most bottomless pit; and are not yet contented to have famished some of the poor citizens heretofore to death and to put other of them even to the mercy of the plague, but afresh they have procured a voluntary war, to the end they would leave behind no kind of misery and ill wherewith the poor silly people should not be plagued; and only because they are weary to serve the rich.

The common people, being set on a broil and bravery with these words, would not appear when the Consuls called their names by a bill to prest them for the wars; neither would they be sent out to this new colony; insomuch as the Senate knew not well what to say or do in the matter. Martius then, who was now grown to great credit, and a stout man besides, and of great reputation with the noblest men of Rome, rose up and openly spake against these flattering Tribunes. And, for the replenishing of the city of Velitres, he did compel those that were chosen to go thither and to depart the city, upon great penalties to him that should disobey. But to the wars, the people by no means would be brought or constrained.

So Martius, taking his friends and followers with him and such as he could by fair words entreat to go with him, did run certain forays into the dominion of the Antiates, where he met with great plenty of corn and had a marvellous great spoil, as well of cattle as 28 of men he had taken prisoners, whom he brought away with him and reserved nothing for himself. Afterwards, having brought back

28 MARTIUS:     The Volsces have much corn; take these rats thither
To gnaw their garners.                       (I, I, 254)

again all his men that went out with him safe and sound to Rome, and every man rich and loaden with spoil, then the home-tarriers and 9 house-doves, that kept Rome still, began to repent them that it was not their hap to go with him; and so envied both them that had sped so well in this journey, and also, of malice to Martius, they spited to see his credit and estimation increase still more and more, because they accounted him to be a great hinderer of the people.

Shortly after this, Martius stood for the Consulship; and the common people favoured his suit, thinking it would be a shame to them to deny and refuse the chiefest nobleman of blood and most worthy person of Rome, and specially him that had done so great 0 service and good to the commonwealth. For the custom of Rome was, at that time, that such as did sue for any office should for certain days before be in the market-place, only with a poor gown on their backs and without any coat underneath, to pray the citizens to remember them at the day of election; which was thus devised, either to move the people the more by requesting them in such mean apparel, or else because they might show them their wounds they had gotten in the wars in the service of the commonwealth, as manifest marks 1 and testimony of their valiantness.

9 MARTIUS: They'll sit by the fire, and presume to know
What's done i' the Capitol ... (I, 1, 195)

0 CITIZEN: Once, if he do require our voices, we ought not to deny
him. (II, 3, 1)

2nd OFFICER: He hath deserved worthily of his country; and his ascent is not by such easy degrees as those who, having been supple and courteous to the people, bonneted, without any further deed to have them at all into their estimation and report; but he hath so planted his honours in their eyes, and his actions in their hearts, that for their tongues to be silent, and not confess so much, were a kind of ingrateful injury; to report otherwise, were a malice, that, giving itself the lie, would pluck reproof and rebuke from every ear that heard it. (II, 2, 27)

1 BRUTUS: I heard him swear,
Were he to stand for consul, never would he
Appear i' the market-place nor on him put

Now it is not to be thought that the suitors went thus loose in a simple gown in the market-place, without any coat under it, for fear and suspicion of the common people. For offices of dignity in the city were not then given by favour or corruption. It was but of late time, and long after this, that buying and selling fell out in election of officers, and that the voices of the electors were bought for money. But after corruption had once gotten way into the election of offices, it hath run from man to man, even to the very sentence of judges, and also among captains in the wars; so as, in the end, that only turned commonwealths into kingdoms, by making arms subject to money. Therefore methinks he had reason that said:
'He that first made banquets and gave money to the common people was the first that took away authority and destroyed commonwealth.'
But this pestilence crept in by little and little, and did secretly win ground still, continuing a long time in Rome before it was openly known and discovered. For no man can tell who was the first man

----

|  |  |
|---|---|
|  | The napless vesture of humility; |
|  | Nor, showing, as the manner is, his wounds |
|  | To the people, beg their stinking breaths.    (II, 1, 247) |
| MENENIUS: | It then remains |
|  | That you do speak to the people. |
| CORIOLANUS: | I do beseech you, |
|  | Let me o'erleap that custom, for I cannot |
|  | Put on the gown, stand naked and entreat them, |
|  | For my wounds' sake, to give their suffrage: please you |
|  | That I may pass this doing. |
| SICINIUS: | Sir, the people |
|  | Must have their voices; neither will they bate |
|  | One jot of ceremony. |
| MENENIUS: | Put them not to't: |
|  | Pray you, go fit you to the custom and |
|  | Take to you, as your predecessors have, |
|  | Your honour with your form.    (II, 2, 138) |
| CITIZEN: | Here he comes, and in the gown of humility . . . |
| CORIOLANUS: | I have here the customary gown.    (II, 3, 44; 93) |

that bought the people's voices for money, nor that corrupted the sentence of the judges. Howbeit at Athens some hold opinion that Anytus, the son of Anthemion, was the first man that fed the judges with money, about the end of the wars of Peloponnesus, being accused of treason for yielding up the fort of Pyle, at that time, when the golden and unfoiled age remained yet whole in judgement at Rome.

Now Martius, following this custom, showed many wounds and cuts upon his body, which he had received in seventeen years' service at the wars and in many sundry battles, being ever the foremost man that did set out feet to fight. So that there was not a man among the people but was ashamed of himself to refuse so valiant a man. And one of them said to another:

'We must needs choose him Consul; there is no remedy.'

COMINIUS: And in the brunt of seventeen battles since
He lurch'd all swords of the garland. (II, 2, 104)

CORIOLANUS: I have wounds to show you, which shall be yours in private. Your good voice, sir: what say you? ...

4th CITIZEN: You have received many wounds for your country.

CORIOLANUS: I will not seal your knowledge with showing them ...
Why in this woolvish toge should I stand here,
To beg of Hob and Dick, that do appear,
Their needless vouches? Custom calls me to't ...

2nd CITIZEN: He used us scornfully: he should have show'd us
His marks of merit, wounds received for's country.

SICINIUS: Why, so he did, I am sure.

CITIZENS: No, no: no man saw'em. (II, 3, 82; 115; 122; 171)

3rd CITIZEN: We have power in ourselves to do it, but it is a power that we have no power to do; for if he show us his wounds and tell us his deeds, we are to put our tongues into those wounds and speak for them; so, if he tell us his noble deeds, we must also tell him our noble acceptance of them. Ingratitude is monstrous, and for the multitude to be ingrateful, were to make a monster of the multitude ...

6th CITIZEN: He has done nobly, and cannot go without any honest man's voice.

7th CITIZEN: Therefore let him be consul. (II, 3, 4; 139)

But when the day of election was come, and that Martius came to the market-place with great pomp, accompanied with all the Senate and the whole nobility of the city about him, who sought to make him Consul with the greatest instance and entreaty they could or ever attempted for any man or matter, then the love and good-will of the common people turned straight to an hate and envy toward him, fearing to put this office of sovereign authority into his hands, being a man somewhat partial toward the nobility and of great credit and authority amongst the patricians, and as one they 35 might doubt would take away altogether the liberty from the people. Whereupon, for these considerations, they refused Martius in the end, and made two other that were suitors Consuls.

The Senate, being marvellously offended with the people, did accompt the shame of this refusal rather to redound to themselves than to Martius. But Martius took it in far worse part than the Senate and was out of all patience. For he was a man too full of passion and choler, and too much given to over self-will and opinion, as one of a high mind and great courage, that lacked the gravity and affability that is gotten with judgement of learning and reason, which only is to be looked for in a governor of state; and that remembered

35 CORIOLANUS: Behold, these are the tribunes of the people,
The tongues o' the common mouth: I do despise them;
For they do prank them in authority,
Against all noble sufferance.

SICINIUS:                                          Pass no further.
CORIOLANUS: Ha! what is that?
BRUTUS:       It will be dangerous to go on: no further.
CORIOLANUS: What makes this change?
MENENIUS:    The matter?
COMINIUS:     Hath he not pass'd the noble and the common?
BRUTUS:       Cominius, no.
CORIOLANUS:                        Have I had children's voices?
1st SENATOR: Tribunes, give way; he shall to the market-place.
BRUTUS:       The people are incensed against him.
SICINIUS:                                          Stop,
Or all will fall in broil.                              (III, I, 21)

not how wilfulness is the thing of the world which a governor of a commonwealth for pleasing should shun, being that which Plato called 'solitariness'; as, in the end, all men that are wilfully given to a self-opinion and obstinate mind and who will never yield to others' reason but to their own, remain without company and forsaken of all men. For a man that will live in the world must needs
6 have patience, which lusty bloods make but a mock at.

So Martius, being a stout man of nature, that never yielded in any respect, as one thinking that to overcome always and to have the upper hand in all matters was a token of magnanimity and of no base and faint courage, which spitteth out anger from the most weak and passioned part of the heart, much like the matter of an impostume, went home to his house full freighted with spite and malice against the people, being accompanied with all the lustiest young gentlemen, whose minds were nobly bent as those that came of noble race, and commonly used for to follow and honour him. But then specially they flocked about him and kept him company – to his much harm. For they did but kindle and inflame his choler more and more, being sorry with him for the injury the people offered him, because he was their captain and leader to the wars, that taught them all martial discipline and stirred up in them a noble emulation of honour and valiantness, and yet without envy, praising them that deserved best.

In the mean season there came great plenty of corn to Rome, that had been bought part in Italy and part was sent out of Sicilia, as given by Gelon, the tyrant of Syracusa; so that many stood in great hope that, the dearth of victuals being holpen, the civil dissension would also cease. The Senate sat in council upon it immediately. The common people stood also about the palace where the council was kept, gaping what resolution would fall out, persuading themselves that the corn they had bought should be sold good cheap and that which was given should be divided by the poll without paying any

36 BRUTUS:                    He hath been used
                    Ever to conquer, and to have his worth
                    Of contradiction: being once chafed, he cannot
                    Be rein'd again to temperance.                    (III, 3, 25)

penny; and the rather, because certain of the Senators amongst them
did so wish and persuade the same.

But Martius, standing upon his feet, did somewhat sharply take
up those who went about to gratify the people therein, and called
37 them people-pleasers and traitors to the nobility. Moreover, he
said, they nourished against themselves the naughty seed and cockle
of insolency and sedition, which had been sowed and scattered abroad
amongst the people, whom they should have cut off, if they had been
38 wise, and have prevented their greatness; and not, to their own
destruction, to have suffered the people to stablish a magistrate for
themselves, of so great power and authority as that man had to
whom they had granted it; who was also to be feared because he
obtained what he would, and did nothing but what he listed, neither
passed for any obedience to the Consuls, but lived in all liberty,
acknowledging no superior to command him, saving the only heads
39 and authors of their faction, whom he called his magistrates.

37 BRUTUS:       The people cry you mock'd them, and of late,
                     When corn was given them gratis, you repin'd;
                     Scandal'd the suppliants for the people, call'd them
                     Time-pleasers, flatterers, foes to nobleness. (III, 1, 42)

38 CORIOLANUS: In soothing them, we nourish 'gainst our senate
                     The cockle of rebellion, insolence, sedition,
                     Which we ourselves have plough'd for, sow'd, and scatter'd,
                     By mingling them with us, the honour'd number. (III, 1, 69)

39 CORIOLANUS: O good but most unwise patricians! Why,
                     You grave but reckless senators, have you thus
                     Given Hydra here to choose an officer,
                     That with his peremptory 'shall', being but
                     The horn and noise o' the monster's, wants not spirit
                     To say he'll turn your current in a ditch,
                     And make your channel his? . . .
                                 They choose their magistrate,
                     And such a one as he, who puts his 'shall',
                     His popular 'shall', against a graver bench
                     Than ever frown'd in Greece. By Jove himself!
                     It makes the consuls base: and my soul aches
                     To know, when two authorities are up,

'Therefore,' said he, 'they that gave counsel and persuaded that the
corn should be given out to the common people *gratis*, as they used
to do in the cities of Greece, where the people had more absolute
power, did but only nourish their disobedience, which would
break out in the end, to the utter ruin and overthrow of the whole
state. For they will not think it is done in recompense of their
service past, sithence they know well enough they have so oft
refused to go to the wars when they were commanded; neither for
their mutinies when they went with us, whereby they have rebelled
and forsaken their country; neither for their accusations which their
flatterers have preferred unto them, and they have received, and
made good against the Senate; but they will rather judge we give and
grant them this as abasing ourselves, and standing in fear of them, and
glad to flatter them every way. By this means their disobedience
will still grow worse and worse; and they will never leave to practise
new sedition and uproars. Therefore it were a great folly for us,

40 CORIOLANUS: Whoever gave that counsel, to give forth
               The corn o' the storehouse gratis, as 'twas used
               Sometime in Greece . . .
               Though there the people had more absolute power,
               I say, they nourish'd disobedience, fed
               The ruin of the state . . . They know the corn
               Was not our recompense, resting well assured
               They ne'er did service for't: being press'd to the war,
               Even when the navel of the state was touch'd,
               They would not thread the gates. This kind of service
               Did not deserve corn gratis. Being i' the war,
               Their mutinies and revolts, wherein they show'd
               Most valour, spoke not for them: the accusation
               Which they have often made against the senate,
               All cause unborn, could never be the motive
               Of our so frank donation. Well, what then?
               How shall this bisson multitude digest

               Neither supreme, how soon confusion
               May enter 'twixt the gap of both and take
               The one by the other.           (III, 1, 91; 104)

methinks, to do it. Yea, shall I say more? we should, if we were wise, take from them their Tribuneship, which most manifestly is the embasing of the Consulship and the cause of the division of the city; the state whereof, as it standeth, is not now as it was wont to be; but becometh dismembered in two factions, which maintains always civil dissension and discord between us, and will never suffer us again to be united into one body.'

41

Martius, dilating the matter with many such like reasons, won all the young men and almost all the rich men to his opinion; insomuch they rang it out that he was the only man, and alone in the city who stood out against the people and never flattered them. There were only a few old men that spake against him, fearing lest some mischief might fall out upon it; as indeed there followed no great good afterward.

41 CORIOLANUS: What may be sworn by, both divine and human,
　　　　　　　　Seal what I end withal! This double worship,
　　　　　　　　Where one part does disdain with cause, the other
　　　　　　　　Insult without all reason, where gentry, title, wisdom,
　　　　　　　　Cannot conclude but by the yea and no
　　　　　　　　Of general ignorance, – it must omit
　　　　　　　　Real necessities, and give way the while
　　　　　　　　To unstable slightness . . .
　　　　　　　　What should the people do with these bald tribunes?
　　　　　　　　On whom depending, their obedience fails
　　　　　　　　To the greater bench: in a rebellion,
　　　　　　　　When what's not meet, but what must be, was law,
　　　　　　　　Then were they chosen: in a better hour,
　　　　　　　　Let what is meet be said it must be meet,
　　　　　　　　And throw their power i' the dust.　　(III, I, 141; 164)

　　　　　　　　The senate's courtesy? Let deeds express
　　　　　　　　What's like to be their words: 'We did request it;
　　　　　　　　We are the greater poll, and in true fear
　　　　　　　　They gave us our demands.' Thus we debase
　　　　　　　　The nature of our seats and make the rabble
　　　　　　　　Call our cares fears; which will in time
　　　　　　　　Break ope the locks o' the senate and bring in
　　　　　　　　The crows to peck the eagles.　　(III, I, 113)

For the Tribunes of the People being present at this consultation of the Senate, when they saw that the opinion of Martius was confirmed with the more voices, they left the Senate and went down to the people, crying out for help, and that they would assemble to save their Tribunes. Hereupon the people ran on head in tumult together; before whom the words that Martius spake in the Senate were openly reported; which the people so stomached that even in that fury they were ready to fly upon the whole Senate. But the Tribunes laid all the fault and burden wholly upon Martius and sent their sergeants forthwith to arrest him, presently to appear in person before the people to answer the words he had spoken in the Senate. Martius stoutly withstood these officers that came to arrest him. Then the Tribunes in their own persons, accompanied with the Aediles, went to fetch him by force, and so laid violent hands upon him. Howbeit the noble patricians, gathering together about him, made 42 the Tribunes give back and laid it sore upon the Aediles. So, for that time, the night parted them, and the tumult appeased.

The next morning betimes, the Consuls seeing the people in an uproar running to the market-place out of all parts of the city, they were afraid lest all the city would together by the ears. Wherefore, assembling the Senate in all haste, they declared how it stood them upon, to appease the fury of the people with some gentle words or grateful decrees in their favour; and moreover, like wise men

42 BRUTUS: Lay hands upon him,
And bear him to the rock.
*Coriolanus draws his sword.*
CORIOLANUS: No, I'll die here.
There's some among you have beheld me fighting:
Come, try upon yourselves what you have seen me.
MENENIUS: Down with that sword! Tribunes, withdraw awhile.
BRUTUS: Lay hands upon him.
MENENIUS: Help Martius, help,
You that be noble: help him, young and old!
CITIZENS: Down with him, down with him!
*In this mutiny, the Tribunes, the Aediles, and the People, are beat in.*
(III, I, 222)

325

they should consider it was now no time to stand at defence and in contention, nor yet to fight for honour against the commonalty, they being fallen to so great an extremity and offering such imminent danger. Wherefore they were to consider temperately of things and to deliver some present and gentle pacification. The most part of the Senators that were present at this council thought this opinion best and gave their consents unto it. Whereupon the Consuls, rising out of council, went to speak unto the people as gently as they could; and they did pacify their fury and anger, purging the Senate of all the unjust accusations laid upon them; and used great modesty in persuading them, and also in reproving the faults they had committed. And as for the rest, that touched the sale of corn, they promised there should be no disliking offered them in the price.

So the most part of the people being pacified and appearing so plainly by the great silence and still that was among them, as yielding to the Consuls and liking well of their words, the Tribunes then of the People rose out of their seats, and said: Forasmuch as the Senate yielded unto reason, the people also for their part, as became them, did likewise give place unto them. But notwithstanding they would that Martius should come in person to answer to the articles they had devised. First, whether he had not solicited and procured the Senate to change the present state of the commonweal and to take 43 the sovereign authority out of the people's hands. Next, when he was sent for by authority of their officers, why he did contemptuously resist and disobey. Lastly, seeing he had driven and beaten the Aediles into the market-place before all the world, if, in doing this, he had not done as much as in him lay to raise civil wars and to set 44 one citizen against another.

| 43 | BRUTUS: | In this point charge him home, that he affects Tyrannical power. | (III, 3, 1) |
| | SICINIUS: | We charge you, that you have contrived to take From Rome all season'd office and to wind Yourself into a power tyrannical; For which you are a traitor to the people. | (III, 3, 63) |
| 44 | SICINIUS: | Have we not had a taste of his obedience? Our aediles smote? Ourselves resisted? | (III, 1, 318) |

All this was spoken to one of these two ends: either that Martius against his nature should be constrained to humble himself and to abase his haughty and fierce mind; or else, if he continued still in his stoutness, he should incur the people's displeasure and ill will so far that he should never possibly win them again; which they hoped would rather fall out so than otherwise; as indeed they guessed, unhappily, considering Martius' nature and disposition.

So Martius came and presented himself to answer their accusations against him; and the people held their peace and gave attentive ear to hear what he would say. But where they thought to have heard very humble and lowly words come from him, he began not only to use his wonted boldness of speaking – which of itself was very rough and unpleasant and did more aggravate his accusation than purge his innocency – but also gave himself in his words to thunder and look therewithal so grimly as though he made no reckoning of the matter. This stirred coals among the people, who were in wonderful fury at it; and their hate and malice grew so toward him that they could hold no longer, bear, nor endure his bravery and careless boldness. Whereupon Sicinius, the cruellest and stoutest of

BRUTUS:       This mutiny were better put in hazard,
              Than stay, past doubt, for greater:
              If, as his nature is, he fall in rage
              With their refusal, both observe and answer
              The vantage of his anger.                    (II, 3, 264)

CORIOLANUS:   The fires i' the lowest hell fold in the people!
              Call me their traitor! Thou injurious tribune!
              Within thine eyes sat twenty thousand deaths,
              In thy hands clutch'd as many millions, in
              Thy lying tongue both numbers, I would say
              'Thou liest' unto thee with a voice as free
              As I do pray the gods.                        (III, 3, 68)

SICINIUS:     What you have seen him do and heard him speak,
              Beating your officers, cursing yourselves,
              Opposing laws with strokes and here defying
              Those whose great power must try him.          (III, 3, 77)

the Tribunes, after he had whispered a little with his companions, did openly pronounce, in the face of all the people, Martius as condemned by the Tribunes to die. Then presently he commanded the Aediles to apprehend him and carry him straight to the rock Tarpeian, 47 and to cast him headlong down the same.

When the Aediles came to lay hands upon Martius to do that they were commanded, divers of the people themselves thought it too cruel and violent a deed. The noblemen also, being much troubled 48 to see such force and rigour used, began to cry aloud, 'Help Martius!' So those that laid hands on him being repulsed, they compassed him in round among themselves, and some of them, holding up their hands to the people, besought them not to handle him thus cruelly. But neither their words nor crying out could aught prevail, the tumult and hurly-burly was so great, until such time as the Tribunes' own friends and kinsmen, weighing with themselves the impossibleness to convey Martius to execution without great slaughter and murder of the nobility, did persuade and advise not to proceed in so violent and extraordinary a sort as to put such a man to death without lawful process in law; but that they should refer the sentence of his death to the free voice of the people.

Then Sicinius, bethinking himself a little, did ask the patricians for what cause they took Martius out of the officers' hands that went

47 SICINIUS:                           This deserves death.
   BRUTUS:          Or let us stand to our authority,
                    Or let us lose it. We do here pronounce,
                    Upon the part o' the people, in whose power
                    We were elected theirs, Martius is worthy
                    Of present death.
   SICINIUS:                         Therefore lay hold of him;
                    Bear him to the rock Tarpeian, and from thence
                    Into destruction cast him.
   BRUTUS:                             Aediles, seize him! ...
                    Lay hands upon him,
                    And bear him to the rock.          (III, I, 208; 222)
48 BRUTUS:          Lay hands upon him.
   MENENIUS:                        Help Martius, help,
                    You that be noble.                 (III, I, 227)

to do execution. The patricians asked him again why they would of themselves so cruelly and wickedly put to death so noble and valiant a Roman as Martius was, and that without law or justice.

'Well then,' said Sicinius, 'if that be the matter, let there be no more quarrel or dissension against the people; for they do grant your demand that his cause shall be heard according to the law.'
Therefore said he to Martius:

'We do will and charge you to appear before the people, the third day of our next sitting and assembly here, to make your purgation for such articles as shall be objected against you, that by free voice the people may give sentence upon you as shall please them.'
The noblemen were glad then of the adjournment, and were much pleased they had gotten Martius out of this danger.

SICINIUS:                    Sir, how comes't that you
        Have holp to make this rescue?

MENENIUS:                              Hear me speak:
        As I do know the consul's worthiness,
        So can I name his faults. . . .

SICINIUS:                         Speak briefly then;
        For we are peremptory to dispatch
        This viperous traitor; to eject him hence
        Were but one danger, and to keep him here
        Our certain death: therefore it is decreed
        He dies to-night.

MENENIUS:                         Now the good gods forbid
        That our renowned Rome, whose gratitude
        Towards her deserved children is enroll'd
        In Jove's own book, like an unnatural dam
        Should now eat up her own!            (III, I, 276; 284)

MENENIUS:                         Give me leave,
        I'll go to him, and undertake to bring him
        Where he shall answer, by a lawful form,
        In peace, to his utmost peril.

1st SENATOR:                         Noble tribunes,
        It is the humane way: the other course
        Will prove too bloody, and the end of it
        Unknown to the beginning.

In the mean space, before the third day of their next session came about, the same being kept every ninth day continually at Rome (whereupon they call it now in Latin, *Nundinae*), there fell out war against the Antiates; which gave some hope to the nobility that this adjournment would come to little effect, thinking that this war would hold them so long as that the fury of the people against him would be well swaged, or utterly forgotten, by reason of the trouble of the wars. But, contrary to expectation, the peace was concluded presently with the Antiates, and the people returned again to Rome.

Then the patricians assembled oftentimes together, to consult how they might stand to Martius and keep the Tribunes from occasion to cause the people to mutiny again and rise against the nobility. And there Appius Clodius, one that was taken ever as an heavy enemy to the people, did avow and protest that they would utterly abase the authority of the Senate and destroy the commonweal, if they would suffer the common people to have authority by voices to give judgement against the nobility. On the other side again, the most ancient Senators, and such as were given to favour the common people, said that when the people should see they had authority of life and death in their hands, they would not be so cruel and fierce, but gentle and civil; more also, that it was not for contempt of nobility or the Senate that they sought to have the authority of justice in their hands as a pre-eminence and prerogative of honour, but because they feared that themselves should be contemned and hated of the nobility; so as they were persuaded that, so soon as they

---

SICINIUS:                                          Noble Menenius,
Be you then as the people's officer.
Masters, lay down your weapons.

BRUTUS:                                          Go not home.

SICINIUS: Meet on the market-place. We'll attend you there:
Where, if you bring not Martius, we'll proceed
In our first way.

MENENIUS:                              I'll bring him to you. [*To the Senators*]
Let me desire your company: he must come,
Or what is worst will follow.                    (III, I, 323)

330

gave them authority to judge by voices, so soon would they leave all envy and malice to condemn any.

Martius, seeing the Senate in great doubt how to resolve (partly for the love and good will the nobility did bear him, and partly for the fear they stood in of the people), asked aloud of the Tribunes, what matter they would burden him with. The Tribunes answered him that they would show how he did aspire to be King and would prove that all his actions tended to usurp tyrannical power over
51 Rome. Martius with that, rising up on his feet, said that thereupon he did willingly offer himself to the people, to be tried upon that accusation; and that if it were proved by him he had so much as once thought of any such matter, that he would then refuse no kind of punishment they would offer him:
' – conditionally,' quoth he, 'that you charge me with nothing else besides, and that ye do not also abuse the Senate.'
52 They promised they would not.

Under these conditions the judgement was agreed upon, and the people assembled. And first of all the Tribunes would in any case, whatsoever became of it, that the people would proceed to give
53 their voices by tribes, and not by hundreds; for by this means the multitude of the poor needy people – and all such rabble as had

51 See p. 326 note 43.

52 CORIOLANUS: Shall I be charged no further than this present?
Must all determine here?

SICINIUS:                             I do demand,
If you submit you to the people's voices,
Allow their officers and are content
To suffer lawful censure for such faults
As shall be proved upon you?

CORIOLANUS:                     I am content.     (III, 3, 42)

53 SICINIUS:               Have you a catalogue
Of all the voices that we have procured
Set down by the poll?

AEDILE:                   I have; 'tis ready.

SICINIUS: Have you collected them by tribes?

AEDILE:                       I have.     (III, 3, 8)

nothing to lose and had less regard of honesty before their eyes –
came to be of greater force, because their voices were numbered by
the poll, than the noble honest citizens, whose persons and purse did
dutifully serve the commonwealth in their wars. And then when the
Tribunes saw they could not prove he went about to make himself
King, they began to broach afresh the former words that Martius
had spoken in the Senate, in hindering the distribution of the corn at
mean price unto the common people and persuading also to take the
office of Tribuneship from them. And for the third, they charged
him anew that he had not made the common distribution of the
54 spoil he had gotten in the invading the territories of the Antiates;
but had of his own authority divided it among them who were with
him in that journey. But this matter was most strange of all to
Martius, looking least to have been burdened with that as with any
matter of offence. Whereupon being burdened on the sudden, and
having no ready excuse to make even at that instant, he began to
fall a-praising of the soldiers that had served with him in that
journey. But those that were not with him, being the greater number,
cried out so loud and made such a noise that he could not be heard.

To conclude, when they came to tell the voices of the tribes, there
were three voices odd which condemned him to be banished for life.
After declaration of the sentence the people made such joy as they
never rejoiced more for any battle they had won upon their enemies,
they were so brave and lively; and went home so jocundly from
55 the assembly, for triumph of this sentence. The Senate again in
contrary manner were as sad and heavy, repenting themselves
beyond measure that they had not rather determined to have done
and suffered anything whatsoever, before the common people
56 should so arrogantly and outrageously have abused their authority.

| 54 BRUTUS: | Enforce him with his envy to the people, |  |
|---|---|---|
|  | And that the spoil got on the Antiates |  |
|  | Was ne'er distributed. | (III, 3, 3) |
| 55 AEDILE: | The people's enemy is gone, is gone! |  |
| CITIZENS: | Our enemy is banish'd; He is gone! Hoo! Hoo! |  |
|  | *They all shout, and throw up their caps.* | (III, 3, 136) |
| 56 ROMAN: | For the nobles receive so to heart the banishment of that |  |

There needed no difference of garments, I warrant you, nor outward shows to know a plebeian from a patrician; for they were easily discerned by their looks. For he that was on the people's side looked cheerily on the matter. But he that was sad and hung down his head, he was sure of the noblemen's side – saving Martius alone, who neither in his countenance nor in his gait did ever show himself abashed, or once let fall his great courage; but he only of all other gentlemen that were angry at his fortune did outwardly show no manner of passion, nor care at all of himself. Not that he did patiently bear and temper his good-hap, in respect of any reason he had or by his quiet condition; but because he was so carried away with the vehemency of anger and desire of revenge that he had no sense nor feeling of the hard state he was in, which the common people judge not to be sorrow although indeed it be the very same. For when sorrow, as you would say, is set a-fire, then it is converted into spite and malice, and driveth away for that time all faintness of heart and natural fear. And this is the cause why the choleric man is so altered and mad in his actions, as a man set a-fire with a burning ague. For, when a man's heart is troubled within, his pulse will beat marvellous strongly.

Now, that Martius was even in that taking, it appeared true soon after by his doings. For when he was come home to his house again and had taken his leave of his mother and wife, finding them weeping and shrieking out for sorrow, and had also comforted and persuaded them to be content with his chance, he went immediately to the

CORIOLANUS: Come, leave your tears: a brief farewell ...
            Nay, mother,
Where is your ancient courage? you were used
To say extremity was the trier of spirits ...
            Farewell, my wife! my mother!
I'll do well yet,  [*etc.*]               (IV, 1, 1)

---

worthy Coriolanus, that they are in a ripe aptness to take all power from the people and to pluck from them their tribunes for ever.           (IV, 3, 21)

333

gate of the city, accompanied with a great number of patricians that brought him thither, from whence he went on his way with three or four of his friends only, taking nothing with him nor requesting anything of any man. So he remained a few days in the country at his houses, turmoiled with sundry sorts and kinds of thoughts, such as the fire of his choler did stir up.

In the end, seeing he could resolve no way to take a profitable or honourable course, but only was pricked forward still to be revenged of the Romans, he thought to raise up some great wars against them, by their nearest neighbours. Whereupon he thought it his best way first to stir up the Volsces against them, knowing they were yet able enough in strength and riches to encounter them, notwithstanding their former losses they had received not long before, and that their power was not so much impaired as their malice and desire was increased to be revenged of the Romans.

Now in the city of Antium there was one called Tullus Aufidius, who for his riches, as also for his nobility and valiantness, was honoured among the Volsces as a king. Martius knew very well that Tullus did more malice and envy him than he did all the Romans besides; because that many times in battles where they met, they were ever at the encounter one against another, like lusty courageous youths, striving in all emulation of honour, and had encountered many times together; insomuch as, besides the common quarrel between them, there was bred a marvellous private hate one against
58 another. Yet notwithstanding, considering that Tullus Aufidius was a man of a great mind, and that he above all other of the Volsces

58 MARTIUS:           They have a leader,
Tullus Aufidius, that will put you to't.
I sin in envying his nobility,
And were I any thing but what I am,
I would wish me only he.
COMINIUS:           You have fought together.
MARTIUS:  Were half to half the world by the ears and he
Upon my party, I'ld revolt, to make
Only my wars with him: he is a lion
That I am proud to hunt.          (I, I, 232

334

MARTIUS: I'll fight with none but thee; for I do hate thee
Worse than a promise-breaker.

AUFIDIUS:                     We hate alike.
Not Afric owns a serpent I abhor
More than thy fame and envy.        (1, 8, 1)

AUFIDIUS:                   Five times, Martius,
I have fought with thee; so often hast thou beat me,
And wouldst do so, I think, should we encounter
As often as we eat. By the elements,
If e'er again I meet him beard to beard,
He's mine or I am his: mine emulation
Hath not that honour in't it had; for where
I thought to crush him in an equal force,
True sword to sword, I'll potch at him some way
Or wrath or craft may get him . . .
                           My valour's poison'd
With only suffering stain by him; for him
Shall fly out of itself: nor sleep nor sanctuary,
Being naked, sick, nor fane nor Capitol,
The prayers of priests nor times of sacrifice,
Embarquements all of fury, shall lift up
Their rotten privilege and custom 'gainst
My hate to Martius: where I find him, were it
At home, upon my brother's guard, even there,
Against the hospitable canon, would I
Wash my fierce hand in's heart.        (1, 10, 7)

CORIOLANUS:                 Saw you Aufidius? . . .
Spoke he of me?

LARTIUS:           He did, my lord.

CORIOLANUS:               How? What?

LARTIUS: How often he had met you, sword to sword;
That of all things upon the earth he hated
Your person most, that he would pawn his fortunes
To hopeless restitution, so he might
Be called your vanquisher.

CORIOLANUS:             At Antium lives he?

LARTIUS: At Antium.

CORIOLANUS: I wish I had a cause to seek him there,
To oppose his hatred fully.        (III, 1, 8)

most desired revenge of the Romans, for the injuries they had done unto them, he did an act that confirmed the true words of an ancient poet, who said:

> It is a thing full hard man's anger to withstand,
> If it be stiffly bent to take an enterprise in hand;
> For then most men will have the thing that they desire,
> Although it cost their lives therefore; such force hath wicked ire.

And so did he. For he disguised himself in such array and attire as he thought no man could ever have known him for the person he was, seeing him in that apparel he had upon his back; and, as Homer said of Ulysses,

> So did he enter into the enemy's town.

It was even twilight when he entered the city of Antium; and many people met him in the streets, but no man knew him. So he went 59 directly to Tullus Aufidius' house; and when he came thither, he got him up straight to the chimney hearth, and sat him down, and spake not a word to any man, his face all muffled over. They of the house, spying him, wondered what he should be; and yet they durst not bid him rise. For ill-favouredly muffled and disguised as he was, yet there appeared a certain majesty in his countenance and in his 60 silence. Whereupon they went to Tullus, who was at supper, to tell him of the strange disguising of this man. Tullus rose presently from

59 *Enter Coriolanus in mean apparel, disguised and muffled.*

CORIOLANUS: A good city is this Antium. City,
          'Tis I that made thy widows. . . .
              *Enter a Citizen.*

                                  Save you, sir.
CITIZEN:     And you.
CORIOLANUS:          Direct me, if it be your will,
          Where great Aufidius lies: is he in Antium?    (IV, 4, 1)
60 See IV, 5, especially:
CORIOLANUS: Let me but stand; I will not hurt your hearth.   (IV, 5, 26)
SERVANT:     Nay, I knew by his face that there was something in him:
          he had, sir, a kind of face, methought, – I cannot tell how to
          term it.                            (IV, 5, 162)

the board, and, coming towards him, asked him what he was and wherefore he came. Then Martius unmuffled himself, and after he had paused a while, making no answer, he said unto him:

'If thou knowest me not yet, Tullus, and, seeing me, dost not perhaps believe me to be the man I am indeed, I must of necessity bewray my self to be that I am. I am Caius Martius, who hath done to thyself particularly, and to all the Volsces generally, great hurt and mischief; which I cannot deny, for my surname of Coriolanus that I bear. For I never had other benefit nor recompense of all the true and painful service I have done, and the extreme dangers I have been in, but this only surname – a good memory and witness of the malice and displeasure thou shouldst bear me. Indeed the name only remaineth with me. For, the rest the envy and cruelty of the people of Rome have taken from me, by the sufferance of the dastardly nobility and magistrates, who have forsaken me and let me be banished by the people. This extremity hath now driven me to come as a poor suitor to take thy chimney hearth, not of any hope I have to save my life thereby – for, if I had feared death, I would not have come hither to have put my life in hazard – but pricked forward with spite and desire I have to be revenged of them that thus have banished me, whom now I begin to be avenged on, putting my person between thy enemies. Wherefore, if thou hast any heart to be wrecked of the injuries thy enemies have done thee, speed thee now, and let my misery serve thy turn; and so use it as my service may be a benefit to the Volsces; promising thee, that I will fight with better good will for all you than ever I did when I was against you, knowing that they fight more valiantly, who know the force of their enemy, than such as have never proved it. And if it be so that thou dare not, and that thou art weary to prove fortune any more, then am I also weary to live any longer. And it were no wisdom in thee to save the life of him who hath been heretofore thy mortal enemy and whose service now can nothing help nor pleasure thee.'

61

*61* CORIOLANUS: If, Tullus,
       Not yet thou know'st me, and, seeing me, dost not
       Think me for the man I am, necessity
       Commands me name myself. . . .

Tullus, hearing what he said, was a marvellous glad man, and, taking him by the hand, he said unto him:

'Stand up, O Martius, and be of good cheer; for in proffering thyself unto us thou dost us great honour; and by this means thou mayest hope also of greater things at all the Volsces' hands.'

So he feasted him for that time, and entertained him in the honourablest manner he could, talking with him in no other matters at that present. But, within few days after, they fell to consultation together in what sort they should begin their wars.

---

My name is Caius Martius, who hath done
To thee particularly and to all the Volsces
Great hurt and mischief; thereto witness may
My surname, Coriolanus: the painful service,
The extreme dangers and the drops of blood
Shed for my thankless country are requited
But with that surname; a good memory,
And witness of the malice and displeasure
Which thou shouldst bear me: only that name remains;
The cruelty and envy of the people,
Permitted by our dastard nobles, who
Have all forsook me, hath devour'd the rest;
And suffer'd me by the voice of slaves to be
Whoop'd out of Rome. Now this extremity
Hath brought me to thy hearth; not out of hope –
Mistake me not – to save my life, for if
I had fear'd death, of all the men i' the world
I would have 'voided thee, but in mere spite,
To be full quit of those my banishers,
Stand I before thee here. Then if thou hast
A heart of wreak in thee, that wilt revenge
Thine own particular wrongs and stop those maims
Of shame seen through thy country, speed thee straight,
And make my misery serve thy turn: so use it
That my revengeful services may prove
As benefits to thee, for I will fight
Against my canker'd country with the spleen
Of all the under fiends. But if so be

Now on the other side, the city of Rome was in marvellous uproar and discord, the nobility against the commonalty, and chiefly for Martius' condemnation and banishment. Moreover the priests, the soothsayers, and private men also, came and declared to the Senate certain sights and wonders in the air, which they had seen, and were to be considered of; amongst the which, such a vision happened: There was a citizen of Rome called Titus Latinus, a man of mean quality and condition, but otherwise an honest sober man, given to a quiet life without superstition and much less to vanity or lying. This man had a vision in his dream, in the which he thought that Jupiter appeared unto him and commanded him to signify to the Senate that they had caused a very vile lewd dancer to go before the procession; and said the first time this vision had appeared unto him he made no reckoning of it; and coming again another time into his mind, he made not much more account of the matter than before. In the end, he saw one of his sons die, who had the best nature and condition of all his brethren; and suddenly he himself was so taken in all his limbs that he became lame and impotent. Hereupon he told the whole circumstance of this vision before the Senate, sitting upon his little couch or bed, whereon he was carried on men's arms; and he had no sooner reported this vision to the Senate, but he presently felt his body and limbs restored again to their former strength and use. So raising up himself upon his couch, he got up on his feet at that instant and walked home to his house without help of any man.

The Senate, being amazed at this matter, made diligent inquiry to understand the truth, and in the end they found there was such a

---

Thou darest not this and that to prove more fortunes
Thou'rt tired, then, in a word, I also am
Longer to live most weary, and present
My throat to thee and to thy ancient malice:
Which not to cut would show thee but a fool,
Since I have ever follow'd thee with hate,
Drawn tuns of blood out of thy country's breast,
And cannot live but to thy shame, unless
It be to do thee service.                    (IV, 5, 60; 71)

thing. There was one that had delivered a bondman of his that had offended him into the hands of other slaves and bondmen, and had commanded them to whip him up and down the market-place, and afterwards to kill him; and as they had him in execution, whipping him cruelly, they did so martyr the poor wretch that, for the cruel smart and pain he felt, he turned and writhed his body in strange and pitiful sort. The procession by chance came by even at the same time; and many that followed it were heartily moved and offended with the sight, saying that this was no good sight to behold, nor meet to be met in procession time. But for all this, there was nothing done, saving they blamed and rebuked him that punished his slave so cruelly.

For the Romans at that time did use their bondmen very gently, because they themselves did labour with their own hands and lived with them and among them; and therefore they did use them the more gently and familiarly. For the greatest punishment they gave a slave that had offended was this: they made him carry a limmer on his shoulders that is fastened to the axletree of a coach, and compelled him to go up and down in that sort amongst all their neighbours. He that had once abidden this punishment, and was seen in that manner, was proclaimed and cried in every market-town, so that no man would ever trust him after; and they called him *furcifer*, because the Latins call the wood that runneth into the axletree of the coach *furca*; as much to say as, 'a fork'.

Now, when Latinus had made report to the Senate of the vision that had happened to him, they were devising whom this un-pleasant dancer should be that went before the procession. There-upon certain that stood by remembered the poor slave that was so cruelly whipped through the market-place, whom they after-wards put to death; and the thing that made them remember it was the strange and rare manner of his punishment. The priests hereupon were repaired unto for their advice. They were wholly of opinion that it was the whipping of the slave. So they caused the slave's master to be punished, and began again a new procession and all other shows and sights in honour of Jupiter.

But hereby appeareth plainly how King Numa did wisely ordain all other ceremonies concerning devotion to the gods, and specially this custom which he stablished, to bring the people to religion. For when the magistrates, bishops, priests, or other religious ministers go about any divine service, or matter of religion, an herald ever goeth before them, crying out aloud: *Hoc age:* as to say, 'do this', or 'mind this'. Hereby they are specially commanded wholly to dispose themselves to serve God, leaving all other business and matters aside; knowing well enough, that, whatsoever most men do, they do it as in a manner constrained unto it. But the Romans did ever use to begin again their sacrifices, processions, plays, and such like shows done in honour of the gods, not only upon such an occasion but upon lighter causes than that; as when they went a procession through the city and did carry the images of their gods and such other like holy relics upon open hallowed coaches or charrets called in Latin *tensae*, one of the coach horses that drew them stood still and would draw no more; and because also the coachman took the reins of the bridle with the left hand, they ordained that the procession should be begun again anew. Of later time also they did renew and begin a sacrifice thirty times one after another, because they thought still there fell out one fault or other in the same, so holy and devout were they to the gods.

Now Tullus and Martius had secret conference with the greatest personages of the city of Antium, declaring unto them that now they had good time offered them to make war with the Romans while they were in dissension one with another. They answered them, they were ashamed to break the league, considering that they were sworn to keep peace for two years. Howbeit, shortly after, the Romans gave them great occasion to make war with them. For on a holy day, common plays being kept in Rome, upon some suspicion or false report they made proclamation by sound of trumpet that all the Volsces should avoid out of Rome before sunset. Some think this was a craft and deceit of Martius, who sent one to Rome to the Consuls to accuse the Volsces falsely, advertising them how they had made a conspiracy to set upon them whilst they were busy in seeing these games, and also to set their city a-fire.

This open proclamation made all the Volsces more offended with the Romans than ever they were before; and Tullus, aggravating the matter, did so inflame the Volsces against them that, in the end, they sent their ambassadors to Rome to summon them to deliver their lands and towns again which they had taken from them in times past or to look for present wars. The Romans, hearing this, were marvellously nettled; and made no other answer but thus: if the Volsces be the first that begin war, the Romans will be the last that will end it. Incontinently upon return of the Volsces' ambassadors and delivery of the Romans' answer, Tullus caused an assembly general to be made of the Volsces, and concluded to make war upon the Romans. This done, Tullus did counsel them to take Martius into their service, and not to mistrust him for the remembrance of anything past, but boldly to trust him in any matter to come; for he would do them more service in fighting for them than ever he did them displeasure in fighting against them. So Martius was called forth, who spake so excellently in the presence of them all, that he was thought no less eloquent in tongue than warlike in show; and declared himself both expert in wars, and wise with valiantness. Thus he was joined in commission with Tullus as general of the Volsces, having absolute authority between them to follow and pursue the 62 wars.

But Martius, fearing lest tract of time to bring this army together with all the munition and furniture of the Volsces would rob him of the mean he had to execute his purpose and intent, left order with the rulers and chief of the city to assemble the rest of their power and to prepare all necessary provision for the camp. Then he with the lightest soldiers he had, and that were willing to follow him, stale away upon the sudden, and marched with all speed, and entered the territories of Rome, before the Romans heard any news of his coming; insomuch as the Volsces found such spoil in the fields as

62 LIEUTENANT:           Yet I wish, sir, –
I mean for your particular, – you had not
Join'd in commission with him; but either
Had borne the action of yourself, or else
To him had left it solely.

(IV, 7, 12)

they had more than they could spend in their camp, and were weary
63 to drive and carry away that they had.

Howbeit the gain of the spoil and the hurt they did to the Romans
in this invasion was the least part of his intent. For his chiefest purpose
was to increase still the malice and dissension between the nobility
and the commonalty; and, to draw that on, he was very careful to
keep the noblemen's lands and goods safe from harm and burning,
but spoiled all the whole country besides, and would suffer no man
to take or hurt anything of the noblemen's. This made greater stir and
broil between the nobility and people than was before. For the noblemen fell out with the people, because they had so unjustly banished
64 a man of so great valour and power: The people on the other side
accused the nobility, how they had procured Martius to make these

63 MESSENGER: It is spoke freely out of many mouths –
     How probable I do not know – that Martius,
     Join'd with Aufidius, leads a power 'gainst Rome,
     And vows revenge as spacious as between
     The young'st and oldest thing.
SICINIUS:          This is most likely!
BRUTUS:  Raised only, that the weaker sort may wish
     Good Martius home again . . .
MENENIUS: This is unlikely. . . .
     *Enter a Second Messenger.*
2nd MESSENGER: . . . A fearful army, led by Caius Martius
     Associated with Aufidius, rages
     Upon our territories; and have already
     O'erborne their way, consumed with fire, and took
     What lay before them.     (IV, 6, 64)
64 COMINIUS:     Who shall ask it?
     The tribunes cannot do't for shame; the people
     Deserve such pity of him as the wolf
     Does of the shepherds: for his best friends, if they
     Should say 'Be good to Rome,' they charged him even
     As those should do that had deserved his hate,
     And therein show'd like enemies.  (IV, 6, 108)
MENENIUS:     You have made fair hands,
     You and your crafts! you have crafted fair!

65 wars, to be revenged of them; because it pleased them to see their
goods burnt and spoiled before their eyes, whilst themselves were
well at ease, and did behold the people's losses and misfortunes, and
knowing their own goods safe and out of danger; and how the war
was not made against the noblemen, that had the enemy abroad, to
keep that they had in safety.

Now Martius having done this first exploit, which made the
Volsces bolder and less fearful of the Romans, brought home all the
army again, without loss of any man. After their whole army, which
was marvellous great, and very forward to service, was assembled in
one camp, they agreed to leave part of it for garrison in the country
about; and the other part should go on and make the war upon the
Romans. So Martius bade Tullus choose, and take which of the two
charges he liked best. Tullus made him answer, he knew by experience
that Martius was no less valiant than himself, and how he ever had
better fortune and good-hap in all battles than himself had. Therefore
he thought it best for him to have the leading of those that should
make the wars abroad; and himself would keep home, to provide
for the safety of the cities and of his country and to furnish the camp
also of all necessary provision abroad.

So Martius, being stronger than before, went first of all unto the
city of Cercees, inhabited by the Romans, who willingly yielded
themselves and therefore had no hurt. From thence he entered the
country of the Latins, imagining the Romans would fight with him
there to defend the Latins, who were their confederates and had
many times sent unto the Romans for their aid. But on the one side

| | |
|---|---|
| 65 BRUTUS: | Raised only, that the weaker sort may wish<br>Good Martius home again. |
| SICINIUS: | The very trick on't.  (IV, 6, 69) |
| COMINIUS: | You have brought<br>A trembling upon Rome, such as was never<br>So incapable of help. |
| BOTH TRIBUNES: | Say not we brought it. |
| MENENIUS: | How! Was it we? we loved him; but, like beasts<br>And cowardly nobles, gave way unto your clusters,<br>Who did hoot him out o' the city.  (IV, 6, 117) |

the people of Rome were very ill willing to go; and on the other side the Consuls, being upon their going out of their office, would not hazard themselves for so small a time; so that the ambassadors of the Latins returned home again and did no good. Then Martius did besiege their cities, and having taken by force the towns of the Tolerinians, Vicanians, Pedanians, and the Bolanians, who made resistance, he sacked all their goods and took them prisoners. Such as did yield themselves willingly unto him, he was as careful as possible might be to defend them from hurt; and because they should receive no damage by his will, he removed his camp as far from their confines as he could. Afterwards he took the city of Boles by assault (being about an hundred furlong from Rome) where he had a marvellous great spoil and put every man to the sword that was able to carry weapon. The other Volsces that were appointed to remain in garrison for defence of their country, hearing this good news, would tarry no longer at home, but armed themselves, and ran to Martius' camp, saying they did acknowledge no other captain but him. Hereupon his fame ran through all Italy; and every one praised him for a valiant captain, for that, by change of one man for another, such and so strange events fell out in the state.

In this while, all went still to wrack at Rome. For, to come into the field to fight with the enemy, they could not abide to hear of it, they were one so much against another, and full of seditious words, the nobility against the people, and the people against the nobility; until they had intelligence at the length that the enemies had laid siege to the city of Lavinium, in the which were all the temples and images of the gods their protectors, and from whence came first their ancient original, for that Aeneas at his first arrival into Italy did build that city. Then fell there out a marvellous sudden change of mind among the people, and far more strange and contrary in the nobility. For the people thought good to repeal the condemnation and exile of

66 Martius. The Senate, assembled upon it, would in no case yield to

| | | |
|---|---|---|
| 66 AUFIDIUS: | The tribunes are no soldiers; and their people Will be as rash in the repeal, as hasty To expel him thence. | (IV, 7, 31) |
| CITIZENS: | Faith, we hear fearful news. | |

that; who either did it of a self-will to be contrary to the people's desire; or because Martius should not return through the grace and favour of the people; or else, because they were throughly angry and offended with him, that he would set upon the whole, being offended but by a few, and in his doings would show himself an open enemy besides unto his country; notwithstanding the most part of them took the wrong they had done him in marvellous ill part, and as if the injury had been done unto themselves. Report being made of the Senate's resolution, the people found themselves in a strait; for they could authorize and confirm nothing by their voices, unless it had been first propounded and ordained by the Senate.

But Martius, hearing this stir about him, was in a greater rage with them than before; insomuch as he raised his siege incontinently before the city of Lavinium, and, going towards Rome, lodged his camp within forty furlong of the city, at the ditches called Cluiliae. His encamping so near Rome did put all the whole city in a wonderful fear; howbeit for the present time it appeased the sedition and dissension betwixt the nobility and the people. For there was no consul, senator, nor magistrate, that durst once contrary the opinion of the people, for the calling home again of Martius. When they saw the women in a marvellous fear, running up and down the city; the temples of the gods full of old people, weeping bitterly in their prayers to the gods; and finally, not a man either wise or hardy to provide for their safety; then they were all of opinion that the people had reason to call home Martius again to reconcile themselves to him, and that the Senate, on the contrary part, were in marvellous great fault to be angry and in choler with him when it stood them upon rather to have gone out and entreated him. So they all agreed together to send ambassadors unto him, to let him understand how

---

1st CITIZEN:                                    For mine own part,
    When I said, banish him, I said, 'twas pity.
2nd CITIZEN: And so did I.
3rd CITIZEN: And so did I; and, to say the truth, so did very many of us:
    that we did, we did for the best; and though we willingly con-
    sented to his banishment, yet it was against our will.  (IV, 6, 138)

his countrymen did call him home again, and restored him to all his goods, and besought him to deliver them from this war.

The ambassadors that were sent were Martius' familiar friends and acquaintance, who looked at the least for a courteous welcome of him, as of their familiar friend and kinsman. Howbeit they found nothing less. For, at their coming, they were brought through the camp to the place where he was set in his chair of state, with a marvellous and an unspeakable majesty, having the chiefest men of the Volsces about him. So he commanded them to declare openly the cause of their coming; which they delivered in the most humble and lowly words they possibly could devise, and with all modest countenance and behaviour agreeable for the same. When they had done their message, for the injury they had done him he answered them very hotly and in great choler. But, as general of the Volsces, he willed them to restore unto the Volsces all their lands and cities they had taken from them in former wars; and, moreover, that they should give them the like honour and freedom of Rome, as they had before given to the Latins. For otherwise they had no other mean to end this war, if they did not grant these honest and just conditions of peace. Thereupon he gave them thirty days' respite to make him answer.

So the ambassadors returned straight to Rome, and Martius forthwith departed with his army out of the territories of the Romans. This was the first matter wherewith the Volsces (that most envied Martius' glory and authority) did charge Martius with. Among those, Tullus was chief; who though he had received no private injury or displeasure of Martius, yet the common fault and imperfection of man's nature wrought in him; and it grieved him to see his own reputation blemished through Martius' great fame and honour, and so himself to be less esteemed of the Volsces than he was before. This fell out the more because every man honoured Martius, and

67 COMINIUS:   I tell you, he does sit in gold.               (v, 1, 63)

MENENIUS:   He sits in his state, as a thing made for Alexander. What he bids be done is finished with his bidding. He wants nothing of a god but eternity and a heaven to throne in.   (v, 4, 23)

68 See IV, 7.

thought he only could do all, and that all other governors and captains must be content with such credit and authority as he would please to countenance them with. From hence they derived all their first accusations and secret murmurings against Martius. For private captains, conspiring against him, were very angry with him; and gave it out, that the removing of the camp was a manifest treason, not of the towns, nor forts, nor of arms, but of time and occasion, which was a loss of great importance, because it was that which in reason might both loose and bind all, and preserve the whole.

Now Martius having given the Romans thirty days' respite for their answer, and specially because the wars have not accustomed to make any great changes in less space of time than that, he thought it good yet, not to lie asleep and idle all the while, but went and destroyed the lands of the enemy's allies, and took seven great cities of theirs well inhabited; and the Romans durst not once put themselves into the field to come to their aid and help – they were so faint-hearted, so mistrustful, and loth besides to make wars; insomuch as they properly resembled the bodies paralytic and loosed of their limbs and members; as those which through the palsy have lost all their sense and feeling. Wherefore, the time of peace expired, Martius being returned into the dominions of the Romans again with all his army, they sent another ambassade unto him, to pray peace and the remove of the Volsces out of their country, that afterwards they might with better leisure fall to such agreements together as should be thought most meet and necessary; for the Romans were no men that would ever yield for fear. But if he thought the Volsces had any ground to demand reasonable articles and conditions, all that they would reasonably ask should be granted unto by the Romans, who of themselves would willingly yield to reason, conditionally that they did lay down arms.

Martius to that answered that as general of the Volsces he would reply nothing unto it; but yet as a Roman citizen he would counsel them to let fall their pride and to be conformable to reason, if they were wise; and that they should return again within three days, delivering up the articles agreed upon, which he had first delivered them; or otherwise, that he would no more give them assurance or safe conduct to return again into his camp with such vain and frivolous messages.

When the ambassadors were returned to Rome and had reported Martius' answer to the Senate, their city being in extreme danger and as it were in a terrible storm or tempest, they threw out (as the common proverb saith) their holy anchor. For then they appointed all the bishops, priests, ministers of the gods, and keepers of holy things, and all the augurs or soothsayers (which foreshow things to come by observation of the flying of birds, which is an old ancient kind of prophesying and divination amongst the Romans), to go to Martius apparelled as when they do their sacrifices; and first to entreat him to leave off war, and then that he would speak to his countrymen and conclude peace with the Volsces. Martius suffered them to come into his camp, but yet he granted them nothing the more, neither did he entertain them or speak more courteously to them than he did the first time that they came unto him, saving only that he willed them to take the one of the two: either to accept peace under the first conditions offered, or else to receive war.

When all this goodly rabble of superstition and priests were returned, it was determined in council that none should go out of the gates of the city and that they should watch and ward upon the walls, to repulse their enemies if they came to assault them; referring themselves and all their hope to time and fortune's uncertain favour, not knowing otherwise how to remedy the danger. Now all the city was full of tumult, fear, and marvellous doubt what would happen; until at the length there fell out such a like matter as Homer ofttimes said they would least have thought of. For in great matters, that happen seldom, Homer saith and crieth out in this sort:

> *The goddess Pallas she, with her fair glist'ring eyes,*
> *Did put into his mind such thoughts and made him so devise.*

And in another place:

> *But sure some god hath ta'en out of the people's mind*
> *Both wit and understanding eke, and have therewith assign'd*
> *Some other simple spirit instead thereof to bide,*
> *That so they might their doings all for lack of wit misguide.*

And in another place:

> The people of themselves did either it consider,
> Or else some god instructed them, and so they join'd together.

Many reckon not of Homer, as referring matters unpossible and fables of no likelihood or troth unto man's reason, free will, or judgement; which indeed is not his meaning. But things true and likely he maketh to depend of our own free will and reason. For he oft speaketh these words:

> I have thought it in my noble heart.

And in another place:

> Achilles angry was, and sorry for to hear
> Him so to say; his heavy breast was fraught with pensive fear.

And again in another place:

> Bellerophon she could not move with her fair tongue;
> So honest and so virtuous he was the rest among.

But in wondrous and extraordinary things, which are done by secret inspirations and motions, he doth not say that God taketh away from man his choice and freedom of will, but that he doth move it; neither that he doth work desire in us, but objecteth to our minds certain imaginations whereby we are led to desire; and thereby doth not make this our action forced, but openeth the way to our will, and addeth thereto courage and hope of success. For either we must say that the gods meddle not with the causes and beginnings of our actions; or else what other means have they to help and further men? It is apparent that they handle not our bodies, nor move not our feet and hands when there is occasion to use them; but that part of our mind, from which these motions proceed, is induced thereto or carried away by such objects and reasons as God offereth unto it.

Now the Roman ladies and gentlewomen did visit all the temples and gods of the same, to make their prayers unto them. But the greatest ladies, and more part of them, were continually about the altar of Jupiter Capitoline; among which troop by name was

Valeria, Publicola's own sister – the self same Publicola who did such notable service to the Romans, both in peace and wars, and was dead also certain years before, as we have declared in his *Life*. His sister Valeria was greatly honoured and reverenced among all the Romans; and did so modestly and wisely behave herself that she did not shame nor dishonour the house she came of. So she suddenly fell into such a fancy as we have rehearsed before, and had (by some god, as I think) taken hold of a noble device. Whereupon she rose and the other ladies with her, and they all together went straight to the house of Volumnia, Martius' mother; and, coming in to her, found her and Martius' wife, her daughter-in-law, set together, and having her husband Martius' young children in her lap. Now all the train of these ladies sitting in a ring round about her, Valeria first began to speak in this sort unto her:

'We ladies are come to visit you ladies, my lady Volumnia and Virgilia, by no direction from the Senate nor commandment of other magistrate, but through the inspiration, as I take it, of some god above; who, having taken compassion and pity of our prayers, hath moved us to come unto you, to entreat you in a matter, as well beneficial for us, as also for the whole citizens in general; but to your selves in especial, if it please you to credit me, and shall redound to our more fame and glory than the daughters of the Sabines obtained in former age when they procured loving peace, instead of hateful war, between their fathers and their husbands. Come on, good ladies, and let us go all together unto Martius to entreat him to take pity upon us, and also to report the troth unto him, how much you are bound unto the citizens; who notwithstanding they have sustained great hurt and losses by him, yet they have not hitherto sought revenge upon your persons by any discourteous usage, neither ever conceived any such thought or intent against you, but do deliver you safe into his hands, though thereby they look for no better grace or clemency from him.'

9 CORIOLANUS:  The noble sister of Publicola,
                The moon of Rome, chaste as the icicle
                That's curdied by the frost from purest snow
                And hangs on Dian's temple: dear Valeria!     (v, 3, 64)

When Valeria had spoken this unto them, all the other ladies together with one voice confirmed that she had said. Then Volumnia in this sort did answer her:

'My good ladies, we are partakers with you of the common misery and calamity of our country; and yet our grief exceedeth yours the more, by reason of our particular misfortune, to feel the loss of my son Martius' former valiancy and glory and to see his person environed now with our enemies in arms, rather to see him forthcoming and safe kept than of any love to defend his person. But yet the greatest grief of our heaped mishaps is to see our poor country brought to such extremity that all the hope of the safety and preservation thereof is now unfortunately cast upon us simple women; because we know not what account he will make of us, since he hath cast from him all care of his natural country and commonweal, which heretofore he hath holden more dear and precious than either his mother, wife, or children. Notwithstanding, if ye think we can do good, we will willingly do what you will have us. Bring us to him, I pray you. For, if we cannot prevail, we may yet die at his feet, as humble suitors for the safety of our country.'

Her answer ended, she took her daughter-in-law and Martius' children with her, and, being accompanied with all the other Roman ladies, they went in troop together unto the Volsces' camp; whom when they saw, they of themselves did both pity and reverence her; and there was not a man among them that once durst say a word unto her.

70 Now was Martius set then in his chair of state, with all the honours of a general; and, when he had spied the women coming afar off, he marvelled what the matter meant; but afterwards, knowing his wife, which came foremost, he determined at the first to persist in his obstinate and inflexible rancour. But overcome in the end with natural affection, and being altogether altered to see them, his heart would not serve him to tarry their coming to his chair, but, coming down in haste, he went to meet them; and first he kissed his mother and embraced her a pretty while, then his wife and little children; and nature so wrought with him that the tears fell from his

70 See p. 347 note 67.

352

eyes, and he could not keep himself from making much of them, but yielded to the affection of his blood, as if he had been violently carried with the fury of a most swift-running stream.

After he had thus lovingly received them, and perceiving that his mother Volumnia would begin to speak to him, he called the chiefest of the council of the Volsces to hear what she would say. Then she spake in this sort:

CORIOLANUS: Shall I be tempted to infringe my vow
   In the same time 'tis made? I will not.
 *Enter Virgilia, Volumnia, Valeria, young Martius, with attendants.*
   My wife comes foremost; then the honour'd mould
   Wherein this trunk was framed, and in her hand
   The grandchild to her blood. But, out, affection!
   All bond and privilege of nature, break!
   Let it be virtuous to be obstinate.
   What is that curt'sy worth? or those doves' eyes,
   Which can make gods forsworn? I melt, and am not
   Of stronger earth than others. . . .
            I'll never
   Be such a gosling to obey instinct, but stand
   As if a man were author of himself
   And knew no other kin . . .
          Like a dull actor now,
   I have forgot my part, and I am out,
   Even to a full disgrace. Best of my flesh,
   Forgive my tyranny; but do not say
   For that 'Forgive our Romans.' O, a kiss
   Long as my exile, sweet as my revenge!
   Now, by the jealous queen of heaven, that kiss
   I carried from thee, dear; and my true lip
   Hath virgin'd it e'er since. You gods! I prate,
   And the most noble mother of the world
   Leave unsaluted: sink, my knee, i' the earth;
   Of thy deep duty more impression show
   Than that of common sons.     (v, 3, 20; 40)
CORIOLANUS: Aufidius, and you Volsces, mark; for we'll
   Hear nought from Rome in private. Your request?
               (v, 3, 92)

'If we held our peace, my son, and determined not to speak, the state of our poor bodies and present sight of our raiment would easily bewray to thee what life we have led at home, since thy exile and abode abroad. But think now with thyself how much more unfortunately than all the women living we are come hither, considering that the sight which should be most pleasant to all other to behold, spiteful fortune hath made most fearful to us; making myself to see my son, and my daughter here her husband, besieging the walls of his native country; so as that which is the only comfort to all other in their adversity and misery, to pray unto the gods and to call to them for aid, is the only thing which plungeth us into most deep perplexity. For we cannot, alas, together pray both for victory for our country and for safety of thy life also. But a world of grievous curses, yea, more than any mortal enemy can heap upon us, are forcibly wrapped up in our prayers. For the bitter sop of most hard choice is offered thy wife and children, to forgo the one of the two: either to lose the person of thyself or the nurse of their native country. For myself, my son, I am determined not to tarry till fortune in my lifetime do make an end of this war. For if I cannot persuade thee, rather to do good unto both parties than to overthrow and destroy the one, preferring love and nature before the malice and calamity of wars – thou shalt see, my son, and trust unto it, thou shalt no sooner march forward to assault thy country but thy foot shall tread upon thy mother's womb, that brought thee first into 73 this world. And I may not defer to see the day either that my son be

73 VOLUMNIA:    Should we be silent and not speak, our raiment
    And state of bodies would bewray what life
    We have led since thy exile. Think with thyself
    How more unfortunate than all living women
    Are we come hither: since that thy sight, which should
    Make our eyes flow with joy, hearts dance with comforts,
    Constrains them weep and shake with fear and sorrow;
    Making the mother, wife and child to see
    The son, the husband and the father tearing
    His country's bowels out. And to poor we
    Thine enmity's most capital: thou barr'st us

led prisoner in triumph by his natural countrymen, or that he himself do triumph of them and of his natural country. For if it were so, that my request tended to save thy country in destroying the Volsces, I must confess, thou wouldst hardly and doubtfully resolve on that. For, as to destroy thy natural country, it is altogether unmeet and unlawful; so were it not just, and less honourable to betray those that put their trust in thee. But my only demand consisteth, to make a gaol-delivery of all evils, which delivereth equal benefit and safety both to the one and the other; but most honourable for the Volsces. For it shall appear that, having victory in their hands, they have of special favour granted us singular graces, peace, and amity, albeit themselves have no less part of both than we; of which good, if so it came to pass, thyself is the only author and so hast thou the only honour. But if it fail and fall out contrary, thyself alone deservedly shall carry the shameful reproach and burthen of either party. So, though the end of war be uncertain, yet this not-

---

> Our prayers to the gods, which is a comfort
> That all but we enjoy; for how can we,
> Alas, how can we for our country pray,
> Whereto we are bound, together with thy victory,
> Whereto we are bound? alack, or we must lose
> The country, our dear nurse, or else thy person,
> Our comfort in the country. We must find
> An evident calamity, though we had
> Our wish, which side should win: for either thou
> Must, as a foreign recreant, be led
> With manacles thorough our streets, or else
> Triumphantly tread on thy country's ruin,
> And bear the palm for having bravely shed
> Thy wife and children's blood. For myself, son,
> I purpose not to wait on fortune till
> These wars determine: if I cannot persuade thee
> Rather to show a noble grace to both parts
> Than seek the end of one, thou shalt no sooner
> March to assault thy country than to tread –
> Trust to't, thou shalt not – on thy mother's womb,
> That brought thee to this world.                    (v, 3, 94)

withstanding is most certain, that, if it be thy chance to conquer, this benefit shalt thou reap of thy goodly conquest: to be chronicled the plague and destroyer of thy country. And if fortune also overthrow thee, then the world will say that, through desire to revenge thy private injuries, thou hast for ever undone thy good friends, who did 74 most lovingly and courteously receive thee.'

Martius gave good ear unto his mother's words, without interrupting her speech at all; and, after she had said what she would, he held his peace a pretty while and answered not a word. Hereupon she began again to speak unto him, and said:

'My son, why dost thou not answer me? Dost thou think it good altogether to give place unto thy choler and desire of revenge? and thinkest thou it not honesty for thee to grant thy mother's request in so weighty a cause? Dost thou take it honourable for a nobleman to remember the wrongs and injuries done him, and dost not in like case think it an honest nobleman's part to be thankful for the goodness that parents do show to their children, acknowledging the duty and reverence they ought to bear unto them? No man living is more bound to show himself thankful in all parts and respects than thyself, who so unnaturally showeth all ingratitude. Moreover, my son,

74 VOLUMNIA:   If it were so that our request did tend
                To save the Romans, thereby to destroy
                The Volsces whom you serve, you might condemn us,
                As poisonous of your honour: no; our suit
                Is, that you reconcile them: while the Volsces
                May say 'This mercy we have show'd;' the Romans,
                'This we received;' and each in either side
                Give the all-hail to thee, and cry 'Be blest
                For making up this peace!'   Thou know'st, great son,
                The end of war's uncertain, but this certain,
                That, if thou conquer Rome, the benefit
                Which thou shalt thereby reap is such a name,
                 Whose repetition will be dogg'd with curses;
                Whose chronicle thus writ: 'The man was noble,
                But with his last attempt he wiped it out;
                Destroy'd his country, and his name remains
                To the ensuing age abhorr'd.'       (v, 3, 132)

thou hast sorely taken of thy country, exacting grievous payments upon them, in revenge of the injuries offered thee. Besides, thou hast not hitherto showed thy poor mother any courtesy. And therefore it is not only honest, but due unto me, that without compulsion I should obtain my so just and reasonable request of thee. But, since by reason I cannot persuade thee to it, to what purpose do I defer my last hope?'

And with these words herself, his wife, and children fell down
75 upon their knees before him. Martius, seeing that, could refrain no longer, but went straight and lift her up, crying out:
'Oh, mother, what have you done to me?'
And holding her hard by the right hand,
'Oh mother,' said he, 'you have won a happy victory for your country, but mortal and unhappy for your son. For I see myself
76 vanquished by you alone.'

These words being spoken openly, he spake a little apart with his

75 VOLUMNIA:              Why dost not speak?
                  Think'st thou it honourable for a noble man
                  Still to remember wrongs? . . .
                          There's no man in the world
                  More bound to's mother; yet here he lets me prate
                  Like one i' the stocks. Thou hast never in thy life
                  Show'd thy dear mother any courtesy,
                  When she, poor hen, fond of no second brood,
                  Has cluck'd thee to the wars and safely home,
                  Loaden with honour. Say my request's unjust,
                  And spurn me back: but if it be not so,
                  Thou art not honest; and the gods will plague thee,
                  That thou restrain'st from me the duty which
                  To a mother's part belongs. He turns away:
                  Down, ladies; let us shame him with our knees. (v, 3, 153)
76                    *He holds her by the hand, silent.*
   CORIOLANUS:           O mother, mother!
                  What have you done? Behold, the heavens do ope,
                  The gods look down, and this unnatural scene
                  They laugh at. O my mother, mother! O!
                  You have won a happy victory to Rome;

mother and wife, and then let them return again to Rome; for so they did request him; and so, remaining in camp that night, the next
77 morning he dislodged and marched homewards into the Volsces' country again; who were not all of one mind, nor all alike contented. For some misliked him and that he had done. Other, being well pleased that peace should be made, said that neither the one nor the other deserved blame nor reproach. Other, though they misliked that was done, did not think him an ill man for that he did, but said he was not to be blamed, though he yielded to such a forcible extremity. Howbeit no man contraried his departure, but all obeyed his commandment, more for respect of his worthiness and valiancy than for fear of his authority.

Now the citizens of Rome plainly showed in what fear and danger their city stood of this war, when they were delivered. For so soon as the watch upon the walls of the city perceived the Volsces' camp to remove, there was not a temple in the city but was presently set open, and full of men wearing garlands of flowers upon their heads sacrificing to the gods, as they were wont to do upon the
78 news of some great obtained victory. And this common joy was yet more manifestly showed by the honourable courtesies the

77 MESSENGER:   The Volscians are dislodged, and Martius gone.   (v, 4, 44)
78 MESSENGER:   A merrier day did never yet greet Rome,
   No, not the expulsion of the Tarquins.
SICINIUS:                                Friend,
   Art thou certain this is true? is it most certain?
MESSENGER:   As certain as I know the sun is fire:
   Where have you lurk'd, that you make doubt of it?
   Ne'er through an arch so hurried the blown tide,
   As the recomforted through the gates. Why, hark you!
   *Trumpets; hautboys; drums beat; all together.*
   The trumpets, sackbuts, psalteries and fifes,
   Tabors and cymbals and the shouting Romans
   Make the sun dance. Hark you!     *A shout within.*

---

   But for your son, – believe it, O, believe it,
   Most dangerously you have with him prevail'd,
   If not most mortal to him.             (v, 3, 182)

whole Senate and people did bestow on their ladies. For they were all throughly persuaded, and did certainly believe, that the ladies only were cause of the saving of the city and delivering themselves from the instant danger of the war. Whereupon the Senate ordained that the magistrates, to gratify and honour these ladies, should

79 grant them all that they would require. And they only requested that they would build a Temple of Fortune of the Women, for the building whereof they offered themselves to defray the whole charge of the sacrifices and other ceremonies belonging to the service of the gods. Nevertheless, the Senate, commending their good will and forwardness, ordained that the Temple and image should be made

80 at the common charge of the city. Notwithstanding that, the ladies gathered money among them and made with the same a second image of Fortune, which the Romans say did speak as they offered her up in the Temple and did set her in her place; and they affirm that she spake these words:

'Ladies, ye have devoutly offered me up.'

Moreover, that she spake that twice together, making us to believe things that never were, and are not to be credited.

For, to see images that seem to sweat or weep, or to put forth any humour red or bloody, it is not a thing unpossible. For wood and stone do commonly receive certain moisture, whereof is engendered an humour, which do yield of themselves, or do take of the air, many sorts and kinds of spots and colours; by which signs and tokens it is

79 SENATOR:  Behold our patroness, the life of Rome!
Call all your tribes together, praise the gods,
And make triumphant fires; strew flowers before them:
Unshout the noise that banish'd Martius,
Repeal him with the welcome of his mother;
Cry, 'Welcome, ladies, welcome!'                    (V, 5, 1)

80 CORIOLANUS:                              Ladies, you deserve
To have a temple built you.                          (V, 3, 206)

——————

MENENIUS:                              This is good news:
I will go meet the ladies . . .
                              Hark how they joy!
*Sound still, with the shouts.*                      (V, 4, 45)

not amiss, we think, that the gods sometimes do warn men of things to come. And it is possible, also, that these images and statues do sometimes put forth sounds like unto sighs or mourning, when in the midst or bottom of the same there is made some violent separation, or breaking asunder of things blown or devised therein. But that a body which hath neither life nor soul should have any direct or exquisite word formed in it by express voice – that is altogether unpossible. For the soul nor god himself can distinctly speak without a body, having necessary organs and instruments meet for the parts of the same to form and utter distinct words. But where stories many times do force us to believe a thing reported to be true by many grave testimonies, there we must say that it is some passion contrary to our five natural senses, which, being begotten in the imaginative part or understanding, draweth an opinion unto itself, even as we do in our sleeping. For many times we think we hear that we do not hear, and we imagine we see that we see not. Yet notwithstanding, such as are godly bent and zealously given to think upon heavenly things, so as they can no way be drawn from believing that which is spoken of them, they have this reason to ground the foundation of their belief upon: that is, the omnipotency of God, which is wonderful and hath no manner of resemblance or likeliness of proportion unto ours, but is altogether contrary as touching our nature, our moving, our art, and our force; and therefore if he do anything unpossible to us, or do bring forth and devise things without man's common reach and understanding, we must not therefore think it unpossible at all. For, if in other things he is far contrary to us, much more in his works and secret operations he far passeth all the rest. 'But the most part of God's doings,' as Heraclitus saith, 'for lack of faith are hidden and unknown unto us.'

Now when Martius was returned again into the city of Antium from his voyage, Tullus, that hated and could no longer abide him for the fear he had of his authority, sought divers means to make him out of the way, thinking if he let slip that present time he should never recover the like and fit occasion again. Wherefore Tullus, having procured many other of his confederacy, required Martius might be deposed from his estate, to render up account to the Volsces of his charge and government. Martius, fearing to become a private man again under Tullus being general (whose authority was greater otherwise than any other among all the Volsces), answered: he was willing to give up his charge and would resign it into the hands of the lords of the Volsces, if they did all command him, as by all their commandment he received it; and, moreover, that he would not refuse even at that present to give up an account unto the people, if they would tarry the hearing of it. The people hereupon called a common council, in which assembly there were certain orators appointed that stirred up the common people against him; and when they had told their tales, Martius rose up to make them answer. Now, notwithstanding the mutinous people made a marvellous great noise, yet when they saw him, for the reverence they bare unto his valiantness, they quieted themselves and gave still audience to allege with leisure what he could for his purgation. Moreover, the honestest men of the Antiates, and who most rejoiced in peace, showed by their countenance that they would hear him willingly and judge also according to their conscience.

Whereupon Tullus fearing that, if he did let him speak, he would prove his innocency to the people – because amongst other things he had an eloquent tongue, besides that the first good service he had done to the people of the Volsces did win him more favour than these last accusations could purchase him displeasure; and, furthermore, the offence they laid to his charge was a testimony of the good will they ought him, for they would never have thought he had done them wrong for that they took not the city of Rome if they had not been very near taking of it by means of his approach and conduction – for these causes Tullus thought he might no longer delay his pretence and enterprise, neither to tarry for the mutining and rising of the common people against him. Wherefore, those that were of the conspiracy began to cry out that he was not to be heard, nor that they would not suffer a traitor to usurp tyrannical 81 power over the tribe of the Volsces, who would not yield up his

81 AUFIDIUS:                    Read it not, noble lords;
         But tell the traitor, in the high'st degree
         He hath abused your powers.                    (v, 6, 84)

361

estate and authority. And, in saying these words, they all fell upon him and killed him in the market-place, none of the people once 82 offering to rescue him.

Howbeit it is a clear case, that this murder was not generally consented unto of the most part of the Volsces. For men came out of all parts to honour his body, and did honourably bury him, setting out his tomb with great store of armour and spoils, as the tomb of a 83 worthy person and great captain.

The Romans, understanding of his death, showed no other honour or malice, saving that they granted the ladies the request they made that they might mourn ten months for him (and that was the full time they used to wear blacks for the death of their fathers, brethren, or husbands, according to Numa Pompilius' order, who stablished the same, as we have enlarged more amply in the description of his *Life*).

Now Martius being dead, the whole state of the Volsces heartily wished him alive again. For first of all they fell out with the Aeques (who were their friends and confederates) touching pre-eminence and place; and this quarrel grew on so far between them that frays and murders fell out upon it one with another. After that, the Romans overcame them in battle, in which Tullus was slain in the field, and the flower of all their force was put to the sword; so that they were compelled to accept most shameful conditions of peace, in yielding themselves subject unto the conquerors and promising to be obedient at their commandment.

82 ALL PEOPLE:    Tear him to pieces. Do it presently. . . .
AUFIDIUS:                 Insolent villain!
ALL CONSPIRATORS: Kill, kill, kill, kill, kill him!
*Draw both the conspirators and kill Martius, who falls. Aufidius stands on him.*

(v, 6, 121)

83 VOLSCIAN LORD:        Bear from hence his body;
                  And mourn you for him: let him be regarded
                  As the most noble corse that ever herald
                  Did follow to his urn.        (v, 6, 143)

# GLOSSARY

*a-mated*, dismayed, overcome

*antic*, grotesque, clownish

*appeach*, accuse, charge with crime

*assay*, trial, affliction

*bill*, letter, document

*bishop*, (pagan) priest; *chief bishop*, high priest (Pontifex Maximus)

*bishopric*, priesthood

*blood*, disreputable person, roisterer

*bourding*, joking

*bravery*, bravado

*breviary*, abridged version

*burden* (verb), charge, accuse

*carect*, carrack, cargo-ship

*careful*, full of anxiety

*cassock*, long military tunic

*certain* (noun), stated amount

*champion country*, flat open country

*charret*, cart

*cithern*, cittern (an Elizabethan instrument resembling a mandoline)

*clean* (*gold*), pure, solid (gold)

*cockle*, weed

*colour* (noun), excuse

*commodity*, benefit, profit

*composition*, peace-settlement, indemnity

*conceit*, view, opinion

*conceitive*, witty

*contentation*, acquiescence, acceptance of the situation

*convinced*, found guilty, convicted

*copped-tank* (*hat*), high-crowned conical (hat)

*cormorant*, greedy, rapacious

*cranews*, crannies, gaps

*crooked of condition*, of perverse temperament

*dainty: made it dainty*, was wary, reluctant

*discommodity*, disadvantage, setback

*easing*, eaves

*embasing*, debasing, humiliating

*evil away with*, ill put up with

*fardel*, (singular) bundle, (plural) baggage

*feel* (verb), sound (someone for his opinions)

*fetch* (noun), trick

*figure: cast a figure*, calculate a horoscope

*fond*, foolish

*gable*, cable

*gaol-delivery: to make a gaol-delivery of all evils*, to get rid of all evils

*garboil*, confusion, turmoil

*gests*, deeds

363

*gillot: tumbling gillots*, romping whores

*gorbelly*, protuberant belly, (adjective) corpulent

*gravelled*, confounded

*guard*, ornamental border, trimming

*hand over head*, rashly, precipitately

*handy-strokes*, hand to hand fighting

*hap*, fortune, chance; *good-hap*, good fortune (applied ironically to misfortune)

*harborough*, harbour

*hardily*, certainly, assuredly

*hoise (sail)*, hoist (sail)

*house-dove*, stay-at-home

*howboys*, oboes (hautbois)

*hugger-mugger*, secrecy; *in hugger-mugger*, furtively

*huswives*, huzzies, loose women

*impostume*, abscess, festering sore

*incontinently*, straightway, immediately

*journey*, battle (one day's fighting)

*keep*, keep a woman as a mistress, commit adultery with

*lay at*, strike at, attack

*leman*, mistress

*lenity*, mildness, leniency

*let*, (verb) prevent, hinder; (noun) hindrance, obstacle

*libertines*, descendants of a freedman

*limmer*, shaft of a carriage

*lodge*, (of an army) encamp

*loof*, luff, turn into the wind

*maze: in a maze*, bewildered, confused

*mean*, middle, average, humble

*mechanical people*, working-men, labourers

*misery*, miserliness

*mistrust*, suspect

*murrion*, morion, kind of helmet

*myriad*, ten thousand coins

*naughty*, evil

*nice*, scrupulous; *make it nice*, be reluctant

*odd: there were three voices odd which condemned him*, he was condemned by a majority of three votes

*overlaid*, overwhelmed

*pass: passed not of*, did not care about, paid no attention to

*perfumed*, (a) scented, (b) disinfected

*pestered*, (a) crowded, (b) plagued

*pilled*, pillaged, plundered

*policy*, trickery

*polled*, plundered, robbed

*port-sale*, auction

*post alone*, quite alone

*presently*, immediately, at present

*pricking: pricking on a clout*, sewing or embroidering a cloth

*psalterion*, psaltery (a musical instrument like a zither)

*quail*, decline, diminish, fade away

*ramp: ramped of her neck*, flung his arms round her neck

*rap: rap and rend of his side*, seize and tear away for his use

*read*, advise

*reason: have reason*, be right; *it is no reason*, it is useless

*reckon*, esteem

*reins: laid the reins of the bridle upon the soldiers' necks*, gave free rein to the soldiers

*rest: to set up his whole rest upon*, to stake his all on, to set his final hope in *round*, whisper

*ruffe: in their greatest ruffe*, at their most exciting point

*sallet*, helmet

*sallet-oil*, salad-oil

*sea between the lands*, Mediterranean Sea

*sessed*, assessed

*sew*, drain

*sharp: at the sharp*, with sword-points uncovered for piercing; *sword-players* or *fencers at the sharp*, gladiators

*silly*, simple

*sith, sithence*, since

*slents*, sarcastic remarks

*snew*, snowed

*specialties*, bonds, debts

*sperage*, asparagus

*springal*, young man, youth

*stand: how it stood upon them*, how it concerned them; *it stood them upon rather to have gone out*, they should rather have gone out

*stay: to set at a stay*, to settle, to reduce to order

*stickler*, umpire

*strange: made it strange*, took offence

*study: for the study's sake*, for the sake of the period of study they had once spent together

*success*, outcome, result

*sumpter*, pack-horse

*swaged*, assuaged

*table: painted table*, picture

*tallages*, taxes, duties

*tane*, taken

*target*, shield

*tickle*, uncertain, unstable, liable to collapse

*toy*, fancy, frivolous idea

*treen*, wooden

*trice* (verb), pull, haul

*tuition*, protection

*understand*, observe

*unfoiled*, unimpaired, uncorrupted (perhaps misprint for *unsoiled*)

*unrebated swords*, swords without any covering to prevent their cutting and piercing; *fencers at unrebated swords*, gladiators

*vaward*, vanguard

*ward*, upbringing

*well-favouredly*, soundly, severely

*whirt*, sharp blow, box on the ear

*wrecked*, wreaked, avenged

*yarage*, manoeuvrability

# FOR THE BEST IN PAPERBACKS, LOOK FOR THE

In every corner of the world, on every subject under the sun, Penguin represents quality and variety – the very best in publishing today.

For complete information about books available from Penguin – including Puffins, Penguin Classics and Arkana – and how to order them, write to us at the appropriate address below. Please note that for copyright reasons the selection of books varies from country to country.

**In the United Kingdom:** Please write to *Dept E.P., Penguin Books Ltd, Harmondsworth, Middlesex, UB7 0DA.*

If you have any difficulty in obtaining a title, please send your order with the correct money, plus ten per cent for postage and packaging, to *PO Box No 11, West Drayton, Middlesex*

**In the United States:** Please write to *Dept BA, Penguin, 299 Murray Hill Parkway, East Rutherford, New Jersey 07073*

**In Canada:** Please write to *Penguin Books Canada Ltd, 2801 John Street, Markham, Ontario L3R 1B4*

**In Australia:** Please write to the *Marketing Department, Penguin Books Australia Ltd, P.O. Box 257, Ringwood, Victoria 3134*

**In New Zealand:** Please write to the *Marketing Department, Penguin Books (NZ) Ltd, Private Bag, Takapuna, Auckland 9*

**In India:** Please write to *Penguin Overseas Ltd, 706 Eros Apartments, 56 Nehru Place, New Delhi, 110019*

**In the Netherlands:** Please write to *Penguin Books Netherlands B.V., Postbus 195, NL–1380AD Weesp*

**In West Germany:** Please write to *Penguin Books Ltd, Friedrichstrasse 10–12, D–6000 Frankfurt/Main 1*

**In Spain:** Please write to *Alhambra Longman S.A., Fernandez de la Hoz 9, E–28010 Madrid*

**In Italy:** Please write to *Penguin Italia s.r.l., Via Como 4, I-20096 Pioltello (Milano)*

**In France:** Please write to *Penguin Books Ltd, 39 Rue de Montmorency, F-75003 Paris*

**In Japan:** Please write to *Longman Penguin Japan Co Ltd, Yamaguchi Building, 2–12–9 Kanda Jimbocho, Chiyoda-Ku, Tokyo 101*